Transforming America

Transforming America

Politics and Culture in the Reagan Years

Robert M. Collins

COLUMBIA UNIVERSITY

NEW YORK

Columbia University Press
Publishers Since 1893
New York   Chichester, West Sussex
Copyright © 2007 Columbia University Press
All rights reserved
Library of Congress Cataloging-in-Publication Data
Collins, Robert M.
Transforming America: politics and culture in the Reagan years / Robert M. Collins.
p. cm.
Includes bibliographical references and index.
ISBN 978-0-231-12400-3 (clothbound : alk. paper) — ISBN 978-0-231-12401-0 (pbk. :
alk. paper) — ISBN 978-0-231-51130-8 (electronic)
1. United States—Politics and government—1981-1989. 2. United States—Economic
conditions—1981-2001. 3. United States—Social conditions—1980- 4. Reagan, Ronald—
Influence. 5. Right and left (Political science) 6. Politics and culture—United States.
I. Title.
E876.C635 2006
973.927092—dc22   2006003871

∞

Columbia University Press books are printed on permanent and durable acid-free paper.
This book is printed on paper with recycled content.
Printed in the United States of America
c 10 9 8 7 6 5 4 3 2
p 10 9 8 7 6 5 4 3 2
References to Internet Web Sites (URLs) were accurate at the time of writing. Neither
the author nor Columbia University Press is responsible for Web sites that may have
expired or changed since the articles were prepared.

CONTENTS

ACKNOWLEDGMENTS

Finishing a book is always gratifying. One reason is that it offers an occasion to break out of the tendency of academics to bite the hand that feeds them. I teach at a fine large Midwestern state university that encourages scholarship in many ways, and I am grateful to the University of Missouri for its support. Over the years my students there, usually without realizing their ultimate role, have constantly reminded me of the excitement and inherent fascination the study of history provides, and along the way they also helped me sharpen many of the ideas in this book. In this last regard, I thank William E. Roberts in particular.

While I worked on this project, my immediate circle sustained me as always with intellectual stimulation and invaluable good cheer. Mark Carroll and Win Burggraaff are friends I laugh with and learn from. Richard Bienvenu generously read portions of this manuscript and allowed me the benefit of his keen eye for language and ideas. On matters of American cultural history in particular, I have borrowed shamelessly from the knowledge and insight of Steven Watts. Workplace colleagues, fellow historians, and, most important, good friends all, I thank them. From farther afield, Donald Critchlow of St. Louis University helped me in a variety of ways both practical and intellectual. At the Columbia University Press, James Warren, Peter Dimock, Leslie Bialler, Kabir Dandona, Marisa Pagano, and Melissa Renée provided the expert assistance that turns typed pages into real books.

Wrapping up a major project affords one an opportunity for larger reflection on the matter of debts owed as well. In the end, we are all like the proverbial turtle basking in the sun on top of a fence post—it ill behooves us to think we got where we are by ourselves. I have been helped by so many for so long—family, friends, and kind acquaintances—that it would take a long list indeed to express my thanks with any accuracy. I will spare the reader that exercise in bookkeeping, and instead offer the many people to whom I am so indebted the assurance that I know who they are, and remember them with gratitude.

May 1, 2006

Transforming America

INTRODUCTION

When Ronald Reagan died in July 2004, many Americans found themselves shocked at how much they cared. After all, it was a death long anticipated—Reagan was an old man and had been suffering from cruelly debilitating Alzheimer's disease for nearly a decade. Moreover, throughout his public career he had been a highly polarizing figure in American national life. Nevertheless, Reagan's demise touched off an outpouring of affection, sorrow, and solemn reflection unusual in a political culture without much built-in capacity for civic rituals. (His was the first state funeral in the United States since the early 1970s.) "Few men in our history have been held in such warm regard," *Newsweek* observed.[1]

Much of the commentary about Reagan focused warmly on his personality—his irrepressible and infectious optimism, his unfailing decency, and his sense of humor. In some ways the grieving resembled an Irish wake. Nearly everyone had a funny remembrance. His official biographer, Edmund Morris, who had been baffled by his subject in life, seemed newly insightful and more openly affectionate. He recalled Reagan's attendance at a ceremonial dinner held by the Knights of Malta, a Catholic group, in New York City a week before he left the White House. The prominent lay Catholic who presided over the dinner as master of ceremonies had imbibed a bit too much wine and foolishly decided to follow the president's speech with some slurred and all-too-informal remarks of his own. He launched into a tribute to Reagan for protecting the rights of the unborn and opposing abortion, and lauded him for recognizing that all human beings began life as "feces." The master of ceremonies turned to Cardinal John O'Connor and recognized him as "a fece" who had achieved much in life, then, turning back, concluded, "You, too, Mr. President—you were once a fece!" Later, when Reagan joined his aides on Air Force One for the flight back to Washington, he observed with perfect, low-key timing: "Well, that's the first time I've flown to New York in formal attire to be told I was a piece of shit."[2] Reagan's humor was engaging precisely because he so often turned it on himself. He was often the butt of his best jokes. People remembered both the humor and the gentleness.

But when the national funereal discussion turned to Reagan's public record, it became considerably more discordant. Disagreements flared, often expressed in heated language that fairly crackled with intensity of feeling. Many recalled Reagan as a heroic leader who had saved the United States from incipient decline. The columnist George Will declared him "a world figure whose career will interest historians for centuries," and the political commentators Michael Barone and Charles Krauthammer nominated him to stand alongside Franklin Roosevelt as the greatest American leaders of the twentieth century.[3] But others were less laudatory. The *New York Times* in its obituary found fully as much to criticize as to praise, dwelling on mistakes, barely mentioning the taming of inflation (in the eyes of many, Reagan's greatest economic achievement), and chalking up Reagan's Cold War triumphs to good fortune.[4] The great liberal historian Arthur Schlesinger, Jr., damned with faint praise, writing that Reagan had a clear vision but "alas, not too much else," "a genius for simplification" but "no capacity for analysis and no command of detail."[5] Some omitted the faint praise altogether. Christopher Hitchens described Reagan as "a cruel and stupid lizard" who was "dumb as a stump."[6]

The denunciation of Reagan in death sometimes had a feverish quality of the sort that reads better in the white heat of passion than in the cool light of day. Larry Kramer, a well-known AIDS activist, called him America's Hitler. The *New Republic*'s drama critic, Robert Brustein, interrupted an ordinary theater review to lay bare the deceased president's appalling record. Reagan, he wrote, had been the enemy of the poor, the homeless, minorities, and AIDS sufferers. Gorbachev, not "this good-natured, engaging, but utterly inconsequential B-movie actor," was responsible for safely ending the Cold War. The "real legacies" of the Reagan presidency were "harebrained technological stunts such as Star Wars, clandestine adventures such as the Iran-Contra affair, tax cuts for the rich masquerading as economic restoratives, and preemptive strikes against such menaces to democracy and world peace as Granada."[7]

Passionate denunciation was not the monopoly of the nation's coastal elites. My own thoroughly congenial across-the-street neighbor in a distinctly modest, middle-class neighborhood in our medium-sized, Midwestern university town wrote a letter to the editor of the local paper at the time of Reagan's funeral indicting "the Great Prevaricator" for a similar litany of crimes. He added that Reagan "brought us Central American death squads, . . . Bitburg, bloated military budgets, enormous deficits, . . . federal union-busting, AIDS," and the designation by the federal government in the 1980s of "ketchup as a vegetable" in federally supported school lunch programs. "Thus began," he concluded, "the right-wing counter-revolution that led to the present psychotic and criminal Bush administration. Good riddance, Ronnie."[8]

Where in this welter of praise and denunciation lies the truth? Who was Ronald Reagan; what did he do to, and for, his country? And what was happening in the rest of American life in the 1980s, in American culture and society, and in the U.S. economy, while he did it? The chapters that follow address these fundamental questions in an attempt to furnish readers with a useful overview of a critical era in the history of modern America. The answers I provide may fail to satisfy everyone, especially given the division of opinion evident in the national conversation prompted by Reagan's death. That likelihood has not stopped me from making judgments and reaching conclusions. I do not apologize for my interpretations, but I invite the reader to test them against the evidence I adduce. I have tried to be both unblinking and fairminded. E.B. White once suggested that "to pursue truth, one should not be too deeply entrenched in any hole." Like everyone, I have my own hole; but I have tried not to burrow too deeply into it. And I have sought to take seriously the historian's obligation to rise out of it enough to see what all sides thought they were up to.

I hope my book is intensive enough to have analytical bite and extensive enough to assess developments in a number of areas — not only politics, but also culture and society, as well as business and the economy. It does not constitute a survey that seeks to touch, however glancingly, on every noteworthy event and development, but stands rather as a broad-ranging interpretation of the 1980s. In the interest of succinctness and salience, much has been knowingly and necessarily omitted. More than a little has no doubt been unwittingly overlooked. But historical interpretations need focus, and they must start and end somewhere. Chapter 1, "Malaise," sets the stage with a discussion of what went so wrong in the United States in the 1970s as to cause serious and well-intentioned commentators and citizens to believe that the United States had passed her zenith and was perhaps irretrievably set on a path of slow national decline. Chapter 2, "Enter Ronald Reagan, Pragmatic Ideologue," traces the rise of the unlikely figure, the former movie actor Ronald Reagan, to whom Americans turned in the critical election of 1980 to arrest the nation's sclerotic drift. It emphasizes Reagan's personal and political optimism and locates the roots of Reagan's appealing sacramental vision of America. It also portrays Reagan as a more complex political figure than many at the time or since have appreciated — smarter, more engaged, and more deftly pragmatic than the cartoon-like figure of a daft old ideologue constructed by journalists and political partisans.

Reagan's unusual and altogether paradoxical blend of ideological zeal and political pragmatism suffused his policy both at home and abroad. He was arguably at his most radical in the realm of domestic economic policy. Chapter 3, "Reaganomics," explores both the sources and the outcomes, positive and negative, of Reagan's economic initiatives. On the whole, the good outweighed the bad. Clearly, supply-side economics was more than the silly, cult-like delusion of an ignorant, passive president and a handful of his crackpot advisers that it was sometimes painted as being. The supply-side approach had considerable intellectual imprimatur, heft, staying power, and long-run influence. But supply-side economics was no automatic panacea. Both supply-side economics and deregulation, two key enthusiasms of the Reagan White House, demonstrated a potential for significant unintended consequences that would subsequently complicate life considerably for Reagan's successors in the White House.

While commentators and ordinary Americans alike at the time focused on governmental policy as the key to explaining and understanding the performance of the economy, other forces and developments worked beneath the surface to transform the U.S. economy, and in the process helped launch the longest period of sustained prosperity in the nation's history. Chapter 4, "Greed Is Good?" discusses the impact of three such subterranean forces in particular: the revolution in information technology, especially in computers; the increasing globalization of the national economy; and the dramatic restructuring of the corporate system, which led not only to monumental financial scandals but also to the emergence of reinvigorated, leaner, and more competitive business enterprise.

The revitalization of the U.S. economy did not solve all problems, however. Chapter 5, "Social Problems, Societal Issues," discusses several of the vexing social ills that afflicted American society in the 1980s—a seeming epidemic of homelessness; the discovery of an ominously large underclass of alienated, unemployed, and impoverished Americans in the nation's largest inner cities; a troubling rise in economic inequality in the society at large; and the emergence of AIDS, a new disease that struck hardest among the nation's male homosexual population. These were problems that defied easy solution, in part because they were dauntingly complicated—multifaceted, with social, cultural, economic, and political aspects in confusing combination. They were also highly controversial and much misunderstood at the time, and in this chapter I try to dispel some of the mythology and misinformation that built up around them.

Chapter 6, "The Postmodern Moment," maps the cultural landscape of the 1980s, identifying patterns of meaning and significance that were often only dimly recognized at the time. By examining such varied phenomena as MTV and 1980s-vintage self-help gurus, it becomes possible to limn the convergence of postmodernism, therapeutic individualism, and heightened materialism that gave American culture in the 1980s its distinctive contours. Chapter 7, "Culture War" shows how such developments led to a protracted cultural and political conflict pitting traditionalist and religious values, mores, and institutions (in other words, bourgeois culture) against the emergent secular, multicultural, self-referential cultural regime of the 1980s, a culture war that continues to reverberate today.

Chapter 8, "Combating the Evil Empire," and chapter 9, "Winning the Cold War," direct the discussion outward to assess the role the United States played in world affairs in the 1980s, most dramatically in the West's triumph in the Cold War struggle that had dominated international relations since the end of World War II. Although these chapters give Reagan primary credit for the ultimate outcome, they also devote considerable attention to the risks run, the collateral damage imposed, and the costs incurred in the superpower contest that the Reagan administration fought in a variety of ways on fronts all around the world throughout the 1980s. Honest bookkeeping, especially in victory, demands no less.

Out of my survey of the 1980s one overarching theme emerges. It is the argument that the 1980s were a time of fundamental realignment in American life. The reorientation took two main forms. In the realm of politics and public policy, Ronald Reagan in his ascendancy shifted the national political conversation to the right, not so far or so radically as his critics feared, but discernibly, indeed decisively. At the same time, American culture moved away from the bourgeois regime of values, mores, and institutions, which had held sway for most of the twentieth century, toward a new more secular, postmodern, multicultural, and therapeutic cultural order. That movement had, in fact, begun in earlier decades, but it accelerated and came to fruition in the 1980s.

In effect, and paradoxically, politics moved right just as culture moved left. The friction generated by these contemporaneous developments helped spark the so-called culture war of the 1980s and 1990s, a brand of cultural conflict that has strong echoes (as in the debates over gay marriage) in the early years of the twenty-first century. As a result of the recentering of its political and cultural mainstreams, America emerged from the 1980s a different nation. On the whole, I maintain, despite the fears of outraged political liberals and embittered cultural conservatives, it was a better, more efficient, and more tolerant one than it had been before.

In a significant subtheme, Ronald Reagan takes shape in the following chapters as one of the most consequential and successful presidents of the modern era. In retrospect, Reagan was the sort of history-shaping figure the philosopher of history Sidney Hook once labeled the "event-making hero." Such persons shift the apparent course of history by virtue of their unusual qualities of intelligence, judgment, vision, character, or will. They may be good or bad—for Hook the label "hero" did not necessarily imply good deeds, merely consequential ones. Event-making heroes are not merely "in the right place at the right time"; their impact is more profound than that because they are, in a real sense, "irreplaceable." That is to say, they are discernibly different from those of their time who, in their absence, might have undertaken the same tasks or shouldered the same responsibilities. And by virtue of their unique combination of attributes, they alter the course of affairs in ways no one else probably could.[9] In the study you are about to read, Reagan looms as such a figure. But to understand how that happened, we must start at the beginning, when the 1980s actually began, before the 1970s were even over.

Chapter 1

"MALAISE"

"The nation needed a Jimmy Carter," Lyn Nofziger has written, "in order truly to appreciate a Ronald Reagan."[1] Nofziger, who was one of Ronald Reagan's closest political advisers during the Californian's long, slow ascent to national prominence, might be excused the partisan bite of his comment. But he was correct in a more general — and generous — way than he perhaps intended: We do, indeed, need to grasp the nature and extent of America's vexing problems in the 1970s in order to understand Ronald Reagan's presidency and to assess the claim the 1980s make on our attention as a distinctive and significant historical era with a unique tenor. The 1970s were a time of testing for Americans, and many came to fear that the nation had lost its ability to master its problems. The result was a palpable loss of confidence, a disturbing sense that the nation's drift might easily turn into permanent decline. Serious observers began to talk of an American climacteric, of a sclerotic society irreversibly succumbing to the ravages of age. It was in the 1970s, amongst those problems and those fears, that the era of the 1980s actually began.

STAGFLATION

At the heart of America's crisis of confidence lay a dramatic decline in the fortunes of the U.S. economy during the 1970s.[2] The defining event of the decade was the oil embargo engineered by the Organization of Petroleum

Exporting Countries (OPEC) in 1973–1974. A cartel that had been created in 1959 in an effort by the oil-producing states to control their own economic destiny, OPEC seized the opportunity presented by the 1973 Arab–Israeli conflict to begin to raise world oil prices in earnest. When Egypt and Syria attacked Israeli positions in October 1973, beginning the so-called Yom Kippur War, the Arab oil-states immediately cut their production by 10 percent in an attempt to pressure Israel's chief ally, the United States. After some early reversals and a massive resupply effort by the Nixon administration, the Israelis prevailed militarily. The Arab oil producers promptly embargoed the shipment of oil to the United States, Portugal, and Holland as punishment for their aid to Israel. And when the embargo was lifted in the spring of 1974, OPEC continued to raise the world price of oil, which moved from $1.99 per barrel on at the beginning of the Yom Kippur War to over $10 per barrel by the end of 1974.

The impact of the resultant energy crunch was substantial. The massive increase in the cost of energy reverberated throughout the American economy and triggered the recession of 1974–1975, the most serious economic downturn since the Great Depression. Both the GNP and the stock market dropped precipitously. New York City tottered on the brink of bankruptcy. In the spring of 1975, the unemployment rate reached 9 percent, its highest level since 1941. At the same time, skyrocketing energy costs combined with stubbornly entrenched inflationary expectations initially generated by Lyndon B. Johnson's Vietnam War–era guns-and-butter policy to push the annual rate of inflation into double digits. Economists called the combination of low-capacity operation and high unemployment coupled with rapidly rising prices "stagflation." The conventional wisdom that the economy might suffer from stagnation or inflation but never both simultaneously was sadly proven wrong.

Moreover, the stagflation of the 1970s resulted from forces more structural, endogenous, and long-running than the temporary oil embargo and the sudden spike in energy prices. The resurgence of international economic competition from both Europe and Asia had American business reeling. Over the course of the decade, the United States lost 23 percent of its share of the total world market, despite a 40 percent depreciation in the value of the dollar that made U.S. exports cheaper and imports more expensive. By 1979, imported consumer electronics had captured more than half the American market. In a pattern repeated elsewhere in the economy, Japanese manufacturers took an American invention, the videotape recorder (VCR), and mass-produced it so efficiently that their exports soon came to dominate the U.S. market. In the metalworking machinery sector, the West Germans overtook U.S. firms in the world market, while at home foreign firms captured 25 percent of the American market for such goods.

In steel, as American facilities became increasingly outdated and uncompetitive, producers relied on government protection in the form of "voluntary" import quotas and trigger-price mechanisms to defend their hold on the domestic market. At the end of the 1970s, U.S. Steel's Fairfield Works in Alabama was still partially steam-powered! Meanwhile, the Japanese used the cheap, efficient process known as continuous-slab casting (which had been developed in the United States) to manufacture half of all Japanese steel, whereas the U.S. steel industry's use of that technique accounted for only 16 percent of its steel output. When the United States sought to boost tank production after the Yom Kippur War, Secretary of Defense James Schlesinger was stunned to discover that so much American foundry capacity had been closed because of low profitability that he had to turn to foreign suppliers to provide the needed turrets. "No greater change from World War II could be imagined," he later exclaimed: "The great arsenal of democracy without foundry capacity!"[3]

No single industry illustrated America's competitive woes more vividly than auto manufacturing. The 1970s were an unmitigated disaster for Detroit. The competitive arrival of the Japanese carmakers, which at the beginning of the decade made big inroads in California by aiming at the low-price end of the passenger car market, was a particularly devastating development. The American manufacturers, accustomed to easy domination of their domestic market, failed at first to see the danger—when the famous racer Carroll Shelby telephoned the Ford executive Lee Iacocca to say he'd been offered a Toyota dealership in Houston, Iacocca replied, "Let me give you the best advice you'll ever get. Don't take it. . . . Because we're going to kick their asses back into the Pacific Ocean."[4] By 1980, the Japanese had captured 22 percent of the United States market, with imports overall constituting 27 percent of domestic auto sales.[5]

Cars from such Japanese giants as Honda, Toyota, and Datsun (now Nissan) consistently outshone their American counterparts in build quality, durability, fuel efficiency, repair record, and overall consumer ratings, all while posting a cost advantage that averaged $2,000 per unit.[6] Iacocca, who left Ford and ultimately headed the Chrysler Corporation, later reported that "Chrysler's quality had been so poor that the dealers got into the habit of expecting to rebuild cars when they received them."[7] In a sense, the buyers of domestic cars in the 1970s did the factories' quality-control work for them—Ford, for example, counted warranty claims to measure its product quality.[8] In 1979, a professor at the Harvard Business School attracted national attention and grudging nods of agreement with a new book entitled *Japan as Number One*.[9]

At the heart of all these economic problems—stagnation, inflation, and a decline in international competitiveness—lay perhaps the most troubling development of all: a sharp decline in the productivity of American workers. As economists are fond of saying, productivity isn't everything, but it is *almost* everything. When all is said and done, it is productivity—specifically gains in productivity—that drives an economy forward to a higher standard of living. During the impressive postwar quarter-century from 1948 to 1973, output per man-hour grew at over 3 percent per year. Over the next five years, output per man-hour declined by two-thirds to grow at a rate of 1 percent per year. The average for 1977–1978 was a dismal 0.4 percent.[10] Although Americans remained the world's most productive workers, improvement in productivity had slowed dramatically, making it likely that America's most energetic competitors would in the not-too-distant future close the gap in this most fundamental of economic measures.

Economists were, and remain, at a loss to explain conclusively the slowing of productivity growth. A partial answer lay in the entry into the labor force of large numbers of young people—baby boomers come of age—and of female workers. Both groups were relatively inexperienced and thus by definition relatively inefficient workers until they mastered the learning curve in their various endeavors. Increased government regulation also played a role. Carter's Council of Economic Advisers in 1979 estimated that the direct costs of compliance with environmental, health, and safety regulations might have reduced productivity growth by 0.4 percentage points per year since 1973. Meanwhile, the onset of economic tough times saw a drop in business investment in labor-saving equipment and a reduction in overall societal spending for research and development. Finally, the 1970s also witnessed the continuation of a secular shift in the economy away from the manufacture of goods toward the provision of services, and productivity gains in the burgeoning service sector were notoriously difficult both to realize and to measure.[11]

Most striking, the perverse intertwining of economic stagnation, rapid inflation, declining competitiveness, and flatline productivity brought to an end a quarter-century of mass upward economic mobility, the postwar golden age of economic growth and stability. Between 1973 and 1979 real median family income actually fell as the vital signs of the U.S. economy flickered ominously. Make no mistake: At the end of the 1970s, Americans were exceedingly well off by both historical and international standards. But they looked back wistfully on the postwar boom as a past they had lost. Unemployment made them insecure about the present and inflation made them fearful of the future. In 1979, 72 percent of the public agreed with the statement "We are fast coming to a turning point in our history where the 'land of plenty' is becoming the land of want." Writing in *Time* magazine, the journalist Lance Morrow observed, "From the Arab oil boycott in 1973 onward, the decade was bathed in a cold Spenglerian apprehension that the lights were about to go out, that history's astonishing material indulgence of the U.S. was about to end." Americans now confronted harsh economic realities that defied conventional analysis and economic problems that defied easy solution. Worse still, they faced an economic future more uncertain than at any time since the Great Depression.[12]

WATERGATE, VIETNAM, AND THE CONFIDENCE GAP

The bad news of the 1970s was not exclusively economic. Americans suffered still other blows to the national sense of well-being. The world of public affairs contributed two particularly devastating experiences—Watergate and Vietnam. Watergate was both a political scandal and a constitutional crisis. It unfolded slowly but inexorably, and from the initial discovery of the burglars in the headquarters of the Democratic National Committee at the Watergate complex in June 1972 to Richard Nixon's resignation as president in August 1974, Watergate held the attention of the nation throughout. Americans were preoccupied, indeed, nearly transfixed, as the drama played itself out.[13] The new president, Gerald Ford, so feared that Americans would not be able to put Watergate behind them that he risked his own political standing by granting the fallen Nixon a full presidential pardon, in order to assure that Nixon would not continue to dominate the national scene from a courtroom or jail cell. Within days Ford's approval rating plummeted from 71 percent to 50 percent.[14]

Despite Ford's courageous attempt finally to put to rest what he had at his swearing-in ceremony called "our long national nightmare," the toppling of a sitting president left deep scars. Ultimately some seventy individuals, including several cabinet members, two Oval Office aides, and a number of presidential assistants, were convicted of, or pleaded guilty to, Watergate-connected crimes. As the political commentator Elizabeth Drew subsequently reported:

> [Watergate] . . . shook our confidence. We had had a kind of faith that we would never elect a really bad man as president—an incompetent or a fraud, perhaps, but not a man who would preside over criminal activities and seek to take away our liberties. We had a deep, unexamined confidence in the electoral system. The system was messy, but we had come to depend on it to keep us well within the range of safety. And then it didn't.[15]

The ignominious conclusion of the war in Vietnam followed upon Watergate like the second blow of a vicious one-two punch painfully replayed in slow motion. Nixon and his national security adviser, Henry Kissinger, had negotiated an American withdrawal from Vietnam in early 1973, as part of an arrangement that they labeled, all too prematurely, a peace with honor. But the agreement, which left the North Vietnamese army (NVA) in place in South Vietnam, began to unravel almost immediately. In April 1975 the communists swept into power in both Cambodia and South Vietnam in swift and final military offensives.

There was scant honor for the United States in any aspect of the war's sudden conclusion. Cambodia fell to the communists shortly before the endgame in Vietnam. Kissinger, at that time the Secretary of State, read aloud at a somber mid-April cabinet meeting a letter from Sirik Matak, the former Cambodian prime minister, who awaited the entry of the victorious Khmer Rouge communists into the Cambodian capital of Phnom Penh. Turning down an offer by the American ambassador to arrange for his evacuation to safety, Matak wrote stingingly:

Dear Excellency and Friend:
    I thank you very sincerely for your letter and for your offer to transport me towards freedom. I cannot, alas, leave in such a cowardly fashion. As for you, and in particular for your great country, I never believed for a moment that you would have this sentiment of abandoning a people which has chosen liberty. You have refused us your protection, and we can do nothing about it.
    You leave, and my wish is that you and your country will find happiness under this sky. But, mark it well, that if I shall die here on this spot and in my country that I love, it is no matter, because we all are born and must die. I have only committed this mistake of believing in you [the Americans].
    Please accept, Excellency and dear friend, my faithful and friendly sentiments.

Occupying Phnom Penh, the Khmer Rouge promptly executed Matak, shooting him in the stomach and leaving him, without medical assistance, to die three days later.[16]

Matak's death was but a foretaste of his country's fate. Anthony Lewis, then the foreign affairs columnist of the New York Times, had asked just a few weeks earlier, "What future possibility could be more terrible than the reality of what is happening to Cambodia right now [due to fighting in the war]?" Immediately before the fall of Cambodia's anti-Communist regime, the New York Times foreign correspondent Sydney Schanberg—who would receive a Pulitzer Prize for his reporting from Cambodia—wrote in a front-page story that "for the ordinary people of Indochina . . . it is difficult to imagine how their lives could be anything but better with the Americans gone."[17] Unfortunately, the Times' journalistic imagination proved no match for the Khmer Rouge's ruthless determination to create a new society in Cambodia. Over the next several years, America and the world watched with horror as the Khmer Rouge killed somewhere between one and two million Cambodians (of a total population of approximately seven million) in one of the worst episodes of state terror in the history of the exceedingly bloody twentieth century.[18] Using a perverse moral calculus that refused to place the responsibility for such crimes on the direct perpetrators, some observers blamed the Cambodian horror on America's Vietnam war policies; others saw the outcome as the proof that the domino theory advanced to justify U.S. intervention in Indochina had been right after all. Neither line of analysis left Americans with grounds for satisfaction or consolation.

In Vietnam itself, the final images of America's longest war were those of the chaotic American evacuation of Saigon.[19] U.S. officials remained in the beleaguered South Vietnamese capital until the end, fearing that a premature American departure would be seen as abject abandonment, hoping against hope that last-minute negotiations could avoid a total capitulation. Finally, on April 29, 1975, the American disc jockeys at Saigon's Armed Services Radio station played "White Christmas" over and over, a prearranged signal to begin full-scale evacuation; then they put a long-playing tape of John Philip Sousa marches on the air and left. The extrication that followed was successful in a narrow sense, with seventy helicopters taking out 1,373 Americans, 5,595 Vietnamese, and 815 other foreign nationals in the next eighteen hours.[20] But any satisfaction that might be taken in the achievement was overwhelmed by unforgettable scenes of the last helicopters lifting off from the roof of the U.S. embassy while hundreds of desperate Vietnamese scrambled below in the vain hope that they, too, might be taken to safety. As one North Vietnamese commander of the final assault observed, "[The United States] . . . mobilized as many as 6 million American soldiers in rotation, dropped over 10 million tons of bombs, and spent over $300 billion, but in the end the U.S. Ambassador had to crawl up to the helicopter pad looking for a way to flee."[21]

When on April 30, 1975 the last American chopper lifted off carrying the final contingent of the embassy's Marine Corps guards, its crew reported, with unintended poignancy: "All the Americans are out. Repeat Out." Back in Washington, President Ford announced grimly, "The Government of the Republic of Vietnam has surrendered. . . . Vietnam has been a wrenching experience for this nation. . . . History must be the final judge of that which we have done or left undone, in Vietnam and elsewhere. Let us calmly await its verdict."[22] But Americans quickly discovered they could not put Vietnam behind them quite that easily.

Addressing a commencement ceremony audience at Notre Dame University in 1977, President Jimmy Carter reported that the war had "produced a profound moral crisis" that sapped "faith in our own policy and our system of life."[23] Indeed, the spiritual impact of the Vietnam experience was profound and long-lasting, much like the psychic impact of World War I on Europeans. The diplomatic historian George C. Herring has written, "As no other event in the nation's history, [the Vietnam War] . . . challenged Americans' traditional beliefs about themselves, the notion that in their relations with other people they have generally acted with benevolence, the idea that nothing is beyond reach."[24] The war left the American people frustrated and confused about both their collective intentions and capabilities.

The confluence of economic bad news, the Watergate scandal, and a divi-sive, grueling, and unsuccessful war in Southeast Asia contributed importantly to a growing mistrust of traditional institutions and sources of authority. Par-ticularly striking was the fact that the resultant "confidence gap" afflicted so many different private and public institutions at about the same time. As the pollster Daniel Yankelovich reported in 1977:

> We have seen a steady rise of mistrust in our national institutions. . . . Trust in government declined dramatically from almost 80% [sic] in the late 1950s to about 33% in 1976. Confidence in business fell from approximately a 70% level in the late 60s to about 15% today. Confidence in other institutions—the press, the military, the professions—doctors and lawyers—sharply declined from the mid-60s to the mid-70s. . . . One could go on and on. The change is simply massive. Within a ten-to-fifteen-year period, trust in institutions has plunged down and down.[25]

In time the decline in trust of particular societal institutions turned into a more general pessimism, a palpable loss of Americans' renowned national op-timism about the future. In June 1978 the Roper Organization, at the behest of the Department of Labor, conducted what pollsters call a national ladder-scale rating, a questionnaire used since the late 1950s to elicit judgments regarding quality of life in the recent past, the present, and the foreseeable future. The authors of the ladder-scale study reported that for "the first time since these scale ratings have been obtained . . . the U.S. public . . . [does not look] toward some improvement in the future." In 1980 similar inquiries discovered that for the first time American respondents rated their lives "five years ago" more satisfactory than "at the present time." At the end of the 1970s Americans, for the first time in the postwar era, were disappointed with the present and fearful of the future.[26]

THE CENTRIFUGAL ASCENDANT

As Americans came increasingly to distrust their institutions and to lose their traditional faith in the future, other bonds that held their society together seemed to loosen and unravel as well. Beginning during the last third of the nineteenth century, accelerating in the twentieth century, America had been transformed by the impact of its centralizing tendencies. The driving forces of modernization—industrialization, urbanization, the creation of a national market, the development of national norms and standards, waves of organi-zational activity, and relentless bureaucratization—all worked to consolidate and centralize the institutions of society. The island communities characteris-tic of the agricultural order of the nineteenth century gave way to urban cen-ters that exemplified the new industrial regime. The preeminence of the large corporation and the emergence in the 1930s of a powerful, countervailing federal government apparatus underscored the ascendancy of the centripetal impulse. But now, in the 1970s, observers were surprised to see evidence of new centrifugal influences, a seeming fragmentation of American society, with attendant changes in norms and behavior that caused some to speak darkly of a new balkanization of American life.

The ways in which Americans interacted with, and became involved with, others were changing. Ties became less permanent, less intense, less inclusive. The political analyst Kevin Phillips noted a new emphasis on localistic and particularistic identities. "Throughout the 1970s," he wrote, "the symptoms of decomposition appeared throughout the body politic—in the economic, geographic, ethnic, religious, cultural, biological components of our society. Small loyalties have been replacing larger ones. Small views have been replacing larger ones."[27] It was not that all sense of common identity had suddenly died in America; rather, it was a matter of the radius of identification and trust constricting, of a miniaturization of community.

Sometimes the new diversity took shape along lines of economic geography. A resurgence of regionalism pitted the Sunbelt South and Southwest against the Frostbelt states of the industrial Northeast and Midwest (also called the Rustbelt, in a particularly unkind reference to the region's loss of economic competitiveness). States now battled fiercely over how much they paid in federal taxes and got back in federal largess, fearful that Washington was draining them and favoring others. The Southwest and Northeast clashed on energy issues, with the Oil Patch states of Texas, Louisiana, and Oklahoma seeking high prices for, and minimal federal regulation of, their oil and natural gas production and the energy-dependent Northeast demanding government intervention of various sorts to control prices and protect vulnerable consumers. A bumper sticker popular in Dallas and Houston directed drivers to "Drive Fast, Freeze a Yankee." With less humorous intent, *Business Week* warned of a "Second War Between the States."[28]

In a time of centrifugal diversity, the biological markers of life—race, gender, sexual preference, age, ethnic origins—became increasingly salient. More and more Americans came to define themselves primarily by these largely immutable characteristics. After enjoying substantial legal and political success, toward the end of the 1960s the civil rights movement faltered. The most momentous social movement ever in American history found itself exhausted and in disarray—beset by internal divisions, facing a formidable white backlash, and now confronting structures of economic and social inequality more impervious to challenge than had been the South's Jim Crow segregation. In the 1970s, African Americans in increasing numbers turned their backs on their earlier integrationist ideals and abandoned their hope of joining the American mainstream. "Instead," writes the historian Bruce Schulman, "they increasingly saw themselves as a separate nation within a nation, with distinct needs and values."[29] In time, Chicanos, Asian Americans, American Indians, a variety of white ethnics, and gays and lesbians mounted similar claims to cultural autonomy. Assimilation, once seen as a noble goal of the American experiment, in the 1970s became a synonym for cultural oppression.

The women's movement that burst into prominence at the end of the 1960s crested in the succeeding decade, energized by its considerable success in changing both laws and attitudes and by its ongoing struggle to pass into law the Equal Rights Amendment to the U.S. Constitution. But here, too, the struggle proved exhausting, and by the end of the 1970s frustration and disenchantment set in. Acting in accord with Gloria Steinem's famous contention that a woman needs a man like a fish needs a bicycle, activists developed a brand of cultural feminism that emphasized gender differences and sought to create female institutions—a feminist subculture—to provide the nurture and opportunity denied women by the patriarchal mainstream. One result of this reorientation was the creation in the 1970s of more than three hundred new women's studies programs in colleges and universities.[30]

It was not the mere appearance of these centrifugal tendencies that gave observers pause. American history had always been full of diversity of all sorts, with centrifugal impulses sometimes waxing, other times waning, but never absent. But the new fragmentation in American life now seemed to enjoy the encouragement of established elites and the imprimatur of the government. The concept of affirmative action, which had been introduced in a vague formulation by President John F. Kennedy, had by the early 1970s developed into an elaborate but inchoate system of racial preference guided by the institutionalized civil rights lobby, a handful of federal agencies, and the federal courts. In order to rationalize the emergent affirmative action regime, Secretary of Health, Education, and Welfare Caspar Weinberger in 1973 asked the Federal Interagency Committee on Education (FICE) to develop common rules for racial and ethnic classification. The FICE devised a schema of five racial categories (American Indian or Alaskan Native; Asian or Pacific Islander; Black; White; and Hispanic), which was tweaked by the Office of Management and Budget and promulgated as Statistical Directive 15. These categories became the basis for an array of government actions in the areas of education (college admissions), business and employment (access to government contracts), and politics (the gerrymandering of congressional districts). "Once this process [of racial and ethnic quotas] gets legitimated there is no stopping it," Daniel Patrick Moynihan warned the graduating class at the New School for Social Research in 1968.[31] Now the federal government had done just that.

What the centrifugal impulse of the 1970s meant for the future was not clear. Phillips saw it as a sign of national decline, a dangerous weakening of the glue that held a fractious society together. Others saw in a renewed diversity the hope of realizing the full promise of democracy: a nation where people were at last free to be *themselves*. Finally, they believed, the oppressive drive for assimilation, for compelled homogeneity, would give way to a healthy celebration of difference. The debate allowed no ready conclusions. Indeed, it would continue into the new millennium. But in the short run, it was clear that the balkinization of American life in the 1970s made governance increasingly akin to the proverbial herding of cats or frogs, and made leadership an exceedingly difficult task.

THE TRAVAILS OF POLITICAL LEADERSHIP

No one better exemplified the challenges and difficulties of political leadership in the 1970s than Jimmy Carter, who won the presidency in 1976 by campaigning as an outsider untainted by either the corruption of Watergate or the failed policies of his Washington predecessors. Born in the small town of Plains, Georgia, and raised on his family's peanut farm there, Carter struck out for the larger world when he won an appointment to the United States Naval Academy at Annapolis. He served in the navy for a decade, working on atomic-powered submarines under the legendary captain, later admiral, Hyman Rickover, but returned home to take over the family peanut business after his father's death in 1953. Finding an outlet for his ambition, energy, and intelligence in civic leadership, Carter served on the local school board, library board, and hospital authority, and became the district governor for the fifty-four Lion's Clubs of southwestern Georgia. Inevitably electoral politics beckoned; in the 1960s Carter served several terms in the Georgia legislature and in 1970 he won election as governor.

It did not take long for the Georgian to develop national political aspirations. As governor, Carter found himself entertaining a host of national political figures who passed through Atlanta hoping to position themselves for the 1972 Democratic presidential nomination. Possessing what *Time* magazine would later characterize as an "almost arrogant self-confidence," Carter took the measure of his visitors and found himself thinking that he was at least as capable as they. When his picturesque and thoroughly formidable mother, Miss Lillian, teasingly asked what he was going to do when his term as governor was over, Carter told her, "I'm going to run for president." "President of what?" she asked innocently. "Momma, I'm going to run for the President of the U.S., and I'm going to win," he answered earnestly.[32]

Carter's long campaign for the White House began even before the votes were counted in Nixon's overwhelming 1972 re-election victory. It was a steeply uphill struggle. When Carter appeared on the television show *What's My Line?* in early 1973, the panel was stumped. They did not recognize him and failed to guess his job. But running as an outsider enabled him to make a virtue out of his relative obscurity. He might be the little-known, former one-term governor of a middling-sized Southern state, without a clear track record on national issues, experience in foreign affairs, or an arresting national vision, but at least he was untouched by the revelations, scandals, and policy mistakes of the recent past. In place of national experience or ideological zeal, Carter offered voters himself—his character and his technocratic skill as a problem-solver.

In the event, the American people decided that Carter's offer of himself was a good deal. They found reassurance in his campaign promise, "I'll never tell a lie," despite his penchant for seemingly gratuitous exaggeration—for example, he often claimed to be a nuclear *physicist*, when, in fact, he had been the superbly trained chief *engineer* on the *Seawolf*, an early nuclear-powered submarine, a distinction *with* a difference. He was impressively intelligent. He had graduated from the Naval Academy sixtieth in a class of 822, and JFK's highly regarded economic adviser, Walter Heller, opined that the newly elected Democrat would rank easily among the very brightest graduate students at the nation's top universities. James Fallows, a journalist who joined Carter's White House team as a speechwriter, thought he was "probably smarter, in the College Board sense, than any other president in this century." And he was as energetic and tenacious as he was ambitious and bright. As a boy, Carter had prepared his somewhat scrawny body for admission to the Naval Academy by eating huge quantities of bananas in order to meet the minimum-weight standard and by rolling his arches on Coke bottles by the hour in order to minimize the disability of distressingly flat feet. Now he had come from nowhere to win the nation's highest office.[33]

Untainted by national scandal and experience, Carter and the small band of Georgians who accompanied him to Washington as advisers were also innocent of the inside-the-beltway experience so useful—indeed, necessary—for maneuver in the dense social and political environment of the nation's capital. It quickly became evident that beguiling innocence could all too easily translate into costly ineptitude. One early incident quickly became the stuff of Washington legend. When the most powerful figure in Washington's political establishment, the Democratic Speaker of the House, Thomas "Tip" O'Neill of Massachusetts, asked for tickets to an inaugural gala at the Kennedy Center for some relatives and friends, Carter's chief adviser, Hamilton Jordan, sent over a block of seats in the back row of the balcony. There ensued a classic tempest in a teapot. The morning after the event, O'Neill called Jordan in a huff. "Listen, you son of a bitch. When a guy is Speaker of the House and his family gets the worst seats in the room, he figures there's a reason behind it. I have to believe you did that deliberately." When Jordan offered to return O'Neill's money if he was so unhappy, the speaker replied, "Don't be a wise guy. I'll ream your ass before I'm through."[34] Word soon circulated among Beltway insiders that

O'Neill had taken to referring to Jordan as "Hannibal Jerkin." Of Carter and his Georgians, O'Neill later remembered, "They were all parochial. They were incompetent. They came with a chip on their shoulder against the entrenched politicians. Washington to them was evil. They were going to change everything and didn't understand the rudiments of it."[35]

The triviality of Gala-gate was followed by similar but more substantive missteps. Carter's choice of his longtime aide Frank Moore as his chief congressional liaison was unpopular on Capitol Hill. After only a month in office, Carter initiated a predictably costly fight when he unilaterally announced his intention to cut back on a traditional prize of congressional pork-barrel politics by eliminating nineteen previously scheduled federal dam and water projects. As congressional tempers flared, a White House aide reported to the president, "The concern around the Senate is that you are naive or selfish or stubborn, perhaps all three. Most senators already see you as hard-nosed and they respect that, but they also see some signs which, to them, indicate that you are hard-headed and, even worse, high-handed."[36] In the end the administration and the Congress compromised on the number of water projects to be eliminated, an outcome that Carter regretted and Congress resented.

Inexperience was not Carter's only problem. Other failings undercut his leadership as well, most notably his inability to establish clear overarching goals and themes for his presidency. As president, Carter seemed to want to do everything, and all at once. He confessed in his diary, "Everybody has warned me not to take on too many projects so early in the administration, but it's almost impossible for me to delay something that I see needs to be done."[37] Carter seemed to think, as the speechwriter Fallows put it, "in lists, not arguments; as long as items are there, their order does not matter, nor does the hierarchy among them." "I came to think," Fallows continued, "that Carter believes fifty things, but no one thing. He holds explicit, thorough positions on every issue under the sun, but he has no large view of the relations between them, no line indicating which goals . . . will take precedence over which . . . when the goals conflict."[38]

Even close allies corroborated the charge. Hamilton Jordan subsequently recalled that at the end of one congressional session, Tip O'Neill asked Vice President Walter Mondale to identify four or five priority items from a list of more than twenty still-pending legislative initiatives. With the help of Jordan and Frank Moore, Mondale identified five high-priority pieces of legislation and presented the list to Carter for his approval. The president added eleven more items, and then returned to O'Neill a list of sixteen "must-have" selections.[39]

At first, the public embraced Carter's penchant for trees over forests as an engaging, if eccentric, sign of his technocratic competency. In an era over-rich with adversity, Americans had at last found an omniscient problem-solver, someone who seemed to know something about everything. The popular television comedy show *Saturday Night Live* ran a hilarious parody in March 1977 of Carter's real-life attempt at presidential outreach to the public: a live, national radio call-in show moderated by the venerable TV anchorman Walter Cronkite that had Carter answering questions phoned in by ordinary citizens (the show was videotaped and shown later the same day by PBS). In the SNL send-up, Carter (played by a toothsome Dan Ackroyd) establishes his seeming omnicompetence by taking a call from a postal worker in faraway Kansas, who complains about problems plaguing the Postal Service's new MarvEx 3000 mail sorter. Noting to the caller that he and the vice-president had just that morning been discussing the MarvEx 3000, Carter/Akroyd proceeds to explain in hilariously all-knowing detail that changing the three-digit setting of the caliper post on the first-grid sliding armature will keep the letters from clogging and thus solve the caller's problem. The skit concludes with a final call from seventeen-year-old Peter, who reports anxiously that, having taken LSD, he is experiencing a bad trip. Cronkite wants to hang up on the frightened lad, but the president intervenes to talk him down, demonstrating a street dealer's knowledge of the arcania of drug use. Here, clearly, was a problem-solving leader who *did* know everything about everything.

In time, however, Carter's command of minutia came to be seen as problematic, symptomatic not of mastery but of an unhelpful penchant for micromanagement. The revelation in 1979 that Carter had during his first six months in office personally reviewed all requests to use the White House tennis court elicited more eye-rolling than praise, and Carter's earnest denial of having done so at a press conference seemed only to confirm, with inadvertent humor, a weakness for micro-management: "I have never personally monitored who used or did not use the White House tennis court. I have let my secretary, Susan Clough, receive requests from members of the White House staff who wanted to use the tennis court at certain times, so that more than one person would not want to use the same tennis court simultaneously, unless they were either on opposite sides of the net or engaged in a doubles contest."[40]

Not surprisingly, the administration got off to a slow start. Faced with daunting challenges at home and abroad, Carter's concrete achievements were few. When asked by journalists to evaluate his first year's achievements, the president replied tellingly, "I believe that our intentions are recognized as being good. So in all I think it has been a good year for us."[41] In 1978 the administration enjoyed notable foreign policy triumphs, with Senate ratification of the treaties arranging for the return of the Panama Canal to local control and the stunning Camp David agreement between the leaders of Israel and Egypt, which after further difficult and halting negotiations eventuated in an Egyptian-Israeli peace treaty. But success on the domestic front largely eluded the president, who often found himself fighting two-front wars against both congressional liberals (led by Senator Ted Kennedy, whose presidential aspirations rose whenever Carter's political fortunes fell) and Republican conservatives on the high-visibility issues of inflation, energy policy, and health care.

In 1979 things went from bad to worse, and beyond. For Jimmy Carter, it was truly an anno horribilis, with disasters on virtually every front. The U.S. economy, already beset by stubborn stagflation, now suffered a second oil shock. In Iran the Shah's political rule collapsed when he and his family fled the country in January, and the seemingly interminable political unrest and economic disruption that followed caused serious cuts in that nation's oil production; the ever-opportunistic OPEC seized upon the situation to engineer increases in the price of crude from $12.84 to $25 a barrel over the course of the year. Prices on the international spot market (where oil not already under contract is bought for whatever price obtains at the moment) reached as high as $45 a barrel.[42] By summer gas lines reappeared in California and spread across country. In July, 30,000 independent truckers went on strike to protest the cost of fuel, shutting off the flow of agricultural produce and other goods to market. As energy prices rose, inflation once again spiked upward, with the consumer price index increasing 14.4 percent from May 1979 to May 1980.

INTO THE EIGHTIES

The era of the 1980s began on or about July 1979. That is not to say that the singular historical period so closely associated with Ronald Reagan's presidency came clearly and completely into view at that moment; its arrival was not as sudden or as definite as that. But the direction of events shifted. They went down a path that led away from what had been and opened into a distinctly new era in American life. July 1979 swung open like a gate to the future.

The pivot was a strange, dramatic episode that unfolded at Camp David, the presidential retreat in the Choctaw Mountains, 45 miles northwest of Washington, D.C. The location was a sharp twist of historical irony. Less than a year earlier at Camp David, Jimmy Carter had engineered the peak achievement of his presidency, working intimately with the leaders Anwar Sadat and Menachem Begin to frame a workable formula for peace between Egypt and Israel. But in the summer of 1979, the mood at Camp David was one of deep gloom.

Carter had been receiving bad news, and bad reviews, for months. Early in the year, Gerald Rafshoon, a longtime political adviser, had sent the president a lengthy memorandum warning of a "perception among the public and the press that you have so far failed to provide the country with the strong leadership necessary to overcome our major problems." At about the same time, the president's pollster, Patrick Caddell, alerted the White House to a related but more all-encompassing development: the emergence, he reported in an April memo, of a national "crisis of confidence marked by a dwindling faith in the future."[43] In May, Caddell helped arrange a White House dinner party that brought together an array of intellectuals and writers whose work had informed the pollster's notion of a spiritual malaise; their discussion stuck in the president's mind.[44]

While attending a contentious Tokyo economic summit in June 1979, Carter received an urgent communication from his domestic policy adviser Stuart Eizenstat, who warned: "Inflation is higher than ever. A recession is clearly facing us. . . . The polls are lower than they have ever been. . . . And the Congress seems completely beyond anyone's control." On the president's left, Senator Ted Kennedy, a sharp critic and a likely contender for the Democratic nomination in 1980 should Carter falter, circled like a shark in bloody waters; on his right, polls showed Ronald Reagan, a possible Republican candidate, leading Carter in a presidential straw poll by several points. Cutbacks in Middle East oil production caused by unrest in Iran and further OPEC price increases (61 percent so far in 1979) had created a short-term energy crisis that threatened to become a political nightmare for the embattled administration. On the first weekend of the summer in June 1979 some 70 percent of the nation's gas stations were closed. "This would appear," Eizenstat told the president, "to be the worst of times."[45]

Hurrying home from the Tokyo economic summit to shore up his political position, Carter skipped a previously planned vacation stopover in Hawaii and went immediately to Camp David to prepare a previously scheduled national television address on the energy issue. Looking over drafts of the speech with his wife and confidante Rosalynn, he decided that yet another detailed speech on energy policy—his fifth after having declared the energy issue the "moral equivalent of war" at the outset of his term—would as likely antagonize his audience as rally them. The president stunned his staff and the nation's press by canceling the speech and secluding himself at Camp David for a memorable ten days, meeting with a steady stream of invited guests from public and private life in order to gather his presidency for a final stab at the sort of leadership he had seemed to promise when first elected. "What is being talked about," a Carter adviser told the increasingly fascinated press, "is how to give a different direction to the leadership and management of the country without changing presidents."[46]

The 130 or so visitors who trekked to Camp David to confer with the president and his closest advisers and aides included members of Congress; state and local officials; party leaders; religious figures; energy experts from industry and academe; and such miscellaneous luminaries as the archetypal Washington insider Clark Clifford, Lane Kirkland of the AFL-CIO, and the civil rights activist Jesse Jackson. A number of high-powered intellectuals also dropped by, among them the sociologists Robert Bellah and David Riesman and the historian Christopher Lasch. The visitors usually met the casually attired president in an elegant wood-paneled conference room at Laurel Lodge; for the most part, they talked and he listened, often taking notes with a blue felt-tip pen. "I spent 90 percent of my time listening," he noted in his diary on July 9.[47] Carter left his mountaintop retreat only to visit with two groups of "ordinary citizens" brought together in Martinsburg, West Virginia, and Carnegie, Pennsylvania, by Caddell's polling firm. Back at Camp David, he held a final session with several dozen top reporters.

Finally, on July 15, 1979, Carter returned to the White House to deliver his long-delayed nationwide address from the Oval Office. Americans were, he later wrote, "intrigued by the mystery of what I would say," and the White House further pumped up public interest by refusing to make available advance copies of the speech. The television audience, claimed by Carter in his memoirs to be around 100 million, surely an exaggeration, was nonetheless the largest of his entire public career.[48]

The speech itself *was* extraordinary.[49] "It is clear," Carter began, "that the true problems of our Nation are much deeper—deeper than gasoline lines or energy shortages, deeper even than inflation or recession." He reported what he had learned from his many visitors to Camp David, quoting one southern governor as saying, "Mr. President, you are not leading the nation—you're just managing the government." But Carter claimed that his own "just mixed success" as president was only a symptom of the nation's more fundamental malady: Americans faced "a crisis of confidence" that threatened to "destroy the social and the political fabric [of the nation]." Moreover, that erosion of faith in the future was compounded by a falling away from the values of the past. "In a nation that was proud of hard work, strong families, close-knit communities, and our faith in God, too many of us now tend to worship self-indulgence and consumption." The result was a dangerous loss of national will and unity of purpose. The consequences were all around—"paralysis and stagnation and drift." Economic productivity and personal savings were in decline; "disrespect for government and for churches and for schools, the news media, and other institutions" was on the rise; extremist and unyielding special interest groups seemed to rule Washington. The nation had lost its connection to the past and its faith in the future.

"This is not a message of happiness or reassurance," observed Carter in a magnificent understatement, "but it is the truth and it is a warning." The "malaise" speech, as it came to be known despite the fact that the president did not use that particular term in his television text, was an apt depiction of the problems befalling America in the 1970s. As *Time* magazine editor-in-chief Henry A. Grunwald later would write, "The country had faced crises before, but it was hard to find a moment since World War II when so many different ones came together at the same time."[50] In fact, Carter spoke the unhappy truth about a troubled decade.

It was not Carter's focus on adversity that made the speech extraordinary. Rather, the malaise speech stood out because of his decision to understand and explain that adversity in a profoundly pessimistic formulation. Mondale had warned Carter not to be too negative: "You can't castigate the American people or they will turn you off once and for all."[51] In fact, there is good evidence that the American electorate consistently rewards optimism and punishes pessimism.[52] And the malaise speech was definitively pessimistic.

Behavioral scientists in the field of positive psychology who study pessimism (and optimism) often define and measure it in terms of what is called attributional style, the way in which negative outcomes are understood and explained. In that regard, Carter's speech was a textbook example of pessimism in three crucial regards. First, the president emphasized the *pervasive* nature of the adversity Americans faced. The problems were not isolated or discrete, but were interlocked and everywhere, a classic pessimist's perception: "The symptoms of this crisis of the American spirit," said Carter, "are all around us." It was a "crisis of confidence" that "strikes at the very heart and soul and spirit of our national will," one that "was threatening to destroy the social and the political fabric of America."

Second, Carter *personalized* the responsibility for the nation's woes. Psychologists have noted that pessimists characteristically internalize blame for bad outcomes, rather than blaming outside influences, external events, or simple bad luck. Carter himself admitted to having enjoyed "just mixed success" in his own efforts to deal with national problems. "But," he added immediately, "after listening to the American people I have been reminded again that all the legislation in the world can't fix what's wrong with America." In other words, the "paralysis and stagnation and drift" afflicting the United States were the fault of his audience. *They* were the ones who showed disrespect for established institutions, who increasingly failed even to vote, whose "willingness . . . to save for the future has fallen below that of all other people in the Western world," who "now tend to worship self-indulgence and consumption" while their own work ethic atrophied and productivity plummeted.

Finally, the actual language of the malaise speech was imbedded in a larger world-view that accepted the *permanence* of a least a substantial portion of the nation's problems. "Dealing with limits," Carter would write in his memoirs, became "the subliminal theme" of his presidency.[53] The notion that the United States had crossed over into a new, enduring era of shrunken aspirations and capacities was first set out in Carter's inaugural address, when he warned that "even our great nation has its recognized limits, and . . . we can neither answer all questions nor solve all problems. We cannot afford to do everything." He returned to the theme at the dedication of the John F. Kennedy Presidential Library in the fall of 1979: "We can no longer rely on a rising economic tide to lift the boats of the poorest in our society. . . . We have a keener appreciation of limits now—the limits of government, limits on the use of military power abroad; the limits on manipulating, without harm to ourselves, a delicate and a balanced natural environment. We are struggling with a profound transition from a time of abundance to a time of growing scarcity in energy."[54] The notion that the United States was turning a corner into a permanently diminished future provided the final, and perhaps conclusive, note of pessimism to Carter's malaise message.

It was this deep pessimism that made the malaise speech so remarkable. In offering his searching and, in some regards, rather profound analysis of America's woes as a way to salvage his presidency and position himself for re-election, Carter managed to plant his political flag in the inhospitable soil of political pessimism, leaving himself spectacularly vulnerable to challenge from someone better able to provide the electorate with the combination of hopefulness and confidence that, other things being equal, tends to win elections in this most optimistic of political cultures.

Moreover, Carter immediately compounded his mistake. In the wake of the malaise speech, the president sought to underscore his determination to regain control of his political fortunes by dramatically purging his cabinet. In a move that reminded many Washington veterans of Richard Nixon's plan for an administrative housecleaning after his 1972 electoral triumph, Carter requested the resignations of his entire cabinet, plus senior White House staff, and then announced the departure of five cabinet officers. The press and public interpreted the shake-up not as a sign of self-confident renewal but as an indication that the government was imploding. In the immediate aftermath of the malaise speech, Carter had enjoyed a brief dead-cat bounce in his approval rating, but after the cabinet purge the Harris poll reported an immediate drop in his overall rating to the lowest level ever recorded for a modern president. As Walter Mondale remembered, "It went from sugar to shit right there."[55] A joke that started making the rounds on Capitol Hill asked, "What do you do when Jimmy Carter comes at you brandishing a pin?" The punch line: "You run like hell. He's got a grenade in his mouth!"[56]

In the last months of 1979, events halfway around the world conspired to add further tribulations to Carter's year of horrors. Ironically, Carter at first opposed the requests by the deposed and exiled Shah of Iran for admittance to the United States. "Does somebody have the answer," he asked at one meeting, "as to what we do if the diplomats in our embassy are taken hostage?"[57] But in late October he relented in the face of importuning by the Shah's powerful American champions (including such Republican stalwarts as Henry Kissinger and David Rockefeller). When the Shah, suffering from a fatal cancer, entered the country on a tourist visa seeking medical treatment, outraged Islamic radicals made Carter's fear a reality by seizing the staff and Marine Corps guard of the U.S. Embassy in Teheran. The administration worked both in public and behind the scenes to achieve a negotiated solution to the kidnapping of the American diplomats, shuttling the exiled Shah to Panama and freezing billions of dollars in Iranian assets in the United States—all to no avail. Carter watched helplessly as the hostage crisis became a national obsession.

At first, public opinion rallied to the president's support, as Americans interpreted the hostage situation as an assault on their nation. But that support became increasingly soft and frustration set in when the crisis dragged on. "Through TV," wrote Haynes Johnson of the *Washington Post*, "the Iranian crisis became institutionalized and a part of American daily life: the networks began and ended their daily telecasts by numbering each day the Americans had been seized. Reminders of Iran were constant—and, to the TV viewer, inescapable. TV programs were broadcast under such running titles as 'Americans Held Hostage.'"[58] The relentless media coverage made it impossible to escape the realization that the United States had been unable to protect its own diplomats abroad on the nation's business, and was now unable to impose its will on a distant land with but a weak grip on modernity in order to right the perceived wrong.

While America found itself helpless in the hostage crisis, its cold war antagonist was on the march. On Christmas Day, 1979, Soviet forces invaded Afghanistan in order to bolster a Marxist government under attack by a tribal and religious rebellion. The Russians acted under the Brezhnev doctrine, which called for the forces of socialism to intervene internationally in order to prevent the triumph of counterrevolution. Carter responded vigorously, calling the Soviet action "even more serious than Hungary or Czechoslovakia" and "the most serious threat to world peace since World War II."[59] He recalled the U.S. ambassador from Moscow, instituted a grain embargo against the Soviet Union, and banned American athletes from participating in the upcoming summer Olympics in Moscow. But none of those moves had any visible effect on the Soviet intervention.

A final blow to America's sense of itself as a world power came in April 1980, when the administration in desperation launched a necessarily complicated and risky military mission to rescue the hostages. The result was an embarrassing debacle. Because of equipment failures after the mission was underway, at their first refueling stop deep in the Iranian desert the rescuers discovered that they had too few operational helicopters to allow the elite Delta Team force of ninety commandos to proceed further on their planned foray into Tehran. Reluctantly, the commanders on the scene scrubbed the mission. But while the refueling was being completed, one of the copters accidentally lurched into a prop transport with horrific results. The flight crews of the helicopter and the plane were incinerated in a terrible explosion. Hastily abandoning the scene, the rescue force loaded into the remaining transport aircraft and departed, leaving on the ground the burning hulks of the crashed airplane, the now-abandoned helicopters (which were left intact because the commandos feared that blowing them up might block the desert runway with debris), and the charred bodies of eight dead Americans. Gleeful Iranian authorities brought the bodies to Tehran and put them on display at the U.S. Embassy, where militants poked at them for the benefit of television cameras. It now seemed that American impotence was complete.

In the summer of 1980, the journalist William Kowinski chronicled the life and concerns of several middle-class American families. The keynote of his report was anxiety: the "feelings of dismay and confusion that accumulate when inflation and recession change the value of money and all that money means, culturally and psychologically; when the assumptions of several generations about America's expertise and leadership and this country's pre-eminent place in the world are jumbled and wounded; when values are distorted and called into question by economic conditions that affect, in different ways, every class in society." Middle-class Americans, he reported on the basis of his impressionistic study, worried that their dream—the American dream—was slipping from their grasp.[60] The combination of Carter's failure to deal effectively with the nation's vexing problems and the president's pessimistic analysis of those problems and of the nation's future heightened the fear of Americans, and left them increasingly receptive to the blandishments of a former movie actor who still saw America and the future in bright Technicolor hues.

Chapter 2

ENTER RONALD REAGAN, PRAGMATIC IDEOLOGUE

Ronald Reagan was a product of Hollywood in more ways than one. In the literal sense, Americans first met him as an actor on screens large and small, both in movies and on television, over the course of a show business career that spanned four decades. He used his visibility and training as a performer to good advantage in launching a subsequent political career, yet throughout his rise from state to national politics critics routinely dismissed him as merely an actor, someone pretending to be something he was not. For good or ill, his work experience in the movies appeared to matter. But Reagan seemed a product of Hollywood in a grander metaphorical sense as well. His life story read like a movie script celebrating the American Dream. He came from genuinely humble origins in the American heartland, graduated from a small, nondescript, sectarian college at the depth of the Great Depression, and left home for the dream state of California to make his fortune and build his life in the fiercely competitive realms of show business and politics. It was a rise worthy of the silver screen, the story of a man molded by his small-town Midwestern upbringing, his experiences in Hollywood, and his own gradual ideological and political transit from left to right.

GROWING UP IN ILLINOIS

"When I was a child, we moved a lot," Ronald Reagan observed laconically in his later years.[1] Indeed, he did, all over Illinois: Tampico, Chicago, Galesburg,

Monmouth, Tampico again, Dixon, all before he turned ten years of age. His family always rented, sometimes a flat, other times a small house; there was no family farm or store; neither parent had finished high school. His father, Jack Reagan, sold shoes for a living. He was a sometimes-charming man, possessed of the proverbial Irish gift of gab, a great storyteller. But the father's achievements never caught up to his dreams of success, and, perhaps as a consequence, perhaps because of more ingrained and less mutable causes, he went through life an alcoholic. Ronald Reagan's mother Nelle was the kind of person often described as saintly. She worked tirelessly to hold her family together through personal and economic adversity, finding both inspiration and consolation in her deeply held evangelical religious faith as a member of the Christian Church (also known as the Disciples of Christ).[2]

Reagan, nicknamed "Dutch" by his father at birth in 1911, was nine years old when the family finally settled in Dixon, Illinois, a small town of nearly ten thousand that would, for him, be "home." "It was," he recalled, "a small universe where I learned standards and values that would guide me for the rest of my life."[3] He was, literally and figuratively, a son of the Middle West.

Dutch Reagan's childhood was not without its challenges. He came to Dixon, along with his older brother Neil (nicknamed "Moon" by school chums), a new kid in a small town at a time when Americans were less peripatetic than they would subsequently become; the process of fitting in necessarily took a little doing. Like most boys of grade-school age in such places at that time, he wanted to be a sports hero, but his relatively small size and bad eyesight held him back. He would fill out handsomely at puberty and at about the same time would discover that his vision could be corrected with eyeglasses, but that was later. In the meantime, he recalled as an adult, "my troubles in sports, along with always having been the new kid in school, left me with some insecurities." He developed a somewhat introverted nature, finding "a lot of enjoyment during those first years in Dixon in solitary ways—reading, studying wildlife, and exploring the local wilderness."[4] At age ten he took out a library card and thereafter checked out an average of two books a week, mostly boys' adventure stories.[5]

In time, however, the youngest Reagan blossomed in the social hothouse of small-town life. He developed into a superb swimmer and began working summers as a lifeguard at Dixon's local three-hundred-acre Lowell Park, where he became a local legend for rescuing seventy-seven bathers over the course of seven summers from the occasionally swift-running waters of the Rock River. In his senior year at North Dixon High School, Dutch Reagan was senior class president, president of the school drama club, and vice-president of the Boys' Hi-Y; he played on the varsity football and basketball teams, and he dated one of the prettiest girls in Dixon—a minister's daughter. By the time he left to attend Eureka College, a small Disciples of Christ school in rural Illinois some 110 miles away, he had indeed made Dixon his home.

One can see in Reagan's childhood in Dixon, just beneath the surface, the emergence of two particular character traits that significantly colored the whole of his adult life. The first was an emotional aloofness that would plague Reagan in his personal relationships. Reagan had been, in his words, "a little introverted and probably a little slow in making really close friends" during his first years in Dixon. "In some ways," he continued in his post-presidential memoirs, "I think this reluctance to get close to people never left me completely. I've never had trouble making friends, but I've been inclined to hold back a little of myself, reserving it for myself." Neil Reagan has noted that both brothers shared this detachment with their father, and it is tempting to speculate that they perhaps modeled their emotional behavior on his or inherited his emotional style in ways science still does not completely understand. (Peggy Noonan, a Reagan speechwriter and, later, biographer, speculates that Reagan's life-long emotional reserve was typical of children from alcoholic homes. Experts have observed that, because they come to distrust the alcoholic parent, such children often develop "the colossal terror of being close.")[6] Whatever the source, Reagan's emotional self-containment surfaced later in life in his closest relationships, causing considerable pain in his ties with his children and with associates who often found themselves longing for a closeness of connection that Reagan seemed unwilling or unable to provide.

If his father contributed to Reagan's emotional detachment, a second childhood legacy, imparted almost certainly by his mother, proved a more salutary gift. Dutch Reagan grew to become an exceedingly optimistic human being; indeed, that optimism became his signature personality trait. Psychologists estimate that as much as 25 percent of an individual's optimism is heritable.[7] If so, Nelle Reagan must be considered the prime contributor. As Reagan himself recalled, "While my father was a cynic and tended to suspect the worst of people, my mother was the opposite. She always expected to find the best in people and often did."[8] In addition, Nelle provided her younger son with a strong religious foundation and spiritual worldview, which researchers have found to promote feelings of hope, faith, and optimism.[9] Religion was at the center of Nelle's life, and her example led Dutch to ask to be baptized in the Christian Church at age twelve. "Because a lot of Nelle's great sense of religious faith rubbed off on me, I have always prayed a lot," he later recalled.[10] Ronald Reagan was deeply religious in his youth and remained so as an adult (uninformed press commentary to the contrary notwithstanding), which contributed significantly to his sunny nature.

Recent research into the sources and nature of optimism also suggests that how parents, especially primary caretakers (in most cases, mothers), explain adversity to their children—their so-called explanatory or attributional style— has an important influence on the children's later optimism.[11] Mothers incline their children toward optimism if, when explaining life's inevitable adversities, they explain that misfortunes are temporary rather than permanent, specific to one problem rather than pervasive throughout one's life, and external in their causation rather than the result of personal flaws or mistakes. In such matters, Nelle was a textbook case; she was, her son remembered, imbued with "a sense of optimism that ran as deep as the cosmos. . . . [My mother] told me that everything in life happened for a purpose. She said all things were part of God's Plan, even the most disheartening setbacks, and in the end, everything worked out for the best. If something went wrong, she said, you didn't let it get you down: You stepped away from it, stepped over it, and moved on." She repeated constantly "that everything works out for the best and that every reverse in life carries the seeds of something better in the future."[12]

Reagan's optimism came into play as he moved away from the comforts of Dixon and out into the larger world. It took a certain daring and an upbeat sense of the future for a poor boy to be the first member of his family ever to complete high school and then go off to college, at a time when fewer than 7 percent of high school graduates went on to higher education.[13] Reagan's collegiate experience was a happy one. Eureka College consisted of five ivy-covered buildings and had fewer than 250 students; and its scale seemed an extension of the small-town life he had experienced in Dixon. He worked his way through college by means of a needy student scholarship, a tuition deferral, and jobs washing dishes at his fraternity house and at a women's dormitory, along with odd stints working in the school's steam plant. Although he earned only average grades as an economics major, he enjoyed success in the several other realms of American collegiate life, lettering in football and track; coaching and starring on the swim team; serving as student body president and president of the Eureka Boosters Club, basketball cheerleader, and yearbook features editor; and excelling in campus theatrical productions.

A LIFE IN SHOW BUSINESS

When Reagan graduated from Eureka College in 1932, the United States was descending into the lowest depths of the Great Depression. His personal prospects appeared to hit bottom when he lost his bid to become the manager of the sporting goods department in Dixon's Montgomery Ward store, but he rebounded by directing his aspirations upward and outward—he decided to leave Dixon to look for a job in radio. His spirit and determination, coupled with his love of both sport and radio, landed him a job broadcasting Big Ten football games for WOC, a weak 1,000-watt station in Davenport, Iowa. Before long he was working as a sports announcer at WOC's sister station, WHO in Des Moines, one of only fifteen high-powered 50,000-watt clear channel stations in the entire country. He quickly won a name for himself with his ability to re-create Chicago Cubs baseball games by providing a colorful play-by-play version of the contest from a bare-bones telegraphic account of the results. While the nation was still mired in the Great Depression, Reagan, at the age of twenty-two, enjoyed a salary of $75 a week and became a minor celebrity in the Midwest. "If I had stopped there," he later observed, "I believe I would have been happy the rest of my life."[14]

What is striking is that Reagan did not stop there. His amiability cloaked a fierce ambition. Despite his success in radio, Reagan continued to harbor fantasies of an acting career. His mother Nelle had introduced him to dramatic readings and skits as a child, and he had been much influenced by memorable theater teachers in both high school and college. In fact, he had always envisioned radio work as a possible springboard to acting: "I'd seen several movies in which sports announcers played themselves and thought there was a remote possibility the job might lead me into the movies."[15] In 1937 Reagan volunteered his own vacation time to accompany the Chicago Cubs baseball team out to California for its spring training. Through an old radio friend from WHO now enjoying minor success as an actress for RKO, he met an agent who arranged a screen test at Warner Bros., one of the major Hollywood production studios. When he returned to Des Moines, a telegram informed him that Warner Bros. had offered him a seven-year contract, renewable every six months at the studio's discretion, starting at $200 a week. He immediately wired the agent: "SIGN BEFORE THEY CHANGE THEIR MINDS. DUTCH REAGAN." It was, he later recalled, "a fantasy come true."[16] A combination of pluck and luck had taken him a long way—from the nation's depressed heartland, from the small-town America of Tampico and Dixon, Illinois, to fabled Hollywood, the most powerful dream factory in the history of the world.

Reagan's movie career was not a story of instant stardom, but rather the tale of a slow rise to leading-man respectability. He went to work immediately in Warners' "B" movies, which were designed to showcase and test-market industry newcomers. The Bs were low-budget productions, usually shot in just a few weeks with a running time of sixty minutes rather than the ninety minutes of full-fledged "A" feature films. As Reagan was fond of quipping, "They were movies the studio didn't want good, they wanted 'em Thursday."[17] He paid his dues, appearing in a raft of such forgettable films—including a number as Brass Bancroft, a heroic Secret Service agent constantly on the trail of counterfeiters, smugglers, and spies.

The studio system really worked, and Reagan slowly moved into Warners' A-film lineup. In 1940 he won a measure of renown for his role as George Gipp in *Knute Rockne—All American*. Gipp was the insouciant Notre Dame running back who, according to Notre Dame legend, on his deathbed told his coach, the fabled Rockne, "Someday, when the team's up against it, breaks are beating the boys, ask them to go in there with all they've got. Win one for the Gipper."[18] The line was one seared into the fantasy memory of young boys across the land for decades after Reagan's winning performance. The critical highpoint of his acting career came in 1942, when Reagan costarred in *Kings Row*, famously awakening in one scene to find that both his legs have been needlessly amputated by a sadistic doctor, looking down at the sheet lying flat where his legs should have been and crying, "Randy! Where's the *rest* of me?"[19] Reagan appeared in thirty-one films before his career was interrupted by military service during World War II, and a Gallup Poll in early 1942 ranked him seventy-fourth among the top one hundred movie stars, tied for that position with Laurence Olivier.[20] He was clearly not a star of the first magnitude, not a Clark Gable, Jimmy Stewart, or Errol Flynn; but Warner Bros. considered him a dependable craftsman with audience appeal. In 1944 the studio rewarded him with a contract calling for $1 million over seven years (at the rate of $3,500 per week for forty-three weeks in each of the seven years).[21]

Reagan also had a life off-camera, and it was fully as important in his development as his movie successes. He had grown up talking politics with his father, a yellow-dog Democrat who had for a time helped to administer New Deal welfare efforts in Dixon, and carried with him into show business an omnivorous but undisciplined intellectual curiosity. In Hollywood the serious and autodidactic side of his nature became increasing evident. Indeed, his first wife, the talented actress Jane Wyman, whom he married in 1940, observed tartly, "Don't ask Ronnie what time it is because he will tell you how a watch is made."[22] After serving three years during the war as an officer in the army air corps, making military training films in Culver City, California, Reagan returned to civilian life with the liberal sympathies he inherited from his father wholly intact and with a new thirst for civic engagement. He was, he recalled, "a New Dealer to the core" when the war ended and he joined "any organization I could find that guaranteed to save the world," including the Americans for Democratic Action, the United World Federalists, the American Veterans Committee, and the Hollywood Independent Citizens Committee of the Arts, Sciences, and Professions.[23] (Reagan soon resigned from the latter two organizations when he came to believe they were not truly liberal groups, but rather Communist fronts.)

The chief vehicle for Reagan's increasing civic engagement was his profession's labor union, the Screen Actors Guild (SAG). He considered himself "a rabid union man."[24] Reagan first joined SAG in 1937, served as the union's president from 1947 to 1952, and returned for a final presidential term in 1959–60. SAG was a relatively conservative union, interested primarily in "bread and butter" issues involving compensation and working conditions, but under Reagan's leadership it confronted some of the most difficult problems ever to face the movie industry—violent union jurisdictional struggles that convulsed Hollywood in the early postwar years; a bitter battle over Communist influence in the movie industry, accompanied by a highly publicized investigation by the notoriously heavy-handed House Un-American Activities Committee; the demise of the studio system as a result of antitrust litigation; a challenge to the very viability of the movie business by the upstart new medium called television; and a struggle over the issue of residuals (payments to actors for the later sale or commercial use of their creative performances, usually on TV) that led to SAG's first strike in 1960. Reagan's signal achievement as a labor leader was getting residuals for his members, first in 1952 for actors on TV and then in 1960 for actors in films (with retroactive residuals for films made from 1948 to 1959 going to fund a new pension program). Residuals gave SAG members an opportunity to share in both the immediate and the subsequent profits of their creation; they were an innovation in intellectual property relations, one bitterly opposed by the producers in both the television and movie industries.[25]

Reagan's SAG experience was formative for him as an individual in two significant ways. First, it imbued him with an anti-Communism that became a core ingredient of his emergent political identity. "These were eye-opening years for me," he later wrote. He became convinced that, with American films filling up nearly three quarters of the playing time in the world's theaters in the immediate postwar years, "Joseph Stalin had set out to make Hollywood an instrument of propaganda for his program of Soviet expansionism aimed at communizing the world."[26] Reagan—and he was not alone—saw the industry's postwar union jurisdictional disputes and the infiltration of established liberal groups in Hollywood as part of a larger Communist effort to take over the movie industry. He was not making it up: Max Silver, a Los Angeles County Communist leader, subsequently recalled that "the Communist party was very much interested in the success [of its favored union in the jurisdictional struggle]. . . . Its interest lay in the main to establish what we called a progressive center in Hollywood. . . . The party was interested in establishing a nerve center that would be to some extent influenced by party policy and party people."[27] During the labor unrest, Reagan urged SAG members to cross picket lines and continue working, and when anonymously threatened with personal violence for his stand, he followed the suggestion of the Burbank, California, police and carried a handgun in a shoulder holster for seven months. "Now I knew from firsthand experience," he later recalled, "how Communists used lies, deceit, violence, or any other tactic that suited them. . . . I knew from the experience of hand-to-hand combat that America faced no more insidious or evil threat than that of Communism."[28] When the FBI asked him to serve as an informant regarding Communist activity in Hollywood, Reagan readily agreed.[29]

Reagan's SAG experience was formative also in that it helped him become an unusually effective negotiator. Throughout his subsequent political career, Reagan relied on skills that he had developed in long Hollywood negotiating sessions with studio bosses on a variety of contentious work-related issues. "He

was an aggressive man," observed Jack Dales, a SAG executive who represented the union in negotiations along with its elected officers: "Depending upon
the situation he was two men . . . aggressive fighter across the table, then in
conference among ourselves in our caucuses . . . most realistic—'Look, what
are we going to get, what do we need? If we can go this far with A maybe we
can go that far and then we can get a hunk of B'—most reasonable, realistic
in conference, but aggressive to the point of temper in negotiations, of losing
his temper."[30]

Reagan emerged from the SAG presidency with a nuanced approach to the
art of negotiation: He liked to negotiate from strength and was willing to walk
away from the bargaining table in the belief that no agreement was preferable
to a bad one. At the same time, however, he was always ready to compromise
when necessary in order to gain his chief aims, and to take what he could get
in a deal and then come back at some later point for more. His close political
adviser Ed Meese (later his White House counselor and the nation's attorney
general) noted that "the techniques he employed in dealing with the Democrats in Sacramento and Washington, or with Gorbachev at Geneva, were
. . . honed during extensive negotiating sessions with heads of the motion
picture studios."[31]

While Reagan's civic and union engagement blossomed, his acting career
faltered badly. Military service had interrupted his career at a crucial point, just
as he was positioning himself for a possible breakthrough into the first rank of
stars. Although he made twenty-two films after the war, he was unable to recapture his earlier momentum, and his acting ability was not sufficient in itself to
offset the inevitable cost of aging in a business that revolved, even for males,
around youth and personal appearance. Good roles became increasingly hard
to obtain. Moreover, the entire movie industry was caught in a downturn that
many blamed on the competition from television. Reagan hit bottom professionally in 1954 when, in order to pay the bills, he emceed a fifty-minute song-
and-dance revue, complete with a line of chorus girls dressed in a South American motif, at Las Vegas's Last Frontier Hotel for a two-week engagement.

Ironically, it was the upstart medium of TV that resuscitated Reagan's flag-
ging show business career. In late 1954 he signed a contract with General Electric to host (and occasionally star in) that firm's weekly dramatic anthology
television program, the *General Electric Theater*. The series quickly became a
viewing staple, running eight very successful seasons in the 9:00 p.m. Sunday
time-slot. The deal also called upon Reagan to serve as an internal corporate
spokesman for GE, and he succeeded in that role also, spending approximately
sixteen weeks a year on the road touring and speaking to employees in literally
all of the giant firm's 139 plants in thirty-nine states. At first, he spoke about his
adventures in show business, but in time his standard talk became increasingly
political—and his politics were in the process of dramatic change.

Dutch Reagan had worn a "Win with Roosevelt" button on his swimsuit while a lifeguard at Dixon's Lowell Park, and had cast his first presidential vote for FDR, whom he idolized for inspiring the nation with a message of optimism and hope in the dark days of the Great Depression. He continued to identify himself as a liberal and a Democrat during his SAG presidency, and in 1948 he campaigned for both Truman and the crusading liberal Hubert H. Humphrey (who was running for the U.S. Senate from Minnesota on the basis of a strong civil rights record); in 1950 he supported the liberal Democrat Helen Gahagen Douglas in her unsuccessful bid for the U.S. Senate against Richard Nixon. But he was beginning increasingly to see dangers on the left and to view activist government as a problem rather than a solution.

Reagan's conversion to conservatism resulted from several influences. His struggle with Communists in the postwar Hollywood red scare left him deeply antagonistic to the far left and increasingly suspicious of the judgment of liberals, many of whom seemed unable or unwilling to recognize the threat he now saw so clearly. Meanwhile, as his earning power increased, he became increasingly critical of the post-New Deal tax system, which at the highest income tax rate took over 90 cents of the last dollar earned. More and more, he saw government regulation not as a necessary safeguard and protection for the proverbial "little guy" but rather as a constraint on the dynamism of America's real achievers. As his political views changed, so did his political behavior. He voted for Eisenhower in both the 1952 and 1956 presidential elections and by 1960 had become a Republican in all but formal affiliation. He campaigned in 1960 as a Democrat for Nixon, retaining his Democratic registration only because Nixon believed Reagan would be more helpful appearing to cross party lines to give his support. Finally, in 1962, in the midst of supporting Nixon's gubernatorial bid in California, he formally changed his political registration.

Reagan's work for GE reflected his political journey from left to right. Visiting the far-flung GE manufacturing empire, he talked more and more about the depredations of government. "Pretty soon," he later reminisced, "[my speech] became basically a warning to people about the threat of government. Finally, the Hollywood part just got lost and I was out there beating the bushes for private enterprise."[32] But the politicization of Reagan's public persona was not without problems: When he attacked the Tennessee Valley Authority in 1959 as an example of wasteful big-government expansionism, at a time when the TVA was a $50 million-a-year GE customer, Reagan's corporate sponsor gently persuaded him that such was not quite the public relations they were paying for. Later, in 1962, GE insisted he eliminate politics from his speeches and focus more on the wonders of electricity and the firm's product line, but Reagan refused to work as an apolitical pitchman and he and GE parted ways. Reagan kept his hand in television, making a final made-for-TV movie in

1964 and hosting another TV series—the syndicated, non-network *Death Valley Days*—for twenty-one half-hour episodes in 1965–66, but after his contract with GE expired he moved ever more visibly into the world of conservative politics, a realm that now gave him his primary self-identification.

AN ACTOR IN CALIFORNIA POLITICS

In the early 1960s Reagan branched out as a public speaker and began addressing a variety of business groups and anti-Communist organizations. He contributed articles to the conservative journal *Human Events* and joined the national board of the Young Americans for Freedom, a conservative youth group. In 1964 Reagan attended the Republican national convention as an alternate delegate; he later served as the co-chair of Barry Goldwater's presidential campaign in California and taped a television commercial in support of the quixotic Arizonan. When, in the run-up to the election, Goldwater informed some of his West Coast backers that he would be unable to attend a $1,000-a-plate fund-raiser in Los Angeles, they asked Reagan, who by now was well known to conservative activists, to step in.

Reagan wowed his audience with the same basic conservative call-to-arms that he had been polishing for years as a GE spokesman, and Goldwater's local California backers enthusiastically suggested that he repeat his remarks on national television. Reagan agreed to tape the speech before a live audience of invited Republicans, and that version was aired a week before Election Day under the title "A Time for Choosing." The response was electrifying. Replayed at fundraisers in the waning days of the campaign, "The Speech," as it came to be known, ultimately brought in $8 million in contributions for the candidate and the party, an impressive sum at the time. Goldwater suffered a crushing defeat in the election, but the political journalist David Broder called Reagan's performance "the most successful national political debut since William Jennings Bryan electrified the 1896 Democratic Convention with the 'Cross of Gold' speech."[33]

Reagan now found himself a star in a new firmament. Within months, the wealthy California Republicans who had bankrolled his speech for Goldwater approached him to run for statewide office. The fundraisers, who would broaden their number over the years and serve as Reagan's informal "Kitchen Cabinet" throughout his time in public life, were men who already knew Reagan socially. They were the sort of people whose company and views Reagan valued—ideological conservatives, largely self-made men with deep pockets who had come to the Golden State from the Midwest or the Dust Bowl with more ambition than wealth and then had hit it big. Henry Salvatori had come to America from Italy as a child and made a fortune in oil; Holmes Tuttle, part Chickasaw Indian, had left Oklahoma to make a fortune selling cars in

Southern California; Ed Mills was a Dutch immigrant who had moved from stock boy to company chairman at Van de Kamp's Holland Dutch Bakers, Inc. in Los Angeles, a massive retail bakery chain; A.C. "Cy" Rubel was the board chairman of Union Oil. They saw in Reagan a charismatic amateur with a gift for articulating their mutually shared values, and they persuaded him to run for governor of the nation's most dynamic state when the liberal incumbent Pat Brown came up for reelection in 1966.

Reagan announced his candidacy for governor in January 1966. When a reporter noted that Reagan was still appearing on *Death Valley Days* and asked if he'd give Pat Brown equal time, the challenger quipped, "Well sure, our audience is accustomed to seeing both ends of the horse."[34] What was perhaps most surprising about Reagan's subsequent campaign was the pragmatism he displayed. He proved himself an eminently practical politician, one who wanted to win as much as he wanted to put the world on the right track. Chosen by his backers for his staunch conservatism, Reagan ran to the center-right in a conscious effort to win over both moderate Republicans and conservative Democrats. He emphasized the failure of Pat Brown (and California liberalism more generally) to come to grips with urban racial unrest, rising crime, the "mess at Berkeley," and other law-and-order problems, but he took care to couch his indictment in optimistic terms. "Our problems are many," he proclaimed, "but our capacity for solving them is limitless."[35] He countered the vision of a liberal Great Society with his own call for a Creative Society, to be built on individual initiative rather than public action. He also unified a badly fractured Republican Party by invoking the so-called Eleventh Commandment—"Thou shalt not speak ill of any fellow Republican." Putting the precept into action, he incorporated the supporters of his liberal Republican primary opponent, former San Francisco mayor George Christopher, into his own campaign immediately once the general election campaign got underway. At the same time, he avoided offending his own extremist supporters on the GOP's right fringe, observing, "Anyone who chooses to support me has bought my philosophy. I'm not buying theirs."[36]

Reagan had the good fortune to be underestimated by both friend and foe. His former employer Jack Warner, upon first learning of the actor's possible candidacy, is reported to have exclaimed, "Reagan for Governor? No, Jimmy Stewart for Governor, Ronnie Reagan for best friend."[37] The Democrats thought Reagan would be a pushover. As Pat Brown later wrote, "We . . . rubbed our hands in gleeful anticipation of beating this politically inexperienced, right-wing extremist and aging actor in 1966."[38] With expectations so low, Reagan seemed always to be gaining momentum by exceeding them, a not inconsiderable advantage in electoral politics. When the Brown campaign finally woke up to the fact they were in the fight of their lives, they fell back on the discordant and ultimately ineffective strategy of portraying Reagan as simultaneously an idiot actor and an extremist threat to Western Civilization. On Election Day, the overachieving underdog won in a landslide, defeating the incumbent by nearly a million votes, winning by a margin of 58 percent to 42 percent while carrying fifty-five of California's fifty-eight counties.

Winning the election was one thing, governing quite another. When asked soon after his victory what kind of governor he would make, Reagan joked, "I don't know, I've never played a governor."[39] As governor he assumed responsibility for public policy in the nation's most populous state (with more than 20 million inhabitants, California had a larger population than many of the world's nation states) and the sixth largest economy on earth (after the United States itself, the USSR, Britain, France, Japan, and West Germany).[40] As it turned out, Reagan proved himself a fervent conservative who was also highly skilled in the political arts of maneuver and compromise.

At first, Reagan's inexperience (and ideological zeal) showed to less than good advantage. He arrived in Sacramento to greet a full-blown fiscal crisis. The departing Brown administration had changed the state's accounting procedures in ways that managed to hide the fact that California was on the brink of insolvency, spending more than it was taking in. Faced with a budget crunch inherited from his predecessor, Reagan sought to trim state expenditures by instituting a 10 percent across-the-board spending cut, reflecting the conservative belief that all government operations were by definition oversized and wasteful. But that ham-fisted tactic penalized the already lean and rewarded the truly bloated among state agencies. The state legislature insisted on a more discriminating approach and turned down Reagan's first proposed budget. The new governor committed another gaffe of ideological naïveté when he suggested that state employees work voluntarily on the state holidays of Lincoln's and Washington's birthdays, which many interpreted as an insinuation that they failed to work sufficiently hard during their regular hours. Fewer than 2 percent of state workers made the demeaning sacrifice. Still scrambling for a quick-fix solution, Reagan then suffered a self-inflicted public-relations wound when he approved large-scale staff cuts in the state's system of mental hospitals, seeming to validate fears that he was an amiable but cold-blooded extremist.

Reagan proved a fast learner, however, and quickly demonstrated a political nimbleness that surprised his critics. After only two months in office and after having campaigned vigorously as a tax cutter, he called for the largest tax increase in the history of California, or any other state for that matter. Moreover, the $1 billion tax hike Reagan and the Democratic leader of the state assembly, the colorful Jesse M. "Big Daddy" Unruh, cobbled together also reformed the California tax system, moving it, in the judgment of the keenest chronicler of Reagan's political career, Lou Cannon, from "a regressive one that took little account of ability to pay into a reasonably progressive system."[41] State senator George Deukmejian, a future Republican governor of the Golden State, later commented, "A lot of people, including me, thought he would be ideological. We learned quickly that he was very practical."[42]

Reagan's flexible practicality showed in other ways, as well. After opposing the Civil Rights Act of 1964 on what he described as constitutional grounds, he appointed more minorities to office than any of his gubernatorial predecessors. Putting aside his personal beliefs, Reagan signed the Therapeutic Abortion Act of 1967, a liberalized law that allowed for abortion on mental-health, as well as physical-health, grounds. (In the wake of the new law, the number of legal abortions performed in California rose from 518 in 1967 to 199,089 in 1980, and Reagan came to regret his action almost immediately.)[43] He initially opposed the state's adoption of an income tax withholding scheme, fearing that the elimination of burdensome lump-sum tax payments would make it easier to raise taxes. His feet, he told the press, were cast in concrete on the issue. Here, too, he finally surrendered to the suasion of his own state finance director, who argued that the existing lump-sum system put unnecessary strain on the state revenue system. Announcing his change of heart, he explained to amused reporters, "The sound you hear is the concrete cracking around my feet."[44]

Perhaps most surprising to his critics, Reagan as governor carved out an acceptable and somewhat forward-looking environmental record. His appointments in that area were first-rate. Norman "Ike" Livermore, his executive director for resources, among other achievements championed the breeding in captivity of the endangered California condor. William Mott, his state parks director, oversaw the addition of 145,000 acres of land and two vast underwater Pacific Ocean preserves to the state parks system during Reagan's tenure. The administration also succeeded in killing several environmentally unsound projects, despite the fact that their planning was well advanced. Reagan halted the effort to build a massive dam at Dos Rios on the scenic Eel River, and also killed the effort to build a trans-Sierra highway, in order, he said, to "preserve the vast, primitive beauty of this wilderness for generations of Californians yet to come."[45]

Reagan's brand of pragmatic conservatism proved popular enough with voters to enable him to win re-election in 1970 over Speaker Unruh. The margin of victory was only half that of 1966, but the win was still impressive in an election year that saw Republicans lose ground at both the state and national levels.

The major achievements in Reagan's second term came in the form of both victory and, paradoxically, defeat. The triumph was welfare reform. Welfare rolls were growing in a way that troubled practical politicians of all stripes. The number of Californians receiving Aid to Families with Dependent Children (AFDC) benefits rose from 375,000 in 1963 to 769,000 in 1967 and by 1970 had reached 1,566,000 (nearly one out of every thirteen Californians). Negotiating face-to-face with the new state assembly speaker, the young and ambitious

Los Angeles Democrat Bob Moretti, Reagan helped hammer out a compromise welfare reform package, the California Welfare Reform Act of 1971, which tightened eligibility requirements and strengthened safeguards against welfare fraud while at the same time increasing the size of welfare grants for 80 percent of recipients. By 1974, the state's welfare rolls had turned downward to 1,330,000. The new law also provided for an experimental program requiring able-bodied recipients without small children to work in public-sector jobs, so-called workfare. Although the workfare experiment was terminated by Reagan's Democratic successor in 1975, it served as a model for a subsequent experiment in Wisconsin and ultimately for the federal welfare reform of 1996.[46]

If welfare reform showcased Reagan's ability to negotiate and willingness to compromise, the other great effort of his second term demonstrated his ideological fire. Reagan's willingness to take risks and his ability to view old problems in new ways, to be both bold and original, were clearly demonstrated by his campaign in 1973 to hardwire tax and spending limitations into California's constitutional framework. The episode, little noticed by historians, began when Reagan reported that the state had amassed an $850 million budget surplus and asked the legislature to return the money to taxpayers. The Democratic-controlled legislature balked, and Reagan took the issue to the people by organizing an initiative drive to place on the ballot a tax limitation amendment to the state constitution.

As presented to the voters, Proposition 1 was a long (5,700 words), complicated piece of legalese. In essence, it proposed a constitutional limit on the percentage of total personal income within the state that could be collected in revenue in any one year without a special vote of the people, which would have the effect of lowering taxes and tying subsequent state spending increases to the growth in personal income. With iron-clad precision, Prop I would, after a fifteen-year phase-in, limit total state revenue to a little over 7 percent of the total personal income generated in California. In addition, Prop 1 would add to the state constitution the requirement that all tax legislation be approved by a super-majority of two-thirds vote in both houses of the state legislature.

Reagan was the driving force behind Prop 1. He turned to Lewis Uhler, a member of his staff, to oversee the drafting of the proposal, and appointed a former head of the University of Southern California, Dr. Norman Topping, to lead the group Californians for Lower Taxes that spearheaded the fight to get the petition measure on the November 1973 ballot. He also released his top political operative, Michael Deaver, to coordinate the effort to deliver the winning votes on Election Day. Reagan threw all of his political capital into the struggle, making it a personal cause to such a degree that observers interpreted the effort as his opening drive to win the presidency in 1976. (Nixon was, at this point, still safely enjoying his second presidential term, as yet relatively unharmed by the Watergate scandal.) The economist Milton Friedman, by then a nationally recognized free-market guru with a regular column in *Newsweek*, participated in the drafting of Prop 1, and he and Reagan barn-stormed across the state in a small private plane—extraordinary given Reagan's deep aversion to flying—in an effort to build support for the measure. Reagan plumped for the idea at the National Governors' Conference, and mounted an expensive statewide telephone campaign using a pitch for Prop 1 that he himself had recorded.

In the event, Reagan's Prop 1 failed at the ballot box. In November 1973 California's voters defeated the proposal by a 54–46 percent margin. Post-mortems suggested that the measure lost in large part because of its verbose complexity—no one, not even its champions, seemed fully to understand it. Reagan inadvertently shot himself in the foot a week before the election during a television interview, when he was asked whether the average voter would be able to understand the language of the proposal: "No, he shouldn't try," he chuckled. "I don't either."[47] Many Californians went to the polls having read Reagan's careless quip set in large type in full-page ads paid for by the Prop 1 opposition.

But while Reagan lost his personal battle for Prop I, others would take his idea that the only sure way to limit government spending was to limit taxation and go on to win significant victories. As Reagan told a receptive business audience while campaigning for the amendment, "You can lecture your teen-agers about spending too much until you're blue in the face, or you can ac-complish the same goal by cutting their allowance. We think it is time to limit government's allowance—to put a limit on the amount of money they can take from the people in taxes. This is the only way we will ever bring govern-ment spending under control."[48] Reagan's insight, that government spending was best attacked by cutting government revenue, helped launch the modern tax limitation movement.

Reagan's approach became a staple of conservative political economy on both the state and national levels. In 1975, Lewis Uhler, who headed the task force that drafted Prop 1, created the National Tax Limitation Committee, which subsequently spearheaded a struggle for national balanced budget amendment that continued (unsuccessfully) for over two decades. The battle over Prop 1 also prepared the way for the passage of California's famous Prop 13 in 1978, which rolled back property taxes. In the wake of that anti-property tax victory in California, clones of Reagan's original Prop 1 proposal quickly gained approval in Michigan (the Headlee amendment, 1978), California it-self (Prop 4, 1979), and Missouri (the Hancock Amendment, 1980). As the author of one of the major studies of the late-1970s tax revolt has written, "If one wanted to assign a particular starting point to the decade of the tax revolt, the Proposition 1 campaign may be the most logical candidate."[49] Ironically, Reagan's boldness in the losing struggle for Prop 1 helped spark a conservative reawakening that later in the 1970s helped carry him to political triumph on a far larger stage.

Overall, Reagan was, his biographer Lou Cannon has written, "a good governor, but not a great one."[50] He recorded substantive achievements and changed the terms of political debate, to the extent that after his tenure in Sacramento the liberal expansion of California's state government was no longer assumed to be inevitable. His California record made him a credible—indeed, attractive—figure on the national political scene. Over the course of eight years he had proven himself to be a surprisingly effective leader, one who somehow combined true ideological fire with a discriminating political realism. Reagan's ideological drive shaped his strategic vision, while his practicality and ability to compromise enabled him to maneuver adroitly in pursuit of his larger goals.

THE NATIONAL ASCENT

California loomed so large in so many ways in the American mind during the 1960s that Reagan found himself a national political figure from the very start of his first campaign for governor. In a pre-election story in 1966, *Time* magazine put Reagan on its cover and noted that "a victory . . . will inevitably catapult him onto the national scene as the G.O.P.'s Lochinvar from the West. His name is certain to crop up in connection with the party's vice presidential and even presidential nominations in 1968 and 1972."[51] Reagan himself denied having national aspirations, telling *Time* that he would not be a candidate for president in 1968 because "I've got a pretty big job right here."[52] But just nine days after his election, Reagan's advisers met with the governor-to-be and his wife to discuss a stab at the presidential ring. Reagan was lukewarm to the idea, not wanting to overreach and possibly embarrass himself, but his resistance soon weakened.

Reagan was deeply ambitious and competitive, aspects of his nature that his geniality and his passivity in matters that did not interest him often obscured; in truth, he always had an eye out for further opportunity. As governor he accepted speaking engagements in 1967 and 1968 that gave him exposure outside the state (including a nationally televised debate with Senator Robert F. Kennedy, which most observers thought he won). In the end, he settled on a stealth strategy that might deliver him the 1968 Republican nomination if the front-running contenders—George Romney, Nelson Rockefeller, and Richard Nixon—stumbled in their stretch runs. He came to the 1968 Republican National Convention in Miami Beach as California's favorite-son candidate, but Nixon won the game on the first ballot, handily outdistancing Rockefeller and Reagan but in the process barely garnering the necessary majority required by party rules for victory. Ever the master of the *beau geste*, Reagan quickly made his way to the speakers' platform and asked the assembled delegates to nominate Nixon by acclamation. Characteristically, he took his defeat in stride, writing later, "I knew I wasn't ready to be president."[53]

Reagan increasingly *wanted* to be president, however. Nixon was beyond challenge in 1972, as the Democrats found out when he engineered a forty-nine-state landslide victory over challenger George McGovern. However, the scandal and constitutional crisis known as Watergate forced Nixon's resignation before the end of his second term, and his successor, Gerald Ford, already looked politically vulnerable when Reagan left office as governor in January 1975. Reagan had planned to run for president when Nixon stepped down in 1976; despite the changed circumstances, he now decided to stick to his time-table and undertake the daunting political task of challenging the sitting president for the Republican nomination.

A mixture of political ambition and ideological zeal motivated Reagan's insurgency. He believed that Ford was an ideologically mushy lightweight likely incapable of winning the White House in his own right in the 1976 general election. Conservatives particularly resented Ford's selection as vice president of their *bête noire*, the liberal Republican Nelson Rockefeller; his waffling attempts to finesse the abortion issue; and his support for the Equal Rights Amendment (ERA) that Congress sent to the states for ratification in 1972. They also strongly criticized Ford's foreign policy—especially the embrace of the policy of détente vis-à-vis the Soviet Union, which conservatives saw as a form of disguised surrender, and the willingness to negotiate away U.S. control of the Panama Canal.

The struggle for the 1976 Republican nomination went down to the wire. Reagan battled the sitting president through a long season of bruising primaries and state caucuses, and surprised observers with the boldness of his attempts to define himself as a viable alternative to the incumbent. Well before the first primary in New Hampshire, Reagan made news and generated controversy by calling for the massive transfer of some $90 billion in federal programs back to the states, in what he touted as "a program of creative federalism for America's third century."[54] The proposal was carelessly conceived, however, and the boldness backfired, alarming Republican voters in New Hampshire that they might have to institute a state income tax for the first time in order to cover their state's new responsibilities under Reagan's proposed plan. In another example of political audacity (tinctured with growing desperation), just days before the Republican National Convention, Reagan broke with precedent and announced that if victorious he would name Pennsylvania's liberal Republican senator Richard Schweiker as his vice presidential running mate. The surprise move smacked of political expediency—Reagan hoped the gambit would help him win over the possibly crucial votes of the Pennsylvania delegation—and stunned and dismayed the purists among his ideological supporters. Going into the Kansas City convention, neither candidate had enough committed delegates to be assured victory. In the end, Ford marshaled the powers available to an incumbent president and eked out a win on the first ballot by a slim margin, 1,187 votes to 1,070.

Although he lost, Reagan emerged from the intra-party contest in surprisingly good shape. In a show of party unity, the victorious Ford called for Reagan to join him on the platform after his acceptance speech on the convention's last night. With Secret Service agents clearing a path, Reagan slowly made his way from his skybox to the podium, where he proceeded to steal the show. He spoke eloquently to the Republican delegates for six minutes on the stakes in the upcoming election, highlighting both the challenge to individual freedom from government encroachment and the danger of nuclear annihilation, and in that short span he seemed to win over the hall in an emotional way that left more than a few delegates thinking that perhaps the convention had nominated the wrong man after all. "In the time it took for Reagan to speak," Craig Shirley has written, "the Republican Party escaped the clutches of its moderate establishment and fell into Reagan's lap."[55] The next morning, biding farewell to his tearful supporters, he recited from memory the lines of an English ballad he had learned as a child: "Lay me down and bleed a while. Though I am wounded, I am not slain. I shall rise and fight again." He meant it.[56]

While some of his closest aides, including both Lyn Nofziger and Michael Deaver, believed that he was probably too old to make yet another run at the presidency in 1980, Reagan set out almost immediately to maintain his political visibility. In actuality, he began running for president long before he formally declared his candidacy in November 1979. Shortly after the 1976 convention, he wrote to a Texas conservative, "Our cause is not lost and may even be more possible in the days ahead. Don't lose faith and don't think the war is over. I'm starting my five-day-a-week radio commentaries, newspaper column and speaking tours immediately." He confided to Richard Nixon that he would soon "be doing business at the same old stand and for the same old cause." Shortly after Carter's victory in the November election, Reagan formed a political action committee, Citizens for the Republic, which he bankrolled with $1 million in campaign funds left over from his effort to unseat Ford. [57]

In the late 1970s the historical moment was more auspicious for Reagan. Carter's presidential woes invited, indeed excited, political challenges from both within his own party and without. As the Georgian's fortunes sank, Reagan's rose. Equally important, Reagan now was catching the cresting wave of a conservative resurgence that was beginning to wash over American public life.

The signs of a conservative revival abounded. The U.S. business community rediscovered its political voice in the 1970s with the formation of the Business Roundtable, an organization made up of the chief executives of most of the nation's largest corporations (seventy of *Fortune* magazine's top one hundred in 1975) that spoke with special authority on behalf of a strongly pro-business agenda. By mid-decade corporations were forming political action committees (PACs) at more than twice the rate of organized labor. Increased business support for conservative causes in turn helped finance the rise of conservative think tanks, from the long-established American Enterprise Institute, which enjoyed massive growth in the 1970s, to such new undertakings as the Heritage Foundation, founded in 1973 by the conservative industrialist Joseph Coors, and the libertarian Cato Institute established in 1977. Such centers issued a steady stream of conservative ideas and policy prescriptions.[58]

Meanwhile, the articulation in the 1970s of a perspective known as neo-conservatism imparted a new intellectual energy to conservative thought. The "neocons" were, for the most part, intellectuals formerly identified with the left who, the saying went, had been mugged by reality. They recoiled from the radicalism of the 1960s, in both its political and cultural guises; questioned the efficacy of statist social engineering and liberal welfare-state initiatives; called for a strong national defense and for a vigorous anti-Communism in foreign affairs; trusted markets more than government intervention in economic matters; believed that the sources of, and hence solutions to, social ills were more likely to be found in the realm of culture than in the world of politics; and, accordingly, celebrated the bourgeois ethos, not merely because of its essential moral content but also because middle-class values worked so well in practical ways to position people to take advantage of the opportunities available in America's fluid society.[59] The neoconservatives were a small intellectual elite, but their analytical rigor and sophistication gave their particular ideas, which fitted comfortably at numerous points with Reagan's approach to governance, both currency and legitimacy.

Most significant, in the late 1970s conservatism began to coalesce as a grass-roots political movement around both social and economic issues. On one side, conservative activists, often women, mobilized to fight against the Equal Rights Amendment and abortion. As the historian Donald Critchlow has pointed out, by mid-decade the campaign against the Equal Rights Amendment initiated by the stalwart Republican activist Phyllis Schlafly reached beyond party regulars to draw new support from evangelical and fundamentalist Christian groups in state contests to defeat the ERA or rescind prior approval. At the same time, evangelical Protestants and Catholics, many of whom had been Democrats, played an increasingly significant role in grass-roots efforts to contest the abortion issue.[60] On the economic front, the tax revolt originally sparked by Reagan's Prop 1 encouraged conservatives around the country to organize locally in attempts to replicate the successful passage of California's Proposition 13 in the states where they lived. By the end of the 1970s, as Reagan made his final stab at the White House, conservatism stood resurgent, a movement with growing political clout and funding, serious ideas, and grass-roots energy and savvy.

Despite the promising backdrop for Reagan's candidacy, the presidential election of 1980 turned out to be a hard-fought contest, much closer for far longer than the final vote tally might suggest.[61] Only the first step, winning the Republican nomination, proved relatively easy. Reagan faced a crowded field of six other declared candidates. George H.W. Bush broke from the gate early and won the Iowa caucuses, but a week later Reagan won the New Hampshire primary and the race for the nomination quickly became a two-man contest. Reagan prevailed handily, winning twenty-nine of the thirty-three primaries in which he and Bush met head-to-head and taking the nomination on the first ballot at the Republican National Convention in Detroit that July with 1,939 of the 1,994 total votes.

The contest against the sitting Democratic president Jimmy Carter proved more difficult. On Labor Day the polls had the race within their margin of error, a statistical tossup. Carter was an ineffective and unpopular leader, but Reagan had still to overcome doubts that he was up to the challenge of being president, and fears that he was too old for the job. If elected, he would turn seventy just a few weeks into his presidency. More than a few potential voters worried about Democratic charges that he was an ignorant and reckless extremist. Reagan's penchant for factual misstatements, colorful gaffes, and controversial assertions served to heighten such concerns. The Vietnam War was, he declared, a noble cause. He maintained that creationism should be taught in public schools alongside evolution. The press had a field day with his confused claims that "air pollution has been substantially controlled" and that trees and vegetation contributed significantly to dangerous chemical levels in the atmosphere. Hilariously, a day after Reagan's plane was diverted from the Hollywood-Burbank Airport to Los Angeles International because of thick smog, he visited the campus of Claremont College and was greeted by a poster attached to a nearby tree that read, "Chop Me Down Before I Kill Again."[62]

As late as mid-October, the race remained neck and neck. Reagan's own pollster, Richard Wirthlin, found Carter up by two percentage points on October 14, and both the Gallup and the CBS/New York Times polls similarly reported the incumbent with a hair's-breadth lead. "For the first time," the Democratic pollster Peter Hart reported, "I feel the election may be starting to elude Ronald Reagan's grasp." "I sleep like a baby these nights," Carter's campaign manager told a reporter.[63]

The election did turn dramatically at the end, but not in the direction Carter's supporters hoped. The campaign's only public debate between the two presidential contenders on October 28, exactly one week before voters went to the polls, proved significant. Carter and Reagan squared off before a television audience estimated at 100 million, the largest political audience in the nation's history. At the end of the ninety minutes, the Carter camp was elated, certain the president had won the debate on substantive grounds. But the meaning and significance of the debate's cut and thrust lay elsewhere—in Reagan's ability both to create a favorable impression of himself as a plausible national leader rather than a right-wing extremist and to encapsulate in a memorable formulation just why voters should turn to him. He achieved the first when, in response to Carter's questioning of his early opposition to Medicare in the 1960s, Reagan turned and with a smile said genially, "There you go again," in a phrase dismissing all of Carter's efforts to demonize him as a mean-spirited ideologue. He achieved the second in his closing statement when he suggested that voters ask themselves, "Are you better off than you were four years ago? Is it easier for you to go buy things in the stores than it was four years ago? Is there more or less unemployment in the country than there was four years ago? Is America respected throughout the world as it was?" The predictable answers were devastating to Carter.[64]

Also working powerfully in Reagan's favor was the fact that his campaign managed to project a profoundly optimistic vision of American renewal. He promised to revitalize the economy, restore U.S power and prestige in world affairs, and reverse what he saw as the dangerous drift in the direction of a European welfare state. Reagan successfully (and not unfairly) painted his opponent as a pessimist bent on leading the nation into a new "age of limits." "Our optimism," Reagan insisted during the campaign, "has once again been turned loose. And all of us recognize that these people who keep talking about the age of limits are really talking about their own limitations, not America's." Carter, he declared, "mistook the malaise among his own advisers, and in the Washington establishment in general, for a malady afflicting the nation as a whole."[65] Carter's America, he suggested, was in retreat; Reagan's America would be on the march.

The final public polls, which appeared on the weekend before Election Day, indicated that the race was too close to call. Then, in the campaign's final two days, the dam at last burst and the unusually large undecided vote surged to Reagan. On Election Day the Republican challenger won the popular vote by a margin of 51.6 percent to 41.7 percent (6.7 percent went to the third-party candidate, John Anderson) and captured forty-four states to win the electoral vote 489 to 49. What mere days before had appeared to be a tossup instead turned out to be a decisive victory. Ronald Reagan of Dixon, Illinois and Hollywood, U.S.A. had been elected president.

THE MAN IN THE WHITE HOUSE

Reagan's presidency began auspiciously. He took the oath of office on January 20, 1981, on the west side of the Capitol, a break with precedent that begged for metaphorical interpretation. Even the Iranians seemed to be working from his script. In the final days of his administration, Carter had at last broken through and negotiated the release of the fifty-two American hostages in exchange for the unfreezing of some $12 billion in Iranian assets impounded by the U.S. government. The deal, especially the transfer of funds, was complicated and not a few observers suspected that Tehran was dragging its feet in order to deny Carter even this last-minute achievement. In the event, the planes carrying the released hostages did not take off until after Reagan had taken the oath of office. It was the new president, not the old, who announced the fact of the release and basked in the rejoicing that overtook a nation tired of reversals.

Reagan's inaugural speech itself was not one of his most memorable, and its best line, reminiscent of FDR's brave first inaugural address nearly five decades earlier, was little noted at the time. The nation's problems, Reagan told his audience, required "our best effort and our willingness to believe in ourselves and to believe in our capacity to perform great deeds, to believe . . . we can and will resolve the problems which now confront us." "And after all," he added in a line that captured his personal and political essence, "why shouldn't we believe that? We are Americans."[66]

Despite the pep talk, not all Americans were certain that great deeds would follow from Reagan's leadership. Many doubted that Reagan was up to the job and believed he was too stupid, lazy, and passively disengaged to succeed as president in such troubled times. It remained to be seen just what sort of chief executive the American people had chosen. Critics fixed on Reagan's supposed intellectual inadequacy, and the off-hand remark by the well-connected Democratic insider Clark Clifford that the new president was an "amiable dunce" quickly established itself in Washington lore. Over the years, Clifford's dismissive epithet hardened into a definitive judgment widely shared by a variety of the president's detractors (the list was long and distinguished). Reagan demonstrated, wrote Jack Beatty in the *New Republic* in the spring of 1982, "an intellectual slovenliness which, in a job where power could not disguise incapacity, would brand a man a fool." The journalist David Broder of the *Washington Post*, widely regarded as the soul of fair-minded moderation, wrote of "the desert between Ronald Reagan's ears." Even Peggy Noonan, who wrote speeches for Reagan, later, in what she subsequently described apologetically as "a moment of exasperation," referred to his mind as "such barren terrain."[67]

The originality, sweep, and analytical power of Reagan's thought were, in truth, not impressive (although he *was* often bold and original in his political leadership). There were notable soft spots in Reagan's mental makeup. He had large gaps in his knowledge of the world, particularly in areas that did not interest him. His tendency to think anecdotally, while undoubtedly helpful in communicating his ideas to others, did not make for analytical rigor. Richard Darman, who in his capacity as assistant to the president spent several hours each day with his boss over the course of the first term, believed the president's "natural analytic facility" had atrophied "because his charm, good looks, and memory served to get him a long way without additional effort." Darman described him as "a biased empiricist, tending to remember only the evidence that reinforced his ideological predilections." And as Reagan got older, his authorized biographer Edmund Morris has written, he lost the noteworthy curiosity of his youth and his "considerable intelligence" narrowed its focus.[68]

Such caveats notwithstanding, however, the available evidence indicates that Reagan was an intelligent and generally knowledgeable political leader who thought seriously about the issues of his day. Darman also admitted, "More than we condescending Easterners had assumed, or than he let the general public know, he was intelligent, disciplined, and hard working." He recalled that the president benefited from "a near-photographic memory" and "a clearheaded capacity for writing and editing."[69]

In recent years, scholars have discovered and published many of the hundreds of radio scripts that Reagan himself drafted in longhand during the late 1970s, when he was preparing for his 1980 run for the presidency, and these have provided a new window on Reagan's thinking. The scripts amounted to short essays on a wide range of issues, and in them Reagan demonstrated an ability to engage complex ideas and translate them into straightforward and sinewy prose without doing inordinate harm to the subtlety or complexity of the matters being discussed.[70] Researchers have also gained access to Reagan's personal presidential correspondence, which provides yet another window on his thought processes. Reagan often answered his own mail, setting apart time to draft in longhand personal replies to incoming correspondence that had been selected by his staff. Predictably, much of the mail forwarded to him was from friends and so was usually complementary and supportive; but his staff regularly forwarded critical letters as well, which Reagan often answered in an earnest effort to explain his own thinking and position. (This was hardly standard presidential practice. Franklin D. Roosevelt received voluminous mail, but neither he nor his White House staff ever answered or acknowledged negative letters.)[71] The correspondence shows Reagan to be engaged in, and knowledgeable about, the affairs of his presidency. As with the radio scripts, Reagan's hand-drafted personal letters demonstrate an unusual ability to render complicated issues into spare, clear, accessible, and compelling prose. His thoughts moved from his mind to the handwritten page in an unbroken and coherent stream, with relatively few cross-outs or emendations and none of the problems of syntax or lucidity that occasionally marred his contemporaneous oral performances.[72]

Reagan was also a hard worker, belying the impression fostered by his own humor that he loafed through his eight years in the White House. He liked to joke that things were so busy he was "burning the midday oil." But as Nancy Reagan put it, "Ronnie's easygoing manner is deceiving. Although he isn't as driven or as intense as some of his predecessors in the White House, underneath that calm exterior is a tenacious, stubborn, and very competitive man." Reagan's personal secretary, Helene Von Damm, who accompanied him from California, noted that Reagan's typical daily routine was "non-stop." He usually ate lunch in the Oval Office. Given a detailed schedule of his day every morning, Reagan ticked off each task completed with the discipline of someone who, in Darman's words, had "a compulsive insistence upon completing whatever work was given him." Moreover, he was not simply a nine-to-five worker. "Each evening," Damm reported, "President Reagan left with a great sheaf of papers under his arm, and would go through them in the study on the second floor of the residence, sometimes drafting memos and even letters to constituents on yellow legal pads. Whenever he had time to spare, in cars, on airplane trips, or between meetings, the President would open his briefcase and dig in." Edward Rollins, who was the White House political director from 1981–85 and ran the president's successful 1984 reelection campaign, observed that Reagan had "a clean desk attitude. If you give him four hours of reading, he'll do it all. He won't talk about it. But you'll see his notes on page 40." Reagan worked diligently at everything he undertook in life, whether acting in movies, clearing brush at his California ranch, or being president. It was simply in his nature and upbringing.[73]

As chief executive, however, Reagan practiced a hands-off style of management that often left the impression he was sleepwalking through his presidency.[74] Lou Cannon has written that he "managed by indirection when he managed at all."[75] But here, too, things were more complicated than they at first appeared. Reagan described his management approach in characteristically simple terms: "Surround yourself with the best people you can find, delegate authority, and don't interfere as long as the policy you've decided upon is being carried out."[76] The president's role, as he envisioned it, was to set forth an overarching agenda for his administration, articulate its tone and philosophy, and establish the general direction of its policy. Executing policy and attending to the innumerable details of governance fell to others. Reagan was often disconcertingly passive and uninformed regarding matters unrelated or tangential to his handful of major goals, and was content to let issues and problems come to him. Martin Anderson likened his style to that of an ancient king or Turkish pasha: "Rarely did he ask searching questions and demand to know why someone had or had not done something. He just sat back in a supremely calm, relaxed manner and waited until the important things were brought to him."[77] When confronted with choices, he made decisions carefully but with dispatch, and he stuck to them.

Reagan's system worked well when it worked well, unleashing the creativity and talent of those around and under him. It also allowed him to husband his personal and political resources for the instances and issues that in his judgment mattered most. But the approach was not without its flaws and dangers. It left underlings, even cabinet members such as Secretary of State Alexander

Haig and Secretary of the Treasury Donald Regan, adrift, uncertain about policy and their roles in the so-called Reagan Revolution. Haig, who resigned under pressure in 1982, complained that "the White House was as mysterious as a ghost ship; you heard the creak of the rigging and the groan of the timbers and sometimes even glimpsed the crew on deck. But which of the crew had the helm?" Regan, who served in the cabinet for four years, observed that in terms of presidential direction "from first day to last at Treasury, I was flying by the seat of my pants." Reagan, he reported, "seemed to believe that his public statements were all the guidance his private advisers required."[78]

Reagan's relaxed management style also invited more than the usual amount of internecine squabbling within the administration, thereby possibly wasting as much energy as it unleashed. In the eyes of critics, Reagan's style fairly invited the very sort of mismanagement and scandal that conservatives were always complaining about. And it could be substantively and politically disastrous if the president's free-wheeling subordinates dropped the ball—in the Iran-Contra affair (which is discussed below in chapter 9), Reagan's approach left him appearing a hapless bystander to his own presidency.

Yet, on the large matters that counted most—the issues central to his agenda of revitalizing the economy, rebuilding U.S. military strength and international influence, and restraining the growth of government—Reagan was firmly in charge. It was he who ultimately called the shots that mattered, often over considerable opposition from within the White House circle, from Congress, and from the public at large. Regarding tax cuts, the struggle against inflation, the ratcheting up of military spending, the launching of the Strategic Defense Initiative anti-ballistic missile program (SDI or, more popularly, Star Wars), and the twists and turns of Cold War policy, Reagan's personal actions and decisions at crucial points determined the course of both policy and affairs. Moreover, in all those cases the president personally worked hard to mobilize the popular and political support he needed to prevail. It was with some justification that Reagan complained in a letter to a Texas conservative: "Some in the media delight in trying to portray me as being manipulated and led around by the nose. . . . I'm in charge here and my people are helping to carry out the policies I set."[79]

If Reagan was not stupid, lazy, or passive to the point of disengagement, what then were the salient features of the man that shaped the broad outlines of his presidency? The two that stand out most clearly in retrospect were first, his optimism; and second, his unusual combination of ideological fervor and moderating political pragmatism. As president, Reagan's optimism remained his signal personality trait. The pundit George Will observed that the president had a "talent for happiness." David Gergen, Reagan's director of communications, agreed: "He had a quiet assurance about life, so that he seemed to glide, serene in his belief that everything would turn out for the better. People felt

good being around him, as if everything would be all right for them, too."
George Shultz, who would replace Haig as Secretary of State, wrote: "He appealed to people's best hopes, not their fears, to their confidence rather than
their doubts." Reagan's sunny nature was a central element of both his personal
charm and his political charisma.[80]

When asked about his optimistic nature, Reagan often trotted out a favorite story, one polished to a high sheen by frequent repetition. It involved two
youngsters, one an incurable malcontent and the other an incorrigible optimist. The boys' parents decided one Christmas to give them different presents
in the hope of modulating their temperamental predispositions. Given a room-
ful of toys, the malcontent just sat in the corner and cried, certain that all his
wonderful presents would just break on him. Meanwhile, his brother, given a
pile of horse manure, dove in with great relish, exclaiming with a huge grin as
he shoveled away with both hands, "I just know there's a pony in here somewhere!" It was clear in the telling which boy the president of the United States
identified with.[81]

Reagan's optimism was more complex than it seemed at first blush. As with
many virtues, it was not without its defects. Reagan's irrepressible sunniness
sometimes caused him to see certain unpleasant aspects of reality less clearly
than he arguably should have. Psychologists tell us that optimists are usually
not the most objectively realistic of people, and Reagan sometimes illustrated
the point.[82] There was in his personal life the instance of his strange assertion
after doctors in 1985 removed a golf ball-sized malignant tumor from his colon
that "I didn't have cancer." Rather, his wife Nancy has recalled, he insisted on
telling people, "I had something inside of me that had cancer in it, and it was
removed." "That's Ronnie, my beloved optimist," wrote the first lady.[83] It was
an incident where optimism shaded into denial. The same tendency occasionally manifested itself in the public realm. It could be seen in Reagan's slow-
ness in recognizing that his huge budget deficits constituted a serious problem
and in the difficulty he had taking the full measure of social problems that
might point to systemic flaws in the country he reverently called "the shining
city on a hill."

In most contexts and in general, however, Reagan's sanguinity worked to his
advantage. It undergirded his daring and boldness, his willingness to pursue
innovative programs such as supply-side economics and the Strategic Defense
Initiative. It inspired him to "stay the course" in the painful struggle against
inflation, and to both prosecute the Cold War with victory in mind and then
help end it. It led him to challenge the conventional wisdom on arms control
and thus to achieve historic arms reduction. Not least, it served as the enduring
basis of his political appeal. Reagan's optimism helped get him elected in 1980
and made the "It's Morning Again in America" theme of his successful 1984
reelection campaign credible and effective.

Less recognized at the time was the dualism at the core of Reagan's political identity. Lou Cannon has since observed that "on nearly all issues, Reagan was simultaneously an ideologue and a pragmatist." The ideological half of Reagan's dual political nature was the more obvious and better known. It was his avowed conservatism that excited his supporters, frightened his liberal opponents, and left independents uneasy. Reagan saw his election as an ideological victory as well as personal one. Addressing the Conservative Political Action Conference two months into his presidency, he spoke of "our victory"—"not so much a victory of politics as . . . a victory of ideas, not so much a victory for any one man or party as a . . . victory for a set of principles." Reagan provided both rhetorical and substantive support for conservative ideas and principles throughout his presidency. His goals were a smaller government, lower taxes, a stronger military, and a more vigorously anti-Communist foreign policy. He celebrated religion, family, and traditional moral values, condemned abortion, and called for a return to the practice of school prayer. Overall, both at home and abroad, he sought to achieve what he called "man's age old dream"—"the ultimate in individual freedom consistent with an orderly society."[84]

The other side of Reagan's dualistic political identity tended often to moderate the sharper edges of his ideological vision, however. He was a politician who liked to win, not simply for his own sake (although that surely mattered) but also in order to solve problems and perhaps at the same time actually advance, if only partially, the conservative agenda. "He was," recalled his speechwriter Noonan, "in many ways, a pragmatist in full-throated pursuit of that least romantic of goals, the practical solution. . . . He believed in negotiation and compromise; he was inclined to split the difference." Reagan's director of management and budget, David Stockman, who had hoped that the president would be a revolutionary, ruefully agreed that he "was a consensus politician, not an ideologue." Darman observed that Reagan "would sacrifice the purity of his ideology for the practical necessities of governance" and "was prepared to abandon the purists' version of the Reagan Revolution in order to assure a popular Reagan presidency." Of course, the point should not be oversimplified or misconstrued—Reagan remained always a staunch conservative, and he could be a very stubborn one; but he was also surprisingly adroit and flexible.[85] It was the oxymoronic intertwining of the two characteristics, each noteworthy and genuine in its own right, that constituted Reagan's special political genius.

In truth, Reagan had been a pragmatist, in the sense of inclining toward practical compromise as a mode of positive action, even longer than he had been a conservative. The experience of his Hollywood labor negotiations as the head of the Screen Actors Guild had, in fact, been formative. He wrote to a Guild compatriot from the old days, "You know, those people who thought being an actor was no proper training for this job were way off base. Everyday I find myself thankful for those long days at the negotiating table with Henry

Cohen, Freeman, the brothers Warner et al."[86] When he entered public life to serve as governor of California, Reagan got still more practice at the art of maneuver and bargaining, necessary skills since the Democrats controlled the state legislature for six of his eight years in Sacramento. The optimist in Reagan saw compromise not as a form of losing but rather as a technique for winning, the taking of half a loaf with the determination to come back for the rest later.

First lady Nancy Reagan usually reinforced her husband's pragmatic inclinations. She was, White House spokesman Larry Speakes has written, the president's "one indispensable adviser," and she cared more about his popularity and historical reputation than about any ideology. "Her only agenda was Ronald Reagan," commented Deaver.[87] They had wed in 1952, several years after Reagan's divorce from his first wife, Jane Wyman, and remained an intensely close couple throughout their long marriage. As first lady Nancy Reagan proved highly controversial, the victim of her own foibles and an unmerciful press. Although she never had quite the influence over her husband's decisions that some attributed to her, her protectiveness of the president's political image and standing often caused her to urge on him the virtues of moderation.

The double-sidedness of Reagan's political persona—ideologue and practical politician—was reflected in the makeup of the new administration, which included a mix of both sorts of individuals. "In some respects, the Reagan presidency was like a coalition government," Edwin Meese, a member of Reagan's initial "troika" of top aides, has written, "albeit a coalition among different varieties of Republicans." Deaver, a second member of the original troika, agreed that the White House staff "was split right down the middle between the moderates and the conservatives." The administration's ideological conservatives were referred to variously as the true believers, the Reaganauts or Reaganites, or sometimes simply the Californians, since many had been with the president since his days in California politics. They included Meese, policy adviser Martin Anderson, political adviser Lyn Nofziger, defense secretary Caspar Weinberger, and national security advisers Richard Allen and William Clark. The pragmatists or moderate conservatives included White House chief of staff James Baker, the third member of the Troika; his deputy Richard Darman, known to his ideological opponents as "the Black Prince of Centrism"; Deaver; communications director David Gergen; and Secretary of State Shultz.[88]

While virtually all those concerned could fairly be labeled conservatives, the differences between the Reaganites and the pragmatists were real and significant in their policy implications. Edwin Feulner, Jr., the head of the Heritage Foundation, which had the reputation of being "Reagan's think tank," observed at the time: "Pragmatists want to resolve problems, and the true believers want to change institutions and leave a lasting legacy for this administration."[89] Meese, who distinguished between the two groups in a slightly different fashion, has said that "the original Reaganites were chiefly interested in changing the existing way of doing things in the direction of Reagan's thinking; the pragmatists were often interested in adjusting Reagan to fit more closely with the existing way of doing things."[90] The two groups constantly maneuvered to gain Reagan's ear, and the infighting between them, as with squabbles within families, was often fierce. (To liberal critics looking on from the outside, the inbred quarrels reflected at best the bitterness of small differences.) Moreover, the disagreements were frequently exacerbated by the personal and jurisdictional rivalries that inevitably crop up in any bureaucratic enterprise. "Machiavelli would have felt right at home [in the Reagan White House]," Gergen has written: "The quarrels were intense . . . [and] knives could come from anywhere." Gergen avers that the tensions within the administration in the end made for creativity, motivating and enabling both camps to serve well the larger cause of Reagan presidency, but others, certainly Haig and Shultz, took a more negative view and found the internecine conflict wearying and counterproductive.[91]

The tension between the administration's hard-shell conservatives and its pragmatic moderates constituted a fundamental theme and helped give the administration's policy its unique right-center orientation. Over the course of two presidential terms Reagan came under fire from the right for not being ideological enough in his appointments, for not expending more of his considerable political capital on behalf of the administration's declared social and cultural agenda, and for negotiating arms reduction with the Soviets. With equal vigor, the left assailed him for being too ideological in his appointments, for opposing women's choice in the matter of abortion and being the tool of the religious right on cultural and social issues, and for his hardline anti-Communism. The interplay of ideological zeal and pragmatic calculation in the president's own political makeup and among his advisers gave the Reagan presidency its distinctive coloration. It produced a political transformation that altered substantially the terms of debate in American politics and public life, while at the same time ensuring that the changes wrought would be short of revolutionary. That was, it appears, precisely what the majority of Americans wanted.

Chapter 3

REAGANOMICS

President Ronald Reagan's most profound impact on public policy came in the realm of political economy. This was the area in which his intentions were most radical, and where his radical intentions coincided with the collapse of the old Keynesian order that had dominated policy throughout the postwar era and the resulting reorientation of economic thought. Economists refer to such changes as inflection points, shifts in direction; historians speak of watersheds. Whatever the particular term, the label fits the 1980s. The changes in economic thought and economic policy that took hold in the 1980s were substantial and, as such matters go, long-lasting, continuing at least into the early years of the new millennium. The economist Lawrence B. Lindsey has observed that "in terms of economic performance, government policy, and the effect on the thinking of professional economists, the 1980s and 1990s form a continuous era radically different from what preceded it."[1] What contemporaries somewhat derisively called "Reaganomics" cast a long shadow.

THE SUPPLY-SIDE REVOLUTION

In July 1980, the Democratic senator from New York Daniel Patrick Moynihan reported, "Of a sudden, the GOP has become a party of ideas."[2] Nowhere did that seem truer than in the realm of economic policy. The idea that took conservative Republicans by storm in the 1980s was supply-side economics, and its most effective evangelist was the unlikely Jack Kemp, a retired pro football player with a penchant for serious thought

The supply-side revolution had begun simultaneously in the 1970s in the worlds of politics and economic analysis. On the political side, the tax-cutting proposals advanced by Representative Jack Kemp were central. A Republican first elected in 1970 from the congressional district around Buffalo, New York, Kemp was an improbable champion of new economic ideas. He came to political economy by way of a professional football career that included two broken ankles, two broken shoulders, a broken knee, and eleven concussions along with his considerable gridiron success. A native Californian, Kemp had been an uninspired student while majoring in physical education at Occidental College; instead of excelling at academics, he channeled his abundant energy into football. He played quarterback well enough to lead small-college passers in accuracy, and in 1957 graduated into the professional game. In the mid-1960s, Kemp led the Buffalo Bills of the upstart American Football League to two league championships and won recognition as the AFL's player of the year in 1964. He also gained important experience as the elected president of the AFL Players Association, a players' union he helped to establish.

Along the way Kemp became a voracious reader of serious writers, especially those of a conservative bent. He encountered the works of Friedrich von Hayek, like Friedman a champion of the free market, and later recalled, "From then on it was Katie-bar-the-door. I read everything I could get my hands on about economics and political philosophy."[3] His natural ebullience now compounded by the drive of the autodidact, he developed an interest in public affairs that brought him to an internship on the staff of California's newly elected Governor Ronald Reagan.

In 1970, local Republicans in Buffalo recruited Kemp to run for Congress. He won that first election in a squeaker and ultimately served eighteen years, enjoying so much support that he sometimes ran unopposed. In Congress, Kemp marched to his own drummer. A fierce and dependable conservative on many issues, he was from the beginning what he later characterized as a "bleeding heart conservative": he opposed abortion but strongly supported the Equal Rights Amendment, and he opposed school busing to achieve integration but became one of the Republican Party's most credible champions of racial equality.[4] Most of all, Kemp loved ideas, and the idea dearest to him was economic growth.

Kemp was more an "opportunity populist" than a traditional Republican conservative, and growth appealed to him because it seemed to be the wellspring of opportunity. Growth would enable the blue-collar voters of Buffalo and its Rustbelt environs to bounce back from the ravages of stagflation. Growth would extend the ladder of opportunity to those born on the margins of American society. Growth would allow many social problems "to take care of themselves," he wrote, and would make those that remained "more manageable." Since the late 1960s, he complained, Americans had had "imprinted on the national consciousness a sense of futility about our ability to regain economic vitality."⁵ Irrepressibly optimistic, Kemp built his political career on the effort to prove such gloom and doom wrong.

The Buffalo congressman seized upon tax reduction as the key to economic growth. Tax relief was "not so much an end in itself," he claimed, as it was "a means of getting this economy moving again."⁶ Significantly, the congressman from Buffalo developed a new supply-side rationale for his tax-cutting proclivities. In September 1975, Kemp argued in a *Washington Star* op-ed piece that tax reduction done the right way would have its chief impact not by boosting demand but rather by affecting supply-side incentives, and he suggested that the broadest improvement of incentives could be obtained by reducing the marginal rates in the income tax. To that end, Kemp joined with Delaware's Republican Senator William Roth in 1977 to introduce the Kemp-Roth Tax Reduction Bill, which called for a 30 percent reduction in personal income rates, to be phased in over three years. The Republican leadership in the House and the Republican National Committee quickly endorsed the bill, and within months Kemp-Roth emerged as the chief Republican solution to America's stagflation malaise.

Kemp-Roth struck a resonant chord with the general public. A 1978 Roper Poll reported that the public supported a 30 percent tax cut by a two-to-one margin. The popular mood had finally caught up with Kemp. Antitax sentiment swelled as inflation relentlessly drove people into higher and higher tax-rate brackets without really having made them richer—the dreaded phenomenon known as "bracket creep." The most dramatic manifestation of antitax sentiment came in the great California tax revolt of 1978, when voters handily approved Proposition 13, which capped the maximum rate of property taxation and prohibited the state and the local California governments from raising existing taxes or imposing new ones without a two-thirds majority vote in the affected jurisdiction. A less noticed but equally significant straw in the wind was the passage in the fall of 1978 of a federal capital-gains tax cut that effectively reduced the maximum tax rate on capital gains from roughly 49 to 28 percent. The cut was enacted by strong bipartisan majorities in both houses despite the opposition of the Carter administration, whose spokesmen reviled the proposal as the "Millionaire's Relief Act of 1978."⁷

Despite such favorable developments, at decade's end Kemp-Roth remained stuck in the legislative mill. Republicans had rallied to the cause but could not pass their program. On the several occasions when they managed to bring their handiwork to a vote, Kemp-Roth was defeated. But in another sense, Kemp and his allies had succeeded wildly by seizing control of the debate about the future shape of the economy and direction of policy. The Kemp-Roth tax-cut proposal helped touch off a fundamental reconsideration of the Keynesian demand-side analysis and prescription that had dominated national economic policy since the end of World War II.

Kemp's tax-cutting approach gained influence in part because of the sustenance and support it derived from developments within the discipline of economics itself. The rise of a number of new theoretical insights emerging from the routine cut and thrust of intellectual life, together with the apparent inadequacy of existing theory to explain and deal with stagflation, resulted in a fierce challenge to the Keynesian analytical orthodoxy. Once this challenge had weakened the regnant demand-side paradigm, the way was open for the rise of a new, alternative school of supply-side economic analysis, of which Kemp-Roth quickly became the premier policy embodiment.

The challenge to the Keynesian paradigm, which unfolded largely within the economics profession's mainstream channels of discussion, came in three distinct waves. The first began with Milton Friedman's warning in the late 1960s that the conventional wisdom regarding the mutual exclusivity of stagnation and inflation, embodied in the widely accepted Phillips curve, was simply wrong. "There is always a temporary trade-off between inflation and unemployment," Friedman concluded, "[but] there is no permanent trade-off."[8] The hope of trading a decrease in unemployment below the economy's "natural" or structural level for only a modicum of inflation was chimerical. If Friedman was right—and he was—the activist Keynesian paradigm and the U.S. economy were in for serious trouble (as the subsequent experience of the 1970s seemed to prove).

The second wave of the assault on Keynesianism came in the 1970s in the work of the Nobel Prize-winning economist Robert Lucas and his followers of the so-called rational expectations school. Although they elaborated their theories in dauntingly dense and complex formulations, Lucas and his adherents pointed to a deceptively simple conclusion: They argued that predictable government intervention was destined to be futile and ineffectual because economic actors would anticipate it. Thus, government activism of any sort was suspect. In his presidential address to the American Economic Association in 1976, Franco Modigliani called the incorporation of the rational expectations hypothesis into Friedman's critique "the death blow to the already battered Keynesian position"[9] Modigliani spoke somewhat ironically, in defense of a chastened Keynesianism, but an increasing number of young economists thought his remark literally on target.

A third and somewhat more oblique attack on Keynesian orthodoxy came in the field that soon came to be called the New Public Finance. This school of thought argued that existing tax disincentives—the ways in which the tax system discouraged desirable economic behavior—were greater than Keynesians admitted, that they seriously distorted saving and investment decisions, and

that the inflation of the 1970s was exacerbating those effects by pushing individual and corporate tax payers into ever-higher brackets based on inflationary,
nominal rather than real, gains. By 1980, the work of the New Public Finance
school—Harvard's Martin Feldstein and Lawrence Summers, and Stanford's
Michael Boskin—had, according to Paul Krugman, "convinced many economists that U.S. taxes were in fact a significant obstacle to investment."[10]

By the end of the 1970s, the combined weight of these professional challenges had left the Keynesian paradigm in tatters. "By about 1980, it was hard
to find an American academic macroeconomist under the age of 40 who pro-
fessed to be a Keynesian," lamented Alan Blinder, himself an economist of
such inclination at Princeton University. That this "intellectual turnabout"
had transpired "in less than a decade" was, in his eyes, "astonishing."[11] With less
sadness, Robert Lucas wrote in 1981 that Keynesianism was "in deep trouble,
the deepest kind of trouble in which an applied body of theory can find itself:
It appears to be giving wrong answers to the most basic questions of macroeconomic policy."[12] Pragmatists and policymakers in the middle, who gave allegiance wholly to neither Keynes nor his academic detractors, found themselves
adrift on the currents of academic debate and real-world ineffectiveness. As
Paul Volcker explained to a journalist, "We're all Keynesians now—in terms
of the way we look at things. National income statistics are a Keynesian view
of the world, and the language of economists tends to be Keynesian. But if
you mean by Keynesian that we've got to pump up the economy, that all these
relationships are pretty clear and simple, that this gives us a tool for eternal
prosperity if we do it right, that's all bullshit."[13]

The weakening of the Keynesian consensus in both macroeconomics (because of intellectual challenges) and policy (because of the practical failure to
deal effectively with stagflation) opened the way for the emergence of a new,
competing approach to economic problems. Whereas the attacks on the existing Keynesian consensus had taken place within the economics discipline's
traditional channels of professionally scrutinized theoretical disputation—in
refereed journals and the like—the framing of the supply-side alternative occurred more in the rough-and-tumble of policy debate and was, therefore, a
more haphazard and inchoate process.

The basic outlines of the supply-side approach were nevertheless clear.
First, the supply-siders emphasized that supply matters greatly, an economic
truism that had been under-appreciated since the triumph of Keynes, who
had emphasized the maintenance of sufficiently high aggregate demand to
keep pace with the economy's recurrent tendency toward overproduction.
Supply-siders shifted attention back to the problem of productivity and how
to raise it. Second, in achieving this rediscovery of the relative significance of
supply, the supply-siders also necessarily shifted attention away from macroeconomics, with its concern for aggregate behavior, and back to the behavior

of discrete economic actors—individuals and firms. Third, following the logic of their broad suppositions, the supply-siders believed that the way to achieve prosperity without inflation was to expand supply by increasing the incentives for individuals to work, save, and invest. The surest way to achieve such results was to cut taxes, especially the existing high marginal rates—those tax rates that applied to the last dollar of income and that therefore most discouraged extra effort and enterprise. Such a tax reduction, they claimed, would raise real output—not by increasing demand but by operating on the supply side of the economy. Full-bore supply-siders went so far as to assert that such tax cuts would be so powerful as to actually generate more revenue than would be lost by the cuts themselves.[14]

The theoretical base for these supply-side ideas derived partly from the classical economics of the nineteenth century and partly from more recent developments at the margin of economic discourse in the early 1970s. The foundation of the supply-side approach derived from the insights of Adam Smith, Jean-Baptiste Say, and Alfred Marshall. The point of good economics and good government, Say had asserted early in the nineteenth century, was to stimulate production, not consumption. Supply-siders asserted that the enduring wisdom of Say's insight had been obscured by the wrenching experience of the Great Depression and the subsequent sway enjoyed by Keynes's emphasis on the necessity of maintaining aggregate demand.[15]

Arthur Laffer, who taught at the University of Southern California and had worked at the Office of Management and Budget (OMB) in the Nixon years, and Robert Mundell of Columbia University provided what little updating accompanied the modern formulation of supply-side theory in the 1970s. Both were academic outsiders. After having made significant contributions in the field of international economics early in his career, Mundell served as an eccentric, long-haired economic guru to the right, organizing conferences at his own Italian villa, increasingly removed from the professional mainstream even as his influence among policy entrepreneurs grew. Laffer remained similarly aloof from the conventional world of academe, but became widely known for authoring the central heuristic device of the supply-side crusade, the so-called Laffer curve, which illustrated the truism that tax rates set too high were as ineffective at raising revenue as tax rates set too low. Laffer was, Martin Anderson, President Ronald Reagan's chief domestic and economic policy adviser, subsequently wrote, "the first person who took the simple idea of supply-side tax effects that has been around since the dawn of economics and painted a picture of it." It was indicative of the professional remove of the supply-side theoreticians that insiders would subsequently celebrate the fact that Laffer first drew the curve that bore his name on a paper cocktail napkin during a legendary meeting with a White House staffer from the Ford administration at the Two Continents Restaurant across the street from the Treasury Department in

Washington. The chief attraction of the Laffer curve was its suggestion that a reduction of tax rates could conceivably pay for itself by generating more revenue, a generally dubious proposition that would ultimately make the device as controversial and professionally suspect as it was politically seductive—no small feat for a truism.[16]

In the mid-1970s, Mundell and Laffer spread their ideas by means of an ongoing, informal, supply-side economics seminar cum dinner that convened at Michael I, a Wall Street area restaurant in Manhattan. The other participants in the Michael I discussions included Jude Wanniski, an editorialist for the *Wall Street Journal*, who would serve as the emergent movement's energetic and hyperbolic publicist, and Robert Bartley, the *Journal*'s editor-in-chief. These two powerful business journalists quickly made their newspaper's op-ed page into, as Bartley put it, "a daily bulletin board" for supply-side ideas. Wanniski helped spread the supply-side message to Irving Kristol, a founding father of the neoconservative movement then starting to blossom, and soon the readers of Kristol's increasingly influential journal of opinion, *The Public Interest*, were exposed to approving discussions of supply-side doctrine. Wanniski penned the burgeoning movement's most complete manifesto in 1978, a book that he, with characteristic zeal, entitled *The Way the World Works*. The basic economic prescription formulated at Michael I and subsequently publicized in these neoconservative forums was tight money to curb inflation and supply-side (i.e., incentive-creating) tax cuts for economic growth.

Meanwhile, the same supply-side approach to fiscal policy was emerging independently in a very practical way on Capitol Hill in the Kemp-Roth tax cut proposals. Kemp soon became the linchpin that joined the several wings of the supply-side crusade together. In 1975, Bartley met Kemp in Washington and upon his return to New York told his *Wall Street Journal* colleague Wanniski, "You'd better get by and meet this guy Kemp; he's quite a piece of horseflesh." Wanniski sought out the young congressman and in short order introduced him to Laffer and Kristol. By mid-1976, the *Wall Street Journal* had begun to champion Kemp as the chief political spokesman for the new intellectual movement. As Kemp emerged as America's first supply-side politician and the movement's political drum major, both the New York theoreticians and publicists and the Washington political economists rallied around him, thereby giving the appearance of unity to a movement that had in reality appeared in different guises and in different places virtually simultaneously.[17]

By April 1976, the new movement had cohered sufficiently to gain its own appellation. In a paper delivered to a meeting of economists, Herbert Stein sketched a taxonomy of economic orientations that included a group he identified as "supply-side fiscalists." Contrary to the myth that soon grew up among supply-siders, a myth nurtured by the tendency of some movement faithful to accentuate their challenge to establishment economics, Stein did not intend the label to be pejorative (although he would quickly become a spirited critic of supply-side doctrine). Audacious pamphleteer that he was, Wanniski seized upon the label but dropped the term "fiscalist" as too limiting. Supply-side economics now had a name.[18]

The noted Keynesian economist Paul Krugman dismissed the supply-side movement as a collection of "cranks" pushing a political agenda rather than an economic analysis, less a valid school of conservative economic thought than a "cult" or "sect." Lawrence Klein, a Nobel Prize–winning Keynesian economist, commented that "if there were Nuremberg trials for economists, supply-siders would be in the dock." Having already given the movement its generic name, Herbert Stein in 1981 identified what he perceived as egregiously unsupportable oversimplifications of the doctrine as "punk supply-sidism." He applied the label to brands of supply-side doctrine that he considered "extreme to the point of being bizarre," versions that offered both a "universal explanation" and a "universal solution" and that in the process crowded out more responsible, if more complicated and difficult, diagnoses and prescriptions.[19]

To dismiss moderate supply-siders as religious cultists or professional war criminals, to focus on "punk supply-sidism," obscured the crucial fact that the supply-siders were not wholly isolated in their essential analysis and policy recommendations. In truth, by the end of the 1970s supply-side ideas had a significant place in serious discussions of the U.S. political economy. For example, the congressional Joint Economic Committee (JEC), controlled by Democrats, gave supply-side thinking an increasingly receptive hearing. The JEC chairman Lloyd Bentsen, a Texas Democrat who would later serve as Bill Clinton's first treasury secretary, became an increasingly outspoken champion of the supply-side approach. In his introduction to the JEC's 1979 yearly economic report, Bentsen wrote that whereas the chief preoccupation of postwar economists had for thirty years been how to ensure an adequate level of aggregate demand, the dramatic changes of the 1970s had finally begun "to force the attention of the country and its economic experts on the supply side of the economy." A year later, he proclaimed "the start of a new era of economic thinking." "For too long," he told the press, "we have focused on short-run policies to stimulate spending, or demand, while neglecting supply—labor, savings, investment and production. Consequently, demand has been overstimulated and supply has been strangled." To correct the policy imbalance, the JEC in its 1980 annual report recommended "a comprehensive set of policies designed to enhance the productive side, the supply side of the economy."[20]

Although the community of academic economists accorded supply-side analysis a distinctly mixed reception, Harvard's Martin Feldstein made the National Bureau of Economic Research (NBER) an outpost of supply-side emphasis, if not doctrine, when he became the organization's president in the mid-1970s. When the NBER held a two-day conference in January 1980 to review the postwar experience of the U.S. economy, Feldstein reported approvingly that "there are at present some signs of growing public and governmental interest in increasing the rate of capital formation." "The Keynesian fear of saving that has dominated thinking . . . for more than thirty years is finally giving way," he told his audience, "to a concern about the low rates of productivity increase and of investment."[21]

Thus, by 1980 supply-side economics was both less and more than met the eye. While the claims of its champions were overwrought, so too were the denunciations of its detractors. It remained more a policy vision than a scientific analysis, but it seemed to fill a real void that was theoretical as well as practical. Much of the supply-side approach was already familiar to economists, and the parts that seemed freshest were, in fact, the doctrine's most dubious aspects. Supply-side thinking remained outside the mainstream, but its policy particulars and its conceptual underpinnings enjoyed notable support.

In retrospect, the emergence of the supply-side doctrine was highly significant. First, it offered policymakers a fundamental change in perspective, a new way in which to envision the nation's economic problems and their solutions. Second, it enabled the Republican Party to rebound from the disaster of Watergate, as the GOP, in Jude Wanniski's joyous phrase, was "reborn as a party of economic growth."[22] Finally, it gave conservatives a powerful rationale for the lower-taxes, smaller-government agenda that they viscerally preferred.

"The GOP is in the process of rediscovering growth," Jack Kemp crowed in 1979, "and with the discovery is coming a political success it will not soon forget." There was a "tidal wave" coming, he predicted, similar to that which had swept FDR into the presidency in 1932.[23] At the time, some thought that Kemp might be the Republican to ride that wave into the White House, but that was not to be. Instead, the Republican to benefit from the confluence of his party's rebirth and Jimmy Carter's political self-destruction was Ronald Reagan.

THE REAGAN ECONOMIC PROGRAM

Reagan's economic program demonstrated the incoming administration's ability to focus at the outset on a few essentials and to sustain that focus over time. In August 1979, Martin Anderson, Reagan's chief domestic policy adviser, drafted the Reagan for President Campaign's "Policy Memorandum No. 1," which sketched out the economic strategy the Californian would take to the voters. "It is time the United States began moving forward again," Anderson told the candidate, "with new inventions, new products, greater productivity, more jobs, and a rapidly rising standard of living that means more goods and services for all of us." To regain the economy's former momentum, Anderson suggested across-the-board tax cuts of at least three years duration in conjunction with the indexation of federal income tax brackets, reduction in the rate of increase in federal spending, the balancing of the federal budget, vigorous deregulation, and a consistent and stringent monetary policy to deal with inflation. Despite George Bush's stinging criticism during the primary campaign that, when combined with the massive military buildup Reagan promised, such a program constituted "voodoo economics," Reagan stuck to the blueprint laid out in Policy Memorandum No. 1. With only minor adjustments and some change in emphasis—a slight downplaying of the balanced-budget goal, attainment of which was pushed further into the future, and an underscoring of the immediate need to fight inflation—that early strategy was the program President Ronald Reagan presented to the American people in February 1981. As Anderson later wrote, "Again and again, in the campaign, during the transition, and all during his tenure as president, . . . [Reagan] adjusted his economic plan to accommodate changes in the economy and political opposition in the Congress, but he did not adjust the blueprint." Both its champions and its critics labeled the blueprint Reaganomics.[24]

The rationale behind Reaganomics was varied. Several members of Reagan's Council of Economic Advisers have noted that there was much more agreement on *what* things the administration should do than on *why* it should do them.[25] The President's commitment to the regimen of tax cuts and spending constraints, tight money, and deregulation reflected, in large part, his own emotional and experiential view of economics. He abhorred big government and had a primordial dislike of high taxes rooted in his own experiences in the film industry. During his peak earning years as an actor at Warner Brothers, Reagan found himself in the 94 percent marginal tax bracket: "The IRS took such a big chunk of my earnings," he remembered, "that after a while I began asking myself whether it was worth it to keep on taking work. Something was wrong with a system like that."

Moreover, the problem was not simply the confiscatory level of taxation but also the ultimate economic impact of such disincentives to work: "If I decided to do one less picture," Reagan later wrote, "that meant other people at the studio in lower tax brackets wouldn't work as much either; the effect filtered down, and there were fewer total jobs available." When the Californian left acting to become an increasingly visible spokesman for American conservatism in the early 1960s, he told his audiences that the progressive income tax had come "directly from Karl Marx who designed it as the prime essential of a socialist state."[26] Reagan's disdain for the progressive income tax, together with his alarm at the growth of the federal government, predisposed him to favor the supply-side approach championed by Jack Kemp and his politico-intellectual allies. The practical preferences were marrow-deep, the theoretical rationale skin-deep, but both counted. Reagan's sunny nature reinforced his inclinations, pushing him further toward a doctrine suffused with optimism as boundless as his own. "Jack [Kemp] was basically pushing on an open door," recalled Ed Meese, because Ronald Reagan "was a 'supply-sider' long before the term was invented." For Reagan, such ideas were less economic doctrine than simple "common sense."[27]

It nevertheless helped immensely that Reagan's version of common sense coincided with an economic dogma that legitimated and bolstered his predilections. Supply-side economics provided a coherent, if controversial, rationale for Reagan's policies and exercised a decisive influence on a number of his key advisers. Martin Anderson, the author of the Reagan for President Campaign's Policy Memorandum No.1, was an early convert to the supply-side approach and in 1976, while reviewing grant applications for the Richardson Foundation, helped Jude Wanniski get the funding that allowed him to leave the *Wall Street Journal* in order to write his supply-side tract *The Way the World Works.* During the race to the presidency, Anderson took what he called "the simple idea that was supply-side economics" and helped make it into "an important part of President Reagan's economic program."[28]

Supply-side ideas also influenced Reagan's "economic professionals" on the Council of Economic Advisers. In announcing the administration's Program for Economic Recovery in February 1981, Murray Weidenbaum, the first of Reagan's several CEA chairmen, noted that "in contrast to the inflationary demand-led booms of the 1970s, the most significant growth of economic activity will occur in the supply side of the economy." When the CEA later set forth the philosophical and intellectual underpinnings of the administration's economic program in the 1982 Economic Report, it embraced a supply-side perspective. While never persuaded that tax cuts would so stimulate economic activity as to automatically and immediately make up for lost revenue—Stein's "punk supply-sidism"—Weidenbaum and his CEA colleagues subsequently recalled that they nevertheless "really believed in supply-side economics."[29]

Shaped by both personal experience and economic doctrine, Reaganomics also had a larger inspiration and rationale. The Reagan program was, at bottom, yet another expression of postwar economic growthmanship. William Brock, the Republican Party chairman, later recalled the "very clear sense that . . . the basic aim of the policy we were trying to implement was to restore growth." Reaganomics, Kemp observed, was "really the classical prescription for economic growth." It was no coincidence that Reagan entitled his major 1980 campaign speech on economic policy "A Strategy for Growth: The American Economy in the 1980s." In his first presidential address on the economy, he reminded his live national television audience, "Our aim is to increase our national wealth so all will have more, not just redistribute what we already have which is just a sharing of scarcity."[30]

In this way, Reagan stole the Democrats' most potent politico-economic appeal and placed it at the center of his conservative Republicanism. Running for reelection in 1984, he joyfully offered voters a choice "between two different visions of the future, two fundamentally different ways of govern-ing—their government of pessimism, fear, and limits, or ours of hope, con-fidence, and growth."[31] Moreover, Reagan harnessed growth to a larger ideo-logical crusade—the dismantling of the modern welfare state.

For conservatives, the brilliance of Reagan's approach and much of its consequent appeal lay in the fact that the same mechanisms that would spur economic growth—tax cuts, spending controls, and deregulation—would also serve to restrain the growth of the federal government. Reagan's disdain for gov-ernment was real and ran deep. In January 1982, he complained in his diary, "The press is trying to paint me as trying to undo the New Deal. I remind them I voted for FDR four times." As Reagan saw it, the charge was off the mark, if only by a little: "I'm trying to undo the Great Society. It was LBJ's war on poverty that led us to our present mess." Believing that the federal government would "grow forever unless you do something to starve it," Reagan perceived his own growth program to be both good economics and good ideology. "By cutting taxes," he later wrote, "I wanted not only to stimulate the economy but to curb the growth of government and reduce its intrusion into the economic life of the country." As both candidate and president, Reagan gave top prior-ity to an economic program designed to stimulate economic growth and to achieve these larger, heroic objectives as well. The relationship between the goals was reciprocal: the tax and spending cuts designed to generate economic growth would shrink government, and the shrinkage of government would in turn contribute to still more economic growth. Reagan's growthmanship served as both vehicle and camouflage for a larger ideological agenda.[32]

DEFICITS AND THE DEFUNDING OF
THE WELFARE STATE

Reagan fought hard to get his economic program approved, energetically twist-ing arms and making personal appeals to individual members of Congress. The administration also benefited mightily from the surge of public affection for the president generated by his graceful performance after an assassination attempt only weeks into his first term in the spring of 1981. On March 13, as Reagan exited a Washington hotel after addressing a meeting of trade union-ists, a deranged young man named John Hinckley fired a quick handgun burst from a .22-caliber pistol—six shots in some two seconds—into the president's entourage before being wrestled to the ground. The assassin used special ex-plosive ammunition, bullets known as Devastators that were designed to ex-plode inside the target in order to cause the greatest possible damage. Hinckley wounded a secret service agent and a District of Columbia policeman, and nearly killed Jim Brady, Reagan's press secretary, with an exploding shot to the head that left him permanently brain-damaged. Agents pushed the president onto the backseat floor of his limousine and it sped from the scene; initially the secret service thought Reagan had escaped injury, but when he started to spit up frothy, bright red blood, the motorcade rushed to a nearby hospital. Struck by a ricocheting bullet that collapsed his left lung and lodged within an inch of his heart but failed to explode, Reagan walked to the emergency room entrance under his own power and then slumped into the arms of secret service agents and hospital staff. Deputy press secretary Larry Speakes, who rushed to the scene, followed his professional instincts and scribbled a note: "Doctors believe bleeding to death. Can't find a wound. 'Think we're going to lose him' [one doctor said]. Rapid loss of blood pressure. Touch and go." The physicians finally located the small entry wound created by the deformed bullet in Reagan's side under his left arm, began to stabilize his condition with transfusions, and wheeled him into surgery.[33]

Most Americans did not realize at the time how seriously Reagan had been wounded, but the nation marveled nonetheless at his grace under pressure. "Honey, I forgot to duck," he told Nancy, echoing the famous comment of boxer Jack Dempsey after Gene Tunney had knocked him out for the heavyweight crown in one of the most famous fights of the 1920s. As he was being wheeled into surgery he reassured his good friend Senator Paul Laxalt, a Nevada Republican, "Don't worry about me. I'll make it." To the surgical team preparing to operate, he quipped, "I hope you're all Republicans."[34]

The seventy-year-old Reagan had the physical constitution of a much younger person and recovered with amazing speed. When he returned from the hospital to the White House within a month, he assumed an almost mythic standing, fixed in the popular mind as someone who had faced grave personal danger with cheerful courage, precisely as did heroes in movies and just the way most Americans secretly wished and hoped they themselves would act in such circumstances. *Newsweek* magazine wrote glowingly of Reagan "grinning like the Sundance Kid into the face of death," and then upped the iconic ante by likening him to "the Duke [John Wayne] defending the Alamo." "Because of the attempted assassination," House speaker Tip O'Neill, Washington's most powerful Democrat, observed, "the President has become a hero. We can't argue with a man as popular as he is."[35]

The combination of purposefulness and popularity enabled the administration to implement large parts of its economic program with a speed that stunned its Democratic opponents. In August, Congress passed the Economic Recovery Tax Act of 1981 (ERTA), which phased in a 23 percent cumulative reduction in personal income tax rates over three years, lowered immediately the top marginal personal income tax rate from 70 to 50 percent, committed the federal government to begin indexing the personal income tax for inflation in 1985, and liberalized depreciation guidelines and increased the business investment tax credit. It was the largest tax cut in U.S. history, and it was permanent.[36]

Reagan achieved similar success on the monetary front, although there he necessarily acted mainly by indirection while the notionally independent Federal Reserve took the lead. Encouraged by Reagan's campaign commitment to fight inflation unmercifully, the Fed, which had already adopted a more strictly monetarist policy approach in October 1979, tightened monetary policy soon after the 1980 election and again in May 1981. Most important, when critics both inside and outside the administration clamored for relief from the economic pain caused by the Fed's attempt to wring inflation out of the economy once and for all, Reagan protected the central bank politically. The president was "steadfast in supporting the Fed's stance of monetary restraint," Reagan confidant Edwin Meese has written: "He never wavered. . . . I was frequently involved in meetings with Federal Reserve Board Chairman Paul Volcker, and the message was always the same—the President backed the board's approach."

In addition, to the extent that the battle against inflation was psychological, and it surely was partly so, Reagan's firmness in firing the 11,400 air traffic controllers, federal employees all, who went out on strike over a pay dispute in August 1981 made an important symbolic contribution. As Volcker later recalled, "The significance was that someone finally took on an aggressive, well-organized union and said no." Equally important for the campaign against inflation, Reagan's strong action against the air traffic controllers— ironically, a lonely source of union support for him in the 1980 presidential campaign—dramatically established his determination and willingness to court short-term risks and to absorb short-term costs in the pursuit of larger goals or principles. The decision to fight the 1982 midterm elections under the slogan "Stay the Course" and the subsequent reappointment of Volcker to a new term as Fed chairman in 1983 drove home the anti-inflation message. Although the Fed's tight money campaign came at an exceedingly high price in both joblessness and lost production—the policy played a major role in bringing about the sharpest recession of the postwar era in 1981–82—the payoff was considerable: in 1982, the consumer price index increased only 3.8 percent, and it remained in that vicinity for the remainder of the decade. As the economist Michael Mussa has observed, "the demon of inflation . . . had finally been tamed."[37]

The administration also made some initial progress in the attempt to reduce the growth of federal spending. Reagan's first budget proposal, presented in February 1981 for fiscal year 1982, called for spending cuts of slightly more than $45 billion; in the end, the legislative package passed in August was estimated to trim spending by $35 billion. The latter figure was sufficient to cause the Democratic chairman of the House Budget Committee to claim that the reduction in spending constituted "the most monumental and historic turn-around in fiscal policy that has ever occurred."[38]

However, the administration's substantial initial progress in all these areas was quickly overtaken and overshadowed by a budgetary crisis that developed even as the basic building blocks of Reaganomics were being put into place in the summer of 1981. Weeks before the president signed the Economic Recovery Tax Act of 1981 into law, OMB director David Stockman warned of a brewing fiscal disaster. From the outset Stockman, a former Michigan congressman, had been a driving force in the framing and implementation of Reaganomics. He possessed, his colleague Martin Anderson has written, "the zeal of a newly born-again Christian, the body of a thirty-four year old, and the drive to work fourteen-hour days, including Saturdays and some Sundays." His personality wore better with some people than with others—Treasury Secretary Donald Regan thought him "arrogant and antidemocrat"—but his intellectual grasp of budgetary matters impressed both friend and foe and made him a powerful figure in White House circles and beyond. Nobody in the administration, perhaps the whole government, knew as much about the budget, and in early August 1981 Stockman told Reagan and his top aides, "The scent of victory is still in the air, but I'm not going to mince words. We're heading for a crash landing on the budget. We're facing potential deficit numbers so big that they could wreck the President's entire economic program."[39]

The problem that Stockman presented to the president and his aides was real, and it quickly got worse. The administration's predicament could be stated all too simply: revenue growth lagged more than originally anticipated, but spending continued to rise. The widening gap between intake and outgo threatened to eventuate in a round of the biggest deficits in peacetime U.S. history. The reasons for the fiscal debacle were somewhat more complicated than the distressingly simple arithmetic that underlay them. On the revenue side of the fiscal equation, several factors were at work. First, the administration won not simply the largest tax cut in the nation's history, but a tax cut far larger overall than even it had originally envisioned. Tax cutting was obviously a political exercise—there were benefits to be gained and disadvantages to be avoided—and, once underway, the process touched off a congressional frenzy, a bidding war in which both political parties courted support by offering special tax relief for favored constituencies. Consequently, the Economic Recovery Tax Act of 1981 came to include not merely the massive reductions in the personal income tax a la Kemp-Roth but also a host of lesser "ornamental" tax breaks, income-tax indexation (a big revenue loser when it corrected the individual income tax structure for inflation from 1985 onward), and large cuts in business, estate, and gift taxes.[40] In addition, the administration had based its initial budget projection of a balanced budget by fiscal year 1984 on a very optimistic forecast, which came to be known as the "Rosy Scenario." As it turned out, economic growth—and hence revenue growth—was much slower than projected, in part because the much-heralded incentive effects of supply-side policies proved both less potent and less immediate in their impact than some had predicted, and in part because when the Fed constricted the money supply to battle inflation, it helped trigger a recession in 1981–82 that further weakened the flow of revenue. Ironically, even the Fed's success in bringing down inflation worked against the administration's hope for a balanced budget, since the slackening of inflation meant less bracket creep in the tax system and consequently less revenue, even before indexation took effect.[41]

Developments on the spending side of the ledger proved similarly disastrous to the administration's initial projections of a balanced budget by 1984. As revenues lagged, expenditures continued to grow. Here, too, the reasons were several. First, even the most dedicated budget slashers within the administration found that gutting the modern welfare state was easier said than done. Stockman was a true radical, an ideologue who wanted a revolutionary reduction in the size and scope of the federal government, what he later termed "a frontal assault on the American welfare state." But, as he himself admitted, his "blueprint for sweeping, wrenching change in national economic governance would have hurt millions of people in the short run." To his disappointment, Stockman discovered that although Reagan genuinely wanted to slow the growth of the federal apparatus, the president was temperamentally "too kind, gentle, and sentimental" for the kind of draconian expenditure reductions his budget director thought necessary to balance the budget and dismantle the existing welfare state. Liberals took a rather different view, complaining that Reagan's cuts in domestic spending signaled "the return of social Darwinism," this time presided over by a former movie actor playing "Herbert Hoover with a smile." The truth actually lay somewhere in between these contrasting assessments. Real spending for non-defense programs other than interest on the national debt did grow in the Reagan years, but at an average annual rate—less than one percent—far below that of previous postwar decades.[42]

Reagan was committed to slowing the growth of established federal programs, but he carefully avoided pledges to abolish outright any specific existing ones. Here, as elsewhere, Reagan combined deeply conservative instincts with a healthy measure of political pragmatism. Although he lacked his budget director's command of fiscal detail, he was savvy enough to recognize Stockman's call for "the ruthless dispensation of short-run pain in the name of long-run gain" as political dynamite. After all, Stockman had been *appointed* OMB director; Reagan had been *elected* president; administrative policymaking and electoral politics bred different outlooks and sensibilities.

The president and his pragmatic political advisers entertained hopes for a second term, and their aversion to bloated government, though genuine, was not so great as to incline them to political suicide attacks. When on one occasion Stockman did manage to engineer Reagan's acquiescence in a plan to cut Social Security benefits to early retirees (those who left the workforce at age sixty-two instead of sixty-five), the resulting political outcry persuaded the president and his advisers that Social Security was, in CEA member William Niskanen's phrase, "a minefield for the administration." Consequently, the White House placed such middle-class entitlements as Social Security and Medicare off limits to budget cutters, preferring to believe, erroneously, that just cutting out waste and fraud could lead to large budget reductions.[43]

Moreover, when the administration did move to trim discretionary spending, it encountered resistance from both within and without that in the long run often proved overpowering. When Stockman sought to trim what he called the "vast local transportation pork barrel"—federal funding for the local building and upkeep of streets, roads, and mass transit—he found himself in a losing battle with transportation secretary Drew Lewis, most of the congress, and a huge constituency of state and local officials, contractors, and unions. "In the end," the budget director recounted, "the transportation sector of the pork barrel never even knew the Reagan Revolution had tilted at it." "It was a dramatic case of everything staying the same," he added ruefully, "but it would be only one of many."[44]

Finally, the administration compounded its budget-cutting woes by implementing a massively expensive military buildup even more energetically than the candidate had promised in the 1980 campaign. Stockman at first applauded the appointment of Caspar W. Weinberger as secretary of defense. Weinberger's tightfistedness as Nixon's budget director and secretary of health, education and welfare had earned him the nickname Cap the Knife, and Stockman hoped that Weinberger would be willing to trim some of the more exuberant plans for rearmament. Reagan's budget director supported the military buildup in the abstract but wanted some defense spending reductions, both because he thought the defense effort contained some egregious waste, because he was increasingly desperate for spending cuts wherever they could be found, and because he hoped that cuts in defense spending would "provide political lubricant" for cuts elsewhere. In the event, however, Weinberger proved a fierce champion of the military machine; to Stockman's horror, Cap the Knife had become Cap the Shovel. So successfully did Weinberger fight off OMB oversight of the defense budget that Niskanen subsequently characterized the resulting administration defense budget as "little more than a stapled package of the budget requests from each service." The pace of military spending slowed in his second term, but overall Reagan presided over a defense buildup that totaled nearly $2 trillion.[45]

In this fashion, a combination of ineluctable arithmetic and the vagaries of politics immersed the Reagan presidency in a tide of red ink. By the end of the administration's second year, the fiscal picture was, Stockman later admitted, "an utter, mind-numbing catastrophe." It worsened with time. The final Reagan record on deficits was unprecedentedly bad: all eight of the administration's budgets ran deficits, the smallest $127.9 billion (current dollars) in FY 1982 and the largest $221.2 billion in FY1986; in FY 1983 the deficit reached a peacetime record of 6.3 percent of GNP; and, overall, the national debt tripled on Reagan's watch, from $914 billion in FY 1980 to $2.7 trillion in FY 1989. James M. Poterba, an MIT economist, has estimated that one-third of the deficit growth under Reagan resulted from tax reduction, two-thirds from expenditure growth in the form chiefly of increased transfer payments to individuals, increased interest payments on federal borrowing, and increased defense spending.[46]

The reaction to this budgetary distress was a series of grudging tactical retreats that came to dominate federal budget policy for the remainder of the 1980s and beyond. For the most part, the impetus for these efforts to recapture a measure of fiscal probity came from fiscal moderates and old-style budget-balancers in Congress, abetted by those of Reagan's advisers, the budget wizards Stockman and his OMB deputy Richard Darman foremost among them, who too late recognized that their original economic design contained, in the so-called "out years" of their own projections, the seeds of fiscal havoc. The salvaging effort took the form chiefly of corrective tax increases (the Tax Equity and Fiscal Responsibility Act of 1982, the 1983 Social Security Amendments, the Deficit Reduction Act of 1984, and the Omnibus Budget Reconciliation Act of 1987) and spending-control measures (Gramm-Rudman-Hollings, passed in 1985, and Gramm-Rudman of 1987) that set precise deficit targets and specified the mechanisms to achieve them. In the end, these efforts, rather than eliminating the deficit as a problem, merely underscored the fact that record budget deficits and the tripled national debt had become the central economic and political realities of the Reagan era.

As a result of the unprecedented red ink, the decade from the mid-1980s through the mid-1990s came to be dominated by budget concerns. Between 1982 and 1995, the federal government was technically forced twelve times to halt operations, however briefly, for lack of funds. Former presidents Gerald Ford and Jimmy Carter warned Reagan's Republican successor, George H. W. Bush, before his inauguration that the federal deficit had come to dominate decisionmaking "in Congress, in the White House, throughout the Federal government." By the end of the 1980s, observed the political scientists Joseph White and Aaron Wildavsky, the budget had become "to our era what civil rights, communism, the depression, industrialization, and slavery were at other times." Extravagant perhaps, but Senator Daniel Patrick Moynihan agreed that the deficit had become "the first fact of national government."[47]

The overriding political consequence of this defining fact of governance was its shattering impact on the sort of federal activism strongly identified with Democratic liberalism. The Reagan administration's persistent efforts to dismantle social programs by restricting eligibility, slashing benefits, and privatizing activities met with only uneven success, but where direct assault failed, fiscal policy succeeded by indirection: Reagan's budget deficits effectively defunded the welfare state. The recurring deficits and growing national debt forced liberals to scurry to protect existing social programs from budget cuts and made it almost impossible for them to mount new efforts at the federal level. The fiscal crisis was "Reagan's revenge," complained the liberal historian Alan Brinkley, "a back door for doing what many on the right had been unable to achieve with their frontal assaults in the 1950s and 1960s." As Reagan White House aide Tom Griscom observed with palpable satisfaction, "You can no longer just say, 'Well, let's do this and not worry about either where the money is going to come from or whether we are going to have to take away from another program or shift priorities.'"[48]

Moynihan believed the outcome to be deliberate. The senator from New York favored a supply-side tax cut of some sort in 1981 in order to improve incentives and boost investment, but he distrusted the promises of the enthusiastic supply-siders around Reagan, observing that they bore the same relationship to genuine conservatives that anarchists did to liberals. Moynihan realized almost immediately that the 1981 tax cut was too large, and he predicted presciently that it would result in crushing deficits. Within weeks of its passage, he asked a New York business audience, "Do we really want a decade in which the issue of public discourse, over and over and over, will be how big must the budget cuts be in order to prevent the deficit from being even bigger. Surely, larger, more noble purposes ought to engage us."[49]

By the end of 1983 the senator became convinced, partly on the basis of conversations with Stockman, who had been a Moynihan protégé (and that family's live-in babysitter) while studying at Harvard Divinity School, that "the early Reagan deficits had been deliberate, that there had been a hidden agenda." Writing in the *New Republic* in December, Moynihan argued that the "deficits for the president's initial budgets" were "purposeful," although he conceded that they "were expected to disappear" in later years.[50]

Had there been a conspiracy purposely to generate huge deficits in order to bring the welfare state to its knees by "starving the beast"? Stockman denied the allegation, asserting that both the administration's "rosy scenario" forecast and the Congressional Budget Office projections used by Congress in developing the 1981 tax cut had predicted falling deficits under the administration's budget proposals. He also denied that anyone within the administration really believed they were creating huge deficits that could be used effectively to discipline congressional spending. In other words, the deficits were too much a surprise to have been put to the conspiratorial uses suggested by Moynihan. Stockman's deputy at OMB, Richard Darman, called Moynihan's charge "way overdrawn," but granted that both Reagan and Stockman had believed that the threat or reality of reduced revenue could be used to rein in the spending habits of the profligate Congress.[51]

Moynihan was onto something, but something considerably more complicated than his conspiracy theory suggested. Stockman's denial notwithstanding, it is clear that a number of conservatives thought that the way to arrest the
growth of the welfare state was to cut off its revenue and let the threat of subsequent deficits help move Congress to restrain expenditures. For too long, they
believed, Republicans had attacked the burgeoning liberal state by trying to
curb spending, an approach that left them at the disadvantage of opposing popular liberal "give-away" programs and then, when defeated, calling for painful
tax increases to cover the excesses of Democratic big spenders. To the critics,
that approach was tantamount to "root-canal economics" and had all the political appeal of a trip to the dentist. As was often the case, Milton Friedman
was in the forefront of those calling for a change in strategy. As early as 1967, he
wrote in his *Newsweek* column that "those of us who believe that government
has reached a size at which it threatens to become our master rather than our
servant" needed to oppose any tax increase and accept larger deficits as "the
lesser of evils." The Chicago economist, who served on Reagan's pre-election
Economic Policy Coordinating Committee and then on the President's Economic Policy Advisory Board, put an even finer point on the idea in another
Newsweek column weeks after Reagan's inauguration: "If the tax cut threatens
bigger deficits, the political appeal of balancing the budget is harnessed to reducing government spending rather than to raising taxes. That . . . is the way
that President Reagan proposes to follow."[52]

Reagan and his advisers did not want the actuality of large budget deficits,
but were perfectly willing to use the threat of them to force Congress to control spending. Reagan himself continued to believe that cutting government's
allowance would force more responsible spending behavior. Despite his occasional denial, Stockman obviously thought along precisely this line. As he
recalled in his political memoir (published even before the Reagan red ink had
dried), the OMB director realized as early as mid-February 1981 that a looming
budget deficit "would become a powerful battering ram. It would force Congress to shrink the welfare state. It would give me an excuse to come back to
them [for spending cuts] again and again."[53] As conspiracies go, however, this
one was, for those willing to read between the lines of public pronouncements,
a rather poorly kept secret. Repeating his familiar trope, Reagan himself told
the National Association of Manufacturers in a March 1982 speech, "Increasing taxes only encourages government to continue its irresponsible spending
habits. We can lecture it about extravagance till we're blue in the face, or we
can discipline it by cutting its allowance."[54] It was the threat of budget deficits
that gave this disciplinary tactic its coercive power.

But the budgetary politics of the 1980s were further complicated by the fact
that attitudes were ambivalent and ambiguous, sometimes even schizophren-
ic. Those most responsible for the fiscal carnage of the 1980s certainly did not

welcome the deficits when they first appeared. When the threat of red ink failed to elicit the spending cuts needed to balance the budget and the large deficits became reality, some of the key plotters in Moynihan's supposed conspiracy panicked. Stockman, who later joked that he was one-half supply-sider and one-half "recidivist Hooverite," quickly became a leading exponent of tax increases to stanch the fiscal hemorrhaging. This offended the more zealous supply-siders: Wanniski commented acidly, "Stockman was part of the small band of revolutionaries, and he went over"; Edwin Meese complained that the OMB director became "a tax-hike mole in a tax-cutting government." Stockman, however, was not the only one spooked by the emergent deficit overhang.[55]

Reagan, too, grew worried, as his diary entries over the course of 1982 indicate. In January, the president was resolute: "I told our guys I couldn't go for tax increases," he wrote. "If I have to be criticized, I'd rather be criticized for a deficit rather [sic] than for backing away from our economic program." But after a budget briefing on Election Day in November (an off-year contest that saw the Republicans lose twenty-five seats in the House), his tone was more distressed: "We really are in trouble. Our one time projections, pre-recession, are all out the window and we look at $200 billion deficits if we can't pull some miracles." In early January 1983, he shared his growing anguish with his Budget Review Board: "We can't live with out-year deficits. I don't care if we have to blow up the Capitol, we have to restore the economy."[56] Expressing his concern several weeks later in his 1983 state of the union address, the president himself broke with his hardcore supply-side supporters, calling the deficit problem "a clear and present danger to the basic health of our Republic" and proposing a standby tax "because we must ensure reduction and eventual elimination of deficits over the next several years." At the time of his 1984 re-election campaign, Reagan considered cutting the deficit and balancing the budget the chief domestic tasks for his second term.[57] Even treasury secretary Donald Regan, one of the administration's most dedicated supply-siders, came to believe that the projected $221 billion deficit for fiscal year 1986 meant the administration had "reached the danger point."[58]

Although Reagan had long recognized the political usefulness of the deficit threat, there is compelling reason, beyond the clear evidence of his growing concern already cited, to doubt that he purposely engineered the series of deficits that actually occurred. The administration wanted the intimidation of potential deficits, not the reality of actual ones. For one thing, the conservative advisers closest to the president were convinced that the supply-side tax cut would so boost growth as to leave the federal government with more, not less, revenue after the tax cuts. As Stockman wrote derisively, "The whole California gang had taken . . . [the Laffer Curve] literally (and primitively)." The revenue increase generated by the tax cut was called "reflow," a label that gave wishful thinking the aura of economic science.[59] Those who worried about the

lost revenue were deemed not sufficiently appreciative of the "reflow" principle.[60] Throughout 1981, Reagan invoked the reflow concept, pointing reas-
suringly to historical precedent to prove his point. "There's still that belief on
the part of many people," he observed sadly but sagaciously to reporters in
February 1981, "that a cut in tax rates automatically means a cut in revenues.
And if they'll only look at history, it doesn't. A cut in tax rates can very often be
reflected in an increase in government revenues because of the broadening of
the base of the economy."[61]

In Reagan's case, the stubborn belief in reflow was both an intellectual
infatuation with punk supply-sidism and a particularly vivid example of the
way that his unquenchable optimism significantly influenced public policy.
In December 1981, the president complained to an interviewer about those
"who kind of chickened a little" in the face of yawning deficit projections,
whereas his "own feeling—you could call it optimism—is, we haven't even
seen the [supply-side tax cut] program work yet." Martin Feldstein, chair of
the CEA in 1982–84, has remarked that, despite the Council's increasingly
grim deficit projections, Reagan "continued to hope that higher growth would
come to his rescue."[62]

Moreover, in this case Reagan's optimism was determinative. It cannot be
dismissed as the affectation of a figurehead leader who specialized in presidential pomp and public relations while leaving the heavy lifting of policymaking
to staffers. Rather, the president himself called the shots that determined the
parameters of policy. For example, it was Reagan who decided in the summer of 1981 that the administration would not compromise with those congressional Democrats who insisted that the third year of the Reagan personal
income tax cut be made contingent on further progress in reducing spending.
"I can win this," he told Murray Weidenbaum, who served as the first chair
of Reagan's CEA, and thus the die was cast. "I wonder," the economist later
mused, "if we would have those remaining triple digit-budget deficits if he had
compromised."[63]

Even as growth failed him and the unprecedented deficits began to pile
up, Reagan's optimism held firm and he put the best face possible on developments. Weidenbaum observed the remarkable evolution of the president's
thought: "In the beginning, he said that big deficits would not occur because
dismal scientists were underestimating the strength of the American economy.
When the deficits came about, his initial reaction was that they would shrink as
the economy recovered. When they endured, he shifted to a third explanation.
After all, deficits served a useful purpose: They keep the liberals from voting on
big new spending programs."[64]

Of course, in the end, Reagan was correct: the unprecedented string of
huge deficits did prove exceedingly friendly to his antistatist inclinations. Although Stockman would criticize the president for lacking the nerve to deliver

a killing blow to big government and other conservatives would bemoan the resilience of federal spending programs and the political clout of their constituencies, the fact is that Reagan's deficit overhang severely limited the ability of liberals to expand existing programs or establish new ones. Although the administration's record of programmatic retrenchment was uneven, fiscal defunding succeeded. The introduction of costly new social policy initiatives became virtually unthinkable. The welfare state was not dismantled, but it *was* put on hold, arguably more through inadvertence and misplaced optimism than by conspiratorial design.

DEREGULATION

Another area fraught with controversy was deregulation. Reagan came into office promising to provide regulatory relief for American business. To underscore that commitment, his first official act as president on inauguration day was to sign an executive order removing the federal government's remaining price controls on oil and gasoline, and he also moved promptly to institute a temporary freeze on all pending regulatory orders. He named Vice President George Bush to head a new Task Force on Regulatory Relief, and he appointed aggressive deregulators to leadership positions at the Council of Economic Advisers, the Federal Communications Commission, the Federal Trade Commission, the Federal Energy Regulatory Commission, the Occupational Safety and Health Administration, the Environmental Protection Agency, the National Highway Traffic Safety Administration, the Office of Management and Budget, and the Department of the Interior. On February 17, 1981, Reagan signed executive order 12291, which institutionalized the use of cost-benefit analysis as a key criterion in deciding whether the government should undertake new regulatory action—potential benefits would henceforth have to be weighed against the potential costs of action. "So we were able," recalled Christopher DeMuth, the administrator of information and regulatory affairs at OMB in Reagan's first term, "to eliminate a lot of harmful regulations at the top while maintaining a great deal of disagreement on what the appropriate level of spending should be lower down."[65] The administration managed in its first term to cut back slightly both spending for regulatory purposes (down 3 percent in constant dollars) and the employment of regulatory personnel (reduced from 119,000 to 101,000).[66]

The administration's most comprehensive attempt at deregulation came in the form of a relief package for U.S. auto makers, who complained that environmental, fuel economy, and safety regulations were driving up their costs while overseas competitors, especially the Japanese, were pummeling them in the marketplace. Responding to Detroit's entreaties, the Reagan administration delayed the scheduled implementation of some regulations (auto paint shop pollution standards and tougher vehicle emission standards, for example), suspended rules regarding the provision of tire safety information to consumers, and delayed and then revoked the requirement for passive vehicle passenger restraints (air bags); the latter recision was eventually overturned by a Supreme Court ruling.

But the deregulatory ardor of the new administration was misleading in several regards. It formed in the popular mind an identification of Reagan with deregulation, which obscured the central fact that deregulation was essentially a phenomenon of the 1970s. By the time Reagan took office in 1981, the deregulation of the airline, trucking, and railroad industries had been largely completed, and the deregulation of financial services, natural gas, and electric power had all been initiated. Clearly, Reagan was a latecomer to the deregulatory push. Historian Richard H. K. Vietor of the Harvard Business School has concluded that the administration initiated further deregulation only in banking and cable television.[67] The deregulation movement of the 1970s was driven less by an abstract devotion to laissez-faire or some incipient version of Reaganomics than by changing economic circumstances, compelling evidence of the failure of regulation to achieve its stated purposes, and the widely shared concern that government microeconomic regulation traded efficiency for order, a particularly bad bargain in an economy beset by stagflation. Moreover, the drive toward deregulation was bipartisan in nature—airline deregulation got a major push from Senator Edward Kennedy's highly publicized 1975 hearings on the regulatory activities of the Civil Aeronautics Board. Deregulation was the product not of a small band of Reaganauts in the 1980s, but of a diverse coalition of regulators, legislators, judges, and presidents of both parties and all ideological stripes in the 1970s.

The Reagan administration discovered early on that much of the New Deal-era economic regulatory regime aimed at the microeconomic stabilization of specific industries and sectors was already in the process of being dismantled or significantly recast. But when the administration then turned its attention to the social regulatory regime that had been put in place more recently, in the 1960s and early 1970s, to regulate matters of the environment, health, and safety, it found those programs much more resistant to attack: they seemed to work, they had powerful special-interest lobbies to protect them, and they enjoyed broad and deep popular support. The administration could snipe at the EPA and OSHA, but it could not prevail in a frontal attack on them. Scandals that resulted in the resignation of the administrator of the EPA and the secretary of the interior in 1983 further weakened the cause of deregulation and galvanized its opponents, and in the face of such developments Reagan's pragmatic White House advisers counseled retreat.

In Reagan's second term, consequently, deregulation seemed largely to disappear from the administration's agenda. Reagan's key achievement was not further deregulation but rather the prevention of re-regulation. But the second term also witnessed a massive disaster befall the newly deregulated thrift industry, an episode that illustrated both the necessity of economic deregulation and the complexity and pitfalls that attended such change.

The administration's object lesson in the dangers of deregulation came in a most unlikely episode of financial scandal and public policy failure. Few institutions enjoyed as wholesome a reputation in the collective mind as America's so-called "thrifts," the nation's savings and loan associations. The thrifts' public relations success owed much to the vagaries of the entertainment industry. When Frank Capra's 1946 movie *It's a Wonderful Life* fell into the public domain in the mid-1970s, television stations looking for inexpensive holiday programming seized on the film as a bargain and ran it seemingly continuously during the Christmas holiday season. The film's protagonist, the restless but responsible George Bailey (played by Jimmy Stewart), personified the virtues of small-town America, and the savings and loan that he headed became inextricably associated in viewers' minds with those values. In mythical Bedford Falls (Anywhere, U.S.A.), George Bailey's savings and loan was the People's institution: fair, compassionate, populist—dedicated to the progress of all, not the profit of a few. In the face of such powerful images, ordinary Americans in the 1980s found it hard to think of savings and loan associations as possibly sinister institutions that required the closest scrutiny. Yet precisely that proved to be the case, as the deregulation of the savings and loan sector led to the collapse of the entire industry and to the single largest government bailout in U.S. history.[68]

As the 1970s began, the nation's savings and loans (S&Ls) operated in a stable, highly regulated world. The government utilized the famous Regulation Q to fix the rate of interest S&Ls could pay on depositors' savings accounts (the only accounts allowed). To keep the generally small S&Ls competitive with larger banks, the government allowed them to pay depositors slightly higher interest rates; and the government mandated that the S&Ls' loans be restricted to housing mortgages. Wags referred to the resulting regime as the 3–6–3 formula: S&L officials paid a fixed 3 percent interest on depositors' savings accounts, lent the money deposited for long-term home mortgages at a profitable fixed rate of 6 percent; and at 3:00 p.m. went off to play golf.

However, the economic vicissitudes of the troubled 1970s caused severe problems for the thrifts. They faced fierce competition for depositors' money from newly created money market mutual funds, which began operation in mid-decade and lured customers with more attractive interest rates than those allowed S&Ls under Regulation Q. At the same time, rising inflation made saving itself appear a game for suckers, with inflation rates outstripping interest rates throughout the economy. Rather than watch inflation whittle away the real value of savings, Americans increasingly chose to spend their money on immediate consumption. As a result of the deadly combination of new competition and debilitating inflation, S&Ls at the end of the decade confronted an all-too-real liquidity crisis; they were, in effect, running out of money as the inflow of new deposits dried up.

Congress attempted to solve the S&Ls' liquidity problem by partially deregulating the industry. The 1980 Depository Institutions Deregulation Act signed into law by President Jimmy Carter sought to increase the flow of new deposits by phasing out the existing interest-rate ceiling. The law also increased the attractiveness of S&Ls to depositors by raising the size of deposits protected by federal insurance from $40,000 to $100,000 per account.

With the striking perversity that so often afflicts well-intentioned human action, Congress's stab at deregulation immediately exacerbated problems at the other end of the S&L deposit (savings account)–loan (home mortgage) pipeline.[69] Paying higher interest rates did indeed attract new deposits, but obviously at a higher cost to the institutions, which were paying more to bring in new money but which were, under government regulations that remained in effect, still saddled with long-term loans (housing mortgages) earning relatively low rates of interest. There promptly arose a new S&L crisis, this time one of profitability; in 1981 fully 85 percent of all thrifts lost money.

Again, Congress stepped in to solve a pressing problem. The Garn-St. Germain Act of 1982 further deregulated S&Ls by allowing them to invest more broadly in new and possibly more profitable areas such as commercial real-estate development (from shopping centers to ski resorts), business loans, and junk bonds. Meanwhile, federal regulators, the Office of Management and Budget, and Congress combined in a burst of deregulatory enthusiasm to curtail federal supervision of S&Ls in other regards, limiting the number of examiners and weakening accounting rules for the newly liberated thrifts. In Texas, which saw more S&L failures than any other state, the number of regulators was cut from fifty-four to twelve between 1981 and 1985. State legislatures, fearful that state-chartered S&Ls might switch to federal charters in order to take advantage of the now wide-open federal rules, quickly passed their own deregulatory packages.

Unfortunately, the combination of cures created a condition more deadly even than the original maladies. The S&Ls' Bedford Falls image soon gave way to visions of the Wild West. The newly deregulated environment invited the entry into the S&L field of a host of sharp operators and crooks as distant from George Bailey as could be imagined, who bought up existing S&Ls and hurried into the business of making highly speculative loans. Some set out purposely to fleece their investors (depositors). Widespread fraud, embezzlement, and unconscionably extravagant management made a bad situation worse. Meanwhile, a good number of the thrift miscreants scurried to provide campaign contributions and personal favors for naive, inattentive, or opportunistic politicians of both parties in exchange for protection from unwelcome government scrutiny. Charles H. Keating, Jr., the high-flying head of California's Lincoln Savings and Loan Association, used the so-called Keating Five—five senators, four Democrats and one Republican—to run interference for him with regulators; ultimately, the five suffered public opprobrium and formal Senate disapproval of their actions, and Keating went to jail. But such tactics worked in the short run to keep the plight of the thrift industry from full public view. Despite spiraling losses, money kept pouring in because professional money managers were putting together "brokered deposits" in bundles of $100,000 to invest anywhere in the country they could find S&Ls paying unrealistically high interest rates; the $100,000 bundles were, of course, now backed by the newly expanded guarantee of federal deposit insurance.

The financial disaster that had been in the offing for nearly a decade finally came to fruition. By the end of the 1980s, 1,000 of the nation's 3,400 S&Ls were bankrupt or were so-called zombies, dead but still walking—technically bankrupt but in operation with a positive cash flow. Estimates of the government bailout required to put the industry back on its feet ran from $200 to $500 billion; some calculations put the cost at between $2,000 to $2,500 in taxes or forgone government services for every man, woman, and child in America. In 1989 Congress created the Resolution Trust Corporation to sort through the wreckage and reconstitute the thrift industry.

As the scale of the S&L debacle became clear, critics rounded up the patently obvious suspects. Some saw greed and moral rot as the culprits. For the left-leaning *Nation* magazine, all clues led to the White House; the S&L scandal revealed "the rotten core of Reaganism beneath the triumphal facade of freedom, prosperity and power." Other observers focused on deregulation itself as the problem. As one business analyst put it: "If the object of government policy had been to destroy the thrift industry, it is doubtful so clever, so toxic, so multifaceted an attack could have been devised."[70]

However, a fair-minded autopsy finds that the S&L collapse of the 1980s defies both easy analysis and glib moralizing. First, the deregulation of the thrift sector was already well under way by the time Reagan took the oath of office, and the deregulatory legislation of 1980 and 1982 was aimed more at resolving real and serious problems afflicting the thrift industry than at furthering some purely ideological, laissez-faire agenda. Second, the responsibility for what happened over the course of the decade fell on a wide variety of players. Surely the thrift officials who broke both the law and ethical norms in the pursuit of profit bore a burden of guilt that no amount of debate regarding the wisdom of deregulation could soften or remove. Sometimes it was a combination of seemingly benign intentions and tunnel vision in the pursuit of self-interest that helped move the episode toward its unhappy end: Consumer and senior citizen groups lobbied hard at the end of the 1970s to drive up the interest rate on deposits while insisting that mortgage interest rates be held artificially low, rather predictably helping to create the problems Congress then addressed so disastrously in the 1982 Garn-St Germain legislation.

Moreover, the political system as a whole proved unwilling to accept the ineluctable logic of laissez faire—the weak must be allowed to fail. Officials of both parties, at all levels, flinched at each of the numerous points in the development of the S&L problem when damage could have been contained by simply letting weak institutions go belly-up. They did so because the S&Ls still basked in George Bailey's reflected image of local virtue, and because those who ran them were often significant figures in their communities and important campaign contributors. The politics of constituent service (rather than grand ideology) dictated that S&L operators would be protected for as long as possible. Had the plug been pulled in the early and mid-1980s when the S&Ls' problems, though large, were still manageable, the ultimate economic cost to the industry and to the public would have been much less.

Nevertheless, no matter how widely the responsibility for the S&L collapse of the 1980s can be distributed, the episode did constitute a catastrophic failure of the process of deregulation. This is not to say that the previous regulatory regime had been working well—it was dismantled because it was hidebound and unable to adapt to the swift-running currents of economic change that overcame it in the 1970s. But all involved in the S&L deregulation process (including both Congress and Reagan administration officials at the White House, in OMB, and at Treasury) failed to appreciate adequately the inherent complexity, the trickiness and difficulty, of deregulation—the need to think through relentlessly the many possibilities for unintended consequences. As had been true of the original drive to regulate earlier in the century, deregulation clearly shaped markets in many ways, not a few of them unanticipated.

In retrospect, two key misjudgments stand out. First, officials in both the executive and legislative branches failed to grasp that the deregulation of a complex industry—even, or perhaps especially, partial deregulation—required the government to *increase* its supervision of the economic landscape it was reconfiguring in new ways. In the S&L episode, officials failed to exercise the prudent oversight that successful deregulation required. Second, by expanding federal deposit insurance coverage at the very time they were encouraging S&Ls to engage in predictably riskier behavior, deregulators significantly weakened the "fear factor"—the knowledge that to take undue risks is to court utter failure—that normally instills discipline in a truly free market. Thus, deregulation of the thrift industry became a perfect occasion for privatizing profits while socializing losses, a proposition dubious in the abstract and disastrous in actuality. Ironically, it could be said that S&L deregulation was most fundamentally undone by the one form of regulation, deposit insurance, that no politician interested in reelection would ever suggest dismantling.

Better supervision would not have eliminated that problem entirely, but it could have minimized its ultimate impact and cost. The Reagan administration did not create the S&L crisis, but it was guilty of not monitoring the industry closely enough to catch the problems attending deregulation before they grew to catastrophic proportions. The failure was one of governance, in the old-fashioned sense, more than of the concept of deregulation per se. As the former Reagan insider David Gergen concluded, "A clear lesson is that in shrinking government programs or turning over federal responsibilities to private hands, the executive branch must still count on a strong corps of civil servants for oversight."[71] The transition to deregulated competition paradoxically required heightened, not lessened, oversight of the rules and guidelines that remained in place, and necessitated a new attentiveness to the forces and unintended consequences of deregulation itself. As lessons go, that one proved extraordinarily expensive.

REAGANOMICS IN RETROSPECT

The economic policies of the 1980s were controversial at the time and have remained so. Debating Reagan's economic performance as president has long been a parlor game for the politically inclined, but one typically generating more heat than light, with prejudices often trumping facts. The initial assessments of Reaganomics were largely negative, often mocking, as if the dramatic shift in ideas and policy had truly been merely the mischief of a daft old man. But time has not been kind to the naysayers. As Reagan's not uncritical, but always-astute biographer Lou Cannon has written in updating his superlative study *President Reagan: The Role of a Lifetime,* "Mark Twain liked to say that Wagner's music was better than it sounds, and it can now [2000] be said that Reagan's economic policy was better than it looked when he left office."[72]

For one thing, the fundamental statistics of the economy's performance during the Reagan years were impressive. To be sure, statistics are famously open to manipulation and interpretation, and both the critics and the champions of Reaganomics have adduced numbers of all sorts to "prove" their diametrically opposed arguments.[73] But statistics are nevertheless necessary if we are to go beyond anecdotal special pleading. The Harvard economist Robert J. Barro, a conservative, has created a matrix for judging the performance of the economy during presidential administrations that measures over the course of an entire presidential term the movement of inflation, unemployment, long-term interest rates, and GDP growth relative to the postwar historical average. Because it covers entire four-year periods, the matrix avoids the many disputes that typically arise from the use of statistics that capture only a frozen moment in time or from the "cherry-picking" of statistical beginning and ending dates. Using Barro's approach with official government data covering the period 1949–1998,

one finds Reagan's two terms ranking at the top of the thirteen postwar administrations, neck and neck with the Bill Clinton's two terms (seemingly an
indicator of the measuring rod's partisan neutrality).[74]

In more qualitative terms, Reagan could boast of two particularly noteworthy achievements. The first was breaking the back of the Great Inflation that so
plagued the U.S. economy in the 1970s. The tight money policy that won the
victory over inflation emanated from the Federal Reserve, the nation's largely
autonomous central bank, but it was a policy that could not have been successfully sustained without the president's stalwart political support. It was, without
doubt, a costly victory, purchased at the price of great collateral damage — the
sharpest recession (as measured by the unemployment rate, which reached 10.8
percent) of the postwar period. However, virtually no serious observer disputed
the significance of the achievement. Even Charles L. Schultze, Carter's CEA
chairman, admitted that "the reduction in inflation was worth the pain" of the
1981–82 recession.[75] Moreover, Reagan's resolution was rewarded with good fortune. Real oil prices began to fall steadily in 1981 and collapsed spectacularly
in 1986, helping the administration to sustain its gains in the struggle against
inflation. In this regard, Reagan was as lucky as Carter had been unlucky.[76]

Reagan's second signal achievement, now clear in retrospect, was to set in
motion, in the aftermath of the hard-won triumph over inflation, what economists label "the Great Expansion," an unparalleled twenty-year burst of prosperity at century's end. The expansion began in November 1982 when the
economy emerged from the recession, ran for ninety-two months (at the time,
the longest peacetime expansion on record), paused for a minor recession in
1990–1991, and resumed as the boom of the 1990s, a wholly unprecedented
ten-year expansion that ultimately became the longest in all of U.S. history.
The economist (and former Federal Reserve governor) Lawrence B. Lindsay
maintains, "The years after 1983 are best viewed as a single expansion, with its
roots in the policy changes of the late 1970s and early 1980s. There has never
been a period of comparable length with so much growth and so little contrac-
tion in the history of the United States."[77] While there are limits to how much
credit can reasonably be attributed to Reagan for an expansion that continued
long after he left office, amidst considerable change in both policies and underlying economic circumstances, the fact that the U.S. economy performed
in so stellar a fashion for so long after the changes he initiated went into effect
at the very least calls into question those contemporary critics who asserted he
was single-handedly wrecking the economy.

Reagan's achievements can also be counted in terms of the alternatives he
forestalled, although here judgments more clearly reflect political preferences.
Absent Reagan's free-market and free-trade approach, the U.S. response to international competition and domestic stagflation would likely have gravitated
toward statist programs of industrial policy and strategic trade, both of which

place economic decisionmaking in the hands of policymakers who are deemed to have judgment about the allocation of resources superior to that of the marketplace. At the time such an approach came highly recommended by the success of Japan's vaunted Ministry of International Trade and Industry. With the subsequent stagnation of the Japanese economy, we have seen more clearly the limitations of such governmental micromanagement.

Reagan could also fairly claim, in the words of the White House aide and arch pragmatist Richard Darman, to have "helped prevent America's slide toward a statist, European-style mixed economy."[78] Although not able to *reverse* the trend toward big government, the administration did manage to hold annual increases in real domestic spending to 1 percent, far below the average for other postwar presidents. Conservatives also consoled themselves with the knowledge that the percentage of GNP taken up by federal taxes, which had been projected absent Reagan's tax cuts to reach 24 percent by 1986, stood in Reagan's last full year in office at 19.0 percent, slightly under the level of 1980 (19.4 percent).[79] But these accomplishments were, of course, open to interpretation. What conservatives cheered, liberals castigated and characterized as a hardhearted failure of social vision.

In hindsight, the most telling charges against Reagan's economic leadership remain two—that Reaganomics left the nation with a crushing burden of debt and that the consequences of economic policy by the rich for the rich caused a spectacular rise in inequality. I discuss the former charge immediately and the latter issue at length in chapter 5. In both cases the criticisms contain both a hard kernel of truth and much mitigating complexity.

It is one of the great ironies of the 1980s that Reagan's stumbling success in his ideological endeavor to limit the perceived leftward drift of government ultimately came at the expense of his economic goal of accelerated long-term growth. The deficits that effectively prevented any substantive extension of the welfare state (beyond the inexorable advance of middle-class entitlements) at the same time compromised the drive to make the economy more productive. The administration's record on growth was modest. The Gross National Product grew by a total of 30.4 percent from 1980 to 1990, considerably below the record of the 1950s and 1960s, and even less, albeit barely, than the woeful decade of the 1970s. Reagan's champions attribute the lag to the necessity of first defeating the inflationary spiral Reagan inherited from the 1970s, and their argument has some merit.[80] But the record deficits generated by Reaganomics also appear to have played a negative role, although somewhat indirectly and less calamitously than predicted by critics.

The economic impact of the large Reagan deficits was substantial, but just how substantial and to what degree harmful have proven to be controversial questions. It will not do to oversimplify a complex matter. Even among professional economists, there was much empirical and analytical uncertainty regarding the effect of the Reagan budget "disasters." William Niskanen wrote in 1988 that although economists had been studying the economic effects of government borrowing for years, "the economics community has probably never been more confused about this issue." Another economist noted that the confusion was compounded by the fact that virtually everyone who approached the topic of Reagan's deficit spending had "some kind of ax to grind." Consequently, professional opinion ranged widely: Some said large deficits mattered little, if at all; others saw in them the road to ruin.[81]

If the Reagan deficits were indeed harmful, the damage they did was not immediately obvious to the casual eye. Certainly they were not nearly so catastrophic as liberal critics insisted. The conventional wisdom that large deficits would fuel a runaway inflation proved in this case to be wrong. A massive inflow of foreign capital appeared to mitigate the immediate impact of the deficits on investment in the United States. This was surely not the immediate meltdown some critics predicted.

Nevertheless, the massive deficits constituted a real problem in several regards. First, they required drastically increased interest payments, which themselves came to constitute a significant source of increased federal spending (no small irony!), further distending subsequent budgets in a compounding fashion. Second, as the Harvard economist Benjamin Friedman has written, "Deficits absorb saving. When more of what we save goes to finance the deficit, less is available for other activities that also depend on borrowed funds. . . . The more of our saving the deficit absorbs, the harder everyone else must compete for the rest and the higher interest rates go." Thus, the sustained large deficits kept real interest rates (that is, interest rates corrected for inflation) high even after the Federal Reserve eased monetary policy to deal with the 1981–82 recession; and those high real interest rates, both short-term and long-term, in turn caused both business and individual net investment (relative to income) to lag significantly in the Reagan years. The end result was, in Friedman's words, an "extraordinary shrinkage of America's capital formation in the 1980's."[82] Third, the string of deficits meant that government subsequently skimped on the sorts of long-term investment in infrastructure and human capital (education and training) required for future economic growth. Finally, the deficits left policymakers with little fiscal purchase for fine-tuning the economy for either growth or stability. Without very much discretionary fiscal income to manipulate through spending and taxing decisions, "all that is left is monetary policy," wrote the economic journalist Thomas Friedman, "[which] is like trying to play a piano with only the black keys." Thus, in the name of growth, the Reagan administration ended up damping one of the chief postwar engines of growth.

Paul Krugman of MIT concluded that, all told, the Reagan deficits constituted "a moderate drag on U.S. economic growth." The administration's policies were, he wrote, "if anything biased against long-term growth." Ironically, the administration's vaunted supply-side approach ended up working more to boost demand in the short run than to effect long-term growth by increasing investment and productivity on the supply side. The result was far less than the calamity claimed by Democratic partisans, but nevertheless a somewhat disappointing outcome for an administration embarked on a supply-side growth crusade.[83]

Moreover, the stultifying impact of the Reagan deficits was broadly psychological as well as narrowly economic. If economic activity does indeed have a psychological component—as notions such as Keynes's "animal spirits," consumer confidence, and depression- and boom-mentalities all imply—then the symbolic impact of the budget woes of the 1980s must also to be taken into account. The deficit overhang became a problem to the extent that it seemed to reflect on the order and legitimacy of the nation's political household. The deficits were threatening in part simply because the political system seemed unable to control them.[84] That failure placed a cloud of uncertainty over both the economic and political future. How could Americans be certain inflation was really dead, and could be kept that way, when the federal government could not keep its own financial house in order? In the face of such a failure of character and nerve, how could anyone be certain U.S. policymakers and politicians would ever be able to do the things that were necessary but also difficult and painful? And without some semblance of reassurance regarding inflation, how could long-term interest rates be brought down from their unusually high level? The failure to control the budget deficits of the 1980s inevitably left hanging the fundamental question of whether the government could be trusted to control itself. Without such confidence, vigorous and sustained economic growth remained uncertain.

But if and when that confidence could be established—as it was by Reagan's successors—the way would be clear for an unprecedented continuation of prosperity, for a continuation of the 1980s expansion into the boom of the 1990s. The laying of the foundation for that sustained prosperity constituted Reagan's chief and enduring economic legacy.

Chapter 4

GREED IS GOOD?

The American Business System in the Eighties

Oliver Stone's 1987 hit movie *Wall Street* introduced viewers to Hollywood's vision of the defining elements of 1980s America—greedy predators and their lackey drones, driven by the money lust that is capitalism, juxtaposed against the weak and vulnerable who struggled to survive in the heartless social order the greedy have created. Movie audiences had scarcely settled in their seats before they were asked viscerally to choose which side they were on in the Manichean struggle. Stone's film was a box-office success despite decidedly mixed reviews, and has since become, in the nation's social memory, a defining representation of what the American business system was all about in an era still remembered as the quintessential decade of greed and excess.

Wall Street pounded home its message via a plot that many commentators found melodramatic and contrived. In the opening sequence viewers meet Bud Fox (played by Charlie Sheen), a strangely innocent young-man-on-the-make who is taken under the wing of a Wall Street land-shark and corporate raider by the name of Gordon Gekko. The actor Michael Douglas played the role of the older, but still indisputably virile Gekko in convincing reptilian style, and won a best-actor Oscar for his compelling performance. Predictably, Bud is slowly but inexorably corrupted by money, power, and sex. As he sells his soul to Gekko, Bud finds himself in charge of one of his boss's newest acquisitions, an airline that happens to employ the young man's wise and honorable aircraft machinist/union leader dad. Gekko's business plan is, of course, to loot, ravage, and then discard the business and all the poor bastards connected with it. Belatedly, Bud realizes what his life has become and what business on the Street is all about. He recoils and successfully foils Gekko's scheme, using all the tricks he has learned during his own moral descent. When the authorities suddenly bust Bud for insider trading, he agrees to wear a wire to gather damning evidence against the mastermind Gekko. Thus, in an ambiguous but strangely uplifting denouement, Bud saves his soul even as he prepares to spend some time behind bars for his own misdeeds. The film's stark moral lesson—what the *Chicago Sun-Times* film critic Roger Ebert characterized as its "radical critique of the capitalist trading mentality"—stands underscored and italicized.

In the end, it was not the contrived story of Bud's ultimate redemption that lodged in the nation's collective memory, but rather the character of Gordon Gekko. He has all of the movie's best lines. "I create nothing. I own," he says, with no hint of apology. Most unforgettable, Gekko dominates both the room and the movie when he makes a speech to a shareholders' meeting: "The point is, ladies and gentlemen, that greed, for lack of a better word, is good. Greed is right. Greed works. Greed clarifies and cuts through and captures the essence of the evolutionary spirit. Greed . . . has marked the upward surge of mankind." In this fashion, from Stone's script, channeled through Douglas's talent, Gekko's self-indicting clichés were transformed by the magic of Hollywood into iconic statements of the 1980s zeitgeist.

Cultural icons are not, however, wholly fabricated or imposed from without, no matter how artful or manipulative their creator. They take root because they resonate powerfully. People believed *Wall Street* because in it they saw art imitating life. The character Gordon Gekko was eminently believable to Americans because it seemed that he had been appropriated from the daily headlines. As it happened, he was. Gekko's "greed is good" speech had already been delivered, in real life, by a genuine Wall Street predator.

"AN ENTIRE NEST OF VIPERS ON WALL STREET"

The Great Wall Street Scandal of the 1980s, like most delicious scandals, began small. On May 12, 1986, the successful investment banker Dennis Levine had breakfast at his Park Avenue apartment with his pregnant wife and his young son, then drove downtown to meet with his staff at the powerhouse firm of Drexel Burnham Lambert. Drexel, which had been a third-tier underwriter of corporate securities in the 1970s, was one of the dazzling success stories of the 1980s. Now the hottest firm on the Street, Drexel had become a genuine rival to the established giants Goldman, Sachs and Morgan Stanley. That afternoon two men, who looked slightly out-of-place to the alert Drexel receptionist, tried to see Levine at his office.

Levine, a man with much to hide, knew that the Securities and Exchange Commission (SEC) had been investigating his offshore banking activities in the Bahamas, and so slipped out of his office and fled, in a fashion befitting a Wall Street trader on the lam. For hours he drove aimlessly around Manhattan in his top-of-the-line BMW (his bright red Ferrari Testarossa would have been too conspicuous), placing frantic calls to his wife, his father, and his boss. While on the phone, he also managed to hire a very high-priced, superstar legal team to represent him as his troubles unfolded.

Later that evening, Dennis Levine drove to the U.S. Attorney's office in lower Manhattan to turn himself in, expecting to be served an embarrassing subpoena and then released so that he could attend a scheduled charity ball to benefit Mt. Sinai Hospital. He wore a dark European suit, a yellow Hermes tie, and black Gucci loafers. To his surprise, he was arrested, frisked, read his rights, and immediately jailed. His cell, he later remembered, smelled "an odor I won't soon forget. It was like an out-of-body experience." He shared his new accommodations with two accused drug dealers. He was, at the time, making over $1 million a year. He had been illegally trading and profiting on insider information for eight years.[1]

Levine sang like the proverbial canary to federal investigators. Facing a possible twenty-year sentence, he agreed to cooperate with prosecutors and pleaded guilty to four criminal charges related to his insider trading activities; he received a two-year prison sentence and paid a $362,000 fine and $11.6 million in restitution to the SEC. The sentencing judge noted Levine's "truly extraordinary" cooperation and observed, "Through the information he has provided, an entire nest of vipers on Wall Street has been exposed."[2]

Levine named the immediate co-conspirators in his insider-trading ring and, most important, gave authorities the name of the famous risk arbitrageur who had also taken advantage of the insider information he had provided—a shadowy Wall Street legend named Ivan Boesky. The moment Levine fingered Boesky, the scandal went big-time.

It is difficult even in retrospect to know just who Ivan Boesky really was. He actually employed a publicist to cultivate his reputation as a transcendent man of mystery. We do know that he was born in Detroit, the son of a Russian immigrant father who had arrived in the United States indigent but later prospered as a restaurant owner. Boesky's own record gets fuzzy almost immediately. He claimed attendance at the elite Cranbrook School, a private boys' school outside Detroit, but neglected to mention that he left there after his sophomore year and graduated from the same public high school as the comedian Eddie Murphy. He always claimed the University of Michigan as his college, but in fact attended classes at Ann Arbor for only a very brief time; he did more class work at the less prestigious Wayne State University and Eastern Michigan University, but never graduated from any college. He finally got a law degree from the distinctly mediocre Detroit College of Law, which did not require a B.A. for admission. Boesky gravitated to Wall Street without having accomplished very much anywhere else.[3]

On Wall Street, Boesky found his calling. He became a risk arbitrageur, an "arb" in the argot of the Street, someone who speculated in takeover stocks, hoping always to play the spread between the purchase price of a stock and its selling price once a merger was consummated. His timing was good, because the 1980s witnessed one of the greatest waves of mergers and acquisitions in the history of U.S. business. Since many proposed mergers fell through, an arb's work was inherently risky business, with the possibility of both big gains and huge losses. Risk arbitrage was also a game where advance, inside information could be priceless. It required the nerve of a cat burglar and sometimes elicited the ethics of that trade as well. Boesky himself once bragged that in his line of work "nervousness is a misallocation of energy." On another occasion, when asked what was in his mind at the moment he decided to press forward with a risky deal, he replied "Two things only. Greed and fear."[4]

Boesky fascinated people in large part because while others merely practiced greed, he celebrated it. He saw it not as one of the more unavoidable of the seven deadly sins, but rather as a laudatory guiding principle for life. He would sometimes entertain visitors to his vast, white-carpeted office with its panoramic view of New York City by displaying a T-shirt emblazoned, "He who owns the most when he dies, wins."[5] Invited to be the commencement speaker for the University of California at Berkeley's Business School in 1986, Boesky punctuated a dull speech by expounding extemporaneously: "Greed is all right, by the way. I want you to know that. I think greed is healthy. You can be greedy and still feel good about yourself." The audience erupted in spontaneous applause.[6] Somewhere in Hollywood, the muse of scriptwriters smiled.

Boesky also created a lifestyle befitting his philosophy. He lived with his wife and four children on a 200-acre estate in suburban Westchester County, complete with formal gardens, indoor handball and squash courts, saunas, spas, pools and pool houses, indoor and outdoor tennis courts, and art and antiques of great value. "It's definitely how people live in books," said an admiring friend.[7]

Boesky's interior life, however, was Spartan. Dressed always in a signature black three-piece suit with a gold chain that looked to the unknowing like a Phi Beta Kappa key, he worked incessantly. He usually slept but two or three hours a night, ate little, and fueled himself with endless cups of coffee. He talked only business, even at social occasions. "He is," said a lawyer and close friend, "a financially driven person. I think it's hard to understand artists, because they have this crazy commitment, and that's what Ivan has—except it's not to the ballet but to the art of making money."[8] It was also the relentless, single-minded regimen of the predator.

The revelation that Boesky had built his success on insider information, illegally obtained from his connections in some of Wall Street's premier firms and sometimes paid for with suitcases full of cash, brought his career to an abrupt halt and the emerging scandal to a new level. In January 1987 *Fortune* denounced Boesky, the erstwhile man of mystery, as "one of history's great crooks."[9] Boesky, like Levine, cooperated with U.S. Attorney Rudolph Giuliani's increasingly aggressive investigators in the hope of gaining leniency. He ultimately received a three-year sentence, and had to pay the government $100 million in penalties (half of which he subsequently wrote off on his federal taxes). But he was permitted to choose the minimum-security federal prison camp where he would do his time. In a particularly dubious concession by authorities, he was also allowed to liquidate much of his stock portfolio before the charges against him were made public, thereby in a sense profiting from his own personal insider information about his future. Even at the end, he played all the angles.

As his part of the deal with authorities, Boesky betrayed the biggest name on the Street. He allowed investigators to tap his phone and agreed to wear a wire in order to record his fellow conspirators making incriminating statements in private conversation with him. Among the people he recorded was the one person who was credited with having "invented" the great merger boom of the 1980s, Michael Milken. With Milken, the Great Wall Street Scandal of the Eighties simultaneously reached its peak and its nadir.

Milken was the undisputed master of Wall Street's universe in the 1980s. Whereas Boesky was a super-rich throwback to the earlier free-booting robber barons of the Gilded Age, Milken was the even wealthier boy genius who was single-handedly creating tomorrow's new economy.

The *Economist* magazine called him "probably the most influential American financier since J. P. Morgan." *Fortune* labeled him "the premier financier of his generation." *Forbes* magazine observed that he was "almost surely . . . the chief architect of America's corporate restructuring in the Eighties."[10]

Milken's rise on Wall Street had hardly been preordained. He was a classic outsider: a West Coast Jew, the son of a middle-class accountant, who rose to the top of an industry long dominated by so-called "white-shoe" WASP patricians. Raised in the comfortable Los Angeles suburb of Van Nuys, he attended the University of California at Berkeley, where he joined a fraternity, majored in economics, and was elected to Phi Beta Kappa. At college he became known for sleeping only three or four hours a night; he often played poker until dawn and then went down to a local stockbroker's office to check the market. He made it clear to friends that he wanted to get very rich. After graduation Milken married his high school sweetheart and went east to the Wharton School at the University of Pennsylvania for an MBA. It was there he stumbled upon the insight that would make him a billionaire and cause him to play an indispensable role in the corporate restructuring of American business.

At Wharton Milken was an operations research major, studying how to apply mathematics to organizational or business problems, but his interest took a turn when he became fascinated by so-called junk bonds. Such long-term debt instruments were issued by new or relatively shaky companies with less than solid credit ratings and prospects, and therefore paid higher than normal yields to cover the greater risk of default. As the name implies, junk bonds were considered distinctly dubious investments. Through careful study, however, Milken came to the realization that in fact they were not as risky as investors believed, and that the risk they did entail was richly rewarded by their higher yields. In 1973 he co-authored a paper with a Wharton professor entitled "Managing the Corporate Financial Structure" and presented it at a Financial Management Association conference. But the kind of money Milken dreamt about making was not available to reward scholarship even in the finest business schools.

Milken took a job with Drexel and pursued his passion for junk bonds professionally with rapidly increasing success. By 1978 he was making so much money for Drexel that he was able to persuade the firm to let him move his junk bond operation to Beverly Hills, California. Milken prospered in part because he was extraordinarily smart and hard-working; but it undoubtedly helped that Milken saw himself on a mission to save the U.S. economy by providing the small, innovative entrepreneur access to capital beyond the expensive short-term financing offered by banks. When he began to capitalize the takeovers of existing large businesses, he claimed to be engaged in a crusade to shake up a complacent, stodgy, and entrenched corporate establishment that had lost the will and ability to innovate. Milken was indeed fueled by greed, but it was a greed for history-making achievement as well as wealth.

The wealth came, in great measure. Milken raised tens of billions of dollars in capital for the likes of MCI, Time Warner, Turner Broadcasting and CNN, and for the takeovers of National Can, TWA, Revlon, and CBS; and for such efforts he was well rewarded—in 1987 alone Drexel paid him an unprecedented $550 million. He chose to invest his vast personal fortune rather than spend it in the pursuit of Boesky-like opulence, and lived quietly with his wife and three children in a comfortable but relatively modest five-bedroom home on a one-acre plot in the hills of suburban Encino, California. But a relatively modest life-style and a penchant for privacy could not insulate him from the spreading Wall Street Scandal.

The government's pursuit of Milken proved more difficult and more controversial than its earlier efforts against the lesser malefactors. After Boesky cooperated with authorities in order to cut a favorable deal for himself, the government took an exceedingly long time to develop its case against Milken, which caused his defenders (and he had many, whereas Boesky had few) to argue that the case was a forced one. When the government invoked the fearsome RICO statute (the Racketeer Influenced and Corrupt Organizations Act) against

Milken, his defenders seized upon the action as proof of government heavy-handedness and the flimsy nature of the case in its more ordinary aspects. But the pressure was inexorable. In 1989 Drexel pleaded guilty to six counts of mail and securities fraud, paid a $650 million fine, and as part of its settlement with the government severed its ties to Milken, who was allowed to resign. In February 1990 Drexel, the highest flyer on the Street in the mid-1980s, when even the secretaries had typically received 35 percent bonuses at year's-end, filed for bankruptcy. Finally, in April 1990 Milken pleaded guilty to six felonies involving conspiracy and securities, mail, and tax violations. He was sentenced to ten years in prison (but actually served only twenty-two months), paid the largest fine in U.S. history, $900 million, and was barred from the securities industry for life.[11]

With Drexel's demise and Milken's conviction, the Great Wall Street Scandal of the 1980s came to an end. In all, fourteen people were convicted of criminal behavior. Rudolph Giuliani, the hard-driving and publicity-savvy federal attorney, left office in 1989 having built a national reputation as the prosecutor who cleaned up the Wall Street mess and went on to a successful political career as the mayor of New York City.

Controversy continued to swirl around Milken. Was he a villain or a victim? One loyalist cracked, "They should find Mike guilty and make him Secretary of the Treasury."[12] Other defenders claimed that he was punished for being rich. No doubt envy did fuel some of the animus against him. Writing in the *New Republic*, the columnist James Gibney exclaimed, "I want Milken to suffer because he's filthy rich. What better way to close out an eight-year era of officially sponsored greed than to go after one of its prime movers?"[13] Still others wondered if he was punished simply for being what he was—a financier. Richard Cohen, a columnist for the *Washington Post*, wrote of Milken with great indignation and a seemingly complete innocence of the role capital markets play in a capitalist society: "The man produces nothing. He manufactures nothing. He has dug no wells, cut no record, made no movie."[14] The *New York Times* editorialists, however, had a keener sense of how Wall Street worked and of the coexisting truths that Milken had both committed criminal acts and revolutionized corporate finance: "Michael Milken is a convicted felon. But he is also a financial genius who transformed high-risk bonds—junk bonds—into a lifeline of credit for hundreds of emerging companies. Snubbed by the banks, these businesses would otherwise have shriveled. . . . There is no condoning Mr. Milken's criminality. But if overzealous government regulators overreact by dismantling his junk-bond legacy, they will wind up crushing the most dynamic parts of the economy."[15]

The notes of ambiguity and ambivalence sounded by the *New York Times* hinted at an essential fact—that beneath the media focus on Wall Street criminality, there was something else happening in the American economy in the

1980s. It is in this sense in particular that the continuing iconic resonance of the movie *Wall Street* and the character Gordon Gekko misleads. Greed was, in fact as well as in the movies, a powerful force in the upper echelons of American capitalism in the 1980s, corruption a constant danger, criminality an indisputable matter of judicial record. But it is a fundamental error to mistake a part of the story—the reality of scandal and misfeasance—for the larger whole. While many Americans fixated on the scandals and the decade-of-greed theme they seemed to validate, there were other, more significant developments and forces at work revolutionizing the American business system. Those changes coursed powerfully, on and often beneath the surface, and were so large in scope and influence as to be sometimes difficult to discern; their ill-defined vastness left them hard to personalize in any all-encompassing way. They were not inherently invisible to moral scrutiny, but neither did they lend themselves to easy moralizing (except when they could be tied to Wall Street greed). In the end, globalization, the personal computer revolution and the coming of the Information Age, and the transformation and reorientation of the corporate economy influenced the American business system and, ultimately, the way people live in the United States and around the world far more than did the highly publicized depredations on Wall Street.

GLOBALIZATION

In announcing his candidacy for the presidency in November 1979, Ronald Reagan called for a "North American Accord" to tie together more closely the economies of the United States, Canada, and Mexico. The proposal went largely overlooked in the subsequent campaign, but it was a harbinger of the future. As the 1980s unfolded, both Democrats and Republicans observed that the United States was becoming more economically interdependent with the rest of the world. Ira Magaziner and Robert Reich, two prominent Democratic policy mavens, wrote in 1982 that Americans needed to "acknowledge that the nation is dependent on a dynamic world economy that must be better understood." Similarly, the President's Commission on Industrial Competitiveness warned in the mid-1980s, "We must acknowledge the reality of a new global economy—an economic era that has come quietly, without fanfare." They were, of course, correct. By the time Reagan left office, the United States had implemented the Caribbean Basin Initiative to encourage trade and investment in Central America (1982–83), concluded a free trade pact with Canada (1988), and advanced a negotiating framework for a similar deal with Mexico— steps that eventuated in the North American Free Trade Agreement (NAFTA) that became operative on January 1, 1994. With hindsight, we can now see clearly that the United States in the 1980s became increasingly enmeshed in the process we call globalization.[16]

Transnational economic integration was not an entirely new phenomenon. In the fifty years before World War I, the Western world (essentially North America, Western Europe, and Australia) had witnessed a dramatic increase in international commerce as capital, goods, and labor flowed across national boundaries with a new ease. In fact, the share of exports in world output peaked in 1913 at a level that would not be surpassed until 1970.[17] Economic historians have attributed that early blossoming of international commerce in large part to technological developments in transportation, especially the impact of railroads and steamships. The outbreak of World War I initiated a return to economic autarky, however, a movement that was subsequently reinforced by the onset of the Great Depression, when many nations, including the United States, scurried for the cover of high tariffs and other protective devices to shield limping home industries.[18]

The new turn toward truly global economic integration that crested in the last decades of the twentieth century took shape initially in the efforts to rebuild and recast the world economy in the wake of the Second World War. The Bretton Woods Conference of 1944 created a number of new institutions to facilitate a renewal of world commerce, among them the International Monetary Fund (IMF) to supervise international exchange, the World Bank to help finance reconstruction and development, and the General Agreement on Tariffs and Trade (GATT) to reduce barriers to trade. The Bretton Woods regime outlawed discriminatory currency practices and exchange restrictions and established adjustable exchange rates pegged to the dollar and ultimately to gold. The legendary Marshall Plan, introduced in 1947 to provide massive amounts of U.S. aid for the rebuilding of the war-torn economies of Western Europe, played a role by insisting that recipient governments liberalize their trading relations. In the effort to jump-start the national economies of Europe, the Marshall Plan even permitted the recipients of U.S. aid to temporarily levy higher tariffs on American goods than on European ones.[19]

The early postwar efforts enjoyed considerable success. So much so that the economic resurgence of Europe and Japan in time overwhelmed the original system of adjustable, pegged exchange rates, and consequently the Bretton Woods monetary regime was fundamentally altered in 1973 to allow floating exchange rates. The change created still another strand of international interconnection, a global foreign exchange market, and the resurgence in world trade continued unabated. Moreover, the long postwar movement in the direction of global economic integration proved to be both more extensive and more intensive than the pre–World War I experience—more extensive because now global really meant global, including Asia, Latin America, and even Africa; and more intensive in that the actual ties of economic interconnection were both more numerous and stronger than before.

By the 1980s the accelerating process of globalization was altering the U.S. economy in profound ways. Trade was one good place to see its imprint. Trade as a percentage of overall U.S. economic activity (GDP) doubled from 7 percent in 1960 to 14 percent in 1983.[20] *Life* magazine, estimating in the fall of 1989 that Americans had thus far through the 1980s purchased $3.41 trillion in imported goods while exporting $2.46 trillion, decided to run a story examining how "shopping in the international mall" had affected a typical suburban family. Zeroing in on the Palm family—husband, wife, and three children ages fourteen, eight, and five—living in suburban Los Angeles, *Life* calculated that they owned more than $50,000 in merchandise either imported from abroad or manufactured in the United States by foreign-owned firms. For the accompanying signature *Life* photo layout, the family placed all their belongings of foreign origin in their front yard, arranged in clusters around the flag of their country of origin. The array was impressive in both sheer quantity and global sweep—fully seventeen nations contributed to the international flavor of the Palms' material possessions, with Japan contributing the most products.[21] Moreover, trade was becoming more important for other countries as well. For all the world's industrialized countries taken together, trade as a percentage of GDP rose from 23.3 percent in the 1950s to 24.6 percent in the 1960s, 32 percent in the 1970s, and 37 percent in the 1980s.[22]

The globalization of finance also became a significant fact of life in the 1980s. The cross-border flow of goods in trade was more than matched by a cross-border flow of investment. "Capital now chases round the world at the touch of a button," observed the *Economist* magazine in 1989.[23] The button was, of course, attached to a computer, as developments in information technology and communication helped shrink the world. Electronic connections obliterated both space and time. International markets for bonds, equities, and foreign exchange (currency) became networks that spanned the globe and operated somewhere—and therefore everywhere—in the world twenty-four hours a day, communicating via computers, telephones, and fax and telex machines. A significant sign of the new level of global interconnectivity was the fact that between 1978 and 1988 American investment overseas grew by some 180 percent, and foreign investment in the United States ballooned by about 380 percent.[24]

Globalization represented the silent revolution of the 1980s. It was in evidence in virtually every area of American economic life, but emerged in such a gradual and piecemeal fashion and was so pervasive that it was hard to appreciate its broadest outlines as a multifaceted but singular phenomenon. Ordinary Americans focused on it most when it pinched badly, as when severe international competition drove U.S. producers to the wall or when Americans learned to their astonishment and dismay that Japanese investors had purchased such citadels of American capitalism as New York City's Rockefeller

Center. Otherwise, globalization remained a slightly fuzzy notion that lacked the concrete quality of the Great Wall Street Scandal. But clearly the phenomenon that became a buzzword in the 1990s had already significantly altered the U.S. economy in the previous decade.[25]

A COMPUTER REVOLUTION AND THE COMING OF THE INFORMATION AGE

The U.S. economy was also profoundly altered by the signal technological developments of the 1980s, the birth and diffusion of the personal computer and the concomitant transition to an Information Age. Computers had been around since World War II, but the information revolution came upon America in the shape of a new smaller version of the very large and expensive mainframe machines that had defined electronic computing in its earliest decades. The revolutionary innovation was the smaller personal computer, the PC. The story of the personal computer went back to the early 1970s, when Intel, a leading manufacturer of semiconductors, created the enabling technology, the microprocessor. When asked by a Japanese manufacturer to design a customized logic chip for new calculator, Intel developed a general-purpose chip that could be programmed for a variety of purposes. But then, not fully realizing the multipurpose advantages of its own creation, Intel granted an exclusive license for its microprocessor design to the Japanese electronic calculator firm. The Japanese firm went bankrupt not long afterward, but before it did Intel found the wit to renegotiate and so regained the right to market the chip to others as a separate product.

The new Intel 4004 chip was, its initial advertising explained, "a microprogrammable computer on a chip." Intel boasted in 1971 that it promised "a new era of integrated electronics." It certainly seemed that way to the nation's electronics hobbyists, who were always looking for, and finding, new uses for technical breakthroughs.[26] In 1975 Micro Instrumentation Telemetry Systems (MITS), a small electronics kit supplier located between a Laundromat and a massage parlor in an Albuquerque, New Mexico, strip mall, used an updated version of the Intel microprocessor chip as the basis for its Altair 8800, considered by experts to be the first real personal computer. MITS named the Altair 8800 for a planet on the *Star Trek* television series, and sold it for $397 in kit form to be assembled by hobbyists. *Popular Electronics* magazine, a bible for electronics buffs of the day, proclaimed on its January 1975 cover: "PROJECT BREAKTHROUGH! World's First Minicomputer Kit to Rival Commercial Models . . . ALTAIR 8800."[27] When assembled by consumers, a task that took considerable time, the new machine appeared deceptively simple—a metal box housing a power supply unit and a central processor, with a panel on the front containing numerous switches and neon bulbs. The machine's memory consisted of 256 bytes, the rough equivalent of one paragraph of information. There was no display, no keyboard. The user communicated to the Altair by laboriously flipping the switches, one flip for each byte of information. It was a process that took even the most practiced users several minutes, and just one mistake meant the programmer had to begin all over. This was a revolution with crude and humble beginnings.

The Altair 8800 excited electronics hobbyists across America despite its shortcomings. Or perhaps because of them. The machine was poised on a new road to somewhere, but it cried out for helping hands in order even to start the journey. In March 1975 a group of hobbyists interested in sharing their passion with others and in checking out the heralded new machine met for the first time in a San Francisco Bay Area garage. They began calling themselves the Homebrew Computer Club, but the folksy name proved somewhat misleading when the membership quickly outgrew the garage. Soon regular meetings in the auditorium at the Stanford Linear Accelerator Center attracted crowds of more than five hundred. Much attention was paid first to getting one's Altair 8800 just to work, and then to somehow improving it. The Homebrew Computer Club, as two of the chief chroniclers of the computer revolution have written, served not only as "the spawning ground of many Silicon Valley microcomputer companies" but also "the intellectual nutrient in which they first swam."[28]

Meanwhile, on other side of the country the coverage of the Altair 8800 in *Popular Electronics* caught the eye of two temporarily transplanted young men who had grown up together in Seattle, Paul Allen and Bill Gates. Both were nerds with considerable experience in the world of mainframe computing. Gates was at Harvard trying to decide on a major—his family wanted him to prepare for a legal career—when Allen, who had studied computer science at Washington State, came running through Harvard Square to show him the *Popular Electronics* cover article on the new microcomputer. They immediately called the manufacturer of the Altair 8800 and offered to develop a usable programming system for the new machine based on an increasingly popular computer language known as BASIC. Working day and night, they delivered their barely finished product to MITS in six weeks. It worked well enough that MITS promptly hired Allen as its software director, and both he and Gates moved to Albuquerque. Micro-Soft (the hyphen would soon disappear), the partnership the two friends had hurriedly formed, had made its first sale.

While some worked to exploit or improve the Altair 8800, others sought to supplant it. The young Californians Stephen Wozniak and Steven Jobs did so spectacularly. The Woz, as he was called, was a brilliant hands-on engineer; Jobs was a visionary who might easily be mistaken for a longhaired, sandal-wearing hippie with electronics skills. Together they made a powerful team. While still students, Jobs in high school and Wozniak at Berkeley, they joined forces to sell so-called blue boxes, devices designed to gain illegal access to telephone lines. Jobs and Wozniak became early members of the Homebrew Computer Club: "It changed my life," recalled the Woz. "My interest was renewed, and every two weeks the club meeting was the big thing in my life."[29] In 1975 Wozniak built his own computer, which he and Jobs, apparently out of sheer whimsy, named the Apple. Using the Jobs family garage as their workshop, the two hand-assembled about two hundred machines and managed to sell them all. Encouraged by their success, Wozniak worked to design a successor model, and Jobs went looking for venture-capital and business advice. By the time the Apple II was introduced in April 1977, their company was up and running, and the new machine was both a technical and commercial success. With its CPU, display screen, and keyboard all fully encased in an attractive plastic housing, the Apple II actually looked like a finished consumer product, rather than a hobbyist's dream kit project. The company began a national advertising campaign aimed at a broad consumer audience, with color copy even appearing in *Playboy* magazine. The firm's attractive new logo—an apple with a bite taken out—quickly became a familiar icon. By the end of the year Apple Computer was doubling production every three to four months and returning a profit for its investors.[30]

As the original Altair 8800 and its hobbyist ethos receded in the distance, the Apple II was joined on the personal computer cutting edge by other consumer-oriented machines, notably the Tandy TRS-80 and the Commodore PET. The move in the direction of a broader public presented the nascent industry with a new problem. In the early, hobbyist phase, it was enough that microprocessor-based machines merely worked, that they performed at higher and higher levels of technical proficiency. But by the late 1970s, less technologically adept customers were asking just what useful tasks the machines could do for them. That question in turn set up a new demand for software applications that went beyond mere recreational gaming. In December 1979, the firm Personal Software launched a new program called VisiCalc (for Visible Calculator), which enjoyed immediate success. Visicalc was wholly original in its ability to lay out a spreadsheet and allow the user to make "what if?" entries that would then show how all the other dependent variables would respond to any given input change. Originally available only on an Apple disk, the program seemed to take what had been a hobbyist's infatuation and make it into an invaluable business tool. At about the same time, a new word-processing software program called WordStar exploded onto the market, giving the newer and more powerful machines the ability to display on screen the precise layout of the finished printed page (WYSIWYG, or what you see is what you get, technology). The personal computer's usefulness for working with both numbers and words was now firmly established. That made it impossible for the biggest player in information technology to remain aloof.

IBM struck swiftly. In 1980 the world's premier computer firm decided to launch a crash project, Project Chess, to develop its own microcomputer and bring it to market within a year. Big Blue's introduction of the IBM Personal Computer (soon known by its shorter label, the IBM PC) in August 1981 legitimated the personal computer for the U.S. business community and in the process helped significantly to entrench the personal computer in American life. If IBM made them, then the technology was real and those things really were business machines. Showcasing the considerable technological advances made since the earliest microprocessors, the IBM PC was built around an Intel 8088 chip with 29,000 transistors aboard, capable of processing .33 MIPS (million instructions per second). The first machines shipped to Sears Business Centers and ComputerLand stores for general retail sale (a sharp departure from traditional IBM practice) came with 64 kilobytes of memory and a floppy disk drive, and sold for $2,880. They were not cheap, but they flew off the shelves anyway—IBM sold nearly 200,000 PCs in the first year.[31]

In its rush to market, IBM broke with company tradition by outsourcing the project, relying on other manufacturers for power supplies, floppy disk drives, printers, and software. Most significant, IBM turned to Paul Allen and Bill Gates of Microsoft to provide the PC's operating system (MS-DOS, short for Microsoft Disk Operating System) and BASIC programming. Since the IBM PC's innards and operating system were not proprietary, a host of imitators began producing clone machines that ran the same software. Compaq, a manufacturer based in Houston, took the early lead in developing IBM clones, but was quickly joined by other major manufacturers, including Tandy, Commodore, and Zenith. In that fashion, the IBM PC design architecture quickly became the industry standard, and that pattern in turn further excited the attention and efforts of software developers. Now their products could be used interchangeably on a majority of personal computers in use in the United States and, increasingly, around the world; the dollar signs in their eyes began to dance as in a video game.

In January 1983, *Time* magazine affirmed the impact of the microcomputer revolution by replacing its traditional "man of the year" choice with the selection of the computer as the "machine of the year" for 1982. The choice was unusual—it was the first time in fifty-six years that the award did not go to a person or some human collectivity. But *Time* believed the departure from precedent imperative. The United States, it reported, was in the grip of a "giddy passion for the personal computer." The magazine reported that sales of the new personal computers had grown from 724,000 in 1980 to 2.8 million units in 1982. Such numbers, *Time* asserted, conveyed a significant message: "The 'information revolution' that futurists have long predicted has arrived, bringing with it the promise of dramatic changes in the way people live and work, perhaps even in the way they think. America will never be the same." Looking ahead, *Time* concluded its cover story on "The Machine of the Year" by quoting Adam Osborne, whose 24-pound Osborne I machines for the moment represented the cutting edge of truly portable computers. "The future," Osborne asserted, "lies in designing and selling computers that people don't realize are computers at all."[32]

For the American public, that particular future arrived with a bang during the 1984 Super Bowl. Viewers watching the third quarter of a one-sided contest between the then-L.A. Raiders and the Washington Redskins were treated to what is widely considered the single most influential American TV commercial ever made.[33] Directed by Ridley Scott, a highly regarded Hollywood filmmaker, and produced on a record-high $700,000 budget, the ad opens with a scene of human drones marching in lockstep through a futuristic system of tunnels into a cavernous auditorium. The auditorium is dominated by a huge video screen, on which appears a larger-than-life Big Brother figure who lectures the pathetic assemblage on the glory and necessity of conformity:

"Today, we celebrate the first glorious anniversary of the Information Purification Directives. We have created, for the first time in all history, a garden of pure ideology. Where each worker may bloom secure from the pests of contradictory and confusing truths. . . .

"We are one people, with one will, one resolve, one cause. . . . We shall prevail!"

Suddenly, the gray, dystopian mood is interrupted by the appearance of a shapely, tanned, highly athletic young woman, who runs into the auditorium pursued by menacing authority figures resembling Darth Vader's starship troopers from the 1977 epic film *Star Wars*. She wears a white tank top bearing the Apple logo, red athletic shorts, and running shoes, and she carries a large sledgehammer, which she, with an audible grunt, winds up and hurls into the giant screen. As the screen image of Big Brother explodes, a visible shock wave of light (freedom?) washes over the assembled drones while an off-camera voice intones: "On January 24, Apple Computer will introduce the Macintosh. And you'll see why 1984 won't be like '1984.'" The theme of Apple's classic sixty-second commercial was clearly the empowerment of the individual, and that was indeed a resonant aspect of the appeal of all personal computers. There was a liberationist strain that ran through the thought of many computer pioneers, and Apple's ad powerfully expressed that message. But the ultimate significance of the Macintosh lay elsewhere — in its particular technology.

The Macintosh spoke directly to the need Adam Osborne had articulated for a computer that people would not realize was a computer. The small eight-person Macintosh design group at Apple (ultimately expanded to forty-seven as development proceeded) had set to work sequestered in a separate building at the Apple headquarters complex, over which flew a pirate's flag. Apple co-founder Steve Jobs directed the Macintosh project to incorporate new technology that he had observed several years earlier during visits to the Xerox Corporation's famed electronics lab cum think-tank known as the Palo Alto Research Center (PARC). PARC was a most unusual place, where engineers routinely pushed computer technology to the farthest limits, usually unconstrained by the necessity of designing commercial products. There Jobs encountered graphical user interface (GUI, pronounced gooey) technology, which used graphics—windows, icons, and pull-down menus—chosen by an "X-Y Position Indicator for a Display System" (i.e., a mouse) to direct the personal computer's operations. The brilliance of the approach lay in its intuitive aspect—it caused the intimidating personal computer figuratively to "disappear," replacing it with a largely self-evident, user-friendly desktop that could navigated and manipulated with ease.

Although Macintosh never gained more than 10 percent of the personal computer market, it nevertheless made GUI-technology a must for the entire industry. The gravitational pull of the GUI approach proved irresistible. The remaining task was somehow to bring GUI technology to the vast number of personal computers using IBM PC architecture and the MS-DOS operating system. Once again, Bill Gates and Microsoft were able to provide the crucial product at the right time. In 1985 Microsoft launched its first version of Windows, a new layer of software that rested on the MS-DOS operating system and virtually replicated the Macintosh's visual layout (necessitating an initial licensing agreement with Apple). The first version operated notoriously slowly, and only when subsequent, more robust versions were introduced (Windows 2.0 in 1987, Windows 3.0 in 1990, Windows 95 in 1995, and on and on) and microprocessor speeds increased did Windows become truly dominant. But by 1989 Microsoft had sold 2 million copies of the program and GUI technology was firmly entrenched.[34]

The early 1990s brought still another set of signal breakthroughs, the most significant of which involved linking computers together into networks. First, the Pentagon's ARPANET (i.e., the network of the Advanced Research Projects Agency), created in the late 1960s to link together the computers of a handful of American universities—four so-called nodes were operational in 1970—gradually morphed into the wholly civilian and much larger Internet, which in 1992 connected more than a million host sites (and ten times that number four years later).[35] Next, in 1990 Tim Berners-Lee, a scientist at the CERN High-energy Physics Lab in Geneva, Switzerland, developed a hypertext system, HTML, that would allow users to leap from one Internet document to another, creating a so-called World Wide Web of information that was stretched over the framework of the Internet. Finally, in the early 1990s a number of browsers and search engines were developed to help users navigate the Web. Among the browsers, "Gopher," developed at the University of Minnesota, and "Mosaic," developed by a group of graduate students at the

University of Illinois, pioneered the way, with more sophisticated commercial ventures such as Netscape Navigator and Microsoft's Internet Explorer following in their wake. Search engines with names such as Yahoo!, Alta Vista, and Google were soon running on the browsers and enabling users to further focus and direct their search for information. With these developments, the computer revolution heralded by *Time's* Machine of the Year cover story in 1982 had come to a full, if surely not final, fruition.

It is no exaggeration to say that in the 1980s and early 1990s the United States moved from the Industrial Age to the Information Age. The U.S. economy became what economic historians call "a first mover" in the development of both the computer and software industries, and in the larger shift from a natural resources-based economy to one whose strength derived from specialized human capital (i.e., knowledge). Manufacturing personal computers and creating software also became important industries in their own right. By 1988, the manufacture of personal computers was bringing in more revenue than the sales of mainframe units, and the U.S. software industry was amassing roughly $27 billion in yearly revenue.[36]

Moreover, the new information technology was transforming the way the rest of the economy operated. "New technology, based on computers and microelectronics, appears to be everywhere . . . [and] few workplaces are exempt from the extraordinary changes now [in 1985] taking place," observed one researcher.[37] "There is hardly a segment of the U.S. economy that has not been penetrated by some form of computer-based technology," reported a Harvard Business School scholar in 1988.[38] In the service sector, computers enabled businesses to control and analyze an ever-increasing flow of information in new, more powerful ways. In continuous-process manufacturing industries, such as refining, chemical processing, and food and beverage production, computers proved particularly useful for monitoring and controlling the flow of product through the manufacturing process. In the manufacture of discrete parts into finished products, such as cars, farm equipment, or consumer electronics, computers provided the capability of computer-aided design for drafting and engineering and of computer-aided manufacturing using numerically controlled machines and robots for actual production. So-called CAD/CAM manufacturing capability was often more talked about than realized in the 1980s, but General Motors, using CAD/CAM software and tools, was able to shift from producing 1988 models to manufacturing new 1989 models over the course of just one weekend.[39] The shape of the future was unmistakable.

Finally, in the 1980s using a computer at home, at school, and at work became an increasingly common feature of everyday life of in the United States. The Census Bureau reported a "dramatic rise in computer use," with some 28 percent of adults and 46 percent of children using computers with some regularity in 1989. The percentage of households owning a computer doubled between 1984 and 1989 to 15 percent. Of a total of 116 million employed adults, 37 percent used a computer at work in 1989.[40]

As computers became more widespread, Americans also discovered that the new technology brought with it costs as well as benefits. One California psychotherapist described the dangers of something called "technostress." In those unable to cope easily or successfully with computer technology, technostress was said to cause anxiety, irritability, headaches, and nightmares. In others who adapted too well to the computer culture, technostress fostered an unhealthy identification with the new technology, causing a loss of the capacity to feel and to relate to others.[41] In short, Americans were damned if they didn't and damned if they did. Now *that* was a familiar syndrome. There was some comfort in knowing that even in the Information Age some of life's traditional dirty tricks still obtained.

THE TRANSFORMATION OF U.S. BUSINESS

Perhaps the most overlooked significant development of the 1980s, all but lost in the furor over business greed and scandal, was the restructuring and reorientation of the U.S. business system. The business historian Louis Galambos has described what happened in the 1980s as "the most formidable transformation" in the history of American business.[42] Responding to the woeful economic performance of the 1970s, American corporations in the following decade restructured themselves, reoriented their management culture, and adopted some of their international competitors' best ideas and practices. In the process they reconfigured the business landscape and paved the way for a nearly two-decade-long economic boom at century's end.

The backdrop for this remaking of the American business system lay in the confluence of several powerful trends and developments that came together in the 1960s and 1970s. The first was the trend in American business toward conglomeration, the growth of firms via the acquisition of subsidiaries that operated in seemingly unrelated areas and dealt with a dizzying variety of products and technologies. A classic example was ITT, a firm specializing in high-technology communications, which in the 1970s owned the Sheraton hotel chain and Continental Baking, a company best known as the creator of one of America's best loved junk snacks, the Twinkie. The second development was the rise of intense international economic competition. Japan and Western Europe rebounded from the lingering effects of World War II and reasserted themselves as formidable economic competitors, while at same time a number of less-developed countries also mounted challenges to U.S. economic preeminence in particular market niches. When the two trends of conglomeration and intense international economic competition converged against the backdrop of the stagflation of the 1970s, the result for U.S. business was disaster.

The rise of conglomeration as an organizing principle for America's large corporations significantly hindered their ability to respond effectively to the international challenge. Awkward and unwieldy, such corporate giants performed under pressure like dinosaurs. They often proved to be out of touch with their own products and markets, a remove that compromised both efficiency and creativity. Although they usually had in place highly sophisticated systems of financial control, conglomerates tended to lose their more fundamental expertise regarding their products and their customers. Moreover, it proved very difficult amidst the diversity of a conglomerate's endeavors to develop a common corporate culture that could sustain the firm in hard times or point the way to better days. "Conglomeration," the business historians Louis Galambos and Joseph Pratt conclude, "left many American firms poorly equipped to develop and sustain the sort of concentrated focus and expertise needed to produce quality products capable of competing in international markets."[43]

In the 1980s U.S. firms reacted to that problematic state of affairs. Their response constituted nothing less than a major reordering of U.S. corporate system. It was a transformation that began in late 1970s, altered the business landscape throughout the 1980s, and achieved impressive results in the 1990s, when the United States enjoyed the longest uninterrupted economic expansion its history. The shift away from conglomeration in the organizing of corporate activity was an important part of a more general change in the 1980s from an emphasis on security and equality to an emphasis on innovation and efficiency.

Several notable changes in public policy helped push the reorganization along. The Reagan administration saw all too clearly the daunting challenge of international competition and the difficulty U.S. firms had in responding to their foreign competitors. Attorney General William French Smith told the cabinet council on legal policy in March 1983 that "the recent emergence of strong foreign competitors in numerous global markets, often with full government backing, makes it imperative that U.S. regulatory policies do not unnecessarily limit the flexibility of American business to respond to challenges and opportunities both here and abroad."[44] The deregulation begun under Carter and continued in the 1980s helped along the process of reorganization by exposing formerly sequestered firms in finance, transportation, communications, and energy to market discipline. Deregulation placed a premium on innovation and efficiency, and the firms in deregulated industries often restructured their operations in the pursuit of those goals.

Most important, the Reagan administration instituted a significant change in the nation's antitrust policy. Under the leadership of Assistant Attorney General William Baxter, the government first brought the long-running antitrust suit against AT&T to a private settlement that effectively broke up the Bell System; then it dropped the major antitrust action against IBM that had been pending for years. With the deck thus cleared, Baxter pushed the nation's antitrust policy in a dramatically new direction by virtually suspending the enforcement of section 2 of the famous Sherman Anti-Trust Act, the part of the statute that prohibited monopoly. "My immediate purpose in writing the Merger Guidelines," Baxter has recalled, "was to facilitate the movement in the direction of deconglomeration."[45] The result, in the judgment of one prominent business historian, was a "decisive shift in policy" that "encouraged firms to combine in new ways, to establish strategic alliances with erstwhile competitors, and in general to experiment with structural changes that would have been difficult if not impossible to achieve at any time prior to 1981."[46] Andrei Shleifer and Robert W. Vishny, two careful scholars of the 1980s merger movement, agree: "The evidence suggests that takeovers in the 1980s represent a comeback to specialized, focused firms after years of diversification." In their judgment, the takeover wave was "to a large extent a response to the disappointment with conglomerates" and reflected "the deconglomeration of American business."[47]

With the open support of a business-friendly administration willing to act in this and numerous smaller ways, the U.S. corporate system in the 1980s embarked on a massive internal overhaul. The corporate restructuring that followed took advantage of a number of recently introduced financial innovations. The new financial practices and devices that many contemporary journalistic observers viewed in the context of greed and scandal—leveraged buyouts (LBOs), managerial buyouts (MBOs), hostile takeovers, and junk bonds—appear in hindsight to have been crucial in financing the restructuring, and thus the deconglomeration, of American business. The easy availability of funding through LBOs, MBOs, and the sale of junk bonds made takeovers affordable, and the relaxed antitrust policy encouraged the merger of firms in the same industry.

The resultant takeover wave of the 1980s was historic by several measures—some $1.3 trillion in assets changed hands and at least 143, or 28 percent, of the 500 largest corporations in 1980 had been taken over by new owners by 1989.[48] The dominant rationale for much of the takeover activity was to break up conglomerates in order to sell off their extraneous parts to specialized buyers and refocus the firm on its core business. IT&T went back to the basics of providing high technology communications products and services for world markets, in the process divesting itself of thirty-three other businesses between 1979 and 1981.[49] Gulf and Western, which had been one of the better-performing conglomerates, began to spin off subsidiaries in profusion. Exxon stopped putting its name on computers and returned to a focus on oil technology and markets.

The tide of conglomeration was clearly receding. To be sure, some conglomeration-style diversification continued, as Du Pont bought up Conoco and U.S. Steel (USX) swallowed Marathon Oil. But it was noteworthy that the new models of 1980s business success were firms that eschewed conglomeration. When

Thomas J. Peters and Robert H. Waterman published the best-selling and most influential business book of the 1980s, *In Search of Excellence: Lessons from America's Best-Run Companies*, they held up as models firms that "stuck to their knitting." One was Johnson & Johnson, whose founder, Robert Wood Johnson, had told his successor, "Never acquire any businesses you don't know how to run." Another was Proctor & Gamble, whose former head was quoted as saying, "This company has never left its base. We seek to be anything but a conglomerate."[50]

The restructuring of American business in the 1980s also involved other sorts of downsizing besides deconglomeration. It was not uncommon for large firms that were not conglomerates also to break into smaller autonomous units, sometimes turning divisions into separate companies in order to focus more tightly on product and market. Another aspect of downsizing involved companies trimming their managerial staffs, in an effort to become organizationally leaner and more efficient. Downsizing in the white-collar ranks reflected a conscious effort to flatten the corporation by pushing discretionary power down to lower levels within the firm, in the belief that those levels were closer to markets and products and therefore best positioned to make tactical decisions. Still other forms of downsizing involved large blue-collar layoffs, transferring production offshore to take advantage of cheaper foreign labor, outsourcing ancillary operations to outside specialty firms, increasing the use of temporary workers, and depending more and more on consultants to solve specialized problems.

The 1980s restructuring of American business via deconglomeration and downsizing was complemented by a distinctive reorientation of another sort, as U.S. businesses adopted many of the managerial values and practices of their international competitors. The Ford Motor Company was a good example of that softer sort of conceptual and behavioral change.[51] Few firms so badly needed to turn themselves around. At the end of the 1970s Ford was a basket case, laid low by its own ineptitude, two oil shocks, and the onslaught of overseas competition. In 1980 it lost $1.5 billion, and the losses continued for three consecutive years. In an effort to stanch the flow of red ink, the company shut down thirteen plants and laid-off 191,000 workers by 1983.

Ford's resurgence in the 1980s, as the business historian David Hounshell makes clear, was built on innovation in the managerial culture, in the design of new products, and in the production process itself. First, Ford changed its management culture by adopting the ideas of W. Edwards Deming, an American who had gone to Japan in the early postwar years as a consultant and become a revered management guru to Japanese industry. Deming specialized in quality control, but his real message was at once broader and deeper than mere statistical quality control; he was the prophet of total quality, the philosophy that product quality had to be central to everything a company did. It was a value system the Japanese borrowed, internalized, and then used to clean the clocks of their American competitors.[52]

Ford adopted Deming's philosophy in the 1980s to halt its slide toward oblivion. The company created an Executive Development Center so that Deming himself and his assistants and converts could teach Ford's managers Deming's Total Quality Management or TQM system. Ford adopted "Quality Is Job One" as an advertising slogan, but more importantly used it as an organizing principle within the firm. Soon the emphasis on teamwork, empowerment, and continuous improvement filtered into the business of designing and manufacturing cars, especially Ford's new mid-size offering, the Taurus. The new model's design team brought together in a newly integrated way input from designers, engineers, marketers, and potential customers (via focus groups) all through the process of bringing the Taurus from clay model to production automobile.

Ford's reorientation also changed the way the Taurus was actually put together. Under the influence of Deming's worker-friendly ideas, Ford softened its longstanding adversarial approach to the United Auto Workers (UAW). In exchange for a relaxation of work rules and job classifications (which gave managers a new flexibility), Ford offered workers a share in the company's profits. To draw workers into fuller participation in the actual production process, the company formed so-called quality circles, or Employee Involvement programs, where quality issues could be discussed. For the first time, Ford granted workers the power to temporarily shut down the production line in order to fix a problem. The result of the new attitudes, organization, and practices was a new car that went on to become the best-selling model in the U.S. market several years running. In 1986, the first full year of Taurus production, Ford earned more money than its chief competitor GM for the first time since 1924, and the following year Ford's after-tax earnings set an auto industry record.

Like the coming of globalization and the Computer Revolution and the Information Age, the restructuring and reorientation of American business in the 1980s constituted a success story of historic proportion. The changes involved were so large and ran so deep that they were at times hard to discern, and they were sufficiently long-running that their payoff was not always immediately evident. For example, economists note that the application of advances in information and communications technology in the 1980s was analogous to the spread of electricity in an earlier era in that they both constituted "general purpose technologies," with powerful and pervasive benefits that required years if not decades before being fully translated into productivity gains.[53]

By the end of the decade, however, it was clear that the business system that had entered the 1980s reeling from both its own self-inflicted wounds and the impact of international competition was emerging as a dynamic and innovative powerhouse. A major analysis of comparative international competitiveness by the McKinsey Global Institute, using productivity or output per worker as the basic measure, found that in 1990 a full-time American worker was 12 percent more productive than his German counterpart, 30 percent more than Japanese workers, and 34 percent more than British employees.[54] Moreover, researchers have found that the U.S. economy has become distinctly less volatile since 1984, on both the up-side and the down-side of the business cycle. The spread of new computer-based inventory management and ordering systems and the increased use of just-in-time manufacturing in leaner and more nimble firms allow businesses now to better stabilize inventories relative to market demand.[55] A decade that had begun amidst talk of American economic decline ended with commentators around the globe marveling at the "American Solution"—the ability and willingness of U.S. policymakers, business leaders, and workers to respond to competitive challenges by accepting the necessity of disruptive and often painful change.

Chapter 5

SOCIAL PROBLEMS, SOCIETAL ISSUES

If the economic success of the 1980s was real, so too were the problems confronting American society in an era of change and adaptation. Some of those problems resulted from the economy's restructuring and reorientation, and they were largely economic in nature. Others were social or cultural in essence. Many had a political aspect. But the most vexed and vexing problems spilled over into all of those categories, and often seemed more worrisome and resistant of solution for that reason. What the most serious had in common, beyond such nettlesome complexity, were a scale, scope, and systemic quality that transcended, and often overwhelmed, individual efforts to deal effectively with them. Such issues perforce constituted society's burden and society's agenda, and presented especially difficult challenges at a time when both politics and culture tended to stress the individualistic elements of the American Creed rather than its egalitarian and communitarian ones.

HOMELESSNESS

Nearly everyone who spent time in America's large cities in the 1980s rubbed up against them in some fashion, even if only by virtue of carefully striving to avoid them. They seemed to old-timers to have appeared almost overnight — "It wasn't always like this," people who had grown up in the city muttered — overflowing from homeless shelters to colonize urban street corners and public spaces. They carried their worldly belongings in the disposable trash bags of an alien, affluent civilization, and the term "bag lady" insinuated itself into the American vocabulary. The overcrowded shelters were soul-crushing places, despite the best efforts of more than a few saintly volunteers and social workers, but they at least offered some physical safety and protection from the elements. The homeless not in shelters slept in cardboard boxes on much coveted steam grates or in abandoned buildings or in the bowels of the subway system, and ran heightened risks to life and limb. Choose your steam grate unwisely or forget to wrap up in cardboard or newspaper to block the moisture and you might get so wet from the steam that you'd freeze later in the night.[1] By mid-decade, homelessness had become a national scandal. It also became a national cause: in the words of the *New Republic*, "the social issue of the eighties"—"stylish enough to lure Hollywood to Washington" and "established enough to warrant routine updates in the daily papers." [2]

Mitch Snyder, one of the more poignant figures in the history of American social activism, played a major role in forcing America to confront the issue of homelessness and in determining how the media and the public came to understand the problem. Snyder came to social protest in a roundabout fashion. Born to a Jewish family in Brooklyn, he had a troubled youth. His father ran off with another woman when Mitch was nine. "I grew up swearing never, ever to do to my kids what my father had done to me," he later recalled.[3] He dropped out of high school and served time in reform school for vandalizing parking meters. As an adult, Snyder got married and worked a myriad of jobs, but never seemed to find a rhythm in his life or peace in his own skin. After six years of marriage, he abandoned his wife and two sons to hit the road. Within a year, he was arrested and charged with transporting a stolen vehicle across state lines. Convicted, he served more than two years in federal prison.

It was while he was imprisoned at the federal correctional facility in Danbury, Connecticut, that Snyder's life changed direction. There he met the legendary Roman Catholic social activists Daniel and Philip Berrigan, who were serving time for their antiwar activities, and their influence altered his life forever. Under their tutelage, Snyder discovered within himself a fervor for social justice that rivaled their own. Released from prison in 1972, Snyder began a new life, joining Washington's Community for Creative Non-Violence (CCNV), an antiwar group that in time also turned to advocating the cause of the increasing numbers of homeless appearing in America's major cities. In 1982 Snyder fasted for sixty-three days to protest the proposed naming of a submarine *Corpus Christi* (Body of Christ); the protest succeeded, as authorities beat a tactical retreat and ultimately christened the offending vessel the *City of Corpus Christi*. By that time Snyder, too, was moving from peace activism to advocacy for the homeless, and it was there he left an indelible mark.

Snyder gained lasting fame in 1984 by going on a fifty-one-day hunger strike that ended just before Election Day, in a successful effort to force the Reagan administration to lease and refurbish the federally owned building at the corner of Second and D Streets NW in downtown Washington, D.C., that housed the large, ramshackle CCNV homeless shelter. Just hours after Snyder declared victory and stopped his fast, Mike Wallace canonized him a secular saint on CBS's highly rated 60 Minutes news magazine program. After introducing him as "the shepherd of the homeless in Washington, the nation's capital," Wallace ended the interview with the suggestive question: "Gandhi, Mother Theresa, Martin Luther King—Mitch Snyder?" The wraithlike Snyder (he had lost sixty pounds), looking with his ruffled hair and army-surplus wardrobe like the genuine zealot and ascetic he was, modestly demurred.[4] But for many Americans, the comparison was apt; and thus validated by the media, a hero was born and an issue took life. Hollywood quickly came calling, and in 1986 CBS produced the made-for-TV docu-drama Samaritan: The Mitch Snyder Story, starring Martin Sheen as the protagonist. A more traditional documentary followed.

As a result of such intense publicity and his close identification with the issue, Snyder had a defining influence on how the media and the public perceived the problem of homelessness. In 1982 he and his CCNV colleague Mary Ellen Hombs published Homelessness in America: A Forced March to Nowhere, in which they estimated that between 2 and 3 million Americans were homeless. Their figure, which commentators and politicians tended always to round up, constituted more than 1 percent of U.S. population. In part because it was so large as to capture attention, the number stuck and came to be treated as an established fact, despite having been pulled from thin air and being wildly wrong.

Snyder knew his numbers were wrong. "These numbers are in fact meaningless," he subsequently explained to a congressional hearing. "We have tried to satisfy your gnawing curiosity for a number because we are all Americans with Western little minds that have to quantify everything in sight, whether we can or not." His co-author Hombs later explained: "I can't even begin to tell you how we got the numbers. It's not a productive exercise. . . . What's the difference, really, what the numbers are? Whether it's 300,000 or 3 million, the homeless are out there. They have to be turned away from shelters every night. If the federal government built the housing these people needed, the problem would practically be nonexistent. Instead of spending money on counting the homeless, we could be spending money on housing them."[5]

Moreover, Snyder and other reformers resisted attempts to develop a more accurate portrait of homelessness. When Reagan's Department of Housing and Urban Development tried to develop its own tally in 1984, Snyder denounced the results (much lower than his) as "tripe." Acceptance of the lower HUD numbers, he confided to Ted Koppel of ABC Television's *Nightline*, might "take some of the power away . . . some of our potential impact . . . and some of the resources we might have access to."[6] Later, when the federal government decided to count the homeless as part of the 1990 census, Snyder advised non-cooperation and refused to allow census takers access to the CCNV shelter, the nation's largest, again fearing the political consequences of too low a count.[7]

We now know just how far off Snyder and the commentators who followed his lead were in their estimates of the scale of homelessness. HUD, the Urban Institute, and the U.S. Conference of Mayors all developed authoritative contemporary estimates that were much lower than Snyder's figure of 3 million. The best scholarly analysis of homelessness, by the sociologist Christopher Jencks, estimates that the number of homeless increased dramatically over the course of the 1980s, rising from 125,000 in 1980 to 216,000 in 1984 and 402,000 in 1988, before dropping to 324,000 in 1990.[8] If Jencks's numbers are correct (they are likely the best we will ever get), Snyder's estimate overstated the numerical extent of homelessness in 1984 by roughly a factor of thirteen.

Advocates for the homeless, including Snyder, also misinformed the public regarding the salient characteristics of that population. For a long time, advocates and the media relied on the trope that the homeless were really "just like you and me," although people's personal observation of the homeless, admittedly usually limited and hardly unbiased, often said otherwise. The notion that all that separated the general public from life on the streets was some bad luck had its uses, however. It humanized the homeless and encouraged people to see them as deserving of help. But at the same time, as Jencks observed, the failure honestly to confront the empirical characteristics of the homeless population confused "sentimentality for compassion" and hindered the search for effective solutions to what was, withal, a serious national problem.[9]

At the end of the decade, the *New York Times* finally reported on its front page that "drug and alcohol abuse have emerged as a major reason for the homelessness of men, women, and families, complicating the search for solutions, advocates for the homeless say. . . . Advocates like Robert M. Hayes [a former Sullivan and Cromwell lawyer who founded of National Coalition for the Homeless] say that they have shied away from discussing the problem of addiction in the past, in part because they feared that the public would lose its sympathy for the homeless."[10] The sanitized and misleading portrait of the homeless was too well entrenched to be easily dislodged by a late turn to candor, however. A study of the news coverage of homelessness by the three major broadcast TV networks (CBS, NBC, and ABC) over the period November 1986–February 1989, surveying more than a hundred stories in all, found that only 3 percent of the homeless persons profiled were described as substance abusers, only 8 percent as mentally ill, and only 12 percent as unemployed.[11] That was reportage from another planet.

The sad, complicating reality was that the homeless were not typical Americans simply down on their luck. The vast majority were unemployed. Most were single adults, not families. Nearly a quarter had spent time in a mental institution; roughly 40 percent had spent time in prison or jail; a third were currently seriously mentally ill (delusional in the sense of hearing voices or having visions); a third had serious problems with alcohol abuse; and following the troubling spread of crack cocaine use in the mid-1980s, it was estimated that a third of all homeless single adults regularly used that highly destructive drug. Many were socially isolated and existentially alone — 36 percent reported having no friends and 31 percent reported having no contact with their relatives.[12] These problems, which many of the homeless carried with them everywhere, constituted a sort of permanent bad luck rather different from the roll-of-the-dice variety advocates sought to portray. Such problems made finding practical solutions to plight of the homeless enormously difficult.

Miscounting and mischaracterizing the homeless invariably led to misconstruing who or what was responsible for their plight and what best to do about it. Snyder blamed bad leaders and a morally benighted system. He considered Reagan an "ignorant . . . maniac" and America "one of the most heinous cultures the world has ever seen."[13] Robert M. Hayes of the National Coalition for the Homeless called the homeless "the most egregious symbol of a cruel economy, an unresponsive government, a festering value system."[14] Insistence that the homeless were just ordinary folks down on their luck, best understood as the victims of a sick system, enabled homeless advocates to overlook what harder-headed analysts saw as the chief causes of the increase in homelessness of the 1980s — the wholesale deinstitutionalization of the mentally ill in the preceding decades; the subsequent failure to provide alternative housing and treatment for those thus turned out; the virtual abolition of anti-vagrancy laws and of involuntary commitment for the mentally ill who ended up on the streets, no matter what the danger to their health, safety, and human dignity; the crack epidemic; increased long-term joblessness; and the gradual disappearance of flophouses and other sorts of disreputable Skid Row housing that had previously sheltered the most down and out.[15] Instead Snyder, Hayes, Jonathan Kozol, and a host of other advocates argued that the homeless were separated from the mainstream public only by the lack of a home, and pushed a simple, and fatally simplistic, solution to the problem — in Hayes's famous formulation: "Housing, housing, housing."[16]

Advocates usually combined their demand for more housing with the accusation that federal housing programs were being cut dramatically in the 1980s as part of Reagan's assault on the welfare state. What the Reagan administration actually did was redirect money from public-housing projects to Section Eight housing allowances to help low-income individuals and families rent from private landlords. Federal outlays for low-budget housing (i.e., the money

actually spent) doubled in real dollar terms, and the number of federally subsidized rental units increased from 2.9 million to 4.7 million between 1980 and
1992. Over the same period, the number of new low-income tenants assisted
by federal programs grew by 60 percent. Much of the credit for such increases
belonged to congressional Democrats, but the fact remained that under the
Reagan and George H.W. Bush administrations federal spending for low-income housing grew faster than actual outlays for social security or defense.[17]
Unfortunately, there was more to solving the problem of homelessness than
just "housing, housing, housing."

What prominent activists failed to address was the difficulty in getting the
hardcore homeless to come in off the streets for housing when it was available.
For example, in 1994 New York City's Times Square Business Improvement
District (BID) undertook a large-scale and expensive outreach program to lure
an estimated two hundred homeless individuals from that well-known neighborhood into available government-subsidized housing. After a year and the expenditure of $700,000, the outreach project managed to persuade only two of
the 206 homeless individuals contacted and courted to accept the housing that
was being urged on them. Clearly, homelessness was a complex social, economic, and cultural problem that required more than well-intentioned calls
for more housing.[18] There would be no magic bullet cure—the sort Americans
of all political inclinations liked best—only slow incremental progress against
one symptom or another.

The seeming intractability of the homelessness problem weighed on Snyder, who sensed correctly, as the 1980s became the 1990s, that public sympathy
for his cause was waning. He began to talk dispiritedly of what he saw as a widespread "psychic numbing" in attitudes toward the homeless.[19] In large cities,
Americans were coming to view the homeless less in terms of their suffering
and more in terms of their impact on the quality of urban life for everyone else.
Aggressive, indeed intimidating, panhandling became endemic in places such
as New York City, and, whether fairly or not, people identified that problem
with homelessness. In 1988 the *New York Times* reported in a front-page story
that "some psychologists, social-service workers and city officials fear that the
rise in begging is further hardening New Yorkers against their fellow citizens
and eroding the quality of life." "It provides a new target for my homicidal
fantasies," exclaimed an Upper East Side psychoanalyst who had been confronted coming out of a Manhattan doughnut shop by a menacing beggar who
demanded half his doughnut.[20]

As his cause foundered, Snyder's life collapsed in around him. Exhausted,
he told friends in April 1990 that he planned to take a leave and withdraw to
a Trappist monastery. He learned he was under investigation by the Internal
Revenue Service in connection with his royalties from the CBS docu-drama of
his life. In early July, his longtime girlfriend and co-crusader, Carol Fennelly,

broke off their relationship, which she would years later claim had long been marred by his physical and emotional abuse. Two days later, Mitch Snyder did a most uncharacteristic thing—he gave up. After carefully locking and unlocking the doors of his room so that his former lover would likely be the one to find him (she was not), he hanged himself using an electric cord. His suicide note, addressed to Fennelly, read: "I loved you an awful lot. All I wanted was for you to love me more than anyone else in the world. Sorry for all the pain I caused you in the last 13 years."

The world took note of Mitch Snyder's passing. Speaking to the 2,500 mourners at a memorial service held outside the huge CCNV shelter, Philip Berrigan recalled, "He literally walked around in the skin of the poor. He put on the poor as Christians are called to put on Jesus Christ."[21] Appropriately, the proceedings ended with a protest march on behalf of the homeless to City Hall, where thirty-seven mourners were arrested for unlawful assembly. Snyder, who over the course of many life-endangering protest fasts had given much thought to his funeral, literally had wanted it that way.

Snyder's life and legacy were fully as tangled as the social problem to which he had devoted himself. He was, wrote one insightful journalist, "a jumbled zealot, a man who embodied all the virtues and shortcomings contained in that special breed."[22] He was a disturber of the peace who in his own life found too little of that precious commodity. His achievements were considerable. He helped the homeless in the most elemental of ways and demanded that others do the same. His relentless agitation and seeking after publicity raised the alarum about a serious social problem that was escalating rapidly in the 1980s. He doubtless helped improve federal funding for homeless programs and likely increased charitable giving for the homeless as well.

Snyder's flaws and mistakes had consequences also. He and the other red-hot homeless advocates so misrepresented, exaggerated, and oversimplified the issue as to invite an inevitable backlash when the truth in all its complexity in the end became undeniable. They promoted simplistic solutions that bore scant relevance to the complicated phenomenon they were fighting. The episode raised troubling questions as to whether advocacy groups could be trusted to provide the realistic portrait of a problem that good public policy demanded in order to be effective, and whether the media actually had the objectivity and critical faculties necessary to puzzle through well-intentioned but bogus claims and explanations in relation to vexed social issues. The speakers at Mitch Snyder's funeral likened him to Martin Luther King Jr., Malcolm X, Nelson Mandela, Mother Teresa, and Jesus. Carol Fennelly, who would remain at the CCNV shelter to carry on the struggle, struck a somewhat different note, describing him as "P. T. Barnum incarnate."[23] She appeared to mean it lovingly, but the characterization lingers uncomfortably in the mind.

THE SPECTER OF AN AMERICAN UNDERCLASS

However vexing an issue, homelessness was not the most worrisome of the social problems afflicting urban America in the 1980s. That dubious honor fell to what Senator Edward Kennedy (D, Massachusetts) described to a National Association for the Advancement of Colored People meeting in 1978 as "the great unmentioned problem of America today—the growth, rapid and insidious, of a group in our midst, perhaps more dangerous, more bereft of hope, more difficult to confront, than any for which our history has prepared us. It is a group that threatens to become what America has never known—a permanent underclass in our society."[24]

The term underclass identified a seemingly recent phenomenon in the nation's urban ghettos: the rise of a debilitating complex of persistent poverty in conjunction with sustained unemployment and welfare dependency, family breakdown, school failure, rampant drug use, escalating and increasingly violent crime, and high rates of teenage pregnancy. *Time* magazine in 1977 warned that a combination of grinding poverty and pathologically self-defeating behavior had produced in the nation's big city ghettos "a large group of people who are more intractable, more socially alien and more hostile than almost anyone had imagined. They are the unreachables: the American underclass."[25] According to the Urban Institute, using 1980 census data, 57 percent of families with children in underclass neighborhoods were headed by a woman (the U.S. average was 17 percent). Forty-two percent of teenagers in such neighborhoods dropped out of high school, compared to a national average of 14 percent. By 1987 the illegitimacy rate in the underclass neighborhood of New York City's Central Harlem was roughly 80 percent, and two of every five such "fatherless" babies were born to teenage mothers.[26]

Defined as it was by behavioral and attitudinal characteristics as well as by demographics, the size of the underclass was impossible to determine with anything approaching precision. Informed estimates in the 1980s ran from half a million to over 4 million, largely black or Hispanic, located chiefly in the inner cities.[27] No matter what the rough count, the underclass was relatively small, a clear minority of the nation's poor, but what worried Americans was the fact that its influence and consequences seemed so much larger and more destructive than its sheer numbers might suggest. The phenomenon's strong racial overtone, which awakened both racial fears and racial guilt, made the issue both more urgent and more incendiary. Not surprisingly, in the 1980s the problem of the underclass attracted the attention of some of the nation's finest social analysts, who labored from a variety of analytical and political perspectives to come up with explanations for what was happening and with prescriptions for how to fix it.

Charles Murray was among the first to weigh in, with a politically conservative analysis that had a considerable influence on Reagan administration policymakers and remarkable staying power in the ongoing national discussion of welfare policy. Born and raised in Newton, Iowa, a modern company town where his father worked for the Maytag Company, Murray attended Harvard as an undergraduate and received a Ph.D. in political science from the Massachusetts Institute of Technology. He saw poverty close-up while serving for five years in village health programs as a Peace Corps volunteer in Thailand in the late 1960s. In the 1970s he conducted evaluations of numerous federally subsidized social programs, and gradually concluded that, despite the good intentions and "uncommon energy and dedication" of those administering them, government social programs usually failed to help the poor in any lasting way.[28] Murray's skepticism about the success of the Great Society initiatives attracted the support of conservative foundations, and in the early 1980s the Manhattan Institute for Policy Research subsidized his writing a full-blown analysis of the impact of government programs on the poor.

In *Losing Ground: American Social Policy, 1950–1980*, published in 1984, Murray set out to answer a deceptively simple question. Why, he asked, had so many of the indicators of well-being and social stability for the working-aged poor—including dependence on welfare, labor-force participation, educational achievement, single-parent household formation, illegitimacy, and crime—taken a negative turn beginning in the Great Society heyday of the 1960s, precisely when government outlawed some of the most overt forms of racial discrimination and when federal social welfare spending kicked into high gear? Murray never invoked the term "underclass," but the behavioral pattern he discussed was that commonly identified with the concept. His answer was as straightforward as his question. Things had gotten worse for the working-aged poor because government had through its policies and programs changed the "rules of the game" in such ways as to "make it profitable for the poor to behave in the short term in ways that were destructive in the long term." In other words, federal social policy had created disincentives to work and inducements to "bad" or economically and sociologically self-defeating behavior. The nation, Murray claimed, had subsidized poverty and produced more poor, subsidized births outside of marriage and gotten dramatically higher rates of illegitimacy. Social policy had provided "official sanction to reject personal responsibility for one's actions," and the result was an increase in antisocial and imprudent behavior. "We tried," he wrote, "to remove the barriers to escape from poverty, and inadvertently built a trap." The solution, in the end, could only be Alexandrian—"Cut the knot, for there is no way to untie it," Murray concluded. Americans needed to scrap the entire federal welfare and income-support apparatus for those of working age.[29]

In essence, Murray blamed federal social welfare policies for creating the underclass. For this he was uncritically celebrated by the right and reflexively denounced by the left. The explosions of disagreement and moral outrage that greeted Murray's analysis were deafening. Critics attacked his statistical evidence, which was indeed vulnerable in spots, and answered his study with their own wholly positive assessments of federal policy over the same period.[30] At the time few people found it possible to take seriously his draconian ultimate solution. But the thrust of his analysis was not easily dismissed. Murray over-argued in suggesting that government caused the underclass, but in the face of his unblinking analysis it was difficult to deny that welfare policies played a significant contributory role in sustaining some of the most debilitating ills plaguing the underclass. He pointed out in an unequivocal fashion that the emperor had no clothes, a truth that many observers suspected but few had uttered so baldly and compellingly. Murray's notion of "welfare dependency" would influence debates on the underclass and welfare policy both in the United States and elsewhere for decades.[31]

The chief liberal alternative to Murray's analysis came in the form of an exquisite analysis of the underclass phenomenon by William Julius Wilson, who in 1987 published *The Truly Disadvantaged: The Inner City, the Underclass, and Public Policy*.[32] Wilson had been born into a working-class family in Pennsylvania, and lived in straitened circumstances after his father, a coal miner, died of lung disease when "Billy" was twelve. His widowed mother worked as a domestic, and the family scraped by, suffering privation but never hopelessness. "We were poor," Wilson subsequently remembered, "but there was always the feeling that things would improve and get better."[33] Although neither of his parents had graduated from high school, all six Wilson children managed to obtain higher-education degrees. William Julius Wilson graduated from Ohio's Wilberforce University, a historically black school, and after a stint in the army continued his studies, earning a Ph.D. in sociology from Washington State University in 1966. He enjoyed great success in his subsequent academic career, and in the mid-1980s was a distinguished service professor in one of the most renowned sociology departments in the world at the University of Chicago.

In writing *The Truly Disadvantaged* Wilson self-consciously set out to offer a liberal alternative to Murray's argument. The field was wide open, for liberals had shied away from serious discussions of the underclass phenomenon ever since the unhappy experience of Daniel Patrick Moynihan in the mid-1960s. While serving as a mid-level official in the labor department in early 1965, Moynihan had written a famous memorandum entitled "The Case for National Action: The Negro Family," in which he warned that victory in the struggle against Jim Crow segregation would not by itself bring about true racial equality in America. The next stage in the national struggle for racial equality, he

suggested, required an all-out attack both on the racial prejudice that continued to poison American life and on the troubling problem of a crumbling family structure within the black lower class.

Moynihan wrote that poor blacks were trapped in a "tangle of pathology"
and argued that the matriarchal system that prevailed among them was responsible, directly or indirectly, for "most of the aberrant, inadequate, or antisocial
behavior" that plagued the racial ghettos of the nation's large cities.[34] In the su-
percharged emotional atmosphere that had grown up around considerations of
race at the height of the black freedom struggle, Moynihan's candor provoked
a ferocious response, with accusations in the *Nation* and elsewhere that he was
a sociological faker and an encourager, albeit unintentional, of "a new form of
subtle racism" that blamed the victim for the consequences of white oppression.[35] The abuse came in torrents, from both blacks and white liberals, and
Moynihan was astonished at how few in the liberal community defended him.
As a result, he subsequently distanced himself from issues centering on race
during his long career as the U.S. Senate's resident intellectual statesman. As
Wilson explained at the outset of *The Truly Disadvantaged*, the episode served
as an object lesson for others as well, creating "an atmosphere that discouraged
many social scientists from researching certain aspects of lower-class black
life."[36] Serious discussion of the social pathologies on the rise in the ghetto was,
in effect, off-limits for liberals because of the fear that it could be twisted to
validate racist stereotypes. Even worse than silence, some on the left chose to
see in the weakening of traditional values, mores, and institutions among the
underclass not self-destructive devolution but rather heretofore unrecognized
cultural creativity and adaptability. Wilson, an African American and self-proclaimed social democrat, courageously confronted head-on the indisputable
evidence of social dislocation in the ghetto underclass. In so doing, he regained
for the liberal perspective a claim to realism that had for a season been lost.

Wilson's intellectual tour de force in *The Truly Disadvantaged* lay in his
combining elements of the major competing (and seemingly conflicting) interpretations of the underclass into a provocative new synthesis that was much
more than the sum of its parts. He accepted that racial discrimination was indeed a part of the explanation for the rise of the underclass, but maintained
that contemporary discrimination no longer played a defining role. Rather, it
was historical racial discrimination that had created the concentration of impoverished masses of African Americans in urban centers in the first place,
with all of the so-called concentration effects that followed.

Wilson also accepted that there was a cultural dimension to the plight of
the underclass, but he interpreted that culture as one of social isolation, not
a permanently internalized culture of poverty. The culture of social isolation
was as dysfunctional as the liberal Moynihan and the conservative Murray had
claimed; but rather than being an autonomous and self-perpetuating construct,

Wilson saw it as the cultural consequence of what was the single most important cause behind the rise of the underclass—the loss of jobs available to inner-city residents in the wake of massive economic change in recent decades.
Having thus integrated elements of what might be labeled the "racism" and
"culture of poverty" models of explanation, Wilson placed them in the service
of his own structural interpretation.

For Wilson, the key to understanding the rise of the underclass lay in the
structure of society, particularly the loss of employment opportunities in the
inner city. The United States had for some time been in the process of shifting
economic resources and opportunities from manufacturing to the service sector, inter-regionally from North to South and West, and locally from central
cities to suburbs. The result was a steady loss of jobs available to inner-city
blacks. And as the jobs moved away, so too did those higher-income African
Americans with sufficient resources to follow them, an out-migration ironically facilitated by the victories of the civil rights movement in breaking down
racial barriers. As a result, the inner city ghettos became increasingly socially
isolated, ever more impoverished and vulnerable to the social pathologies
that accompanied joblessness, dependency, and hopelessness. Change in the
economy begat change in the social structure, which begat change in the culture—an endless cycle of mutually reinforcing cause and effect that spiraled
ever downward.

The only way to break the spiral, according to Wilson, was through a massive national effort—on the scale of the Marshall Plan, not race-specific but
universal in scope—to bring employment to all Americans. He called for expensive programs of macro- and microeconomic state intervention, seeming to
include everything but the proverbial kitchen sink. Read closely, his proposal
was painfully vague and hopelessly quixotic—one would never have guessed
that inflation and governmental efficiency had recently been burning political issues, that the previous large federal jobs program, CETA, had over the
course of the 1970s become mired in controversy, or that the 1984 election had
returned to the White House by a historic margin a Republican dedicated to
restraining the growth of government. Nevertheless, the sheer elegance of Wilson's analysis, his ability to pull together the strands of seemingly competing
explanations into one grand theory with striking explanatory power, marked
the arrival of an intellectual superstar.

Wilson was not without his critics, however. From the left, a reviewer in
the Nation savaged him for his "disturbing and retrograde" emphasis on social
pathology in the ghetto (shades of Moynihan!) and for his "deeply patriarchal
vision" of family structure, views that left him the unwitting prisoner of "the
antidemocratic, Reaganite frame of reference."[37] Among less ideological readers, there remained a suspicion that Wilson had underestimated the cultural
component of the underclass phenomenon.

In 1986 the liberal writer Nicholas Lemann published a long, two-part essay in the *Atlantic Monthly* on the origins of the underclass, in which he argued for an anthropological or cultural, rather than economic (either welfare- or jobs-centered), interpretation. "Every aspect of the underclass culture in the ghettos," he wrote, "is directly traceable to roots in the [sharecropper] South." That culture had come to the nation's urban ghettos in the massive migration over the period 1940–1970 of millions of African Americans, including the nascent sharecropper underclass, out of the rural South and into Northern cities. The out-migration of working class and middle class blacks who left the inner city to pursue the opportunities opened up by successes of the civil-rights movement removed important counterweights to the amplification and entrenchment of underclass norms and mores transplanted from the rural South. Social disorganization followed, perhaps exacerbated by welfare policies and the loss of jobs, but not caused by them.[38]

Still other critics wondered whether all the jobs available to low-skill workers had indeed fled America's central cities. The Harvard economist Richard Freeman reported that 70 percent of the unemployed underclass youth he interviewed in 1980 admitted they could easily find a job, but they disdained the readily available work as "chump-change," dead-end propositions.[39] However, many of the immigrants streaming into American cities in the 1970s and 1980s found such jobs to be an entry-point to long-term economic success.[40] Again, cultural attitudes seemed to be salient.

In the end, the intellectual and policy debate over the underclass was never fully resolved. There was no all-out, universal governmental intervention of the sort recommended by Wilson, but the economic expansion begun in 1983 continued through the end of the century with only one relatively short and mild interruption. By the mid-1990s the buoyant economy gradually began to generate the sort of tight labor market conditions capable of driving down unemployment to levels approximating full employment, in the process absorbing workers from even the poorest neighborhoods.[41] According to the Urban Institute, the absolute number of poor people in underclass neighborhoods, which had risen from 4.9 million in 1980 to 7.1 million in 1990, actually declined to 6.7 million in 2000. At the same time, conditions in high-poverty neighborhoods improved slightly in terms of school achievement and two-parent family stability (the latter viewed as an economic advantage, not as a moral matter), while welfare dependency dropped dramatically. Given the pessimism that had prevailed regarding the intractability of the underclass phenomenon, the Urban Institute characterized the good news as "astonishing." Clearly, said liberals (and the non-partisan Urban Institute agreed), the turnaround vindicated Wilson and his theory: The availability of jobs had been the key.[42]

At about the same time, the nation's welfare system was radically transformed. A process of welfare reform that had begun when Reagan inserted into the 1981 budget a provision allowing individual states to experiment with new, work-oriented approaches to welfare culminated in the Personal Responsibility and Work Opportunity Reconciliation Act of 1996, passed by a Republican congress and signed into law by a Democratic president, Bill Clinton. The new law effectively ended welfare as a federal entitlement by eliminating the old welfare mainstay, Aid to Families with Dependent Children (AFDC); requiring recipients of the new state programs that replaced AFDC under broad general federal guidelines to seek work; and capping lifetime welfare eligibility for the new arrangements at five years. The *Economist* magazine saw welfare reform, not economic structure and jobs, as the cause of the subsequent improvement in the fortunes of the underclass: "For decades, the underclass has loomed as America's deepest social problem. In just five years [1996–2001], [welfare] reform has halved the size of the problem and made it possible to move on to the next stage."[43] For conservatives, the news validated both Murray's stress on the importance of government policy and, in a larger sense, the interpretation of the underclass issue as fundamentally a cultural phenomenon.

In truth, we do not fully understand what caused the turnaround of the 1990s. It seems reasonable to suspect that both economic and cultural forces were at work. If Ronald Reagan's economic policies and cultural messages provided a foundation for the good news of the 1990s, clearly Bill Clinton's initiatives, including his massive expansion of the Earned Income Tax Credit and increased spending for child care, as well as his defense of welfare reform in the face of great criticism from within his own party, gave developments a crucial push.

In any event, the underclass did not melt away. The problem had merely been ameliorated; it had not disappeared. Americans were not certain it would not take new and perhaps more widespread and virulent forms. Murray warned that the coarsening of life he associated with underclass values and behavior was, like the rap music that represented itself as the artistic expression of the most downtrodden, spreading throughout all of American society.[44] Reports came in from new precincts, including such Midwestern industrial cities as Davenport, Iowa, of an entrenched white underclass manifesting precisely the same patterns of alienation and self-defeating and pathological behavior that had been seen in the inner cities of the 1980s.[45] Others warned of a "rainbow underclass" forming among new immigrants to the nation's cities.[46] Perhaps the only certainty was the fact that anyone seeking to understand either the old problem or its new permutations would have first to stand on the shoulders of the social thinkers of the 1980s, who could not solve the problem or agree among themselves but nevertheless managed to usefully illuminate a deep societal ill.

THE GROWING INEQUALITY GAP

The least visible societal issue of the 1980s was one that seemed at first blush a mere statistical artifact but in truth struck at the heart of the nation's self-identity: a troubling increase in economic inequality. Americans have long prided themselves on the egalitarian nature of their society. Upon visiting the United States in the early 1830s, Alexis de Tocqueville wrote, "No novelty in the United States struck me more vividly during my stay there than the equality of conditions."[47] In reality, however, the equality of position Tocqueville noted was eroding even as he wrote, and over the course of the nineteenth century the process of industrialization further widened the dispersion of income and wealth.

In the late 1930s and throughout the 1940s, however, there occurred what economic historians call the Great Compression, an extraordinary period of wage compression that produced a wage structure more equal than the nation had witnessed previously in the twentieth century.[48] President Harry S. Truman bragged in his 1953 farewell address that the nation had achieved the fairest distribution of income in recent history.[49] Moreover, that distribution seemed to hold steady in succeeding decades. A specialist with the Brookings Institution wrote in 1978 that tracking changes in the U.S. distribution of income was "like watching grass grow."[50] But beginning in the mid-1970s, a discernible trend toward greater inequality took hold and continued through the 1980s and 1990s.

The study of economic inequality is a complex area of analysis, but researchers using a variety of approaches and measures have generally agreed that the United States became more economically unequal in the 1980s. Republican partisans have sometimes challenged those findings, seeing implicit in them an attack on their economic leadership and preference for marketplace solutions, but the professional consensus runs against them.[51] Researchers looking at *wages* have found that inequality grew significantly—between 1970 and 1990 workers at the 90th percentile (near the top of the economic ladder) gained 15 percent in real terms, while workers at the 10th percentile lost about 25 percent.[52] Looking at *income* rather than wages, the Harvard economist Richard Freeman has found that between 1979 and 1996 the share of income going to the top fifth of families rose by 13 percent, while the share going to the bottom fifth of families fell by 22 percent.[53] Experts looking from a slightly different angle, at the *income of households rather than families*, and using the Gini coefficient, a standard measure of inequality named for the Italian statistician Corrado Gini, which establishes a scale running from perfect equality at 0 to perfect inequality at 1.0, have discovered that the inequality of household income rose from 0.398 in 1976 to 0.431 in 1989 and 0.455 in 1996. In short, the inequality of household income had returned to where it had been in the early 1940s, before the Great Compression.[54] Finally, the economist James P. Smith of the RAND Corporation has found that the inequality of *household wealth* (as opposed to income) also spiked sharply beginning in the mid-1980s, due primarily to unequal sharing in the stock market boom that saw the Standard and Poor's Index of 500 stocks rise in real terms by 250 percent between 1984 and 1994, with more to follow before the market bubble burst in 2001.[55]

What caused the rise in inequality observed in the 1980s? Critics rushed to blame Reagan's conservative leadership and devotion to what they labeled trickle-down economics. Kevin Phillips, a political commentator who started out working for Richard Nixon's White House but later embraced a left-leaning populism, led the way. In his best-selling 1990 book entitled *The Politics of Rich and Poor: Wealth and the American Electorate in the Reagan Aftermath*, Phillips asserted that the United States had in the 1980s returned to the harsher capitalism—"capitalist overdrive"—of the late-nineteenth-century Gilded Age, when the Robber Barons—the Vanderbilts, Morgans, Carnegies, and Rockefellers—had joined with Republican politicians to engineer a massive concentration of wealth.[56] Phillips saw Reagan's tax cuts, reductions in social spending, deregulation, relaxation of antitrust enforcement, and tight money policies as primary causes for the new inequality in American life.[57]

There are, however, serious problems with the chiefly political explanation for America's rising inequality. The new inequality had, after all, begun to surface before Reagan took office.[58] Moreover, almost all industrialized nations experienced a similar increase in wage inequality in the 1980s and 1990s.[59] The existing research attributes some marginal influence to public policies pertaining to income taxation, the minimum wage, and deregulation, but concludes that on balance their impact was small.[60] (For example, the trend toward greater inequality showed up in pre-tax as well as post-tax earnings.)[61] Also contributing was a sharp decline in union membership, which dropped from 27.9 percent of the nonagricultural workforce in 1970 to 23 percent in 1980 and 17.5 percent in 1986.[62] Immigration, too, played a supporting causal role. An increasing number of immigrants, relatively less skilled than their immediate predecessors, came to the United States in the 1980s and 1990s, and their arrival had a discernible distributional impact, essentially redistributing income from native workers who competed with immigrant labor to those who used the immigrants' services.[63]

The chief culprits behind the rise in inequality were not government leaders or policies, however, but rather powerful economic forces—technological change, which greatly increased the demand for well-educated and highly skilled workers; and global competition, which brought a flood of inexpensive mass-produced imports and thereby lessened the demand for domestic low-skilled labor.[64] Those causes were as impersonal as they were powerful, and they did not lend themselves to partisan polemics as readily as accusations of plutocratic plunder; but they were real. Fundamental economic and social developments, not Ronald Reagan and his policies, caused the increase in inequality of the 1980s, which continued through most of the 1990s.

The left did have a point, however. If Reagan did not cause the rise in inequality, neither did he do very much to mitigate it. Instead of leaning against the trend, the administration leaned with it. In part, that inclination resulted from the president's ideological perspective. Reagan's concern lay more with the efficiency of the U.S. economy than with its equity. Conservatives did care about expanding opportunity via economic growth, and they sometimes interpreted the extraordinary increases in income and wealth at the top of the economic ladder as evidence that Americans were prospering as never before. What could be wrong with that? Conservatives also emphasized the churning that continued to take place within the existing income distribution, the fact that people were in constant motion both within and between income quintiles. However, that sort of mobility over time, as people moved up or down the economic ladder during their lifetimes, held steady but did not increase in the 1980s. Thus, the churning, the very real economic mobility that continued to be a hallmark of American society, failed to offset the secular inequality trend that had taken hold.[65]

The failure to address the new inequality as a pressing problem also reflected the way that Reagan's personal optimism shielded him from confrontations with what might be considered unpleasant realities—flaws or weaknesses—in the American system. Reagan was attuned to individual misfortune and need. He was, in fact, highly empathetic regarding the plight of flesh-and-blood individuals, probably more so than some of his critics for whom humanity remained always an abstraction. He tended to view individuals' problems in an anecdotal frame, however, and to see solutions in terms of classic conservative voluntarism. Throughout his public career he would write checks to individuals whose personal stories of misfortune or adversity came to his attention. He also tithed a regular portion of his income to his "home" church in California. But Reagan's vision, and his leadership, faltered in precisely those areas where problems transcended the individual and could only properly be understood and addressed as systemic. Powerfully committed to the vision of America as "a city upon a hill"—the Puritan John Winthrop's resonant metaphor was a presidential favorite—Reagan had difficulty in coming to grips with deep-seated imperfection in his beloved.

THE SCOURGE OF AIDS

The passage of time has given the story of the outbreak of the Acquired Immune Deficiency Syndrome (AIDS) epidemic a retrospective clarity wholly lacking at the time. Indeed, it is difficult to recapture the pain, puzzlement, and wild fear that accompanied the disease when it first registered in the early 1980s. Certainly it was not expected. The 1970s had been a decade of revolutionary ferment in the gay community. The sexual promiscuity of San Francisco's gay baths and New York City's gay sex clubs came out of the closet at the same time thousands of gay men did. Meanwhile, the movement for homosexual civil rights begun in the aftermath of the so-called Stonewall Rebellion of the late 1960s grew apace, and in October 1979 more than 100,000 people gathered in the nation's capital for an inaugural March on Washington for Lesbian and Gay Rights. It seemed to many gays that sexual liberation and political empowerment were ecstatically intertwined. In 1980, the camp musical group the Village People, for many mainstream Americans the happy face of a carefree gay culture, released an album entitled *Live and Sleazy*, singing on one cut, "I'm ready for the eighties, ready for the time of my life." The lyrics were, it turned out, a cruelly ironic augury.

In 1979 gay men in San Francisco began showing up at local clinics complaining of swollen glands. As a medical resident at the time subsequently recalled, "We advised people to slow down. This was at the end of the seventies in San Francisco, and gay men had many partners, did drugs, and had a lot of STDs [sexually transmitted diseases]. We told patients to shift out of the fast lane for a while to see if their lymph nodes went down. Retrospectively, that was one of our earliest indications that something was amiss."[66] Their problems did not go away. Instead, previously healthy young men with swollen lymph nodes began to die of unusual opportunistic diseases. The rare cancer known as Kaposi's sarcoma and a form of pneumonia not commonly seen in the young, *pneumocystis carinii*, began showing up in medical reports coming in to the federal Centers for Disease Control (CDC) in Atlanta from California and New York. The gay newspaper the *New York Native* scored a scoop when it ran a story in May 1981 about "rumors that an exotic new disease had hit the gay community in New York." In June 1981 the CDC's *Morbidity and Mortality Weekly Report* began alerting doctors nationwide to the new developments. And on July 3, 1981, came the first mention in America's paper of record, the *New York Times*—"Rare Cancer Seen in 41 Homosexuals." The article was short and buried deep inside the paper. America initially became acquainted with the AIDS epidemic piecemeal, without having a clue as to what was really happening.[67]

The nation learned, but all too slowly. In mid-1982 good evidence that the disease was sexually transmitted finally surfaced. By the end of the year the first well-documented case of AIDS transmission via a blood transfusion made it clear the disease was also transmissible by blood. The groups most at risk, the CDC reported in March 1983, were homosexuals (especially those with a history of multiple sex partners), hemophiliacs (from blood transfusions), intravenous drug users (from contaminated bloody needles), and Haitians (predisposing factor unknown, but suspected to be unprotected gay sex with multiple partners).[68] Finally, in April 1984 Secretary of Health and Human Services Margaret Heckler announced that scientists had identified the source of AIDS as a retrovirus, ultimately labeled human immunodeficiency virus (HIV). At the time, there were 4,177 reported cases of AIDS in the United States.[69]

Responses to the epidemic varied widely. For homosexuals, long oppressed, it was a travail like no other. Ben Schatz wrote, "I sometimes feel like gay men are dangling by their fingers from the edges of a roof, and every minute or so you can look over at the man next to you just in time to see him let go and drop. But up on top of the roof, the rest of the country is having a cocktail party—and except for those people who are walking around stepping on your fingers, they're not even aware we're hanging there. Yet man after man lets go and falls, and you're dangling there and thinking, 'Can I really hang on? How long can I hang on? This seems impossible.' And man after man loses his grip and falls to his death, and up above you you hear ice tinkling in the glasses, but the pile of bodies down below is just getting higher and higher."[70]

On the far reaches of the right, some saw AIDS as the proverbial wages of sin, payback of truly Biblical proportions for homosexual immorality. Patrick Buchanan, who would subsequently serve as Reagan's director of communications (1985–87), wrote in his syndicated column in May 1983, "The poor homosexuals; they have declared war upon nature, and now nature is exacting an awful retribution." Jerry Falwell, the Baptist minister who founded the Moral Majority, that same year observed on television, "When you violate moral, health, and hygiene laws, you reap the whirlwind. You cannot shake your fist in God's face and get away with it."[71]

Most Americans engaged in denial. They were still uncomfortable with and disapproving of homosexuality but not immune to the suffering around them, and they were honestly confused and fearful for their own safety and that of their families and immediate communities. In the popular mind, AIDS remained a gay problem, even as the identification of the HIV virus opened up the logical likelihood of the disease's ultimate spread into the heterosexual mainstream. But that denial became increasingly difficult to maintain as AIDS took on a more and more familiar aspect. The death from AIDS of movie star Rock Hudson in 1985 brought the reality of the disease home to millions of Americans and thus constituted a turning point in the history of the plague.

Hudson died in his Beverly Hills home in October 1985 at the age of fifty-nine. His death made the disease that killed him at once less alien and more horrifying. The nation had only recently learned of his illness, and his homosexuality, when he collapsed while visiting Paris in July 1985 for treatment with an experimental AIDS drug not available in the United States. As *Time* magazine put it chillingly, "The disease took its inevitable course." Hudson had lived a poignantly false double life, making sixty-five movies and starring in the 1970s hit TV show *McMillan and Wife* as a paragon of heterosexual masculinity. His was not a great acting talent, but he always stayed within his limitations and enjoyed considerable Hollywood success, at first getting by on his rugged good looks and sex appeal and later finding his niche in light romantic comedy. He won an Academy Award nomination for his role as a Texas patriarch in the 1956 movie *Giant*.

Throughout his time in Hollywood, Hudson and his handlers worked hard to keep his homosexuality from public view. When a gossip magazine threatened to expose him in the mid-1950s, his studio quickly arranged a marriage of convenience. The union did not last, of course, and discreet friends in the Hollywood community later knew full well that he had a long-time male lover. By the early 1980s Hudson had become resentful and bitter at having to live a heterosexual lie. Sadly, through his illness and death Hudson performed a valuable service by bringing AIDS out of the closet with him. As a *Washington Post* reporter mentioned to a gay rights activist at the time, "Sorry we haven't done much on this [AIDS] before now. We just haven't been able to find a handle that would make the story interesting to the general population." (The activist, who himself suffered from AIDS, was not amused at the implication that the death of thousands of faceless gay men had not been sufficiently newsworthy.) Hudson provided that handle. He gave the disease a familiar human face and in so doing both raised public awareness of the epidemic and engendered greater sympathy for its victims.[72]

Ryan White, an adolescent from Kokomo, Indiana, played a similar role. His was the face of childhood innocence. A hemophiliac, White contracted AIDS from a tainted blood transfusion at age thirteen. He became a household name in 1985 when the Kokomo school superintendent barred him from returning to his seventh-grade classes because he had been diagnosed with AIDS and it was feared he might pose a danger to other students. When he finally reentered school under a court order, his fellow students ostracized and harassed him; more than a score of frightened parents pulled their children out of school; vandals broke windows and fired a shot into his family's home; and someone slashed the tires on the family car. Fleeing the rampant hostility, in 1987 the family moved to nearby Cicero, Indiana, a much smaller farming community, and received a more compassionate welcome. Ryan attended high school there, and continued to demonstrate an extraordinary grace under pressure that won attention and admiration.

Without intending or desiring to, Ryan White became a national celebrity in the fight for tolerance for AIDS sufferers. In 1989 ABC Television told *The Ryan White Story* to a national primetime audience in the form of a two-hour made-for-TV movie. As a spokesman for the National Commission on AIDS commented, "After seeing a person like Ryan White—such a fine

and loving and gentle person—it was hard for people to justify discrimination against people who suffer from this terrible disease."[73] When he died
of complications from AIDS in 1990, at age eighteen, during his senior year
of high school, Ryan White stood 5 feet tall and weighed 90 pounds. Most
of that was heart. His funeral attracted 1,500 mourners, including First Lady
Barbara Bush. Fear and meanness died hard, however. In the year following
Ryan White's death, vandals desecrated his grave at the Cicero Cemetery on
four separate occasions.[74]

Many gays believed that it was precisely that sort of fear and meanness that
determined Washington's position on AIDS. Gays and lesbians and administration critics on the left were utterly convinced that Ronald Reagan was homophobic. The accusation was untrue and obscured the larger irony of the
administration's leadership lapse regarding the disease.

Reagan was no homophobe. Working in the film industry had brought him
and his wife into close contact with many homosexuals. While governor, Reagan became embroiled in scandal involving a "homosexual ring" operating in
his office. The individuals implicated were let go—for political and job-perfor-
mance reasons, not moralistic ones—but Reagan lied (denying that homosexuality was involved in the departures) to protect the privacy of those involved,
even at the risk of prolonging the political fallout and endangering his own
political standing. His biographer Lou Cannon described Reagan's conduct
throughout the episode as "decent and principled."[75] Later, after he had left the
governorship, Reagan courageously and outspokenly opposed the Briggs Initiative (also known as Proposition 6), a 1978 ballot measure that called for the firing of any California teacher who advocated homosexuality either publicly or
privately. "Whatever else it is," Reagan wrote publicly at the time, "homosexuality is not a contagious disease like the measles. Prevailing scientific opinion
is that an individual's sexuality is determined at a very early age and a child's
teachers do not really influence this."[76]

The available evidence indicates that Reagan was personally tolerant of
homosexuality and took the basic libertarian position that gays and lesbians
should be left alone. He never used homosexuality as a wedge political issue.
However, he stopped short of affirming homosexuality. In writing to a friend
regarding the 1984 Democratic Party platform plank on sexual orientation,
Reagan observed, "You know . . . I'm not one to suggest . . . [homosexuals]
should be persecuted in any way but they are demanding recognition and approval of their lifestyle and no one has a right to demand that."[77] Like many
Americans of his generation, Reagan was most comfortable with homosexuality when he did not have to think about it. However, when the issue of homosexuality hit closer to home, Reagan betrayed in small, personal gestures the
cultural views and anxieties of a male born in 1911 and raised in the American
Midwest. For example, when Reagan wrote a friend that his younger son,

Ronald Prescott Reagan, had decided to enter upon a career as a ballet danc-
er, the president-to-be made certain to add, "I hasten to assure you he is an
athlete and all man."[78]

Fairly judging Reagan's performance on the AIDS issue is rather more complex than critics usually admit. The federal establishment played a key role
in responding to the AIDS crisis from the very beginning. It was, after all, the
CDC that first recognized the epidemic in 1981. In May 1983 Assistant Secretary of Health and Human Services (HHS) Edward Brandt proclaimed AIDS
the administration's "number-one [health] priority."[79] In April 1984 HHS Secretary Margaret Heckler announced that government researchers had isolated
the cause of AIDS, the human immunodeficiency virus (HIV). Federal spending on HIV/AIDS rose by at least 75 percent every fiscal year from 1983 through
1989, with increases of 450 percent in FY1983, 134 percent in FY1984, and 148
percent in FY1986. Admittedly, the increases were in no small part the result of
pressure by Democrats in Congress—of the total of $5.6 billion actually spent
between FY1984 and FY1989, the Reagan administration had proposed $2.8
billion—but the record was hardly that of a do-nothing administration.[80]

Cannon, Reagan's most searching biographer, has written that the president's response to the AIDS crisis was "halting and ineffective."[81] Reagan was
slow to use the bully pulpit to address the AIDS issue, although he was urged
to do so by the first lady. The hard-line social conservatives in the administration, especially William Bennett, Secretary of Education, and Gary Bauer, the
White House domestic policy adviser, fought hard to keep the president and
Surgeon General C. Everett Koop from exercising forceful national leadership
on the AIDS issue. According to Koop, Reagan did know and care about AIDS,
but was constantly told by the hard-core conservatives among his advisers that
the issue was political dynamite. "He listened," remembered the surgeon general, "to those who he thought were acting on his best behalf."[82]

Context matters, however, and it is important to remember the utter confusion that enshrouded the AIDS epidemic at its outset. What does one say
from the presidential pulpit when the *Journal of the American Medical Association* reports with seeming authority in May 1983 that AIDS can be transmitted by casual household contact? When French researchers at the prestigious
Pasteur Institute report as late as September 1986 that they have found traces
of the AIDS virus in the genes of some fifty varieties of African insects and
French newspapers run headlines screaming "MOSQUITOES COULD TRANSMIT
AIDS VIRUS." Mervyn Silverman, the director of the San Francisco Department
of Health in the early 1980s, has recalled Reagan's "silence" on AIDS as "deafening" and "tragic." Yet, Silverman had official oversight of San Francisco's
notorious bathhouses, which all serious analysts agree played a pivotal role in
amplifying the spread of AIDS throughout the gay community in that hard-hit
city in the crucial early years of the epidemic, and because of well-documented

political opposition within the gay community he waited until October 1984 before getting up the courage to close down the remaining fourteen bathhouses and sex clubs in his jurisdiction. Fine indeed are the scales that can distinguish among so many varieties of tragic miscalculation.[83]

Still, the critics make a point. Reagan can be faulted for not speaking up earlier and more forcefully. Even in the absence of definitive scientific knowledge, he could have rallied the country with an acknowledgment that AIDS was a serious problem that required citizens, as in the past, to unite against panic and to marshal their compassion in a united response to a communal crisis. Later, once the scientific nature of the threat had been more fully identified and the death toll continued to mount, he should have engaged more fully his great powers of communication and consolation to provide solace to the sufferers. Such efforts would have been largely symbolic, but throughout his presidency Reagan proved time and again the power and significance of symbolism.

In the end, it was the slow, cumulative unfolding of scientific research that brought about the progress that finally was achieved in the struggle against AIDS. By the mid-1990s, research at last yielded drug therapies capable of at least moderating the progression of the disease in individuals. There is little reason to believe that Reagan, or any other political leader, could have hurried that process along in any significant way. As Andrew Sullivan, himself gay and HIV-positive, has written, "An instant cure for HIV was never going to be possible. Science takes time."[84]

The great irony is that Reagan's hesitance to play a stronger leadership role on AIDS, if only rhetorically, created a void that invited, indeed forced, the gay community to coalesce politically in novel ways, with a new, desperate energy, to fight the disease on its own. The administration thus unwittingly facilitated one of the most paradoxical developments of the 1980s—the emergence from a decade dominated politically by the most popular and effective conservative American leader of the twentieth century of a gay and lesbian rights movement stronger, better organized, and more ambitious than ever before.[85]

Because homosexual men bore the brunt of the AIDS epidemic, the gay community and its supporters of necessity played a leading role in coping with the ravages of the disease and combating its spread. One of most important crusaders against the disease was Dr. Mathilde Krim, who for her efforts was named a "Hetero Hero" by *The Advocate*, the national gay and lesbian newsmagazine, and *Ms.* magazine's 1985 Woman of the Year.[86] Krim's life story sounded like the stuff of fiction. She was born in Como, Italy, in the mid-1920s to a Swiss father and a Czech mother. The family moved to Geneva, Switzerland, when she was still a young child, and she was raised and educated there, ultimately earning a Ph.D. in genetics from the University of Geneva.

As she entered young adulthood, Krim developed a powerful empathy for marginalized minorities that became a lifelong hallmark of her character. Her parents were, she later recalled, "sort of gently anti-Semitic. I didn't question it when my parents said that Jews were dirty, or not very honest." All that changed shortly after the end of World War II when she saw newsreel footage of German concentration camps. "I was shocked out of my wits. I went around crying for a week afterward," she recounted.[87] But what set Krim apart from so many people who recoiled at the sight of the horrible consequences of Nazi anti-Semitism was that she really did act on her revulsion. She joined a group of Jewish activists at the University of Geneva and ultimately made her way into the Zionist underground movement, joining the Irgun, a terrorist group led by the later prime minister of Israel Manachem Begin. For a time, she worked in the south of France smuggling guns for shipment to the Zionist forces fighting in Palestine. She also converted to Judaism, married a fellow Irgun member, and in 1953 immigrated to Israel with her new husband. In disgust, her parents disowned her.

In Israel, Krim's life took a storybook turn. She and her husband divorced; meanwhile she continued to work as a researcher at the Weizman Institute of Science. In 1956 she gave a tour of the laboratories to a visiting director of the institute, the New York motion-picture executive Arthur Krim, and the two quickly fell in love. They married and she relocated to New York City, where she continued her scientific work, ultimately studying viruses at the Sloan-Kettering Institute for Cancer Research, while also joining Manhattan high society as the wife of an entertainment industry heavyweight who happened also to be an adviser to Democratic presidents and the finance chairman of the Democratic Party.

Krim's research work at Sloan-Kettering proved controversial. In the early 1970s she became interested in the cancer-fighting possibilities of a naturally occurring protein known as interferon. "She more or less singlehandedly rescued the [interferon] field from oblivion," observed a prominent expert. However, she accomplished that feat by wedding the techniques of the evangelist to those of the scientist, lobbying ceaselessly for increased funding for interferon research, and touting the substance as a possible magic-bullet cure for cancer. In the process she became known as "the interferon queen," a less than complimentary sobriquet. Follow-up scientific studies failed to confirm the premature hype, and the scientist who headed a subsequent interferon inquiry for the National Cancer Institute noted, "There are many examples of fine scientists who, when challenged with the possibility of curing cancer, do not demonstrate the same rigor as they do with their own work." Sandra Panem, a science and policy fellow at the liberal Brookings Institution, observed more sharply, "One clear lesson of the interferon crusade is that rational biomedical policy cannot be based on hype."[88] The AIDS crisis of the 1980s put that rigorously scientific view to a test, with new claims and demands based this time less on hype than on desperation, and once again Dr. Mathilde Krim was at the center of controversies that demonstrated just how political and complex the world of "rational" biomedical policy could be.

Krim learned of AIDS even before it had a name. In 1980 an acquaintance with a medical practice in Greenwich Village told her of seeing a puzzling number of patients presenting enlarged lymph nodes and spleens, which looked like reactions to infection, but with no other symptoms. All were gay men. Krim became sufficiently interested to agree to help test some blood samples. And then the patients started dying.

Krim responded to the emerging AIDS epidemic by again combining her penchant for promotion with her scientific expertise and organizational ability. In 1983 she started the AIDS Medical Foundation, which two years later combined with a separate West Coast AIDS research funding agency to form the American Foundation for AIDS Research (AmFAR), one of the most visible and effective private fund-raising groups in the fight against AIDS. Krim brought to her job as co-chair of AmFAR a scientific reputation (and a heavy European accent) that brought her immediate credibility in her many media appearances to publicize the dangers of the new and often misunderstood disease. She also took full advantage of the social connections she enjoyed as the wife of the president of Orion Pictures, tapping the star-studded Hollywood community in particular—Barbra Streisand, Warren Beatty, Woody Allen, and a host of other celebrities—for help in raising both public awareness and funds for a variety of AIDS programs.

Once engaged, Krim held little back and again found herself embroiled in controversy. She appeared on TV's *Phil Donahue Show* to advocate the use of condoms, supported supplying intravenous drug users with clean, disposable hypodermic needles in order to slow the spread of AIDS among that highly vulnerable group, and championed all manner of gay rights once she became aware of the sociological contexts of the AIDS epidemic. But the controversy that mattered most was over the testing and introduction of new AIDS drugs.

In 1986 Krim and other AIDS activists fought to force the Food and Drug Administration to loosen its procedures for the testing and approval of new anti-AIDS drugs. At issue was a new experimental drug called AZT (azidothymidine). Krim opposed the traditional method of double-blind testing, wherein some patients were given the new drug and others a placebo (inert substance). She characterized the use of placebos in a test population dying from full-blown AIDS as inhumane, arguing that "people who are on their last legs should get anything they want. We should just make sure we're not killing them with it." She also argued for greater access to the drug overall while it was being tested.[89]

Krim lost that particular debate, but in the end she and her allies persuaded the FDA to alter the tricky balance in its approach to drug oversight between compassion and speed on the one hand and traditional scientific methodology and prudence on the other. In the future the former would gain new emphasis. Dr. Anthony Fauci, the head of the federal government's AIDS research program, observed in 1989 that "in the beginning, [the activists] had a blanket disgust with us. And it was mutual. Scientists said all trials should be restricted, rigid, and slow. The gay groups said we were killing people with red tape. When the smoke cleared we realized that much of their criticism was absolutely valid."[90] Using the new approach to speed along the drug approval process, researchers by the mid-1990s managed to develop drug combinations, or "cocktails," often AZT and a variety of new "designer drugs," including protease inhibitors, that helped to make AIDS a "manageable disease" rather than an automatic death sentence.

The gay community itself did much of the heavy lifting in the struggle against AIDS. The crisis forced homosexuals to mobilize as never before. No AIDS activist was more visible, or controversial, than the irascible writer Larry Kramer, who became both an important organizational entrepreneur and the brashest provocateur of gay activism in the 1980s. Kramer grew up in suburban Washington, D.C., the son of a government lawyer. He attended Yale University, came out of the closet at the age of thirty in 1965, and by the 1970s had established himself as a writer of screenplays and novels. As the gay rights movement blossomed in the aftermath of Stonewall, Kramer watched from the sidelines and avoided political involvement, but the plague changed all that. When the first reports of, and deaths from, AIDS began to indicate a pattern of threat to homosexuals, Kramer called a meeting in his New York City apartment that led to the creation in 1982 of the Gay Men's Health Crisis (GMHC), an organization of hundreds of volunteers that quickly became the largest provider of services to AIDS patients in the country. However, the agitator in Kramer soon found his own creation too staid. He believed that gays needed to do more than help themselves; they needed also to confront "the system" that was dragging its heels in reacting to the AIDS crisis. Accordingly, in 1987 he spearheaded the formation of ACT UP, the AIDS Coalition to Unleash Power, which became the most notorious agitprop guerrilla group of the decade.[91]

ACT UP did precisely what its name indicated. It specialized in imaginative, some said outrageous, demonstrations to draw attention to the plight and concerns of AIDS victims of all descriptions, and within three years had chapters in about forty U.S. cities and in several cities abroad. Adopting as its symbol a pink triangle (pointing up) set against a black border, inscribed with the haunting words "Silence = Death," ACT UP was anything but silent. It disrupted trading inside the New York Stock Exchange to protest the high costs of AIDS drugs, regularly staged protests at government offices and at various AIDS conferences around the world, and on occasion blocked traffic on New York's Broadway and San Francisco's Golden Gate Bridge. When Northwest Airlines refused to carry passengers with AIDS, ACT UP purchased millions of dollars of tickets from the airline and then refused to pay for them. It often singled its opponents out for individual attention and abuse—once furtively wrapping the Virginia home of the conservative senator Jesse Helms (R, North Carolina) in a huge, custom-made condom. Most notoriously, in December 1989 the group broke up a High Mass at New York City's St. Patrick's Cathedral to protest what it characterized as the Catholic Church's anti-gay stance. The protestors disrupted the sermon of the outspoken conservative Cardinal John O'Connor, threw condoms all over, and chained themselves to pews; one ACT UP activist purposely crumbled a consecrated communion wafer—believed by Catholics to be, via transubstantiation, the actual Body of Christ—onto the floor. When questioned about the incident, Kramer answered with characteristic defiance: "If you're asking me to apologize, I'm not going to. We're prepared to leave the Catholic Church alone if the Catholic Church will leave us alone."[92]

In addition to taking the lead in creating the GMHC and ACT UP, Kramer played the role of provocateur as vigorously as anyone of his era. He managed to enrage people of all sorts and on all sides. In Kramer's 1985 play about the AIDS crisis, *The Normal Heart*, one of the major characters observes, "There is not a good word to be said for anybody's behavior in this whole mess," and the playwright himself certainly acted on that premise.[93] A critic of gay sexual promiscuity even before AIDS surfaced, Kramer proclaimed early and loudly that "there's no question that the sexual promiscuity of some gay men was unwittingly responsible for AIDS killing so many of us," which caused his gay critics to accuse him of being "sex-negative" and earned him the enmity of gays who feared he was providing their enemies with just the ammunition they desired.[94] For those in power who seemed to be dragging their heels in the fight against AIDS—whether in government, the medical establishment, or at the *New York Times*—Kramer and ACT UP had unbridled contempt. He viewed the world in simplistic, moralistic terms, and typically denounced all adversaries as liars, hypocrites, fools, killers, and Nazis, causing one critic to describe him in 1989 as "a rabble-rousing hysteric venting a 10-year old temper tantrum."[95] Despite, or perhaps because of, his shrill and contrarian nature, Kramer was one of the most visible and influential activists of his day. When it came to raising the consciousness of both gays and mainstream Americans regarding the issues surrounding AIDS, Kramer had no equal. In his inimitable style, he opened the way for others who would use more traditional methods to advance the cause.

Those who spoke in lower voices using more measured language scored important practical victories as the 1980s came to a chronological close. The National Organizations Responding to AIDS (NORA), a coalition of national gay groups and other medical, disability, and professional organizations created in 1986, purposely sought to "de-gay" the struggle against AIDS in an effort to gain support for its legislative initiatives. As described by the historian John-Manuel Andriote, the strategy of de-gaying called for lobbyists to play down the suffering of gays (who along with intravenous drug users still constituted the vast majority of AIDS cases in the United States) and to play up, indeed exaggerate, the danger AIDS posed to heterosexuals and children. In the words of one prominent gay rights lobbyist, the point was to "make people afraid in the straight community."[96]

Using the new approach, NORA helped generate broad support for the Ryan White Comprehensive AIDS Resources Emergency (CARE) Act and the Americans with Disabilities Act (ADA), two crucial pieces of legislation passed in 1990. The Ryan White Act provided federal funding to states and localities particularly hard hit by AIDS to pay for patient services for both AIDS patients and those infected with the virus (HIV) that leads to AIDS. The ADA extended new anti-discrimination protection to AIDS sufferers, and required employers to make reasonable accommodations to provide for such workers. De-gaying was purposely deceptive and was, in the eyes of some gay critics, demeaning to gays in that it seemed to internalize the homophobic message that AIDS mattered only to the extent it hurt heterosexual Americans; and traditional lobbying was difficult and unglamorous work; but by the end of the 1980s such efforts produced concrete advances in dealing with the worst ravages of AIDS.

Sadly, there still was no vaccine to prevent the disease or magic drug to cure it, and despite the pharmaceutical advances of the mid-1990s the death toll continued to grow. The CDC reported that as of January 2003 an estimated 886,575 Americans had been diagnosed with AIDS, and of that cumulative total an estimated 501,669 had died from the disease. In the United States, it remained significantly, but hardly exclusively, an epidemic affecting gays. The CDC estimated that homosexual male-to-male contact had been a transmission factor in 480,509 cases, injection drug use in 240,268 cases, and heterosexual contact in 135,628 cases.[97] (This was not necessarily true elsewhere: in AIDS-ravaged sub-Saharan Africa, where the World Health Organization estimated that 29.4 million people were infected with either AIDS or the HIV virus that causes AIDS as of January 2003, the primary means of transmission was heterosexual contact). The numbers, and the human suffering that stretches behind them, beggar the mind.

✽   ✽   ✽

The problems of the 1980s reminded Americans that even in times of relative comfort and considerable achievement there arise issues that challenge and sometimes overwhelm the personal and even the collective capabilities of individuals and their society. All of the problems of the 1980s discussed above— homelessness, the underclass, yawning inequality, and one of the worst epidemics in history—lingered on, most of them in attenuated form, into the new millennium. Some, Americans in the 1980s ameliorated or began successfully to delimit and contain. Others appeared intractable, awaiting perhaps the superior wisdom or innovative technique of new leadership or the arrival of a new generation or the emergence of new economic, social, and cultural arrangements. But when that new leadership or generation or institutional order arrives, serious students of history must know that solving what is left of the problems of the 1980s will ensure that new, as yet barely imagined difficulties will promptly arise to take their place. Only hubris or historical ignorance could allow one to think otherwise.

Chapter 6

THE POSTMODERN MOMENT

Generalizing about the culture of a society as large and complex as that of America in the 1980s is a tricky undertaking. When the final returns were in, the federal census of 1980 counted 226,545,805 persons residing in the United States.[1] They comprised a stunningly diverse cross-section of humanity: the young and old, the rich and poor, the highly educated and the largely unschooled, city dwellers and those who lived on the land, Americans of many colors and creeds, ethnic backgrounds and places of origin. It is doubtful that any other society on earth contained within it so much variation and so many differences.

Nevertheless, one can identify several large themes or currents that ran through American culture in the eighties and early nineties: a cultural phenomenon known as postmodernism; a multifaceted therapeutic impulse; and an exceedingly strong, updated strain of an old staple of American culture, materialism. Together these elements combined in the 1980s to produce a rough but distinctive spirit of the times, a Zeitgeist that colored high culture, popular culture, and the actual behavior of the American people.

POSTMODERNISM

The most ephemeral but perhaps the most pervasive of the cultural currents at work in the long 1980s was something called postmodernism. Contemporary observers used the label expansively, with little agreement as to just what it meant. Sometimes the term identified a discernible philosophy or world-view, sometimes it denoted a particular aesthetic style, and sometimes it served simply to describe the state and trends of contemporary culture. The label's protean ambiguity was part of its charm, simultaneously inviting both application and misuse—this art or that stance or that thing was just "so postmodern."

For most who invoked the term with any pretense of precision, postmodernism referred to a new phase of cultural development that was, in the shadow of the millennium, spawning a distinctive sensibility, artistic manner, and vernacular way of life. Basic to this conception of postmodernism was an incredulity toward all the old "metanarratives," such universal explanatory schema as religion, Marxism, the upward march of science, the progressive triumph of reason or liberty, or a belief in progress of any sort. Even declension narratives, the story of history as a fall from grace, were suspect.

Without the unifying hold of the old transcendental beliefs or systems of explanation, society in its postmodern phase was decentered and chaotic—broken into a multiplicity of voices, groups, interests, claims, perspectives, and material things, all amplified and multiplied by the surge of communications technology. Fragmentation was the (dis)order of the day. In the critic Fredric Jameson's influential formulation, postmodernism transformed reality into multiple images and shattered time into "a series of perpetual presents."[2] The new disorder blurred distinctions and obliterated old boundaries, sometimes by conflating and combining them, often by simply ignoring them. High culture and masscult and popular culture collapsed in on one another; comic books and advertising copy became literary texts, to be deciphered or "deconstructed" alongside Shakespeare. Postmodern culture was in a state of constant flux, but it was change without any discernible direction, underlying pattern, or larger meaning.

The decentered postmodern society was made still more disorienting by its thoroughgoing relativism. Postmodernists held as a core belief that reality was socially constructed. Sometimes this social construction of reality was arbitrary or accidental, but more often than not human groups purposely shaped and defined their world to control pleasure or gain advantage. The established order in any society comprised practices, institutions, and ideas intended to enhance the dominion of some and effect the oppression of others. Hardened postmodernists suspected that what passed for "reason" was just another instrument of such oppression. The "text" was a fundamental intellectual building block of postmodernism in its philosophical guise, but language and words had no fixed meaning—they were always a matter of convention, manipulation, and contestation. The relationship between signifiers and the signified (words and their referents) was arbitrary, and consequently language was a sort of ever-shifting quicksand. Similarly, "signs," objects ranging from commodity goods to advertising copy, were everywhere and all carried messages, but while some of these messages had been carefully embedded by their producers, others were supplied by viewers and consumers who functioned as "readers," with the result that every communication was in the end fraught with a multiplicity of meanings, all claiming authenticity and deserving attention. In this complex postmodern world of multiple voices, signals, and listeners, a belief in transcendent values and distinctions was delusionary. Whether applied to art or ideas or behavior, absolutist judgments of good and bad, right and wrong, were exercises in power rather than valid expressions, or even merely hopeful approximations, of truth. For postmodernists, truth itself was something of a hoax.

Postmodernism's relativism was manifested most dramatically in matters of culture, morality, and truth. Because all cultural arrangements were socially constructed to meet particular needs and conditions, one could not objectively adjudge any one culture, or cultural practice, superior to another. Similarly, postmodernists found it painful, if not impossible, to objectively evaluate personal actions and behavior in terms of moral value. If moral systems were socially constructed conveniences or, worse still, purposeful tools of oppression, distinguishing between good and bad and right and wrong degenerated into a game of semantics and manipulation. With so many competing truth claims vying for attention and validation in the chaotic postmodern culture, the pursuit of *the* truth was chimerical. In the postmodern world, everything was "true"—and so was nothing.

Some observers believed that the decentering at the core of the postmodern experience was spilling over from society to self. The psychologist Kenneth J. Gergen noted that the spread and pervasiveness of the mass media and recent advances in communications technology were creating a "saturated self." "Postmodernism," he observed, "is the product of an array of technologies that have saturated us with the voices of others. We are now immersed in an array of relationships in a way that has not existed at any other time in history." Bombarded by stimuli, "we begin to feel that we have no real center." Whereas earlier conceptions of the self had located the source of personal identity in the soul or the mind, the postmodern self "is located outside us; as we move from one locale and relationship to another, we change."[3] The result was a sort of multiphrenia: "Our identity," Gergen noted, "is continuously reformed and redirected as we move through a sea of changing relationships." If at mid-century David Riesman and his colleagues had in their social-science masterwork *The Lonely Crowd* posited the appearance of an "other-directed" personality that oriented itself by means of its own internal "social radar" set for registering feedback from the social environment, it appeared that postmodern man had gone even further in surrendering control of his inner self, or selves, to external sources and stimuli. Now, in the 1980s, the feedback was in command. "The fully saturated self," wrote Gergen, "becomes no self at all." *Who* you were depended on *where* you were in a swirling, endless series of ever-changing relationships.[4]

As an artistic style, postmodernism took shape first and could be seen most clearly in the field of architecture, where it emerged in the 1960s, became prominent in the late 1970s and 1980s, and remained influential through the 1990s. In characteristic postmodern fashion, the practitioners of the new turn were reacting against the reigning metanarrative of American architecture: the austere formalism of orthodox modernism, which had dominated architecture in the first three-quarters of the twentieth century. As Philip Johnson, a pioneer of modernism now turned champion of its successor, put it: "The day of ideology is thankfully over. Let us celebrate the death of the *idée fixe*. There are no rules, only facts. There is no order, only preference. There are no imperatives, only choice. . . . I am of the opinion we have no faiths. I have none. 'Free at last,' I say to myself."[5]

The postmodernists replaced the formal absolutism of the modernist international style with a new playfulness and eclecticism, using elaborate decorative elements and multiple, hybrid historical details to embellish their work and impart the stamp of their own personal and exaggerated style. Puckish irony abounded, as though every gesture were enclosed by invisible "quotation marks" of ironic amusement. Postmodern architects intended their work to speak to multiple audiences simultaneously; and they became adept at what one influential critic called double or multiple coding, designing their work to speak both in the esoteric aesthetic language of their craft and profession and in the common parlance of the People.[6] They delighted in putting different styles together in new ways. The influential postmodernist Robert Venturi wrote, "I like elements which are hybrid rather than 'pure,' compromising rather than 'clean,' distorted rather than 'straightforward,' ambiguous rather than 'articulated,' . . . inconsistent and equivocal rather than direct or clear. I am for messy vitality over obvious unity."[7] Michael Grave's Public Service Building in Portland, Oregon, combined at least four distinct historical styles—Egyptian, Italian, Art Deco, and modern. Such random appropriation of the past, with its good-natured mimicry of other styles' peculiar mannerisms and twitches, constituted "pastiche," a favorite form of postmodern expression in all areas. Johnson himself gave his stunning AT&T headquarters building in New York City a neo-Georgian cast and modeled his design for the Bobst Library at New York University on a Victorian penitentiary.

Postmodernism architecture clearly was a reaction against the modernism that preceded it. But it was more besides. And those facts raised questions: What prompted the reaction against modernism to arise when it did, and what caused it to take the shape that it assumed? The search for the sources of postmodernism became something of an intellectual parlor game.[8] Perhaps, some suggested, the trends of the 1980s were merely the extrapolation of long-running devolutionary tendencies in American culture. After all, vulgar democratic pluralism has long been a staple of elitist complaint. Americans had, it seemed, always been corrupting their culture. Postmodernism continued that tendency, demolishing existing standards and making serious cultural assessment all but impossible. To charge that something was crass and vulgar invited the postmodern response that the artist was merely playing with the ideas of crassness and vulgarity. The barbarian masses had often in the past appeared to be at the gate, but in the eighties they seemed actually to be sacking the city. Still, why then?

The most persuasive explanations for the rise of postmodernism pointed to contemporary technological change and economic developments. In an important sense, postmodernism was the cultural reaction to the revolutionary spread in the last quarter of the twentieth century of new communication technologies (TV, multichannel cable systems, satellites and their dishes, fax machines, PCs, VCRs, CDs) that increased exponentially the flow of images and voices. At the same time the new technologies shrank the world in the direction of Marshall McLuhan's global village, they made the cultural environment through which individuals maneuvered spectacularly more dense, and that density—the oft-noted multiplicity of "voices," signs, and all manner of saturating stimuli—lay at the core of the postmodern trend and experience. Critics noted archly that postmodern writers worked almost wholly in the present tense, which was the only one TV offered; if television had not invented the fragmentation of time, it had certainly perfected it.

The multiplicity of voices and signals also reflected the impact of the consumption culture of the late twentieth century, a fact that figured significantly in Marxist interpretations of postmodernism. The need to move the merchandise of a market economy awash in things generated many of the messages and images inundating the postmodern saturated self. Steven Waldman, writing in the *New Republic*, complained of the "tyranny of choice" in an era of consumer-goods market segmentation: the typical supermarket that in 1976 had carried nine thousand products by the early 1990s carried more than thirty thousand; the median household that in 1975 received TV signals from six stations now chose from more than thirty on cable; the number of FM radio stations more than doubled in the 1970s and 1980s.[9] Postmodernism's demolition of categories and standards and its incessant recycling of old styles were well suited for a society driven to consume everything in sight and looking for a way not to feel guilty about its appetites.

THE THERAPEUTIC CULTURE

A second defining feature of American culture in the Reagan Era, running alongside and sometimes intersecting with the rise of postmodernism, was the emergence of what scholars and commentators have labeled the therapeutic culture. The therapeutic attitude, which derived originally from the world of psychoanalysis and psychological counseling, focused on the self as the central organizing principle in life. The initial penetration of such views into the general culture was heralded by Phillip Rieff's 1966 book *The Triumph of the Therapeutic*, which, although prescient, was perhaps a bit premature in announcing the victory of the new cultural order; it was in the 1970s and 1980s that the therapeutic approach actually succeeded in permeating the larger culture. In the words of James L. Nolan Jr., "The contemporary cultural condition is such that externally derived points of moral reference are not available to individuals as they once were. Instead, cultural standards for judgment, guideposts for actions, understandings of oneself, and the tools for navigating through social life are likely to be rooted in the self."[10] The result was a therapeutic culture that emphasized self-knowledge and self-realization as the central projects of life.

A complex phenomenon, the therapeutic culture had four identifying features. The first of these was the celebration of the liberated self. To be sure, individualism had been a defining characteristic of American life from the beginning of the nation. Writing in the 1830s, Alexis de Tocqueville put individualism and self-reliance at the center of his interpretation of the American character, recognizing both their liberating strength and their potential for personal isolation. But over time the American brand of individualism changed from one concerned chiefly with *independence within a system of traditional normative expectations and guidelines* to one focused on *freedom from all restraints and impediments to self-fulfillment*. The poet Walt Whitman seemed a harbinger of the new regime when he wrote, "The whole theory of the universe is directed unerringly to one single individual—namely to You."[11] In the nineteenth century Whitman sang an isolated song of eccentric genius; in the late twentieth century, he spoke for multitudes.

Researchers in the 1980s distinguished the new "expressive individualism" from the older utilitarian version. In 1985 a team of scholars led by the sociologist Robert N. Bellah of the University of California at Berkeley assessed American society and culture in a much-discussed book entitled *Habits of the Heart: Individualism and Commitment in American Life*, which reviewers likened to such earlier works as *Middletown* and *The Lonely Crowd* and even Tocqueville's classic *Democracy in America*. Bellah and his colleagues asked, "How ought we to live? How do we think about how to live? Who are we, as Americans? What is our character?" They sought to answer these questions chiefly by means of impressionistic interviews with white, middle-class Americans, and they determined that Americans in the 1980s embraced a strikingly individualistic value system that revolved around "the ideal of a radically unencumbered and improvisational self." The result, they wrote, approached "a society predicated on individual interests and feelings," one whose communal institutions were in danger of being fatally eroded by the new hyper-individualism.[12]

Ronald Inglehart, a political scientist at the University of Michigan who specialized in using international polling data to track shifting values over time, provided additional support for the idea that a new brand of radical individualism was on the rise. Analyzing poll results from 1970 and beyond in a series of important books, Inglehart established that a shift in attitudes was going on both in the United States and throughout the industrialized West away from giving top priority to physical sustenance and safety toward a new emphasis on self-expression, self-esteem, self-realization, and the quality of life.[13] He labeled the shift a move from materialist to postmaterialist values (and in his most recent work has envisioned the movement from materialist to postmaterialist values as a component of an even larger shift to a postmodern cultural configuration). The shift toward postmaterialist values Inglehart uncovered clearly coincided with what Bellah described as the rise of expressive individualism—they were talking about the same phenomenon. Although the turn toward postmaterialist values occurred first in the United States, Europe actually moved faster and further in that direction over time (a fact that would contribute importantly to the increasing gulf between Europe and America that commentators would note in the early twenty-first century). Nevertheless, Inglehart reported that the change in the United States had been substantial: "In 1972, Materialists outnumbered Postmaterialists by 3.5 to 1. In 1987, this ratio had fallen to only 1.5 to one."[14] Moreover, the cultural influence of those who championed postmaterialist values in Inglehart's polls was likely to be all the greater because they were, according to his data, more highly educated, more articulate, and more civically active than materialists. It was Inglehart's postmaterialists and Bellah's expressive individualists who in the 1980s were leading the way in establishing the self as the supreme object of attention and cultivation.

Psychologists also noted the increasingly self-referential quality of American life in the 1980s. In delivering the prestigious G. Stanley Hall Lecture at the 1988 annual meeting of the American Psychological Association, Martin E. P. Seligman of the University of Pennsylvania described contemporary American culture as buffeted by a dangerously synergistic pair of developments—the rise of an individualism based on the imperial self and a simultaneous loss of faith in society's institutions. He observed that the new individualism represented a shift from an older version based on the "New England self" to a new one that revolved around the "California self." "The traditional New England self," he commented, "is a minimal self, more like our grandparents than us. It's a nose-to-the-grindstone, duty-bound self that works hard to earn its rewards; it is certainly not preoccupied with what it feels—if it acknowledges that it feels at all. The California self, by contrast, is the self 'taken to the max,' a self that chooses, feels pleasure and pain, dictates action, and even has things like esteem, efficacy and confidence."[15]

Customers at newsstands and bookstores could hardly miss the evidence of the increasingly solipsistic quality of American culture. *Self* magazine published its first issue in 1979, aiming at an audience of upscale women interested in improving their quality of life and individual satisfaction—aiming, in other words, at an audience of California, not New England, selves. A look at *Books in Print* in 1950 would find 35 books with titles beginning with the word "self"; in 1978, 209 such titles would show up in such a search; in 1994, the number would be 720. Also available in 1994 were 619 books under the subject heading "self-help technique" and 365 listed under "self-esteem."[16]

The attention devoted to self-esteem identified a second essential feature of the therapeutic culture—the rise of an emotive ethic. Feelings were the coin of the realm in the new therapeutic cultural regime. In 1986 the state of California, often an influential pioneer on the frontier of Self, created a publicly funded, twenty-five-member California Task Force to Promote Self-Esteem and Personal and Social Responsibility. Pushed in the state assembly by a Santa Clara Democrat and approved by the state's conservative Republican governor, the task force was awarded $735,000 to undertake a three-year study of self-esteem. Its legislative champion explained that "self-esteem is implicated as the [sic] causal factor in six major social problems. . . . Ideally this task force will let people know where to go for help and how to begin practicing truly nurturing self-esteem."[17] Nearly all of California's fifty-eight counties established their own self-esteem study groups, and the idea radiated outward, as the states of Maryland, Virginia, Louisiana, Illinois, Kentucky, Washington, Michigan, Oregon, and Florida created similar task forces. There followed predictably the creation of a National Council for Self-Esteem with sixty-six local chapters in twenty-nine states.[18]

In 1990 the California Task Force distributed more than sixty thousand copies of its final report, titled *Toward a State of Esteem*.[19] Among its formal recommendations was the suggestion that prospective teachers be required to take courses in self-esteem, an idea that fell on receptive ears. Indeed, the enshrinement of self-esteem and self-discovery as the chief aims of public education was already well underway across the nation. A critic who studied the programs at twenty college or university schools of education in 1990 found that teaching to improve self-esteem was already the dominant educational approach.[20] As one professor in a course on the teaching of "language arts" in the California State University system told her students: "More important than content or thinking is the students' feelings. You are not there to feed them information but to be sensitive to their need for positive reinforcement, for self-esteem."[21]

The therapeutic culture put emotions on display as never before. Television, wrote Bellah and his compatriots, put a premium on "the portrayal of vivid personal feeling." The medium was "much more interested in how people feel than in what they think."[22] Daytime talk show hosts Phil Donahue and Oprah Winfrey, in particular, raised personal revelation to an art form in both their choice of topics and guests and their empathetic interview styles. Oprah (after her show went national in 1986, she quickly joined the ranks of those celebrities who needed only one name for immediate recognition) shared with her audience her own experience as a victim of incestuous sexual abuse, her drug history, and her roller coaster diet adventures. For those who had trouble expressing their feelings with sufficient feeling, the greeting card industry rushed to help with new lines of particularly warm and fuzzy product. To be sure, Joyce Hall, the founder of the Hallmark empire, had long ago made the selling of sentiment a huge business, but the temperature of emotional communication in the mid-1980s was on the rise. Card lines with names such as Soft Sentiments and Personal Touch conveyed an increasingly intimate range of emotions: "The warmth of your hug lingers . . . " and "In this world it's very scary to be open and vulnerable . . . " and "Finally, I have a friend I can trust . . . completely!" "The style today," said the founder of a new San Francisco card firm, "is openness and honesty." "This is really America in therapy," remarked another emotive entrepreneur, David Viscott, the creator of the 144-card In Touch line, "people trying to get themselves together and be whole. . . . Once I heard a voice saying 'Someday you will tell people what they really feel inside,' and that's what I do."[23]

Not surprisingly, the new therapeutic culture of self-regard and feelings had as a third identifying feature the new prominence of its own priestly elite: psychiatrists, psychologists, and other members of the so-called helping professions. Cultural authority was clearly passing to those who specialized in mobilizing the self's internal resources in the pursuit of personal fulfillment. Such specialists were spilling out of American institutions of higher learning in record numbers. The number of clinical psychologists more than tripled between 1968 and 1983; over the decades of the 1970s and 1980s the number of clinical social workers did the same; in 1983 the United States had one-third of all the world's licensed psychiatrists. In the mid-1980s there were more therapists in the United States than librarians, firefighters, or mail carriers.[24]

The dramatic increase in the size of the new therapeutic elite was both a cause and a consequence of the therapeutic culture's fourth hallmark—its distinctive tendency to interpret an ever-larger portion of human behavior in terms of mental illness, emotional disorder, and medical disease. Matters that were once interpreted in terms of self-control, or, more precisely, the lack thereof, were in the 1980s increasingly defined as diseases or pathologies or illnesses to be cured. Sins were out, syndromes in.[25] The new priests of the therapeutic culture, acting through the American Psychiatric Association, rationalized the expansive view of emotional illness by including in their professional bible, the

Diagnostic and Statistical Manual of Mental Disorders, Third Edition, Revised (1987), a host of conditions that in an earlier day might have been understood as failures of character or quirks of personality. The DSM III-R classified a number of conditions as "Impulse Control Disorders," including "Pathological Gambling" and "Intermittent Explosive Disorder," which it described as "discrete episodes of loss of control of aggressive impulses resulting in serious assaultive acts or destruction of property." Expressive individualism seemed to have its own malady in "Narcissistic Personality Disorder," a label attached to patients with "a grandiose sense of self-importance." Avoidant Personality Disorder identified someone with "a pervasive pattern of social discomfort, fear of negative evaluation, and timidity." All of these disorders had previously been understood in different terms, as character flaws (self-control problems, aggressive impulses, insufferable self-centeredness) or simple traits of temperament (just plain shyness).[26]

The changing view of cigarette smoking exemplified the larger cultural shift. The original Surgeon General's report that identified cigarette smoking as a serious health risk in 1964 took care to specify that tobacco was "habituating" rather than "addicting."[27] In other words, the habit was more a matter of will power than physiological compulsion. Scientists had long understood that nicotine was the pharmacological agent contributing to tobacco's hold on smokers, but it was commonly believed that tobacco, though its use was a difficult habit to break, was in that regard more akin to coffee than to opium or heroin. In 1988, however, both because of a more detailed understanding of just how nicotine chemically affected the nervous system and because of the emergent cultural tendency to substitute medical understanding (addiction) for the earlier moral judgment (weakness), the Surgeon General reversed field and declared that "that cigarettes and other forms of tobacco are addicting in the same sense as are drugs such as heroin and cocaine." Accordingly, the Surgeon General's 1988 Report on Smoking proclaimed that tobacco use was "a disorder which can be remedied through medical attention."[28]

As pathologization advanced, self-help groups proliferated. Alcoholics Anonymous, a success dating from the 1930s, provided the basic model, and there followed Alateen, Narcotics Anonymous, Parents Anonymous, CoDependents Anonymous, Adult Children of Alcoholics, Alanon, Youth Emotions Anonymous, Emotional Health Anonymous, Debtors Anonymous, Workaholics Anonymous, Gamblers Anonymous, Overeaters Anonymous, Dual Disorders Anonymous, Batterers Anonymous, Victims Anonymous, Unwed Parents Anonymous, Sex Addicts Anonymous, and S-Anon.[29] It should not be doubted that such groups supplied welcome emotional succor to many anguished individuals. But it is similarly beyond argument that the drive to medicalize behavior also told troubled Americans that they were victims of forces beyond their control, that they were neither individually responsible nor personally at fault.

Victims were everywhere in the therapeutic culture. One of the more interesting turns of phrase in the 1980s identified the dramatic upsurge in crack cocaine use in U.S. cities as a "crack epidemic," implying a natural phenomenon rather than the unfortunate result of a myriad of bad (and criminal) personal decisions. In one particularly egregious and much-noted episode, Joel Steinberg, the wealthy wife beater and child abuser who was convicted in New York City in 1989 of the battering death of his six-year-old illegally adopted daughter Lisa, told the court, "I'm a victim, as was everyone else who knew Lisa."[30] The first response of accused wrong-doers with access to first-rate legal advice seemed to be to voluntarily check oneself in for either psychiatric or substance-abuse treatment; examples included Senator Robert Packwood (accused of sexual harassment), Washington mayor Marion Barry (accused of crack cocaine use), American University president Richard Berendzen (accused of obscene sexual telephone harassment), and Reagan aide Michael Deaver (accused of influence peddling). Confronting the rise of victimhood, the essayist Lance Morrow lamented in 1991 that the old individualism had been replaced by a new solipsistic version: "The frontiersman's self-sufficiency and stoicism in the face of pain belong now in some wax museum of lost American self-images." "What might have once been called whining," wrote Wendy Kaminer in a bestselling commentary entitled *I'm Dysfunctional, You're Dysfunctional*, "is now exalted as a process of exerting self-hood." In its hardly ignoble, collective pursuit of self-discovery, America discovered that its inner child had become a crybaby.[31]

MATERIALISM, EIGHTIES STYLE

A final cultural main current, materialism, had long been a familiar aspect of American life, but now in the 1980s it seemed to be exerting a more powerful influence than ever before. "Money, money, money is the incantation of today. Bewitched by an epidemic of money enchantment, Americans in the Eighties wriggle in a Saint Vitus's dance of materialism unseen since the Gilded Age or the Roaring Twenties. Under the blazing sun of money, all other values shine palely," wrote Myron Magnet in 1987. The comment appeared not in a Marxist academic journal, but in *Fortune* magazine, a slick-paper voice of modern capitalist enterprise.[32] Laurence Shames, in a book whose title conveyed everything one needed to know, *The Hunger for More: Values in an Age of Greed*, disagreed only that the 1980s were in fact "far more gilded, far more mercenary, far more narrowly defined by bucks" than even the Gilded Age. The most celebrated cultural commentator of the 1980s, Tom Wolfe, avoided contentious historical analogies and said simply, "It was a decade of money fever."[33]

Of course, the 1980s hardly invented materialism, which had a history antedating the settlement of the New World. In the nineteenth century, Tocqueville warned that democracies were particularly vulnerable to materialist excess, with the consequent danger that the citizen "may lose the use of his sublimest faculties and . . . may at length degrade himself."[34] Around the same time, the sharp-tongued Frances Trollope wrote that no two Americans ever engaged in conversation "without the word DOLLAR being pronounced between them."[35] At the end of the nineteenth century Henry Cabot Lodge, who thought he was witnessing the final realization of Tocqueville's fears, commented, "The darkest sign of the age is the way in which money and the acquisition of money seems rampant in every portion of the community."[36]

But the 1980s did see a powerful upsurge in the mighty consumer culture that shaped American life even more forcefully than did the newer postmodern trends and therapeutic impulse. Consumer spending and consumer debt (put more positively, credit) reached dizzying new heights. The therapeutic diagnosis "compulsive shopping" became a commonplace, and the bumper-sticker slogans "Born to Shop" and "Shop till You Drop" were among the classics of the era. And shop Americans did: Time-use researchers estimated that at mid-decade Americans spent almost 6 percent of their waking hours shopping.[37] The federal government's Consumer Expenditure Survey charted consumption patterns every year and found particularly dramatic increases over the decade in expenditures for goods and services that saved time (microwave ovens, restaurant dining, housekeeping and child-care services) or provided entertainment (videocassette recorders and associated tape rentals, sound component systems including compact disc players, and personal computers).[38] Increasingly, American consumers paid for their purchases with plastic instead of cash, as the use of credit cards skyrocketed: In 1985 the plastic revolution had placed 93 million Visa cards, 72.4 million MasterCards, and 16.3 million American Express cards in the hands of American consumers; and bumper stickers could be seen asking, only half in jest, "Can I pay off my Mastercharge with my Visa card?" American Express ads warned, "Don't leave home without it," and Americans did not: In 1988 roughly 110 million Americans held an average of seven charge cards each. To live on the plastic frontier of consumer debt had become an integral part of the American way of life.

Much of the nation's consumer spending—by reliable estimate some 50 to 60 percent of America's retail sales in the eighties—took place at the mall, which the historian of shopping William Kowinski called the "cathedral of consumption" and "signature structure of the age." Essentially a planned and coordinated grouping of stores in an enclosed and climate-controlled environment, the modern mall was born in 1956 with the opening of the Southdale Mall in Edina, Minnesota, just outside Minneapolis. By the 1980s, the phenomenon was going full tilt. The statistics on mall utilization were truly stunning: According to one 1985 survey, 78 percent of Americans (approximately 185 million people) had been to a mall within the period of a month, 93 percent within a six-month period; and a separate marketing survey determined that in 1982 the typical mall visit lasted twelve hours![39]

Malls seemed to serve as community centers of a stunted sort, with a sociology all their own. Adolescents, quickly labeled "mall rats," congregated there in packs to socialize, making the mall into an Americanized version of the *corso*, the street or square where young Italians gather and stroll in order to strut their stuff and be seen. The 1982 hit movie *Fast Times at Ridgemont High*, a comedic, almost ethnographic look at Southern California's teen culture, achieves its verisimilitude in part by using the mall as a standard setting and backdrop throughout. Older Americans became "mall walkers," taking advantage of the mall's safety and guaranteed climate to exercise there, forming clubs and developing a distinct camaraderie seemingly at odds with the coldly commercial atmosphere of their surroundings. In time, malls began to host a variety of community events, from blood drives to voter registration, book fairs, fashion shows, and entertainment of virtually every conceivable sort.

As public spaces, the larger malls of the 1980s were truly cathedral-like in their grandeur. Tysons Corner Center just west of Washington, D.C., was a good example of the state of the art. It brought together under one huge roof five department stores and 237 specialty shops, twenty-one restaurants, and two movie theaters. Its commercial edges were softened by the decorative use of thirty-one 32-foot-high Washingtonia palm trees, 2,500 freshly planted daffodils, and two Italian marble fountains. Ads for the complex told newspaper readers: "The joy of cooking. The joy of sex. What's left? The joy of shopping." But while Tyson's Corner advertised heavily, spending $500,000 on local TV spots, other malls seemed content to let the cumulative impact of the consumer culture do that work for them — the manager running the ur-mall Southdale commented in 1986, "It used to be that you had to lure shoppers out of the house. Now we realize that shopping is itself a form of entertainment."[40]

When mall construction slowed toward the end of the 1980s, analysts speculated that the so-called malling of America might gradually come to a halt and perhaps even recede as older units came to the end of their commercially profitable life cycle; but there was one extravaganza left to be realized — the Mall of America, which opened in Bloomington, Minnesota in 1992 as the nation's biggest shopping wonderland. The edifice covered 4.2 million square feet and provided parking for thirteen thousand cars within three hundred feet of its various doors. The megamall employed a work force of ten thousand to staff its four anchor stores, nearly 360 specialty shops, a seven-acre on-site amusement park, and two indoor lakes. Inside grew some four hundred trees and 526 tons of tropical plants. The mall boasted its own director of tourism, and claimed its own official soft drink (Pepsi), official car (Ford), and official airline (Northwest). Doubters thought its arrival was a case of too much, too late, but it, too, prospered.[41]

What the mall did for suburban and middle-class shoppers, Wal-Mart provided to small-town, rural, working-class, and bargain-minded consumers
across America. Wal-Mart was the brainchild of Sam Walton, one of those rare
entrepreneurs who transform the surface of their society by tapping into deep
currents running beneath it.[42] Walton had graduated from the University of
Missouri in 1940 with a degree in economics and hired on as a trainee with
J. C. Penney. After a stint in the Army during World War II, he opened a Ben
Franklin 5 and 10 in Arkansas, eventually becoming that company's largest
franchisee. He seized upon the idea of bringing discount selling to rural areas,
and when Ben Franklin passed on the opportunity to exploit Walton's vision,
he decided to do it himself. In 1962 he and his younger brother Bud opened
the first Wal-Mart Discount City in Rogers, Arkansas; by 1970 the company
had a stable of thirty stores.

In the 1980s Wal-Mart spread throughout the South, Southwest, and Midwest, transforming both retailing and the face of small towns. By 1989 a $1,000
investment in Wal-Mart's initial public offering in 1970 was worth $500,000
and Walton's retail empire comprised 1,300 stores in twenty-five states, chiefly
in small towns with populations in the range of 5,000 to 25,000. Wal-Mart was
the nation's third largest retailer behind Sears and Kmart, and closing in on
both quickly.

Wal-Mart was an enterprise full of surprises and contradictions. It had many
aspects of an aw-shucks operation from top to bottom. Sam Walton himself
became something of an anti-celebrity—well known for being unlike other
well-knowns. He was self-made, plainspoken, and charismatic in a homespun
way. He famously drove an old pickup truck, and would often travel to visit
his stores with his favorite bird dog, Ol' Roy, along for company (hence the
brand name of Wal-Mart's dog food line). And the Waltons lived modestly in
Wal-Mart's headquarters town of Bentonville, Arkansas, which in 1983 had a
population of 8,756.

But Walton was also the richest man in America, and Wal-Mart one of the
nation's best-run and most sophisticated business firms. Sam piloted his own
plane while inspecting his far-flung properties, and Wal-Mart had an air force
all its own: eleven aircraft, mostly turbo props particularly suited to getting
into and out of small airports. The firm installed computers in all its stores in
the mid-1970s and its Bentonville headquarters, as plain in appearance and
decor as the cafeteria in a rural consolidated school, boasted a computer-
communications complex complete with satellite uplinks that was, in the
words of one visitor, "worthy of the Department of Defense." Its distribution
system of regional warehouses was thoroughly computerized and highly
automated, the marvel of the retail industry.

Wal-Mart was a firm of many faces. The celebrated Wal-Mart smile was
self-conscious corporate policy. Greeters stood at the entrance to every store,

ushering in shoppers with a "Welcome to Wal-Mart" or "How are you today?" Helpfulness was mandatory, not optional, for employees, who were called "associates." Wal-Mart's profit-sharing plan left more than a few associates wealthy, despite the niggardly starting wages of hourly workers; management salaries were, by the standards of American business, modest; and the benefits available to all employees were relatively generous for the retail sector. In ways large and small, Wal-Mart encouraged its employees to feel they had a stake in the company. The firm's well-publicized "Bring it home to the USA," which touted the fact that the bulk of Wal-Mart's fifty-thousand-item inventory were products made in the U.S.A., appealed to the economic nationalism running especially strong in the 1980s among the firm's rural and working-class clientele. Wal-Mart shoppers tended to arrive in Fords and Chevies, not BMW's, and the Made in America campaign showed just how well Wal-Mart knew and catered to its customer base during its rise to retail preeminence.

But there was also a ferocious side to Wal-Mart. The firm was notoriously hard on its suppliers, constantly using its burgeoning buying power to squeeze vendors into cutting their prices. Many producers of consumer goods called Wal-Mart their toughest and rudest account, and the giant was notorious for simply taking its business elsewhere if its terms were not met. Slowly, its small-town competitors, often mom and pop stores still living in a retail world of low-volume, high prices, hefty profit margins, spotty selection, and restricted hours (no Sunday or evening hours), found Wal-Mart to be a simply merciless competitor. In the face of the threatened Wal-Martization of small-town America, with the specter and reality of closed shops and empty storefronts, Main Street increasingly clamored for relief, much as it had in the 1920s and 1930s when the arrival of retail chains—Rexall and Walgreen's, True Value Hardware, A&P and Woolworth's—first changed the face of retail selling in the American heartland.

Despite its critics, however, Wal-Mart prospered, largely because of its relentless devotion to meeting the needs of consumers. Wal-Mart and its imitators brought into the whirligig of American materialism those who consumed as much to satisfy elementary material needs as to slake material desires. In the process, Sam Walton's retail giant helped make America a culture of things for everyone.

While the mall and Wal-Mart rebuilt the infrastructure of American materialism in the 1980s, the media projected a striking cult of material success. Money and possession were presented in many ways, some subtle, others not, as the most genuine and satisfying measures of human achievement. Again, the phenomenon was hardly new—Americans had long found not merely pleasure but also social distinction and personal validation in the accumulation of earthly goods. It was the iconoclastic economist Thorstein Veblen, an American midwesterner, who coined the term "conspicuous consumption" at the turn of the century. But even the cynical Veblen might have been surprised by the spectacle of publisher Malcolm Forbes's seventieth birthday party in 1989, when the birthday boy flew eight hundred guests to Morocco on three jets to be greeted by an honor guard of three hundred Berber horsemen and entertained by six hundred acrobats, jugglers, and belly dancers, at a cost of some $2 million.[43]

What set the 1980s apart in this regard was the postmodern profusion of images, signs, and signifiers driving home the infatuation with wealth and material accumulation. Television was a particularly egregious conveyer of materialist values, through both its constant stream of advertising and its programming. Between 1980 and 1985, the weekly hour-long drama *Dallas* was the nation's first or second most-watched television program for five straight television seasons (it was the sixth most-watched program in 1979–80 and 1985–86, as well). Essentially a prime-time soap opera, the program told the story of the fabulously oil-rich Ewing family, who lived a life of glitzy excess on a ranch called South Fork outside Dallas, committing at least several of the seven deadly sins in every episode. The success of *Dallas* inspired a host of imitators: *Dynasty*, among the top ten shows from 1982 through 1986, told of the wealth and greed of the Carrington and Colby clans, who committed their deadly sins in Denver against the backdrop of the Rockies; *Falcon Crest* studied the wine-rich Channing family at home in their California vineyard; and *Knots Landing* followed the doings of some offshoots of the Dallas Ewings who had moved to California. For those who preferred to study great wealth in a more documentary fashion, television provided *Life-Styles of the Rich and Famous*, a show that accompanied the wealthy and well known on shopping trips to Rodeo Drive and into their personal mansions in order to instruct Americans on what and how to covet; the host Robin Leach closed each episode with the tag line, "May you have caviar wishes and champagne dreams."[44]

The cult of material success also surfaced in the emergence of a brand of serious writing that appealed especially to youthful readers and also garnered critical praise from the arbiters of literary taste. In 1984 twenty-nine-year-old Jay McInerney published his first novel, *Bright Lights, Big City*, to immediate acclaim. The next year, Bret Easton Ellis, barely in his twenties, published *Less Than Zero*, a novel one reviewer described rhapsodically as *"Catcher in the Rye* for the MTV generation." Both were novels of lost youth searching for meaning amidst drugs and nihilism. Both sold well and were made into movies. And, most relevant, both fitted into the category the critic Josephine Hendin called "Fictions of Acquisition." "What stands out," she wrote, "is an assimilation, to the point of wholesale adoption, of advertising culture. Labels, name brands, surface signs have become the sole social referents and methods of character definition." In this fiction, characters were what they consumed—materialism and the substance of being became as one. The merging of literary imagination and material culture yielded, wrote Hendin, "a vision of *emotions* as artifacts, of people as objects in a society whose common culture is increasingly standardized." It was a formula that sacrificed traditional literary values—character development and felicity of expression—for a disturbing cultural vision.[45]

The sociology of hypermaterialism added a new term to the standard American lexicon in the 1980s—yuppie. Yuppies were young, urban professionals. Just how many of them there were was uncertain. In its year-end 1984 cover story on "The Year of the Yuppie," *Newsweek* reported that roughly 1.2 million Americans earned $40,000 or more per year in professional or managerial jobs and lived in cities. Using a looser definition that still caught the spirit of the category, upwards of 20 million young, college-educated Americans lived in metropolitan areas and worked at white-collar or technical jobs. But yuppiedom was less a statistical niche than a lifestyle. As *Newsweek* put it, yuppies lived in a state of "Transcendental Acquisition" and were defined by "the perfection of their possessions": the Rolex watch, Gucci briefcase, and Burberry trench coat for men; the Cartier tank watch, Coach handbag, and Hermes scarf for women; the "Beemer" (BMW) sports sedan; gourmet foods (Brie, raspberry vinegar, gourmet mustard, expensive coffee beans, and bottled water); fine-restaurant dining (especially nouvelle cuisine); the exclusive and expensive purebred dog (the Akita was favored for a season); and the health-club membership. *The Yuppie Handbook*, an instruction manual published in 1984 by two typically enterprising members of the clan, provided a crash course in the intricacies of yuppie consumption for newcomers to the lifestyle. To be sure, by the end of the 1980s the term began to be used pejoratively (as in the expression "Die, yuppie scum!"), but that bespoke less a recoil from yuppie values than the self-confidence fostered by the steady incorporation of the yuppie lifestyle into the American mainstream.[46]

I WANT MY MTV

The institution arguably most emblematic of the cultural currents of the 1980s was the communications upstart known as Music Television, or MTV for short. The insight that gave birth to MTV came to Robert Pittman when he thought to himself that the "generations that grew up with TV communicate differently than previous generations."[47] The observation was hardly original, but few have acted on it with greater success. The son of a Southern minister, Pittman had begun a career in communications when he went to work as a teenage DJ for a Mississippi radio station in order to earn extra money to pay for flying lessons he coveted at the time. He quickly discovered that he had talent for programming and for bringing faltering radio stations back to life. In the late 1970s, he was in his mid-twenties and still wearing scruffy blue jeans, but was now working as the programming director for NBC's flagship radio station in New York City. The entrepreneurial Pittman left the world of radio to translate his vision into what he called "a new form for television designed especially for TV babies." The new enterprise would be, he averred, "a channel with no programs, no beginning, no middle, no end."[48] In its 1980s heyday MTV was precisely that, and it introduced millions of viewers, first in the United States and then around the globe, to the postmodern experience.

The new channel's programming loop consisted of music videos, three-to-five-minute-long renditions of popular music, drawn chiefly from the genre of white rock-'n'-roll known as AOR, or album-oriented rock. In the late 1970s, record companies regularly produced such tapes or films as promos to give artists additional exposure. The magical ability of music to evoke personal fantasies and powerful nostalgia was now routinized, as music videos rolled endlessly to provide a television generation with ready-made sensations and images of intimate meaning. Although the videos would come to be touted as an authentic art form, it was difficult to overlook MTV's business aspect: Music videos were fundamentally advertisements, artfully crafted messages designed to sell the recorded music itself and to entice viewers to consider as well the wares—stereo equipment, cars, cosmetics—sold by MTV's paid advertisers. MTV altered the traditional mix of advertising and programming by removing the programming; it was effectively all advertising, all the time. A more thoroughly commercial operation would be hard to envision.

With a suitably epigrammatic introductory announcement ("Ladies and gentlemen, rock and roll . . ."), MTV went on the air at midnight on August 1, 1981. An obscure British band, the Buggles, provided the first video clip, a song presciently entitled "Video Killed the Radio Star." The original store of 120 video clips were rotated by an on-screen staff of five VJs (video-jockeys). The station aimed to reach a demographic audience much favored by advertisers, the difficult to reach 12–34 age-bracket.

The new cable channel enjoyed a meteoric rise. Carried to 1.5 million homes in 1981, MTV reached 10.7 million homes in 1982, 18.9 million in 1983, and 25.5 million in 1984. A clever promotional campaign, which showcased Sting, Mick Jagger, and other rock luminaries declaring "I want my MTV," encouraged viewers to demand that their own local cable service providers make available *their* MTV. In 1984, MTV was cable television's highest-rated program, and its owners, Warner Communications and American Express, took the enterprise public with an initial public offering. In its first year as a publicly held corporation, MTV generated a 20 percent return of pretax profits on its revenue. In the face of such success, cable magnate Ted Turner pulled the plug on his own competing Cable Music Channel after only a month of transmission, ignominiously selling the assets to a triumphant MTV. Capitalizing on its success, MTV launched a slightly more sedate version of itself called

VH-1, which aimed at a slightly older audience (25–54 years old) and began operation on January 1, 1985.

MTV stumbled slightly at mid-decade, when its ratings sagged briefly, but it quickly recovered its upward momentum. The enterprise proved nimble enough to reinvent itself by lessening its reliance on the endless repetition of music videos and creating its own series programming, beginning with a pop-trivia show entitled *Remote Control*. The move was a retreat of sorts in the direction of broadcasting convention, but MTV's original programming remained novel and eccentric enough to retain the loyalty of its target audience. Global expansion provided a further boost.

Within a few years of its founding, MTV had already begun to function as an agent of what might be called cultural globalization. In July 1985, it provided the master television feed for the first of what became a series of benefit mega-concerts aimed at a truly worldwide audience. The "Live Aid" concert to raise money to fight a horrific famine in Africa lasted seventeen hours and brought together more than sixty bands and individual performers. MTV's signal was bounced off sixteen satellites to an audience estimated at 1.5 billion in more than 150 countries. For the moment, said Bob Geldorf, one of the event's organizers, "the planet has one language—pop music." The producer Michael Mitchell saw signs of an even deeper convergence, observing, "All over the planet, at the same time, people will see and hear and feel the same set of emotions. We're using television to catalyze the world."[49] As it happened, MTV did well by doing good. The concert raised $100 million, and also helped create and solidify an audience base for MTV's own further international expansion. In 1984 MTV had agreed to syndicate its programming in Japan; in short order a Latin American version was instituted and in 1987 MTV Europe began operation; in 1990 MTV reached Eastern Europe; and the creation of MTV Asia soon followed in the early 1990s. Ten years after its initial launch, MTV was available on a regular basis to 194 million homes in forty countries around the world.

MTV's rise was not without controversy, however. The music channel was surprisingly slow to provide full access to black artists. As late as 1983, the singer Rick James could complain, "They probably started out with a requirement of no niggers. They're catering to a white audience."[50] White performers such as David Bowie agreed that MTV's play list seemed oddly segregated. In the uproar that followed, MTV's management essentially confirmed the validity of the charge of racial exclusion by defending the racial orientation of the channel's video mix with the claim that black artists generally did not appeal to MTV's target audience.

Michael Jackson's emergence in 1983 as the biggest entertainment superstar of the era helped to resolve MTV's disturbing race problem. Jackson had already experienced success both as a member of a highly popular rock 'n' roll

family act, the Jackson Five, and in his subsequent career as an individual artist. But all that paled in comparison to the acclaim that greeted his 1982 album
entitled *Thriller*, which in time became the best-selling album in history. The
album spawned a set of music videos for its individual songs that in their elabo-
rateness and storytelling creativity virtually reinvented the music video, making
a promotional tool into a distinctive vehicle of artistic expression. One of the
music videos from Jackson's album, "Beat It," a rock-flavored number with a
guitar solo by Eddie Van Halen, became the first black music video to receive
rotational air play on MTV.

Once breached by Michael Jackson, MTV's racial barrier crumbled. Rap
music, strongly syncopated with spoken lyrics, emerged in the late 1970s and
matured in the early 1980s. It told a story of black inner-city street life in an
argot incomprehensible to most adults (of any race), and its increasingly violent, obscene, and misogynistic content predictably elicited both the wrath
of middle-class adults and the devotion of alienated adolescents in suburbs
as well as urban ghettos. Run-DMC, a trio of childhood chums from New
York, released rap's first gold album in 1984, and MTV gradually absorbed
the new style. In 1986 the white rock group Aerosmith and the black rappers
Run-DMC collaborated on a hit single entitled "Run this Way," which helped
bring the rap or hip-hop genre into MTV's commercial mainstream; by the
end of the decade, *Yo, MTV Raps* had become the channel's most popular
programming segment.

More difficult to resolve was the ongoing controversy over MTV's intertwining of commerce and artistry. The 1980s saw giant corporations make increasing use of popular music and recording stars for gigantic ad campaigns. In 1988
the rocker Neil Young complained about the mixing of rock and commerce in
an ad-bashing video based on his song "This Note's for You," which attacked
those who made music in order to sell merchandise ("Ain't singin' for Pepsi,
ain't singin' for Coke. . . . I don't sing for nobody, it makes me look like a
joke"). When MTV refused to air the video, claiming that it broke programming rules by mentioning specific products, Young responded with a public
memo accusing MTV of truckling to its own corporate sponsors: "MTV, you
spineless twerps. You refuse to show my video. What does the "M" in MTV
stand for? Music or money? Long live rock and roll."[51] But, of course, Young
was fighting a battle long over, rushing to the defense of a purity that rock 'n'
roll had lost well before Robert Pittman had gotten the idea that would bring
MTV into being. From the outset, the M in MTV stood for both money *and*
music, in that order.

Despite its teething problems, MTV reflected deep-running cultural and
technological developments and proved itself surprisingly adaptive to continued change. Throughout the 1980s it exerted great influence on America's
popular culture, not least on its own medium of television. MTV helped put

cable TV on the entertainment map. "Really, MTV did for cable," noted Robert Thompson, director of the Center for the Study of Popular Television at Syracuse University, "what Milton Berle did for television. They made it a must have."[52] MTV's success also inspired a number of direct imitators: the Nashville Network extended the MTV approach to the world of country music; Black Entertainment Television instituted its own music video programming; the USA Cable Network televised music videos for sixteen hours a week with its "Night Flight" programming; and both NBC and ABC built children's cartoon shows around rock-video themes. The imitation could be indirect as well: An NBC executive brainstorming for a new show hit the jackpot when he scribbled on a cocktail napkin the words "MTV cops," from which inspiration sprang the hugely successful TV police drama *Miami Vice*. One of television's hottest shows of the 1980s, *Miami Vice* utilized rock music to pace chase and love scenes and borrowed heavily from MTV's store of signature visual imagery, which included exaggerated camera angles and highly stylized decor.

The music channel's influence touched other media as well. Its stylistic demands quickly affected the music itself. Kim Carnes, a singer/songwriter who won a Grammy in 1981 for her rendition of "Bette Davis Eyes," reported that "video changed the way I approach making an album, the way I write songs. As we're recording, we're thinking in terms of what's going on visually."[53] MTV's favored visual effects—quick cuts, sharp editing, cutaways, flash dissolves, slow motion, double trick fadeaways going into colorization—soon became common in both advertising and the movies. Such techniques resulted in a boom in what came to be called "atmospheric advertising," ads driven by music and visuals, with virtually no hard sell of the details of the product. Hit movies such as *Flash Dance* (1983) and *Footloose* (1984) were conceived from the outset as extended music videos.

Beneath the discrete manifestations of MTV's influence lay its ultimate cultural significance: At bottom, MTV was most important for insinuating postmodern values and techniques into the broader culture. As the cultural critic Jon Pareles observed in the *New York Times*, MTV proved "a ravenous cannibalizer of images." "Music video," he wrote, "is quintessentially post-modern, drawing indiscriminately from high and low culture and past and present styles to create an all-encompassing, dizzyingly self-conscious pastiche."[54] MTV obliterated the reigning metanarratives and the linear, sequential sense of time that undergirded them, presenting instead a disoriented (or "decentered") rush of free-associative images, playfully incongruous juxtapositions, and coolly ironic mélanges, all in the present tense. It was all movement with no discernible direction, no sustained narrative drive save the materialistic impulse to sell. The style was set in the early years: MTV adopted as its logo the now familiar television image of an American astronaut planting the flag on the surface of the moon, except that this image replaced the Stars and Stripes with a banner emblazoned "MTV." As Fred Seibert, the MTV executive responsible for the logo, put it at the time: "Why don't we just steal the most important event in the history of television and make it our own?"[55] The logo was ambitious, clever, and, like the institution it represented, thoroughly postmodern; in this last regard, both the logo and the institution were fitting symbols of the age.

POSTER BOY FOR AN AGE

If MTV was the corporate exemplification of postmodern sensibility, Tony Robbins was the therapeutic culture's poster boy. Robbins was only twenty-five when *Life* magazine in 1985 proclaimed him "the classic 80s-style guru." He had grown up in San Bernadino, California, and worked his way to business success in the positive-thinking industry at a tender age, only then to sabotage himself by overeating, deliberately missing meetings, and engaging in a multitude of other self-destructive behaviors. Soon he found himself living in a tiny bachelor apartment, washing his dishes in the bathtub and heating meals on a single-burner hot plate. But he bounced back by developing a new self-help formula for bouncing back. Six-foot-seven, with a lantern jaw of monumental proportions set in a head that one observer said looked like something found on Easter Island, Robbins became a guru who led others to self-discovery by means of a technique he called Neuro-Linguistic Programming and the gimmick of teaching people to walk on red hot coals. Having reinvented himself in classic American style, he devoted himself to helping others do the same: "My life," he announced, "is about making people feel better and better about themselves"[56]

Robbins began to popularize his fire-walking seminars in Vancouver in 1983, and within two years he was the president and 75 percent owner of the Robbins Research Institute, practicing what he called "compassionate capitalism" and earning $1 million a year. "The best way help poor people," he opined, "is not to be one of them."[57] In 1989, the self-proclaimed "peak performance consultant" developed a series of infomercials that quickly made him a ubiquitous presence on cable television. By the mid-1990s, Robbins had sold more than 2 million copies of his books, *Unlimited Power* and *Awaken the Giant Within*, and more than 13 million self-help audiotape cassettes (a set of twenty-four cost "three easy payments of only $59.95").[58]

Reporting on a five-hour-long "Fear into Power" fire-walk seminar circa 1985, a journalist observed, "Tony trots on stage to Rocky's theme. . . . 'This seminar is not about fire walking,' he says. 'The fire walk is only a metaphor for what we think we cannot do. And once you've walked on fire a lot of the impossibilities become possible.' . . . Tony asks us to think of our greatest fear, our goal for tonight, and what we think is most beautiful about ourselves. He asks us to 'share' these with someone. Instantly an eager young man pops smilingly in front of me and says, 'Hi! My name is Steve. My greatest fear is fear of abandonment. My goal tonight is to feel totally confident about my worthiness to be loved. And what's beautiful about me is that I love people.'"

In the end, Robbins's students do indeed walk the length of a 12-foot bed of coals. "How many of you thought tonight was worth your time, energy and capital investment?" he asks the exhausted, exhilarated fire-walkers. Always selling, even while liberating the hidden powers within, he suggests the participants sign up for the next tier experience, the full "Mind Revolution" package. "I guarantee it will be the most important weekend of your life. Put it on MasterCard or Visa—however you have to pay."[59]

Americans did pay, in large numbers. As with MTV and the postmodern sensibility, Robbins and his many self-help imitators both explored *and* exploited self-discovery, bridging in quintessential 1980s fashion the seeming gap between therapeutic quest and commercial gain. The result was a cultural moment of considerable complexity, when traditional middle-class values were being subverted by the new postmodern and therapeutic impulses even as deep expressions of the nation's bourgeois soul in turn gave the new challenges themselves a distinctively American cast and coloration.

Chapter 7

CULTURE WAR

In 1992 Patrick J. Buchanan gave one of the more notorious speeches in recent American politics to the Republican National Convention meeting in Houston, Texas. It was a fire-breathing harangue designed to arouse. "My friends," Buchanan announced, "this election is about much more than who gets what. It is about who we are. It is about what we believe. It is about what we stand for as Americans. There is a religious war going on in our country for the soul of America. It is a cultural war, as critical to the kind of nation we will one day be as was the Cold War itself." The Republican campaign, Buchanan insisted, would be against not only Bill Clinton and his running mate Al Gore, but against a host of cultural ills and dangers, including abortion on demand, homosexual rights, and radical feminism. In a powerful closing that crossed the line into racist appeal, he called on Americans to emulate the army troops sent to restore order in that summer's Los Angeles race riot: "And as they took back the streets of LA, block by block, so we must take back our cities, and take back our culture, and take back our country."[1]

The response to the Buchanan's address was decidedly mixed. Conservative Republicans applauded what they perceived as a long-overdue call to arms. Moderate Republicans cringed. Republican National Committee chairman Rich Bond thought the decision to let Buchanan speak in prime time on the convention's first night was a "flat-out mistake."[2] Liberals decried the speech as a shrill and dangerous attempt to divide Americans for partisan political purposes. Undecided voters decided to look around. When Bush lost on election night, 1992, media analysts generally portrayed the speech as a political blunder that might well have cost him the election. With Buchanan clearly in mind, NBC commentator John Chancellor remarked, "I think that the convention—and certainly all the polling data indicates [sic] this—offended a lot of women, offended a lot of people in the country who thought it was too religious and too hard-edged." Republican moderate conservatives seemed to agree, as Jack Kemp observed that Buchanan's speech sounded "like he wanted to line people up against the wall and shoot them."[3]

Commentators generally agreed that the speech backfired and hurt the Republicans in the general election. As a political appeal it failed disastrously. (Interestingly, the preternaturally gifted politician Bill Clinton viewed the speech in professional terms, and thought Buchanan had actually accomplished his purpose. "His job," Clinton wrote in his memoirs, "was to stop the hemorrhaging on the right by telling conservatives who wanted change that they couldn't vote for me, and he did it well.")[4]

But as a historian, Buchanan had a valid point. There *was* a culture war going on in the United States, one that had raged throughout the 1980s. In their haste to denounce the speech, commentators overlooked the fact that the cultural conflict of which Buchanan spoke had been one of the defining aspects of the Reagan years. An intellectually and sociologically complex phenomenon, the struggle comprised many battles and campaigns on a myriad of fronts, involving shifting coalitions of adversaries, all cloaked in the usual fog of war. Much of the combat involved guerrilla warfare and small skirmishes that did not always register on the national screen at the time, but the occasional set-piece battles did draw media attention. Even those, however, were often viewed in isolation by the media and tended to baffle outside observers. What was the fuss all about?

The label culture war implies a certain neatness that was missing in real life, and in truth even the combatants sometimes had difficulty identifying the conflict's central dynamic. Although it is tempting to view the culture war as pitting left against right, liberal and radical against conservative, in a continuation of partisan political conflict by other means, such ordinary political categories, although salient, are not quite capacious enough. The keenest student of the culture war, James Davison Hunter, a sociologist at the University of Virginia, explains the phenomenon as a multifaceted struggle between different systems of moral understanding. He identifies the contending worldviews—impulses, really, since they were seldom fully elaborated or thoroughly articulated—as the orthodox and the progressive. (Hunter did not mean for the labels to impute value or correctness.) The orthodox impulse, although it took many shapes, at bottom entailed commitment to "an external, definable, and transcendent authority." Such external authority was located variously in cultural tradition, religion, or conceptions of natural law. The progressive impulse, on the other hand, denied such authority and relied instead on subjective values derived from the contemporary zeitgeist. In practice, as Hunter admits, those who embraced the orthodox impulse tended to be political and cultural conservatives, and those who held progressive moral assumptions tended to be liberal or radical in their political and cultural views. The culture war that convulsed the 1980s was, in Hunter's view, a fundamental struggle for domination between these two competing conceptions of moral authority. It was, he wrote in 1991, well before Buchanan's infamous rhetorical flight at the Republican convention, "a clash over national life itself . . . a struggle over national identity—*over the meaning of America*, who we have been in the past, who we are now, and perhaps most important, who we, as a nation, will aspire to become."[5]

Further complicating the culture war was its *Rashomon*-like quality. The participants usually had dramatically differing versions of what was really going on. Those on the cultural left saw the conflict as caused by the attempt by cultural traditionalists to impose a rightwing cultural theocracy, and they viewed the surge of fundamentalist and evangelical Christianity in the 1970s as the precipitating development. Others saw the story unfolding in precisely the opposite fashion, as beleaguered traditionalists took to the battlements to repel the challenges to the established bourgeois order mounted by radicals who were hell-bent on continuing a cultural assault begun in that earlier period of tumult and upheaval, the 1960s. Both sides had a piece of the truth.

As it happened, the American culture war began in the late 1970s and early 1980s with the confluence of two developments. The first was the explosive growth of evangelical Protestant churches, filled with believers in the spiritual centrality of the Bible, the coming of an apocalypse, and the need for personal conversion (being touched by the Holy Spirit and reborn in Christ, hence the label born-again Christians).[6] The evangelical religious revival produced an energetic sociocultural constituency determined to protect traditional values (Hunter's "orthodoxy"), which they interpreted in terms of longstanding Christian beliefs, from the ongoing assaults of modern society and mass culture. The other key development, happening at the same time, was the movement into mainstream American life and into the core institutions of American culture of 1960s radicals and their ideas, and the similar insinuation into American life of postmodern ideology, with, as we have seen in the previous chapter, its denunciation of existing "metanarratives" (systems of moral authority) and its celebration of subjectivity and relativism. The resultant combination of radical politics and postmodern culture exerted a leftward tug on the cultural mainstream, in the direction of the worldview Hunter identified as "progressive." The clash between the older orthodoxy of Christian values and the beleaguered but still dominant bourgeois order on the one hand and the new radical cultural forces on the other constituted the central battle of the culture war.

The influence of 1960s radicalism on the cultural environment of the succeeding decades was more than just the stuff of conservative paranoia. Two of
the nation's most influential radical scholars, the historians Maurice Isserman
and Michael Kazin, in their penetrating 1989 assessment of the legacy of 1960s
radicalism, described in glowing terms how the "young radicals" of the New
Left and the Sixties counterculture "articulated a critique of 'everyday life' in
the United States, which was, in time, taken up by millions of people who had
little notion of where those ideas originated." Although the 1960s radicals left
no significant organizational legacy, they generated "an attitudinal penumbra"
that exerted a powerful subsequent influence. "Significantly," Isserman and
Kazin observed, "many former radicals made careers in the 'information industry,' as academics, journalists, and media specialists." As a result, the historians
concluded, "radicals probably played a larger role in the universities and the
media in the 1980s than at any previous time in American history," as "radical
perspectives, albeit somewhat diluted ones," found their way "into a surprising number of mainstream venues, from National Public Radio programming
to the op-ed pages of the *New York Times* and the *Wall Street Journal*, to the
Smithsonian's National Museum of American History" and elsewhere.[7] The
advance of cultural radicalism helped set the stage for the bitter cultural strife
of the Reagan era.

THE BATTLE JOINED: THE MORAL MAJORITY AND
PEOPLE FOR THE AMERICAN WAY

The culture war was already under way by the time Ronald Reagan was elected
president in November 1980. There had been numerous skirmishes throughout
the 1970s in which conservative groups fought against what they perceived
as attacks on traditional values. Perhaps the best known was the successful
battle waged in 1977 by the former beauty queen Anita Bryant to repeal a
Miami gay rights ordinance. Bryant's "Save Our Children" initiative won by
an overwhelming 71–29 percent margin, and she promptly became involved
in two other victorious repeal efforts in St. Paul, Minnesota, and Eugene,
Oregon. However, similar efforts failed in Seattle and California. A retaliatory
gay-orchestrated boycott of Florida orange juice subsequently cost Bryant her
lucrative contract as media spokeswoman for that industry and her singing
career simultaneously took a nosedive under the pressure of adverse publicity.
Over the course of the 1970s such cultural conflict became increasingly fierce
and sharp-elbowed. As one traditionalist activist put it at the end of the decade,
the struggle was "a war of ideology . . . a war of ideas . . . a war about our way
of life. And it has to be fought with the same intensity, I think, and dedication
as you would fight a shooting war."[8] As the decade drew to a close, a fresh burst
of organizational activity took matters to a new level.

Two new organizations, formed at the end of the 1970s, propelled the struggle for the soul of America into the decade of the 1980s. Both groups appeared at the outset to be largely one-man shows, but quickly became large and sophisticated bureaucratic lobbying machines, raising the cultural struggle from a guerrilla action to an all-out war fought by large, well-organized, and technologically advanced armies. The formation of the Moral Majority and People for the American Way marked the arrival of the modern culture war in its most up-to-date form.

The Moral Majority was the organizational handiwork of the Reverend Jerry Falwell, a self-proclaimed "Baptist preacher from the hills of Appalachia" who rose to national prominence on the wings of a national evangelical revival that relied heavily on radio and television to spread its message. Falwell founded the Thomas Road Baptist Church in his hometown of Lynchburg, Virginia, with an original flock of thirty-five in 1956. He immediately bought radio time to deliver his message and went on TV within a year. He took his television ministry into national syndication in 1970 and soon became one of the nation's premier televangelists; his weekly *Old-Time Gospel Hour* program grossed $63 million in 1981. Falwell used his media success to build a fundamentalist empire—his Thomas Road Baptist Church congregation had by the beginning of the 1980s grown to 18,000, and he also presided over Liberty Baptist College, a fully accredited liberal arts institution with an undergraduate student body of 3,300. Falwell proudly proclaimed that the school was dedicated to "turning out moral revolutionaries." "Liberty Baptist College," he declared, "is becoming to fundamentalist young people what Notre Dame is to Catholics." (He also tried to make it into an intercollegiate athletic powerhouse, like that Midwestern Catholic school, but without much success. It proved difficult to attract talented and sought-after athletes to a school that required students to get a dean's written permission in order to date.)[9]

Falwell created the Moral Majority organization in 1979 in order to combine his religious beliefs with collective political action. He proposed to combat what he saw as the growing influence of so-called secular humanists in government, the media, and education. "Secular humanism," he complained, "has become the religion of America." The humanists' chief sin was their determination to replace Christian doctrine and scripture with human reason as the society's ultimate moral guide and authority. In the eyes of Falwell and his allies, the substitution of all-too-fallible, all-too-fashionable human reason for religion had already done great harm by sanctioning abortion, gay rights, pornography, and a host of other recent social ills. In an important sense, Falwell engaged in a politics of cultural nostalgia, attempting to recapture a cultural order that he feared was slipping away. As the theologian Harvey Cox of the Harvard Divinity School put it at the time, Falwell was motivated by "a heartfelt belief in the old America that he sees threatened."[10]

Falwell's Moral Majority organization was a formidable operation, com-
prising four functional divisions aimed at education, lobbying, the support
of political candidates, and legal aid for those fighting the good fight on the
right side. The group's original board of directors included the ministers of the
nation's five largest church congregations, and the fledgling organization was
able to use the computerized mailing list already generated for Falwell's *Old-
Time Gospel Hour* program to get up and running. It quickly began lobbying
on a variety of issues from school prayer to the Family Protection Act, using
both mass mailings to potential voters and the direct lobbying of legislators.
By the mid-1980s the Moral Majority had a membership that numbered in the
millions and a reputation that almost certainly outran its actual impact.[11]

"Rarely has an organization set so many teeth on edge so rapidly," said *Time*
magazine of Falwell's political organization.[12] Especially after the pollster Lou
Harris credited the Moral Majority with helping to put Ronald Reagan over the
top in the 1980 election, the organization began to attract the sort of criticism
usually reserved for groups of a less religious nature, such as the American Nazis. Lobbying hard for prayer and the teaching of creationism in public schools,
opposing abortion and not only gay and lesbian rights but homosexuality itself,
Falwell and his Christian religious flock frightened cultural progressives to their
core. Rabbi Alexander Schindler held the Moral Majority responsible for "the
most serious outbreak of anti-Semitism since the era of World War II." George
McGovern called Falwell "a menace to the American political process." The
American Civil Liberties Union warned that the Republic was imperiled. The
president of Yale University, A. Bartlett Giamatti, in 1981 took the occasion of
his annual speech to the incoming freshman class to warn that the Moral Majority "licensed a new meanness of spirit in our land, a resurgent bigotry that
manifests itself in racist and discriminatory postures."[13]

One particularly troubled critic reacted with more than just verbal denunciation. Norman Lear was one of the most powerful individuals in Hollywood,
best known to the public as the producer of provocative situation comedies
that transformed the face of television in the 1970s. As the creator of the sit-
coms *All in the Family* and *Maude*, which specialized in finding humor in
socially significant and often controversial issues, Lear brought a new level of
social consciousness to an essentially escapist art form. He also worked more
generally to nudge the entertainment industry in a socially aware and liberal
direction. At the end of the 1970s, Lear was instrumental in putting together a
nonprofit organization known as Microsecond, headed by Norman and Diana
Fleischman. Kept alive by foundation grants, Microsecond, as the Fleischmans
later recalled, "conducted both large and small events for six years—mostly [in]
the homes of industry professionals" in an effort to acquaint Hollywood with a
variety of left-leaning intellectuals and activists. "Our aim," they subsequently
wrote, "[was] consciousness raising among creators of mass entertainment."[14]

While working on a film on televangelism in 1980, Lear became incensed by Falwell and the Moral Majority's blending of religion and politics. The unholy combination was, he believed, "fascism masquerading as Christianity" and "the ultimate obscenity, the spiritual pornography of a debased religiosity."[15] Lear's concern, together with his own political inclinations, prompted him to make a television commercial aimed at exposing the group's tactics. The resultant sixty-second television spot featured a hard-hatted worker standing in front of his forklift, observing, "There's something wrong when anyone, even a preacher, tells us we're good or bad Christians depending on our political point of view. That's not the American way."

In short order, Lear converted the line into a potent organization, People for the American Way, specifically designed to counter and combat the growing influence of the religious right. Father Theodore Hesburgh, the president of Notre Dame, and M. William Howard, the former head of the National Council of Churches, quickly came on board. By 1987, People For—as it was known to political insiders—had a membership of 270,000, an eighty-person staff, and a budget of $10 million.[16]

Lear's outfit proved itself a potent counterpoint to the Moral Majority both in the political clinches and in the war of persuasion. People for the American Way lobbied for two years in the early 1980s to force the Texas Board of Education to rescind the state's antievolution rules for high-school biology textbooks. Because Texas represented fully 10 percent of the national school textbook market, its rules and decisions exerted great pressure on publishers. Finally in 1984, under the threat of legal action by People for the American Way, the Texas Board of Education revoked its decade-old rule requiring biology textbooks used in the state's public schools to carry the notice that "evolution is treated as theory rather than fact." Moreover, Texas soon altered the process of textbook selection so as to minimize the influence of religiously inspired conservatives. A year later, People for the American Way published *A Consumer's Guide to Biology Textbooks* to shepherd education authorities across the country in their selection of textbooks that emphasized evolutionary theory at the expense of creationism.[17]

Lear also put his creative and entrepreneurial talent to work for the cause. In 1982 he put together a star-studded entertainment special for ABC entitled "I Love Liberty," which brought together Barbra Streisand singing "America the Beautiful," Jane Fonda reciting the First Amendment, and Senator Barry Goldwater introducing a "Grand Old Flag" Busby Berkeley-style spectacular complete with marching bands, baton twirlers, dancers, flag girls, roller-skaters, Uncle Sams on stilts, and the release of sixteen thousand red, white, and blue balloons. In a somewhat more pointed segment, an African American, an Hispanic, an American Indian, a woman, a homosexual, and an angry middle-class white male followed one another in explaining to the audience

why they as typical Americans were aggrieved at American society but nevertheless patriotic.

Although the program billed itself as a simple celebration of basic American values, the Moral Majority attacked the show as a promotion of Lear's personal political views. The producer countered that the show's theme was the
lesson that love of country was "not the private province of the far right. The
flag belongs to all of us. It moistens as many eyes on the left or the center as it
does on the right. 'I Love Liberty' is an attempt to show that the country loves
the flag, that it doesn't belong to just a few." Sensing an opportunity, People
for the American Way sent out letters to three thousand selected members
asking them to invite friends to watch the showing of the special in order to
solicit their membership. In words that must have caused considerable pain
within the ranks of the Moral Majority, an ABC vice president concluded,
"When Norman Lear can come to the table and bring these . . . [show business stars] to the show, you're dealing with something that has presence, a
mass-entertainment appeal."[18] Hollywood versus Lynchburg was not quite an
even match-up.

Falwell's Moral Majority and Lear's People for the American Way continued to dominate the news dispatches from the culture war well into the mid-
1980s. In 1984 the Democrats used Falwell as "a no-risk whipping boy" (the
words of a Democratic operative) in their effort to drum up support for Walter
Mondale's presidential candidacy. "Ronald Reagan and Reverend Jerry Falwell
cordially invite you to their party on November 6th," began one Mondale TV
ad. Against the visual backdrop of an engraved invitation with photos of Reagan
and Falwell appearing side-by-side, the ad voice-over continued, "Think about
the people who have taken over the Republican Party. They want their new
platform to be your new Constitution. Think about that." Mondale invoked
Falwell's name three times during his first televised debate with the incumbent
Reagan, and while on the stump continually reminded voters, "If you pull their
lever, you'll be handing over the Supreme Court to Jerry Falwell, who wants to
run the most private questions of your life."[19]

Although they represented irreconcilable worldviews and agreed on almost
nothing, there remained surprising and unsettling similarities between Falwell
and his Moral Majority and Lear and People for the American Way. Both felt
threatened, both claimed to speak for the majority, both sought to cloak their
side in the symbols of legitimacy, and both demonized the other as a mortal
threat to the welfare of society. Falwell and Lear were enormously attractive
and congenial individuals, but in both men those human qualities masked a
remarkable, single-minded determination at the core. Falwell was famous for
his granite convictions and his ability to take outrageously controversial and
unyielding stands while retaining a smile that seemed as genuine as it was
broad. Lear was similarly deceptive, with a genial, soft-spoken, and self-effacing

persona that belied his ability to play a cynical brand of political hardball, as Ronald Reagan learned firsthand.

Lear struck up a correspondence with the president in 1984, initiating an exchange of letters on the relationship between church and state. The Hollywood producer set the tone for his side of the correspondence by voicing his concern that Reagan "not use the office of the presidency as Evangelist in Chief."[20] Reagan responded to Lear's complaints somewhat defensively but cordially. The president was, in fact, quite unusual in his willingness to respond personally to critical mail, and his office files were replete with his private attempts to win over detractors and explain himself to critics. The habit evidenced his native optimism yet again, the hope that a more elaborate presentation of his position might correct some misunderstanding. Reagan's letters, which he himself drafted in longhand, had a warm, personal tone and conveyed a seemingly honest effort to come to grips with the issues Lear raised. The White House staff ultimately prevailed upon Reagan to cut off the correspondence, however, after Lear, with no prior warning, provided the entire correspondence to the *New York Times* and *Harper's* magazine for publication. An annoyed White House counsel Fred F. Fielding complained, "Lear has taken advantage of the President's personal courtesy and sincere interest in this area in an effort to elevate the status of People for the American Way and himself as its founder, and we should provide no further Presidential assistance to that effort."[21] The episode was a minor one, but it underscored the difficulty both sides in the culture war had in identifying and adhering to tactics that most people on the street would identify as the American way.

CULTURE WAR: THE STRUGGLE FOR INSTITUTIONS

Despite all the attention they received, the Moral Majority and its progressive antagonist, People for the American Way, represented only a small part of a much larger phenomenon. The culture war was fought by a wide variety of groups and individuals at points across the length and breadth of American society. Out of the welter emerged a pattern: The struggle pitted those who identified with an orthodoxy rooted in some sort of transcendent moral authority against those progressives who sought to construct a new order based on prevailing cultural and political values and insights. The particular battles fought were of two general kinds. The first involved contests for the control of major cultural institutions, such as the university, the media, and the arts. The second involved contests to shape policy and determine the political outcome of a number of hot-button issues that set in opposition the underlying worldviews of the competing cultural warriors.

No institution witnessed more cultural contention in the 1980s than the American university. The points of conflict were many, but three in particular stood out: debates over the so-called canon, the issue of multiculturalism, and the matter of political correctness. Beginning in 1986, a highly public debate over curriculum convulsed Stanford University for several years and put that institution momentarily at the center of the culture war. At issue was the university's required, year-long, freshman core curriculum sequence on Western culture, which focused on a canon or agreed-upon reading list of masterworks in Western civilization. In the spring of 1986, members of Stanford's Black Student Union complained that the required sequence was racist and sexist because it excluded non-Western thinkers, issues, and approaches. "Western culture does not try to understand the diversity of experiences of different people," charged one Hispanic student; "It was painful to come to Stanford and find that no member of your race was in the required curriculum," added another activist.[22] In the face of increasingly vocal complaints, Stanford's president called for reason to prevail and handed the problem off to a task force (partly, one suspects, in order to diffuse responsibility for whatever might happen next). In the meantime, Stanford's curricular debate attracted national attention: On Martin Luther King Day in January 1987, the Reverend Jesse Jackson spoke at a Stanford rally, denounced the Western culture requirement, and marched in solidarity with five hundred students who chanted "Hey hey, ho ho, Western culture's got to go."[23] Weeks later, a group of student protesters occupied the university president's office in order to encourage a speedy resolution of the issue.

By and large, the critics opposing the proposed curriculum change argued that the Western culture sequence should be retained because it was historically relevant and because it exposed students to universalist standards of excellence that stood apart from the political passions and fashions of the present day. They lost. As soon as the Stanford Faculty Senate approved the scrapping of the existing Western culture program in early 1988, the unabashedly conservative United States secretary of education William J. Bennett swept into Palo Alto to denounce what he characterized as a craven capitulation to "a campaign of pressure politics and intimidation." "The point for contemporary higher education," Bennett declared, "is this: the classics of Western philosophy and literature amount to a great debate on the perennial questions. To deprive students of this debate is to condemn them to improvise their ways of living in ignorance of their real options and the best arguments for each."[24]

In the end, Stanford replaced its Western Culture requirement with a new sequence of three mandated courses on "Cultures, Ideas, and Values." The required reading for the new approach retained some Western classics but complemented them with new selections by Asian, African, and Middle Eastern writers. To give the new sequence the proper political coloration in an era of identity politics, the faculty plan for the program insisted that each course include "works by women, minorities and persons of color" and also that each course include at least one work addressing issues of race, class, and gender.[25]

The curriculum change enjoyed considerable support, especially among younger faculty of a culturally progressive inclination. For some, it seemed self-evident that views would change over time regarding what constituted a classic. Had not the history of the literary canon, to take an example, been one of continual reassessment, debate, and revision? Surely the canon needed to be adjusted periodically if only to ensure its relevance in a changing world. Moreover, in an increasingly global economy and postmodern culture, with barriers of all sorts falling, boundaries dissolving, and flux seemingly the only constant, to remain static in one's approach to knowledge, to hold any tradition inviolate, seemed not merely old-fashioned but perhaps even anti-intellectual.[26] Traditionalists, on the other hand, saw the curricular change as the triumph of politics over knowledge, a politicization of the university that would prove hard to contain or undo. What mattered under the new regime, they complained, was less the intellectual quality of a work than the demographic identity—the race, ethnicity, class, sex, sexual orientation, and political orientation—and victim status of its author.

The critics of the developments at Stanford University were proven correct on at least one point. The debate over the canon—the word itself originally referred to those works the church considered to be part of the Bible—may have been focused on their campus, but it could not be contained there. The questioning of traditional standards of intellectual quality spread throughout the academy. The study of U.S. literature was a field particularly hard hit by the ensuing controversy. Joseph Berger reported in the *New York Times* that "the radical re-examination . . . has now begun to question the very idea of literary quality and has led to the studying of writers principally for what they have to say rather than how well they say it. Once honored standards like grace of style, vigor of prose and originality of expression have been downgraded or questioned while the importance of historical and social impact and rhetorical strength has grown." Many of the professors who argued that a traditional standard of literary quality was hopelessly elitist and needed to be overthrown had been, Berger noted, "students in the rebellious 1960s."[27] Henry Louis Gates, Jr., a rising academic superstar in the fields of literature and black studies, put an even finer point on it: "Ours was the generation that took over buildings in the late 1960s and demanded the creation of Black and Women's Studies programs, and now, like the repressed, we have come back to challenge the traditional curriculum."[28]

As debate raged over the canon, a related but larger and more amorphous dispute arose in academe over the spread of an expansive new creed known as multiculturalism. Multiculturalism was, at its heart, a doctrine that sought to apply the progressive side of the canon debate—the celebration of "the many" and the subversion of external universalistic standards—to virtually every area of university life, both inside and outside the classroom. The champions of the new "ism" viewed it as the means to "open up" the American university. They sought to establish the widest possible diversity in students and faculty, usually defined in terms of immutable characteristics such as race, sex, and ethnicity rather than in terms of intellectual viewpoints (or even class); to establish courses of study and approaches to knowledge beyond the eurocentric, patriarchal, logocentric ones (standard multicultural terminology of opprobrium) embedded in the traditional curriculum; and to fashion the rest of the university into a hospitable environment for the multicultural enterprise. Often unstated, but universally understood, was the political agenda of making acceptable the broadest possible range of human differences in order to overcome the evils of racism, sexism, and the myriad other forms of discrimination man is prone to.

The advocates of multiculturalism presented their program as a benign attempt to bring the university into the modern global age taking shape everywhere beyond the cloistered groves of the academy. It would enable the university to "get right" with the various freedom struggles of women and minorities that had transpired throughout the 1960s and 1970s and with the changing demographic realities of American life. Multiculturalism, they claimed, was nothing more than educational relevance and educational democracy in their latest incarnations, and as such it had a long and noble pedigree in the history of American pluralism. Other multiculturalists, however, were openly political in their assessment of the debate: the historian Jon Wiener wrote candidly in the *Nation* that "the right wing faculty . . . are filled with resentment, because they know it is they who have been marginalized — by the intellectual energy and commitment of the academic left."[29]

Multiculturalism's appeal also derived from the fact that it fitted so congruently with intellectual currents that had already made great inroads in the American academy. The ideas and theories of the French intellectuals Jacques Derrida, Michel Foucault, Jean-Francois Lyotard, and Jean Baudrillard, conceptions that migrated from France to England and the United States in the 1970s and 1980s and won great acclaim in elite academic circles, provided multiculturalism with an instant intellectual cachet. The French thinkers had their most direct impact on the fields of literature, literary criticism, and literary theory, but they took the whole of culture as their purview and developed insights that many believed could be used to transform society. Their theories were wide-ranging and dense — brilliantly sophisticated perceptions in the eyes of followers, masturbatory gobblydegook in the eyes of critics — but their intellectual schemes all shared a fundamental commitment to relativism, subjectivity, and the idea that all standards are socially constructed and the expressions of power relationships. In a sense, multiculturalism represented these celebrated intellectual currents in action, a heady and attractive combination in an institution defined by its attention to ideas.[30]

Multiculturalism also appealed because it reflected so well the larger cultural currents of the 1980s. It was, in a word, postmodern. As Gerald Early, the director of African and Afro-American studies and a professor of literature at Washington University, brilliantly observed by way of analysis rather than endorsement, multiculturalism was "an outgrowth of the postmodern movement" and of America's postmodern zeitgeist.[31] In typical postmodernist fashion, multiculturalism sought "to displace any sort of 'metanarrative' structure to education, or any grand legitimating discourse of validating 'universalist' principles." The debate between educational traditionalists and multiculturalists was really "between the idea of metanarrative versus the idea of a series of pluralistic, differentiated, and antinomian social orders, both fixed and random." The goal of multiculturalism was "the depriviliging [subverting] of the ideas of the 'finished' world vision, the singular set of universalist ideals."

Moreover, Early averred, multiculturalism had a distinctly therapeutic aspect that was perfectly attuned to the larger therapeutic culture that had arisen in the 1980s and early 1990s. "Multiculturalism," he noted, "does not aim to provide students with a body of knowledge that might make them useful to society but with a certain psychological state that would make them useful to themselves. It is the sense of the private, the inward, the spiritual, the psychological that makes multiculturalism so curious and so curiously American. Here is . . . an intense therapeutic aestheticization of the anxieties of self-consciousness." Multiculturalism served its therapeutic purposes by providing the members of claimant groups with an identity based on victimization, which in turn located the individual amidst the "sheer atomism of modern mass education," comforted and consoled, and bestowed moral and political power. Additionally, for whites, who were the beneficiaries of the European exploitation, multiculturalism offered the frisson of guilt and the catharsis of confession. The beauty of multiculturalism was that it made everyone into a victim of something larger than him- or herself. In that, it was thoroughly in tune with its time.

The critics of multiculturalism, on their part, often accepted the wisdom, necessity, and moral rightness of opening up the university, and even the curriculum, to previously excluded groups and "voices." However, they disapproved of what they saw as other, more problematic aspects of multiculturalism—its thoroughgoing relativism, its insistence on deprecating American and Western culture, and its dangerous penchant for indoctrination and its own brand of intolerance. Relativism lay at the heart of multiculturalism. Under the new regime, no one culture could be adjudged better or worse than any other, because there existed no legitimate universalist or transcendent criteria of judgment. Objective truth, reason, morality, and artistic excellence were all mere social constructions and rationalizations, expressions ultimately of the race, class, and gender of the social constructors, weapons manufactured by the powerful to be wielded against the oppressed and the marginalized. The Enlightenment's celebration of reason was a Western white male scam.

The critics of multiculturalism also quarreled with the tendency of the new philosophy to except Western culture from the relativist dictum: thou shalt not judge. Multiculturalists commonly (the critics claimed, ritualistically) denounced Western culture as irredeemably flawed—hopelessly ethnocentric, patriarchal, and racist. In the multiculturalists' version of the world, the only truly bad guys were the Dead White European Males (so commonly invoked that they received their own acronym: DWEMs) who had created and elaborated Western culture and then tried to impose it on others, including presumably the victimized students trapped in the American university.

Most concretely, multiculturalism gave rise to the troubling and controversial phenomenon known as political correctness. More and more in the late 1980s and early 1990s, universities turned to censorship to protect the sensibilities of those who might be offended by the retrograde failure of some to live up to multiculturalism's progressive standards of relativism and unquestioning tolerance. Inevitably, individuals, either willfully or accidentally, committed the new social infraction of being judgmental or disrespectful of other cultures in general or of especially protected groups on campus. As happens in free societies, people now and then said stupid things. And when they did, university administrators increasingly responded by formulating so-called speech codes and harassment policies forbidding or substantially limiting speech of many sorts commonly believed to be protected under the first amendment. (Indeed, in the late 1980s and early 1990s the courts swept aside such codes at Michigan, Wisconsin, and other major public universities on precisely that ground. They continued to linger at hundreds of schools into the twenty-first century, however.)[32] At the University of Connecticut, the University President's Policy on Harassment identified as possible violations "the use of derogatory names," "inconsiderate jokes," "misdirected laughter," and "conspicuous exclusion from conversation."[33]

Sometimes the universities' actions were preemptive and approached the sort of totalitarian thought control most Americans outside academe had the wit to associate with George Orwell's novel 1984 and to abhor. A small but, to traditionalists, telling example involved the University of Pennsylvania, where an unusually weak administration in the thrall of multiculturalism seemed at the end of the 1980s in danger of losing its bearings completely. When Penn instituted mandatory "racism" training as part of its multicultural regime, an undergraduate voiced concern in a memorandum about the right of individuals to be free from coercion. A university administrator bounced the memo back to her having circled the word "individual": "This is a Red FLAG phrase today," the official wrote, "which is considered by many to be RACIST. Arguments that champion the individual over the group ultimately privilege the 'individuals' who belong to the largest or dominant group."[34]

Traditionalists, who had a different view of the place of the individual and who worried about the new trends within the academy, fought back by organizing the National Association of Scholars (NAS) in 1987. The NAS argued that "the surest way to achieve educational opportunity for all and maintain a genuine sense of academic community is to evaluate each individual on the basis of personal achievement and promise. It is only as individuals united in the pursuit of knowledge that we can realize the ideal of a common intellectual life." The group's president and executive director claimed that it was fighting "to redeem American higher education from intellectual and moral servitude to forces having little to do with the life of the mind or the transmission of knowledge." The group attracted some heavy hitters, including John R. Silber, the president of Boston University; the noted Holocaust scholar Lucy Dawidowicz; the political scientist James Q. Wilson; and the sociologist James Coleman. However, even after ten years in business, it had only four thousand members, and was dwarfed by the staunchly multiculturalist Modern Language Association with a membership in excess of twenty thousand.[35]

When the most egregious excesses of political correctness were made public, the resultant criticism (and ridicule) from outside the academy, in concert with resistance from within, occasionally forced the authorities to retreat. But in the new atmosphere of multiculturalism, such outcomes were hardly automatic. When the traditional defender of academic freedom in the United States, the American Association of University Professors (AAUP), issued a formal statement in 1991 on the political correctness controversy, the group surprised at least a few observers by denouncing the critics of political correctness as bigots: "Their [the critics'] assault has involved sloganeering, name-calling, the irresponsible use of anecdotes, and not infrequently the assertion that 'political correctness' is the new McCarthyism that is chilling the climate of debate on campus and subjecting political dissenters to the threat of reprisal. For all its self-righteous verve, this attack has frequently been less candid about its actual origin, which appears to lie in an only partly concealed animosity toward equal opportunity and its first effects of modestly increasing the participation of women and racial and cultural minorities on campus."[36]

The brouhaha over the canon, multiculturalism, and political correctness forced universities to smooth over some of the roughest edges of the new multicultural regime that took hold in academe in the late 1980s and early 1990s. The avatars of multiculturalism were not quite in complete control of the university. They continued to face resistance from traditionalists both outside and inside the academy. But they had, in a very real sense, won. There was no doubt that the traditionalist influence within the American university had been much diminished, and that a core cultural institution had fallen under the influence of the new multicultural vision.

By the mid-1990s the progressive worldview had a strong presence every-where in the academy outside the hard sciences, especially in the overall gov-ernance and communal life of the university. Richard Bernstein, the national cultural correspondent for the *New York Times*, described the new state of affairs in 1995: "Literally from day one—indeed . . . from before day one—freshman and freshwomen are introduced to a twin message. Its first part is: 'You have just entered an institution that is deeply racist, sexist, patriarchal, unfair, un-just, and old-fashioned—an institution, in other words, that is a microcosm of the iniquitous society from which you came.' The second part is: 'Each of you is a member of a group involving race, ethnic background, and sexuality, and you will be seen, and you should see yourself, primarily as a product of the per-spectives, the limitations, and the sufferings of those groups.' Finally, students are told: 'Your first responsibility, the thing that will designate you as a good person, will be to adopt the great cause of multiculturalism as your own.'"[37] The center of gravity in the academy had moved discernibly to the left.

Struggles for influence and control also took place in other cultural institu-tions throughout the 1980s. Conservatives and cultural traditionalists were con-vinced that the left dominated the major media. As the National Right-to-Life Committee exhorted in a 1990 direct mail statement: "ABC, CBS and NBC [have] Declared War . . . on the Movement. . . . We cannot let a handful of network executives and Hollywood writers, actors and directors poison America with their godless attitudes, which are anti- religion, anti-family and anti-life." Regarding Hollywood, an anti-pornography activist complained, "The people in Hollywood are so far removed from the people of Middle America. They have a hostility toward people who believe anything all. They live in a hedonis-tic, materialistic little world."[38]

Although the matter of media bias has remained a hardy perennial, still the stuff of debate in the early years of the twenty-first century, the cultural conser-vatives of the 1980s had a point. Several studies at the time indicated a strong politically liberal and culturally progressivist bias on the part of the mainstream press (both print and television) and the entertainment industry.[39] In addition, two intentionally comparable polls completed in 1984 and 1985 reported that journalists were twice as likely as the general public to be liberal, and only a third as likely to be conservative. Surveys at the time also indicated that on a host of social issues—such as abortion, capital punishment, and government aid to the poor—journalists, in the words of the *Los Angeles Times* reporter who helped draft the questions and write up the results, "took a far more liberal position than the general public."[40]

Political and cultural conservatives fought back against what they perceived as media bias by shining a spotlight on the performance of the media in order to increase their accountability. Reed Irvine, a Mormon from Salt Lake City, retired from government service at the Federal Reserve in the late 1960s and created an organization called Accuracy in Media (AIM) to serve as a conservative watchdog on the prowl for liberal bias. Beginning in the mid-1970s, AIM started filing complaints with the Federal Communications Commission, seeking license revocation for alleged violators of the FCC's Fairness Doctrine. In the mid-1980s Irvine and AIM, along with similar organizations such as the American Legal Foundation and Fairness in Media, were at war with, among others, CBS, National Public Radio, and the Public Broadcasting Service, which Irvine characterized as "the private playpen of left-wingers who use our tax dollars to promote . . . revolutions and denigrate American institutions."[41]

The impact of Irvine's agitation was difficult to measure. The right liked to think that it was considerable even when invisible. As a writer for the *National Review* put it, "Who can tabulate the stories that the papers and TV stations didn't run because they knew that AIM was waiting in ambush?"[42] But upon closer investigation, AIM's clout dissipates. An interesting test case involved one of Irvine's favorite targets. AIM caught Karen DeYoung, a reporter for the *Washington Post* who covered the revolution in Nicaragua, on tape telling a seminar at the left-leaning Institute for Policy Studies that "most journalists now, most Western journalists at least, are very eager to seek out guerrilla groups, leftist groups, because you assume they must be the good guys." The unwanted attention AIM was able to generate with the DeYoung revelation, in the words of a *Post* editor, "caused some people [at the paper] discomfort." But the subsequent course of the reporter's career at the paper was instructive—she ascended to two of the paper's most prestigious positions, foreign editor and London bureau chief. Ben Bradlee, the *Post*'s executive editor, believed Irvine to be "a miserable, carping, retromingent vigilante." The publisher of the *Post*, Donald Graham, agreed, albeit in less colorful language, observing that Irvine would "throw around accusations about people being communists" in a way that "really reduces his effectiveness quite substantially."[43]

Cultural conservatives also tried other ways to gain influence over the national media. In the mid-1980s a group called Fairness in Media (FIM), spearheaded by the arch-conservative Republican senator from North Carolina Jesse Helms, made a serious bid to buy enough common stock to take over CBS and "become Dan Rather's boss." The takeover bid failed, leaving the national media, at least in the eyes of the culturally orthodox, under progressivist control. The defenders of cultural orthodoxy had challenged for control but without great success. They had launched several ideas that would later bear fruit in the emergence in the 1990s of right-wing talk radio programming and the creation in late 1996 of the Fox News Channel on cable TV, but those developments lay in the future. In the meantime, the supporters of cultural orthodoxy made do with the more than 1,300 religious radio stations, more than two hundred religious television stations, and three religious TV networks that sent out regular messages to local and regional audiences at the end of the 1980s.[44]

The arts constituted yet another arena of cultural conflict in the late 1980s. A particularly vigorous controversy in 1989 swirled around the fact that the publicly funded National Endowment for the Arts had indirectly supported works of art roundly condemned by cultural conservatives as obscene and sacrilegious. The protesters focused particular attention on Andres Serrano's "Piss Christ," a photograph of a crucifix immersed in a jar of the artist's own urine, and on the work of Robert Mapplethorpe, whose photographs explored homoerotic themes in what to many was a disconcertingly forthright fashion. Among his most notorious photographs were one that captured a man urinating in another man's mouth and another depicting the artist with a bullwhip inserted in his anus. Karen Finley, a performance artist best known to the public for smearing chocolate pudding over her body to symbolize the scatological mistreatment of women in patriarchal American society, was another target. The art community acclaimed and defended all three as serious artists. Seeing things differently, the American Family Association, a fundamentalist Christian group, took out full-page newspaper advertisements asking readers, "Is this how you want your tax dollars spent?"[45]

The ensuing battle pitted cultural conservatives upset at the putative immorality of the art and the use of tax dollars to support it against progressives who saw themselves as beleaguered defenders of artistic freedom and the opponents of outright censorship. Conservatives argued that the NEA was wrong to support "artists whose forte is ridiculing the values . . . of Americans who are paying for it." On the other side of the cultural divide, liberals sometimes denied that there was any legitimate distinction between out-and-out censorship and disagreement regarding how best to spend public monies responsibly and wisely. For them it all came down to the suppression of artistic freedom. To question NEA funding for controversial art was to throttle artistic expression. In an expansive redefinition of free speech surely not foreseen by the founding fathers, Robert Brustein, the theater critic for the *New Republic*, asserted that "every artist has a First Amendment right to subsidy." In the end, the NEA decided to ask artists seeking support to sign a pledge that their federally funded art would avoid obscenity and indecency. Meanwhile, the artists in question saw the price of their art skyrocket, as they became celebrities and cultural heroes.[46]

Few cultural institutions managed to escape the 1980s unscathed by controversy. What happened in higher education, the media, and the arts was replicated in controversies involving the public schools, charitable foundations, the world of museums, and popular culture. The emergence of rap music in the late 1980s challenged the bourgeois cultural orthodoxy in ways that would not have been imaginable just a generation earlier. In 1989 the rap group 2 Live Crew released an album entitled "As Nasty as They Wanna Be," which employed the word "fuck" over 200 times, used explicit terms for male and female genitalia over 100 times, included 80 descriptions of oral sex, and invoked the word "bitch" more than 150 times.[47] The outcomes of individual episodes varied, but the larger picture that emerged over the course of the decade showed a pattern of orthodoxy under stress and the progressivist ethic on the rise.

CULTURE WAR: THE STRUGGLE OVER ISSUES

Contention over cultural values also played a significant role in a number of public policy debates. What distinguished such issues was, again, the clash of fundamentally different conceptions of moral authority. No single issue touched on the matter of what America was all about more forcefully than abortion. People on both the pro-life and pro-choice sides of the debate believed themselves engaged in a chiliastic struggle for the soul of America. Abortion law and practice in the United States followed the famous 1973 Supreme Court decision *Roe v. Wade*, a 7–2 ruling that established a constitutional right to abortion and struck down existing state bans on the procedure. Justice Harry A. Blackmun's majority opinion in the landmark case stated, "We . . . conclude that the right of personal privacy includes the abortion decision, but that this right is not unqualified and must be considered against important state interests in regulation." The intense debate that followed the Supreme Court's decision involved both the question of whether the newly recognized constitutional right to abortion should be allowed to stand and the related matter of what, if any, legitimate qualifications the state could impose on that right.

In the 1980s, the number of abortions performed annually rose to over 1.5 million and hovered there, and the increasingly fierce debate over *Roe v. Wade* moved out of the courtroom and into other venues, including the street.[48] As one activist put it, "You can't expect it to remain peaceful in these circumstances. It's like the Civil War. There is no suitable middle ground."[49] As the cultural and political argument heated up, the tone and tactics of both the pro-life and pro-choice forces turned more extreme. Each side regularly likened the other to the Nazis, even in what passed for polite discourse. The novelist Walker Percy made the point on the pro-life side in a letter to the editor of the *New York Times*: "Certain consequences, perhaps unforeseen, follow upon the acceptance of the principle of the destruction of human life for what may appear to be the most admirable social reasons. One does not have to look back very far in history for an example of such consequences. Take democratic Germany in the 1920s. . . . It is hardly necessary to say what use the Nazis made of these ideas. . . . Once the line is crossed, once the principle gains acceptance — juridically, medically, socially — innocent human life can be destroyed for whatever reason, for the most admirable socioeconomic, medical, or social reasons—then it does not take a prophet to predict what will happen next, or if not next, then sooner or later." The pro-choice champion professor Laurence Tribe of the Harvard Law School returned the favor by reversing the historical analogy. "The abortion policies of Nazi Germany," he wrote, "best exemplify the potential evil of entrusting government with the power to say which pregnancies are to be terminated and which are not. . . . Abortion and even its facilitation were, in general, serious criminal offenses in Nazi Germany; a network of spies and secret police sought out abortionists, and prosecutions were frequent."[50]

As the demonizing of opponents in polite discussion intensified, both sides also made use of increasingly graphic imagery in the public relations battle to drive home their respective messages. Anti-abortion forces scored first, and mightily, in 1985 with the widely circulated film entitled *The Silent Scream*, which showed a twelve-week-old fetus with unmistakably human features being swept from the womb in an actual abortion procedure. In 1989 the pro-choice Fund for the Feminist Majority countered by circulating to lawmakers videocassette copies of *Abortion: For Survival*, a film that focused on an 84-second-long real-life abortion and that showed two aborted embryos, amounting to about two tablespoons of blood and tissue, in an effort to make the point that most of the more than 90 percent of abortions carried out in the first twelve weeks of pregnancy did not involve well-formed fetuses like those featured in *The Silent Scream*.[51]

As the argument over abortion grew more heated, those taking extreme positions gained influence and notoriety. No one demonstrated that reality more dramatically than Randall A. Terry. The frizzy-haired tire and used-car salesman and anti-abortion activist from Binghamton, New York, was still in his twenties when he founded the organization Operation Rescue in 1986. The purpose of the group was to provide flying squads of activists who would go around the country to demonstrate at abortion clinics in an effort to interfere with their operation and to persuade their clients to consider alternatives to abortion. Terry approached the task the same way George Patton approached war. His opposition to abortion was unyielding even in cases of rape or incest. The battle against abortion was, he believed, "the fiercest battle in a war of ideologies and allegiances" against forces bent on eliminating "virtually every vestige of Christianity from our laws, morals, institutions, and, ultimately, our families."[52] In that struggle, he held back nothing. At one point, Operation Rescue called a press conference in Los Angeles, complete with bright lights, microphones, and television crews. Terry walked to the microphones, welcomed the assembled journalists, and reminded them that it was their duty to tell the American public the truth about the abortion issue. He and an assistant then opened up a small coffin, which contained a dead fetus. "This is

Baby Choice," Terry announced. "She was murdered by a salt solution at 19 weeks. She will answer all your questions." Without further explanation, Terry and his entourage walked out to their cars and drove off.[53]

Operation Rescue brought a new level of nonviolent militancy to the abortion struggle. In the late 1980s the group—Garry Wills called them "uterine warriors"—crisscrossed the country staging large-scale rescue "interventions."[54] In November 1987 Terry led nearly three hundred demonstrators, among them many clergy, in a blockade of the Cherry Hill (New Jersey) Women's Clinic. In 1988, his forces descended on New York City and Long Island for a week-long series of blockades, at which more than 1,500 demonstrators were arrested, including a Roman Catholic bishop, two Catholic monsignors, fifteen priests, four nuns, a Greek Orthodox priest, two rabbis, and more than twenty evangelical ministers. At and around the time of the Democratic National Convention in the Atlanta that year, Operation Rescue staged twenty-four actions and boasted of 1,235 demonstrators arrested. Between May 1988 and August 1990, according to one authoritative estimate, Operation Rescue mounted 683 blockades, with approximately 41,000 volunteers offering themselves up for arrest.[55] Overall, Operation Rescue engaged in civil disobedience on a scale that rivaled that of the civil rights movement of the 1960s.

Yet, the harder the pro-life movement fought, the more entrenched the right to abortion became. To be sure, it did not always seem that way to the contending forces at the time. In a 1989 decision, *Webster v. Reproductive Health Services*, the U.S. Supreme Court upheld a Missouri law that prohibited the use of public facilities or public employees to perform abortions. In an even more important case in 1992, *Planned Parenthood v. Casey*, the Court upheld several restrictions that the state of Pennsylvania had imposed on the right to abortion. Those included the mandatory provision to the mother of state-prescribed information regarding the gestational age of the fetus and the risks of abortion; a mandatory 24-hour waiting period; and a requirement for the approval of a least one parent in the case of minors. Pro-choice groups interpreted the *Planned Parenthood v. Casey* decision as a disastrous setback, a watering-down of what they had interpreted as a largely unqualified right (at least in the first trimester). In reality, what the Court did in *Casey* was to allow some restrictions on the right to abortion so long as they did not constitute an "undue burden" on the mother.

The *Casey* decision actually left *Roe v. Wade* in surprisingly strong shape. As the most searching and judicious historian of *Roe v. Wade*, David Garrow, has observed, *Casey* was decided by a 5–4 vote. The four justices in the minority opposed any restrictions whatsoever on the right to an abortion. Most significant, three of the five conservative justices in the majority specified in their opinion their basic commitment to *Roe v. Wade* and to the "right of a woman to choose to have an abortion" before fetal viability "without undue interference from the state." In effect, after more than a decade of fierce cultural combat, the Supreme Court remained committed to the essence of *Roe v. Wade* by the same 7–2 margin that had obtained in 1973. "Roe will never be overturned," concluded Garrow. "For the Court to consider reversing Roe and Casey [in the future] would be the equivalent of reversing Brown v. Board of education. Roe's weight in history is such that it's impregnable."[56]

Randall Terry and Operation Rescue proved far more vulnerable than *Roe v. Wade*. The civil disobedience offensive by Operation Rescue and similar anti-abortion groups in the 1980s coincided with a dramatic rise in actual violence against abortion providers and abortion clinics. The federal Bureau of Alcohol, Tobacco and Firearms investigated 164 major arson and bombing cases at clinics and doctors' offices between 1982 and 1995. The same period witnessed four abortion-related murders and eight attempted murders. Pro-choice activists and their supporters blamed Terry and Operation Rescue for creating a hostile climate that encouraged the increased violence. The criminal violence turned public opinion against aggressive and civilly disobedient protesters of the Operation Rescue type, even when they remained nonviolent in their activities.

Meanwhile, just breaking the law brought with it a host of serious consequences. Terry found himself under increasing legal and financial pressure, facing large fines and court judgments running into the hundreds of thousands of dollars. Confronted by prosecutors willing to apply the federal RICO anti-racketeering statute against him and his operation, Terry in 1990 closed down Operation Rescue's headquarters and moved the organization's financial operations underground.[57] Having spent considerable time in jail, including some months on a Georgia chain gang, still saddled by huge, outstanding monetary judgments against his person, unsuccessful in a political run for Congress in 1992, Terry in the mid-1990s remained committed to the culture war he believed still raged. The "power bases" of the culture—the media, arts, government, schools—were, he believed, still in the hands of "the humanists, the liberals, the hedonists, the child killers and the homosexuals," but he soldiered on. In a fundraising letter, he promised, "We will succeed in recapturing the power bases from their current tyrannical captors."[58] Operation Rescue was in tatters, but the culture war continued, as did the slow, uneven, and inexorable drift of American culture in new directions.

Chapter 8

COMBATING THE EVIL EMPIRE

A scant two months into the Reagan presidency, Reuters reported that a "high White House official" had in the course of an interview proclaimed that "détente is dead." The remark burst like a bomb, and the resultant outcry was immediate and anguished. The London *Observer*, alluding to a presumed heightened danger of nuclear war in the absence of a conciliatory superpower relationship, proclaimed that "only the vultures want détente to die."[1]

It quickly became known that the White House official in question was Richard Pipes, whose presence in the corridors of power spoke volumes about the direction of the new Reagan administration's foreign policy. Born a Jew in prewar Poland, Pipes had learned early that world affairs have real consequences. He came to the United States as a young refugee shortly after the outbreak of war in Europe, and learned American culture while attending small Muskingum College in rural central Ohio. He was from the outset struck by the confidence and trust in human goodness that he encountered, qualities in short supply in war-ravaged Europe. In 1943 he was drafted into the U.S. Army and assigned to a military language school to learn Russian, the first step down a path that would ultimately lead to a specialization in Russian history and a distinguished teaching career at Harvard.

For Pipes, the study of Russian history was a moral undertaking as well as an academic endeavor. He was profoundly affected by the Holocaust. "I felt and feel to this day," he reported in his memoirs, "that I have been spared not to waste my life on self-indulgence or self-aggrandizement but to spread a moral message by showing, using examples from history, how evil ideas lead to evil consequences."[2] In time, communism presented itself to him as precisely that sort of evil idea. "The more I learned about communism," he recalled, "the more I came to despise it."[3]

Pipes was smart, vain, and prickly, able to start an argument just looking in the mirror. But what made his White House appointment striking and controversial was not his personality but rather his vehement anti-communism and Cold War hawkishness. In the 1970s he had headed up the so-called Team B external audit of the Central Intelligence Agency's performance in assessing the threat posed by the Soviet Union. Cold War hardliners saw the agency as dangerously sanguine in its evaluation of both Soviet intentions and capabilities, and they prevailed upon President Gerald Ford and CIA director George Herbert Walker Bush to allow a small number of outside experts (the so-called Team B) to compare its assessment of agency performance with that of an in-house CIA evaluation team (Team A). Under Pipes's leadership, Team B reported that the CIA had "substantially misperceived the motivations behind Soviet strategic programs" and "tended consistently to underestimate their intensity, scope, and implicit threat."[4] The Team A–Team B episode generated much debate within the foreign policy establishment and made Pipes a star player among America's arch-cold warriors. Immediately on the heels of the Team B exercise, he joined the executive committee of the newly formed Committee on the Present Danger (CPD), a highly visible neoconservative group urging a firmer stance toward the Soviet Union. Ronald Reagan sat on the CPD's board of directors.

Pipes and his CPD colleagues took direct aim at two developments of the 1970s that were threatening to become part of the conventional wisdom of Western intellectuals and opinion-molding elites: the concept of convergence and the policy of détente. Convergence was the idea that the United States and the Soviet Union were in fact becoming increasingly similar over time, two highly bureaucratized and dangerously over-armed superpowers. The Soviet Union appeared to not a few Western intellectuals to be mellowing and losing its Stalinist rough edges even as the United States appeared less and less the genuine champion of freedom around the world, especially in the Third World, where Cold War pressures and other more dubious motives often led to alliances with unsavory, authoritarian (but anticommunist) regimes. The iconic image of convergence was that of the Cold War adversaries as two scorpions trapped in a bottle, both deadly, with no transcendent moral difference between them.

Détente was a policy that dated from the days of Richard Nixon's presidency. It emphasized accommodation and cooperation between the chief Cold War adversaries wherever possible. Some of its champions rallied to détente by way of the implicit logic of convergence—if the two sides truly were becoming more similar, it made sense to dwell more on their shared interests than on their vestigial differences. With its emphasis on accommodation and the reduction of superpower tensions wherever possible, détente also struck many as the only sane alternative in a world where a spiraling arms race threatened all humanity with the possibility of nuclear incineration.

To Pipes, convergence was a lie and détente a comforting formula for disaster, a policy that acquiesced in evil and lulled the West into a fatal complacency that an ever-aggressive Soviet Union was all too ready to exploit. Such views caused *Pravda* to describe him as a "wretched anti-Sovietist" who suffered from a "pathological hatred of the USSR and dense ignorance."[5] The *Washington Post* editorialized that Pipes represented "rank hysteria in scholarly garb."[6] Ignorant he was not, but his disdain for and distrust of the Soviet Union were indeed palpable. And Pipes's appointment as head of the Soviet desk in the incoming Reagan administration's National Security Council signaled that détente, if not dead, was in for some tough sailing.

UNDER NEW MANAGEMENT

The Reagan administration conveyed its determination to take a more aggressive approach to the Cold War in ways both small and large. In his first presidential press conference, Reagan noted, "So far, détente's been a one-way street the Soviet Union has used to pursue its own aims." Soviet leaders, he added gratuitously, were committed to the goal of world revolution and to that end "reserve unto themselves the right to commit any crime: to lie, to cheat."[7] Meeting with the new secretary of state, Alexander Haig, later that same day, Soviet ambassador Anatoly Dobrynin asked plaintively, "What is the purpose of all that? Why should he set such a tone for the new administration from the very beginning?" When Haig explained that the president had telephoned him immediately after making the remarks to explain that he had not meant to offend the Soviets but only to express his deep personal convictions, Dobrynin replied dryly that the clarification only made him feel worse.[8]

For Dobrynin, a diplomat who had represented the USSR in Washington since the days of Camelot, the indications that America was under new, more aggressive management were unmistakably clear. He himself felt a cool chill when he arrived to meet Haig at the State Department for the first time, attempting as had been his practice since the beginning of détente in the early 1970s to enter the premises via the secretary's private basement garage and personal elevator, only to be unceremoniously turned away and made to enter through the main public entrance used by the rest of Washington's diplomatic corps. When the incident was subsequently leaked to the press, Dobrynin interpreted the episode as "a staged political show."[9] Caspar Weinberger,

Reagan's hawkish secretary of defense, not long thereafter met Dobrynin at a Washington dinner party and explained: "People in Washington feel it is important that the Soviets and the world know that the U.S. has changed, and that we have, and will acquire, much greater strength as well as greater firmness and resolve during this Administration." "I assure you," the Russian replied, "that my country knows very well how much the U.S. has changed. I tell them, I am a good reporter."[10]

Reagan and his advisers believed that their new aggressiveness was a necessary response to a voracious Cold War adversary emboldened by America's woes and passivity over the previous decade. As Robert M. Gates, a senior career CIA official and the deputy director of intelligence in the 1980s, has observed, "By the fall 1980, the sense that the Soviets and their surrogates were 'on the march' around the world was palpable in Washington and elsewhere."[11] The ominous list of Communist advances included Angola, Ethiopia, Mozambique, Yemen, Cambodia, Nicaragua, Grenada, and Afghanistan. It was, Haig noted caustically (and somewhat unfairly), a state of affairs invited by "the Carter experiment in obsequiousness."[12] "The conjunction of Soviet ambition and a maturing Soviet global reach," the secretary of state argued, had created a dangerous "worldwide climate of uncertainty."[13]

Reagan was determined to resolve the uncertainty by confronting the Soviet Union directly—as his first national security adviser, Richard V. Allen, put it, "intentionally, deliberately, and in slow motion."[14] In acting assertively, the president sought to leave behind both the doctrine of détente, by actually rolling back the Soviet sphere of influence, and the doctrine of containment, by *initiating* challenges to the USSR rather than simply *responding* to Soviet actions. His plan, although perhaps that term implies more order and internal coherence that actually characterized his various inclinations, was simple. He wanted to rebuild America's military and economic strength, contest Soviet advances around the world, and increase pressure on the Soviet Union itself with the long-term goal of defeating Soviet Communism as a system. He also intended, when the opportunity presented itself, to negotiate with the Soviets from a position of strength in the pursuit of concrete American national interests, one of which he identified as actual arms reduction rather than the then-conventional goal of arms limitation.

Pipes and others worked to embody Reagan's forward-leaning preferences in stated policy. The end result was National Security Decision Directive (NSDD) 75, adopted formally in early 1983, which articulated U.S. policy toward the Soviet Union for the 1980s.[15] The final wording was straightforward, indeed blunt: "U.S. policy toward the Soviet Union will consist of three elements: external resistance to Soviet imperialism; internal pressure on the USSR to weaken the sources of Soviet imperialism; and negotiations to eliminate, on the basis of strict reciprocity, outstanding disagreements."[16] As Richard Allen has noted, NSDD 75 represented a fundamental reorientation of U.S. policy: "The objective was to find weak points in the Soviet structure, to aggravate the weaknesses, and to undermine the system."[17] Here truly was the defining characteristic of Reagan's new approach to the Cold War—he sought to win it.

REAGAN'S COLD WAR: THE MILITARY BUILDUP

At the heart of Reagan's foreign policy lay the rebuilding of America's military might. Secretary of Defense Caspar "Cap" Weinberger quickly proved to be a fierce advocate of U.S. rearmament. The framed quotation from his hero Winston Churchill that hung over Weinberger's Pentagon desk—"Never give in, never give in, never, never, never, never; in nothing great or small, large or petty, never give in"—conveyed fairly his energy and tenacity in battling for higher defense spending.[18] Defense spending had declined by over 20 percent (in real terms, adjusted for inflation) over the decade of the 1970s, but from 1981 to 1989 the Pentagon's yearly budget nearly doubled from $158 to $304 billion, as the Reagan administration spent an overall total of $2.7 trillion for defense. The results included the modernization of both strategic capability and conventional arms; by the mid-1980s the United States had deployed new Trident missile submarines and the new ten-warhead MX/Peacemaker ICBM, three thousand new combat aircraft, a six-hundred-ship Navy, and ten thousand new tanks.[19]

Without doubt, the two aspects of the defense buildup that had the greatest impact were those that also occasioned the greatest controversy: the deployment of the so-called Euromissiles and the development of the Strategic Defense Initiative (SDI), better known as Star Wars. The first proved so difficult that it almost sundered the NATO alliance; the second nearly scuttled arms negotiations between the superpowers and played a murky but crucial role in ending the Cold War on American terms.

The Euromissile controversy had its origins in the deployment by the Soviets beginning in 1977 of a new intermediate range ballistic missile, the formidable three-warhead SS-20, which targeted Western Europe (and would target South Korea and Japan when deployed in Asia in the early 1980s). Moscow's action spooked West German chancellor Helmut Schmidt, who feared that Europe would become vulnerable to Soviet blackmail unless the Western allies acted to redress the new imbalance. After much debate, NATO in 1979 agreed on a "dual-track" response: the United States would answer the Soviet SS-20 threat by preparing to deploy new Pershing II intermediate range ballistic missiles and ground-launched cruise missiles in 1983—first to West Germany, Britain, and Italy, and later to Belgium and the Netherlands—while simultaneously attempting to negotiate the limitation of all such "INF" (intermediate-range nuclear force) missiles on both sides. The Reagan administration inherited that commitment and integrated it into its own assertive defense posture. In November 1981 Reagan suggested going beyond limiting the number of INF missiles to actually eliminating the entire weapons category; he proposed a so-called "zero option," under which the United States would refrain from deploying its Euromissiles if the Soviets dismantled the intermediate-range ballistic missiles (the new SS-20s, as well as older SS-4s and SS-5s) they had already put in place. Negotiations on INF weapons between the Americans and Soviets began in Geneva.

To their dismay, however, Reagan and his advisers encountered a vigorous popular protest movement that gathered steam in both Western Europe and the United States, threatening to block U.S. Euromissile deployment and upset the delicate balance of NATO's dual-track approach. The Nuclear Freeze movement called on both superpowers to bring the nuclear arms race to a halt by freezing the production of new weapons on both sides. However, the movement came to direct most of its moral condemnation and political energy against the United States and those Western European governments that promised to accept the deployment of Euromissiles on their soil should the INF negotiations fail.

The Freeze movement quickly took on massive and international dimensions. In the fall of 1982 some three-quarters of a million demonstrators gathered in New York City's Central Park in the largest protest in the nation's history. One pro-freeze umbrella group, Citizens Against Nuclear War, claimed to speak for twenty-six organizations with a combined membership of some 18 million, including the American Jewish Congress, Friends of the Earth, and the National Education Association. Hollywood celebrities, including Ed Asner, Harry Belafonte, Meryl Streep, Martin Sheen, and Mike Farrell; pop music luminaries, such as Bruce Springsteen, Jackson Browne, and Bonnie Raitt; and leading Establishment figures including George F. Kennan, the intellectual father of the policy of containment, Georgetown University professor and future secretary of state Madeleine Albright, and William Colby, a former director of the Central Intelligence Agency, all publicly endorsed the freeze idea. In May 1983 the Democrat-controlled U.S. House of Representatives approved a freeze resolution by a 278–149 vote.[20]

The Freeze Movement worked both sides of the Atlantic. Several million demonstrators turned out in a series of protests in the major cities of West Germany, England, Holland, and Italy that helped make 1983 the year of the Euromissiles. The anti-nuclear crusade drew together an unlikely coalition of priests and professionals, pacifists and Reds, environmentalists and feminists, housewives and students, radicals and centrists, ideologues and idealists. Europeans in increasing numbers feared that the Reagan administration was not truly committed to the negotiation track and that deployment of U.S. Euromissiles to counter the Soviet SS-20s would simply increase the likelihood of a war that would obliterate their continent. The West German novelist Guenter Grass compared the deployment of Pershing missiles to the Nazi's Wannsee Conference that had planned the details of the Final Solution.[21]

Reagan attacked the Freeze during the 1982 elections, saying that it was "inspired by not the sincere, honest people who want peace, but by some who want the weakening of America and so are manipulating honest people and sincere people."[22] His concern was not entirely without foundation. Predictably, the Soviet Union did attempt to play on Western anxieties. "We had hoped" Dobrynin would later write, "that the popular movement against American missiles in Europe would make the United States and NATO drop the plan."[23] But the CIA, the FBI, and the House Select Committee on Intelligence all reported that while the Soviets were making a concerted effort, both overt and covert, to influence Western public opinion, the success of the Freeze could not be attributed wholly, or even substantially, to Soviet manipulation.[24] Clearly, the Freeze idea had a broad appeal of its own, over and beyond Soviet efforts to exploit the issue. The fact is that many in the West had come to see the arms race itself as a more dangerous threat than the Cold War adversary.

Reagan also argued his case on the merits, maintaining with considerable persuasiveness that the Freeze was a superficially attractive but substantively flawed idea. A halt at present levels would, he insisted, "preserve today's high, unequal and unstable levels of nuclear forces." It would, in effect, make permanent an American disadvantage in theater-range (INF) weapons and a possibly fatal American vulnerability in strategic (intercontinental) arms. To freeze nuclear weapons at present levels would "pull the rug out from under our negotiators in Geneva." The success of the Freeze Movement reflected the fact that Americans were in a hurry to address what they saw as the growing danger of the arms race. "In a negotiation, however, impatience can be a real handicap," Reagan cautioned. "If we appear to be divided—if the Soviets suspect that domestic, political pressure will undercut our position—they will dig in their heels. And that," observed the man who, though genuinely unassuming, took considerable pride in his own experience and skill as a negotiator, "can only delay an agreement and may destroy all hope for an agreement."[25]

Fear of an escalating arms race suffused the key American media event of 1983, the telecast by ABC of the made-for-TV movie *The Day After*, a fictional account of a nuclear attack on the American heartland. The subject was horrifically topical in the year of the Euromissiles, and ABC ginned up a massive publicity drive to build a huge audience—estimated at 100 million—during a so-called sweeps period when TV industry rating services determined viewership numbers that were then used to set future advertising rates.[26]

The Day After, telecast on a Sunday night in November, portrayed in graphic detail the obliteration of Kansas City, Missouri, and the lingering demise of the nearby university town of Lawrence, Kansas. The 128-minute film opened with normal Americans going through the everyday routines of life against a backdrop of barely intruding media reports concerning an obscure incident on the West German border that seems to be escalating in a vaguely familiar fashion. But life goes on—there are weddings to plan, football games to play. Until the chilling moment when a Kansas farm family hears a loud commotion and looks up from their peaceful preoccupations to see the launch of the American ICBMs based in silos on their property. For a moment that seems to unfold in excruciating slow motion, the characters and their audience together think through what they are witnessing and realize that the awesomely beautiful sensory experience they behold—the deafening, convulsive roar and achingly beautiful contrails set against a clear blue Midwestern sky—can only mean one thing: that Soviet missiles are on their way. They have become, through no action or volition of their own, the walking dead. In truth, the film was hardly an overall artistic success, but those few moments were haunting and spoke to the precise fears being mobilized by the Freeze Movement. A *Washington Post* poll taken the day after *The Day After* found that 83 percent of respondents supported the idea of a nuclear freeze.[27] But at the same time, polls also showed Reagan's job-approval rating on the rise to 65 percent.[28]

In the end, the administration stuck to the two-track policy and deployed the Euromissiles—Pershing II ballistic missiles and jet-powered, low-flying cruise missiles—on schedule beginning in the fall of 1983, when negotiations with the Soviets failed to bear fruit. The reelection of the conservative Margaret Thatcher in Britain, the electoral triumph of Helmut Kohl's conservative Christian Democratic Union in West Germany, and the tough pro-NATO stand of France's socialist president Francois Mitterrand together stiffened European resolve to stand by the deployment commitment. The Soviets responded, as they had earlier threatened, by breaking off the existing negotiations on both intermediate-range weapons and strategic weapons. But the Western alliance had stood firm in the face of Soviet threats and critical opposition at home. In time—weeks after Reagan's own landslide reelection victory in 1984—the Soviets came back to the negotiating table, and with the Euromissile deployment providing a powerful incentive to bargain, they ultimately agreed to an INF treaty built precisely on Reagan's zero-option.

A second highly controversial episode in Reagan's military buildup began with the president's surprise announcement in 1983 that the administration would undertake to develop a defensive shield to protect against ballistic missiles, widely acknowledged to be the most threatening strategic weapons of the day. Reagan called the project the Strategic Defense Initiative (SDI), but critics quickly dubbed it "Star Wars," a reference to the wildly popular 1970s George Lucas masterpiece of cinematic science fiction, a label too evocative ever to be dislodged. In truth, the project did have a science-fiction ring to it, and some critics have argued simplistically that Reagan got the idea for his impenetrable space shield from either a movie he starred in during his Hollywood days (*Murder in the Air*, a Warner Brothers "B" spy film in which Reagan appears as secret service agent Brass Bancroft, tasked with protecting a top-secret superweapon known as the "Inertia Projector," which can destroy enemy planes in the air) or one he had presumably seen later (Alfred Hitchcock's 1966 *Torn Curtain*, which features an anti-missile missile as a central plot device).[29]

The actual origins of SDI were more complex and prosaic. Reagan had come to question the doctrine of Mutually Assured Destruction (MAD) even before winning the presidency. He was repelled by the idea that peace in the nuclear age rested on the fact that no nation could protect itself from nuclear annihilation, and that the only choice in the case of a nuclear attack was to respond by utterly devastating the Cold War foe or by expiring with a pacifistic whimper. (Advocates of MAD believed it was the cruel discipline of the arrangement—the madness of MAD—that in fact kept the peace between the superpowers.) The 1972 ABM Treaty essentially institutionalized MAD by forbidding the deployment of new comprehensive defensive anti-ballistic missile systems. "It was," Reagan recalled in his memoirs, "like having two westerners standing in a saloon aiming their guns at each other's head—permanently. There had to be a better way."[30] A visit with his adviser Martin Anderson to the North American Aerospace Defense Command (NORAD) headquarters complex deep inside Cheyenne Mountain in Colorado in 1979 reinforced his doubts, and when Anderson subsequently prepared his "Policy Memorandum No. 3" for the Reagan presidential campaign, he included a call "to seriously reconsider" MAD and to "develop a protective missile system." Accordingly, the 1980 Republican platform pledged "vigorous research and development of an effective anti-ballistic missile system."[31]

Reagan was not alone in his determination to achieve a defensive breakthrough. Over the years a number of specialists had come to believe that new technological developments were opening up the possibility of an effective defense against a ballistic attack. Edward Teller, the so-called father of the hydrogen bomb, was among them. Teller had in 1967 arranged for Governor Reagan to visit the University of California's Lawrence Livermore Laboratory, where he was briefed for several hours on the ballistic missile defense research being conducted there, which involved the use of nuclear explosives to destroy incoming missiles. In the intervening period new work on lasers and other beam weapons and on kinetic energy devices, as well as progress in the development of computers and microprocessors, persuaded the bushy-browed Teller, the iconic Dr. Strangelove figure of postwar science, that the time was ripe for a defensive breakthrough.[32] Retired Lieutenant General Daniel O. Graham, a West Point graduate who had headed the Defense Intelligence Agency and been a member of Richard Pipes's B Team in the 1970s, reached a similar conclusion about the desirability of a missile defense system. In 1981 he put together a nonprofit missile-defense advocacy group called High Frontier, which in time was absorbed by the Heritage Foundation, the highly influential conservative think-tank. In Congress, Senator Malcolm Wallop, a Wyoming Republican, became a cheerleader for the cause. Reagan's presidential science adviser, Jay Keyworth, joined the chorus, as did a number of the president's longstanding friends and informal advisers from his kitchen cabinet.[33]

The Star Wars initiative was controversial both within the administration and outside. The *New York Times* editorialized that SDI was "a pipe dream, a projection of fantasy into policy."[34] George Ball, a veteran Democratic foreign policy expert, called it "one of the most irresponsible acts by any head of state in modern times."[35] Critics argued that the envisioned system could never work, would be too expensive, was not really necessary, and would itself destabilize the fragile balance of terror upon which world peace actually rested. The Soviets proclaimed to the world that SDI was an American attempt to expand the arms race into the very heavens. (In fact, the Soviets were heavily engaged in their own research in the area of missile defense, at work developing a variety of laser weapons and large beryllium mirrors, while actually deploying at Krasnoyarsk, in the interior of the USSR, a sophisticated, directional, phased-array radar system designed to track incoming missiles, in violation of the ABM Treaty.)[36]

SDI occasioned yet another rift between the conservatives and pragmatists around Reagan. The hardline secretary of defense, Weinberger, after some initial hesitation, became, in the words of his military aide General Colin Powell, "more Catholic than the pope on the subject of SDI."[37] Secretary of State George Shultz was deeply skeptical. He doubted the technical feasibility of the program and worried especially about SDI's implications for America's existing obligations under the ABM Treaty, for NATO relations, and for current arms control negotiations.[38] Presidential science adviser Keyworth recalls that at one meeting "Shultz called me a lunatic in front of the President and said the implication of this new initiative was that it would destroy the NATO alliance. It would not work . . . and was the idea of a blooming madman."[39]

Reagan was firmly committed to the project, however, and he personally pushed SDI into development. He was under no illusion that an anti-missile system was actually in the offing, and took care in announcing the initiative to point out that building a missile defense was "a formidable, technical task, one that might not be accomplished before the end of this century." Nor did he have a particular vision in mind. He claimed no technical expertise, writing in a personal letter at the time, "Frankly I have no idea what the nature of such a defense might be."[40] But he was adamant that the effort be made.

Once again, the president's optimism figured significantly in his decision. At a meeting of his national security advisers six months after the SDI speech, Reagan asked how the matter was progressing. Shultz continued to argue for proceeding very slowly so as not to disturb U.S. allies. "Gentlemen," Reagan intervened, "this reminds me of the optimist and the pessimist. I try to consider both sides. If I am a pessimist, and we don't go ahead and develop SDI you can be sure, as our intelligence estimates show us, the Soviets will. Furthermore, you can bet they won't offer to negotiate—they'll blackmail us to our knees. If you are an optimist, if there is any way you can give the American citizens hope that we can develop a ballistic missile defense of some significance, then we should pursue it. That happens to be a very gracious man's way of saying thank you, George, but here is the way we go."[41] And go SDI did, to the tune of $22 billion in federal funding during Reagan's presidency and roughly $50–60 billion by the end of the century, with no finished product clearly in sight.[42]

Shultz also viewed Reagan's optimism as a key to the SDI debate, but questioned whether such optimism was always a strength. "Ronald Reagan had visionary ideas," he later wrote insightfully: "In pursuing them, he displayed some of his strongest qualities: an ability to break through the entrenched thinking of the moment . . . [and] stand by his vision regardless of pressure, scorn, or setback." But, Shultz continued, "at the same time, he could fall prey to a serious weakness: a tendency to rely on his staff and friends to the point of accepting uncritically—even wishfully—advice that was sometimes amateurish and even irresponsible."[43]

Still, Star Wars was not simply a boondoggle for the defense establishment nor wholly without short-term payoff. In fact, SDI contributed significantly to Reagan's energized prosecution of the Cold War. It was, as Robert Gates has argued, "a Soviet nightmare come to life."[44] Nothing Reagan did so disconcerted the Soviets. The high-level Soviet interpreter who later worked for premier Mikhail Gorbachev and foreign minister Eduard Shevardnadze characterized the reaction of the Soviet leadership as "highly emotional . . . in a tone approaching hysteria."[45]

Gorbachev wrote in his memoirs, "Reagan's advocacy of the Strategic Defense Initiative struck me as bizarre. Was it science fiction, a trick to make the Soviet Union more forthcoming, or merely a crude attempt to lull us in order to carry out the mad enterprise—the creation of a shield which would allow a first strike without fear of retaliation."[46] Many Soviet experts believed that a truly impenetrable missile defense was an impossibility. But the Soviet leadership had to take into account the fact that even an only partially successful SDI would call into question their ability to launch a crushingly decisive first strike (the Americans' great fear) or their capacity to mount a sufficiently destructive retaliatory attack after an American first strike (Gorbachev's "mad enterprise" fear). In this regard, SDI presented a challenge no responsible Soviet leader could dismiss.

To compete with the United States in a new arms race to build a missile shield was hardly an inviting option. The West was far ahead of the USSR in the technological areas—especially computer hardware and software, micro-processors, and communications—necessary for such a contest, and the Soviet command economy simply lacked the nimbleness required for a successful shift from an Industrial Age to an Information Age economic regime. More-over, the Soviet economy was already badly distended and groaning under the burden of its existing Cold War military expenditures; Mikhail Gorbachev in his memoirs complained of "the insatiable Moloch of the military-industrial complex." Nevertheless, the Soviets tried to match the American buildup, boosting defense spending in 1983 to about 55 percent over the 1980 level and increasing such expenditures by another 45 percent under Gorbachev after 1985. The effort paid off in terms of military capability but significantly has-tened the deterioration of the Soviet economy into a basket case.[47]

Perhaps the greatest impact of SDI was psychological. By badly shaking Soviet self-confidence, it worked to reverse the perceptual momentum of the Cold War, which to many observers had been running against the United States since Vietnam. SDI forced the Soviet leadership to confront more starkly than otherwise would have been the case the sclerosis afflicting Soviet society. The KGB general Nikolai Leonov subsequently observed that SDI "played a power-ful psychological role. And of course it underlined still more our technological backwardness. It underlined the need for an immediate review of our place in world technological progress."[48]

Given the practical problems it presented to Moscow and the psychological message it conveyed, it is a mistake to view Star Wars as simply the delusion of an aging, not too bright president who had seen, or starred in, one science-fiction movie too many. Certainly the Soviet Union did not view it that way. Reagan had a point when wrote to a friend in 1985, "I wonder why some of our own carping critics who claim SDI is an impractical wasted effort don't ask themselves, if it's no good how come the Russians are so upset about it?"[49] In the Alice-in-Wonderland environment of the Cold War, which interwove perceptions and realities so tightly that it was sometimes hard to distinguish the one from the other, even a seemingly impractical and wasteful weapon could prove exceedingly potent.

REAGAN'S COLD WAR: FIGHTING WORDS

Less tangible but no less important than Reagan's military buildup was his confrontation with the Soviet Union in the area known as "public diploma-cy." The president realized intuitively that the Cold War was not just a tradi-tional, geopolitical, nation-state rivalry, but also a battle between competing visions regarding how best to organize human activity and manage human society. And he was determined to put the Soviets on the defensive in that war of ideas.

The chief weapon at Reagan's disposal was his own bully pulpit. In a series of widely heralded speeches, he attempted to rock the Soviets back on their heels by attacking the legitimacy and morality of Communism and by refuting the claim that history and contemporary world currents were running in its favor. "The West will not contain Communism," he told a commencement crowd at Notre Dame in 1981, "it will transcend communism. We will not bother to renounce it, we'll dismiss it as a bizarre chapter in human history whose last pages are even now being written." Addressing the British Parliament the next year, he predicted that Soviet Communism would end up on "the ash heap of history," a pointed reformulation of Trotsky's prediction for Bolshevism's democratic opponents. Most famously and controversially, Reagan in March 1983 told the annual convention of the National Association of Evangelicals that the USSR was an "evil empire" and "the focus of evil in the modern world."[50] Critics were scandalized by the president's "primitive and dangerous" language. "What must Soviet leaders think?" asked Anthony Lewis of the *New York Times* after the evil empire speech: "However one detests their system, the world's survival depends on mutual restraint."[51] But even Dobrynin admitted, "The Soviet leadership was at times extremely thin-skinned, forgetting that they also engaged in the same kind of propaganda against the United States from time to time." Reagan's chief offense seemed to be that, as the Soviet ambassador later noted, "he was giving . . . [Soviet leaders] a dose of their own medicine."[52]

Reagan also sought to ensure that his message reached a worldwide audience. "We are going forward with all kinds of new plans using Voice of America — Radio Free Europe, etc.," he wrote to a correspondent early in his first term. "We are determined to *stop* losing the propaganda war."[53] In short order, the administration mobilized the nation's overseas broadcasting apparatus for action on the Cold War's front lines. The president installed his close friend and confidante Charles Z. Wick as director of the United States Information Agency and increased the funding for the Voice of America, which broadcast around the globe, and Radio Free Europe and Radio Liberty, which targeted audiences in Eastern Europe and the USSR respectively.

The American propaganda assault enjoyed considerable success. In economic terms, it forced the Soviets to divert scarce resources to jam incoming broadcasts; they spent an estimated $1 billion per year, more than twice the amount the United States spent on the Voice of America and Radio Free Europe-Radio Liberty combined, in a massive but never wholly effective effort to drown out American broadcasting.[54] Moreover, the administration's message had an important psychological impact. The Sovietologist Seweryn Bialer reported on the basis of his three visits to Moscow in 1983–84 that "Reagan's rhetoric has badly shaken the self-esteem and patriotic pride of the Soviet political elites. The administration's self-righteous moralistic tone, its reduction of Soviet achievements to crimes by international outlaws from an 'evil

empire'—such language stunned and humiliated the Soviet leaders . . .
[who] believe that President Reagan is determined to deny the Soviet Union
nothing less than its legitimacy and status as a global power . . . [which] they
thought had been conceded once and for all by Reagan's predecessors."[55] No
doubt the report horrified the readership of the left-leaning *New York Review
of Books*, where it appeared, but the psychological impact it described was
precisely what Reagan had intended.

REAGAN'S COLD WAR: THE ECONOMIC DIMENSION

The least known aspect of Reagan's Cold War offensive occurred in the realm
of economics. The president was personally convinced that, contrary to the conventional wisdom of Western liberals, the Soviet economy was "held together
with baling wire; it was a basket case."[56] He believed that pressure could speed
up the inevitable economic collapse of the entire Eastern bloc. The incoming
administration first took an opportunistic detour to end the embargo President
Jimmy Carter had placed on American grain sales to the USSR as punishment
for the Soviet invasion of Afghanistan, a move dictated by a desire to cement the
political allegiance of farmers and help out the nation's own ailing economy
at the same time. But thereafter ensued what can be fairly summarized as an
elaborate campaign of economic warfare against the Soviet Union.

The definitive statement of U.S. policy toward the USSR, NSDD-75, in early
1983 described the administration's economic warfare goals as the prevention of
the transfer of militarily useful technology; the avoidance of any subsidy to the
Soviet economy that might ease "the burden of Soviet resource allocation decisions" or "dilute pressures for structural change in the Soviet system"; and the reduction of Soviet economic leverage on Western countries.[57] In layman's terms,
Reagan wanted to squeeze the Soviet Union economically until it squeaked.

Energy constituted a major field of contention in Reagan's economic offensive. In 1980 the Soviets announced that they would build the 3,600-mile long,
twin-stranded Yamal pipeline to ship natural gas from Siberia to hook into the
Western European energy system. The pipeline would be constructed largely
with Western expertise and financing at below-market rates. The nations of Western Europe supported the enterprise, seeing in the pipeline project a source of
both new jobs at a time of troublesome high unemployment and affordable energy. But Washington worried that the pipeline, when completed, would earn
the Soviets an additional $10–12 billion per year in hard currency, which they
badly needed in order to buy the Western high technology required to keep
them economically and militarily competitive. Equally ominous in American
eyes, upon completion of the pipeline Western Europe would depend on the
USSR for fully 60 percent of its total gas supplies, leaving the allies vulnerable
to Soviet economic pressure and political manipulation.[58]

After much fruitless discussion with the Europeans, the administration touched off a firestorm of controversy in late 1981 when it forbade American firms from direct participation in the Yamal pipeline project. A domestic political outcry was predictable, given the costs the prohibition imposed on some sixty U.S. companies: General Electric lost $175 million in orders, Caterpillar Tractor $90 million in sales of pipe-laying equipment.[59] The issue heated up further when the White House six months later extended its prohibition to include the European subsidiaries of American companies and foreign firms using U.S. licensed technology. European leaders, including Reagan's personal friend and ally British Prime Minister Margaret Thatcher, complained that the American actions invalidated existing legal contracts and arrogantly imposed U.S. views, law, and policy on the citizens and firms of other sovereign nations.

In the end the administration surrendered to European pressure—the allies' complaints had considerable merit—and terminated the pipeline sanctions. Its actions had failed to foil the Yamal pipeline project completely, but did increase its cost considerably, delay its completion by two years, and reduce it to a single-strand operation (the second strand of the Yamal pipeline was not completed until 1999, a full ten years late). More important, as part of the agreement to end the pipeline sanctions, Washington secured a commitment from the NATO allies to take a more rigorous approach to trade relations with the USSR. They promised to explore alternative Western energy sources, strengthen controls on technology transfer, and monitor financial dealings with an eye toward increasing the interest the Soviets paid for Western loans. Although it provoked withering criticism at home and abroad, the pipeline episode occasioned a significant procedural advance in Reagan's economic campaign.

Washington meanwhile continued to pursue the matter of Soviet energy sales on an even larger playing field. The sale of Soviet petroleum continued to be Moscow's major source of hard currency. Throughout the early 1980s the administration, with Weinberger and CIA Director William Casey taking the lead, lobbied Saudi Arabia, the world's largest oil producer, to hike its production in order to bring down the price of oil on the world market. To gain favor and influence for both their economic and geopolitical preferences, the Americans kept up a steady flow of advanced weaponry to Saudi Arabia's ruling House of Fahd, including sophisticated airborne warning and control (AWACS) aircraft capable of monitoring and directing air battles over vast areas in real time, often in the face of Israeli complaints and congressional opposition. "One of the reasons we were selling the Saudis all those arms was to get lower oil prices," Weinberger subsequently recalled.[60]

In 1985 the Saudis raised their daily oil output from less than 2 million barrels to nearly 9. The price of crude on the world market consequently dropped from $30 a barrel to $12. To be sure, the major benefit of this striking change in the cost of energy was its salutary impact on the domestic U.S. economy.

It also, however, represented a victory in an important skirmish in Reagan's offensive—analysts estimated that the Soviets forfeited between $500 million and $1 billion in hard currency revenues for every $1 drop in the world price of oil, thus totaling some $10 billion in annual hard currency losses.[61] Given its reliance on Western technology that required hard currency for purchase, the blow to the Soviet economy was severe.

A final front in the economic Cold War was the stuff of spy novels and now-it-can-be-told CIA revelations. The Soviet KGB Technology Directorate had since the 1970s been conducting an elaborate covert operation—designated Line X, which by 1975 was running at least seventy-seven secret agents and relying on another forty-two trustworthy contacts—to purchase under false pretenses or steal much-needed Western technology. At the Ottawa "G-7" economic summit held in the summer of 1981, French president Francois Mitterand informed Reagan that French intelligence had a spy, codenamed Farewell, inside the KGB and had obtained from him what they labeled the Farewell Dossier, which included Line X's shopping list for Western technology and lists of working agents and contacts.

Rather than immediately arresting the Soviet operatives, U.S. intelligence decided to use the information in the Farewell Dossier for a campaign of dirty tricks, supplying Line X with faulty equipment and disinformation. For example, with the aid of Texas Instruments' top management, the CIA provided Line X with a computer chip-testing machine that was modified to perform as advertised for long enough to allay any Soviet suspicions and then start salting its output with defective chips. Subtly altered designs for stealth technology and missile defense were passed along in the hope of leading Soviet scientists astray, wasting both time and treasure. Most spectacularly, U.S. intelligence provided the Soviets with computer control equipment for operating pipelines that ran software altered to create pressures far in excess of design specifications for welds and joints. In June 1982 such equipment caused a massive explosion in Siberia, so large (estimated to be the equivalent of 3 kilotons of high explosives) that U.S. satellites picked it up and Western analysts first thought it to be a nuclear blast. The next year Farewell was caught and executed in Moscow, but the damage done did not stop with his demise. Casey then used the names in the Farewell Dossier to roll up the Line X operation. The doubt and suspicion the U.S. campaign of economic dirty tricks necessarily engendered about all of the USSR's technology imports lingered for years.[62]

REAGAN'S COLD WAR: GEOPOLITICS

Reagan's determination to win the Cold War caused the United States to combat Communist influence everywhere in the 1980s, even in areas long under Soviet control and in parts of the world where U.S. interests were only marginally involved. The strategy represented a turn away from the doctrine of containment that had guided earlier U.S. Cold War policy and that had in effect conceded Soviet domination of Eastern Europe as a fait accompli. In its approach to events in Poland, the administration proved willing to contest Communism's grip even within the existing Soviet empire.

The issue of Poland, whether it would enjoy truly free elections and a democratic future or simply be absorbed into an emergent Soviet empire, had in 1945 been the proximate cause of the Cold War. In 1981, the incoming Reagan administration found Poland once again on the Cold War agenda. The Polish Solidarity movement, part labor union and part indigenous anticommunist political protest, was challenging the ruling Communist regime by demanding labor reforms and greater civil rights, and was in the process raising fears of a Soviet invasion. A crackdown did come in late 1981, but not directly at the hands of the USSR. Instead, Poland's communist government acted on its own to impose martial law and arrest Solidarity's leaders, including the charismatic Lech Walsea, an electrician from the Lenin Shipyard in Gdansk who had become the nation's leading political dissident.

The administration responded by imposing economic sanctions against both Poland and the USSR. The sanctions had real bite, but equally significant was the endorsement of the Solidarity movement they represented. To support Solidarity was to contest the very legitimacy of the Soviet bloc. In a secret memo, Robert Gates of the CIA observed at the time, "I believe it is not going too far to say that the successful implantation of pluralism in Poland would represent the beginning of the end of Soviet-style totalitarianism in Eastern Europe, with extraordinary implications for all Europe and for the USSR itself."[63]

The struggle to keep Solidarity alive succeeded. Cooperating with Pope John Paul II, Poland's spiritual leader in absentia, and the Vatican as well as with Western trade unions, the United States paid for and smuggled into Poland the accouterments of a modern political organizing campaign: fax machines, printing presses, radio transmitters, telephones, shortwave sets, video cameras, photocopiers, telex machines, and computers. The administration continued economic sanctions into 1987, easing them only after Warsaw freed its political prisoners, allowed Solidarity to exist without interference from the state, and agreed to enter into discussions with the Catholic Church. In 1989 Polish authorities finally legalized Solidarity and in 1990 the first free elections in over half a century made Lech Walesa the president of Poland. "This," Caspar Weinberger has written, "was the beginning of the end of Soviet-dominated Eastern Europe."[64]

If the administration's approach was a clear success in Poland, it proved more problematic in nature and uneven in result when transferred to the Cold War battlefields of the Third World. Washington's policy for the Third World—the relatively underdeveloped areas of Latin America, Africa, and Asia that stood outside the recognizable camps of the superpowers—came to be known as the Reagan Doctrine, a label supplied not by policymakers but by the journalist Charles Krauthammer.[65] In actuality, Krauthammer supplied, retrospectively, the name for a pattern of foreign policy initiatives that had manifested itself, slowly but discernibly, over the course of the Reagan presidency. The essence of the Reagan Doctrine was that the United States would support "freedom fighters" (a word choice that reflected the administration's genuine talent for public relations) anywhere on the periphery of the Soviet Empire who were attempting to resist or challenge Communist domination.

The new theme of U.S. foreign policy was, Krauthammer asserted, "democratic militance." Reagan fleshed out the concept in an important speech to the Irish Parliament in 1984. The United States, he said, offered "a politics of hope, a forward strategy for freedom." Looking around the globe, one saw "human freedom under God . . . on the march everywhere in the world. All across the world today—in the shipyards of Gdansk, the hills of Nicaragua, the rice paddies of Kampuchea, the mountains of Afghanistan—the cry again is liberty."[66] And he reiterated the point in his 1985 state of the union message, declaring, "We must not break faith with those who are risking their lives—on every continent, from Afghanistan to Nicaragua—to defy Soviet-supported aggression and secure rights which have been ours since birth." "How can we as a country," Secretary of State Shultz asked an audience several weeks later, "say to a young Afghan, Nicaraguan, or Cambodian: 'Learn to live with oppression; only those of us who already have freedom deserve to pass it on to our children.'"[67]

As critics at the time and since have noted, Reagan's avowed commitment to freedom was circumscribed. The litany that ran from Gdansk through Nicaragua and Kampuchea to Afghanistan passed over a host of other places where freedom and liberty were imperiled by noncommunist authoritarian regimes. The Reagan Doctrine was not a policy defined by abstract and open-ended principle (in the fashion of Jimmy Carter's pursuit of human rights), but rather one in which freedom was viewed instrumentally, as a weapon as well as a goal, and always in the context of the Cold War. In this regard, the administration acted on the insight of its U.N. representative, the redoubtable Jeane Kirkpatrick, who had first won Reagan's attention in 1979 with a much-discussed article in Commentary that drew a crucial distinction between authoritarian regimes of the right and totalitarian regimes of the left—the former offered at least the distant possibility of evolutionary reform, whereas the latter had to be resisted and destroyed in order for freedom to have any chance whatsoever. (Although Kirkpatrick's insight was highly controversial and has remained so, one must note that while only roughly one-third of the people of Latin America lived under civilian democratic rule before 1980, by the end of Reagan's second term approximately 90 percent did. At the start of a new century, Washington would point out that every government in Latin America, with the exception of Cuba, had been democratically elected, although that fact unfortunately did not always guarantee the liberties and legal protections typically associated with life in Western industrial democracies.)[68]

The implementation of the Reagan Doctrine was limited in a second significant regard as well. Despite his image among critics at home and abroad as a shoot-from-the-hip cowboy, Reagan was loath to express the new democratic militance by means of direct, large-scale American military intervention, except in those cases where the United States was certain to prevail with ease or where absolutely vital U.S. interests were at stake. As a consequence, the doctrine was typically implemented in an indirect fashion, through the encouragement, funding, and arming of indigenous resistance forces. Indirection had the virtue of minimizing the doctrine's cost in blood and treasure, but the administration would learn the hard way that the exercise of the Reagan Doctrine could sometimes entail very high political costs and bring with it unintended consequences of considerable magnitude.

The premium on indirection meant that the CIA often played a central role in implementing the Reagan Doctrine. CIA director William Casey was precisely where he wanted to be—everywhere and at the center of things—and he was hyperactive on all fronts. A senior CIA official at the time has recalled: "Push. Push. Push. Casey never stopped coming up with ideas—or forwarding those of others—for waging the war against the Soviets more broadly, more aggressively, and more effectively. From New Caledonia to Suriname, from Afghanistan to Nicaragua, from the Sahara to Cambodia, no report of Soviet, Cuban, Libyan, or Vietnamese activity—no matter how insignificant—escaped his notice and his demands that CIA counter it."[69]

The administration pushed increasingly hard in Afghanistan. After invading that neighboring country in 1979, the Soviets found themselves tied down in a protracted struggle against a crude but formidable guerrilla foe known as the mujahidin, who were inspired by both a desire to oust the Soviets and their own fundamentalist Islamic faith. But it was difficult to imagine that the Afghans, armed with bolt-action rifles, could prevail against the 120,000 troops, armor, and helicopter gunships of the USSR's Fortieth Army. In his last year in office, Carter used the CIA to funnel support to the Afghan resistance, and Reagan, with strong bipartisan support in Congress, slowly built on that effort. By mid-1981, the United States had provided more than $100 million to the Afghans and had recruited China, Saudi Arabia, Pakistan, and Egypt into an anti-Soviet coalition to help sustain the mujahidin. The Americans and Saudis served as the primary financial backers while the Chinese became the chief supplier of Soviet-style arms to the guerrillas.

When the struggle of the Afghan resistance dragged on into the mid-1980s, some commentators expressed skepticism that the Soviets could ever be defeated in a contest so close to home. In January 1985, the journalist Richard Cohen wrote in the *Washington Post* that the United States was "covertly supplying arms to guerrillas who don't stand the slightest chance of winning." "Afghanistan," he continued, "is not the Soviet version of Vietnam."[70] But two months later the Reagan administration dramatically escalated its support for the mujahidin and made it into precisely that.

In March 1985 Reagan signed NSDD-166, which called for a further ratcheting up of the American effort in Afghanistan. Funding doubled—Washington sent roughly $2 billion in aid and weaponry to the Afghan resistance in the 1980s—and the United States transformed the war by providing sophisticated and deadly new equipment to the mujahidin. After the approval of NSDD-166 the Americans furnished delayed timing devices for explosives, long-range sniper rifles, targeting devices for mortars that were linked to a U.S. Navy satellite, and wire-guided anti-tank missiles. Most important, the administration delivered deadly accurate Stinger shoulder-fired surface-to-air missiles, which broke the hold of Soviet air power, especially the highly effective helicopter gunships, in the conflict (it was reported that 340 Stingers were actually fired during the war, accounting for 269 Soviet aircraft downed). The CIA also supplied the Afghan resistance with satellite reconnaissance data and intercepts of Soviet communications.[71]

In the end, the increased aid, which constituted the largest covert operation in U.S. history, together with the staying power of the mujahidin turned the war around. After the loss of an estimated fifteen thousand Soviet dead and the expenditure of more than $100 billion, Moscow announced in February 1988 that they would withdraw from Afghanistan over the course of the next year, and they were true to their word.[72] On February 15, 1989, Lt. General Boris V. Gromov, the commander of the Soviet Fortieth Army, strode alone across a bridge over the Amu Darya river, the last Soviet soldier to leave Afghanistan. The Soviets left behind a client communist regime that fought on against the mujahidin, but in 1992 the Afghan resistance took Kabul and Afghanistan's communist experience finally came to an end (with an overall toll of nearly 1 million Afghan dead and one-third of all Afghan villages destroyed.)[73] Washington's Cold War campaign against Soviet adventurism in Afghanistan had achieved its fundamental purpose.

If the administration enjoyed broad-based support for the application of the Reagan Doctrine in far-off Afghanistan, the opposite was true of its efforts in Latin America. Reagan himself admitted that one of his greatest frustrations as president was his "inability to communicate to the American people and to Congress the seriousness of the threat we faced in Central America."[74] The administration's concern centered on Nicaragua, El Salvador, and the tiny island nation of Grenada. Reagan believed that all were threatened by Cuban subversion, backed ultimately by the USSR.

The disquiet regarding Nicaragua dated back to the Carter presidency. In July 1979 an uprising engineered by a broad coalition spearheaded by the rebel group known as the Sandinistas toppled the dictatorship of Anastasio Somoza Debayle. The Carter administration had contributed to the overthrow of Somoza by cutting off U.S. aid to the brutal dictator, but Washington soon began to worry about the leftist leanings of the new Nicaraguan regime. The most radical elements of the Sandinista movement quickly consolidated their power by marginalizing the bourgeois liberals who had fought with them against Somoza. As Humberto Ortega, who would become the Sandinista defense minister, later recalled, "We radicalized our model to look more like Cuba. . . . We wanted to copy in a mechanical way the model that we knew—which was Cuba—and we identified ourselves with it."[75]

Publicly, the Carter administration attempted to nudge the Sandinista regime in the direction of moderation by offering U.S. friendship and economic aid ($120 million from 1979–81), in effect hoping to create a self-fulfilling prophecy. But at the same time Washington confronted the emergent reality on the ground. The new Sandinista government canceled elections, welcomed thousands of Cuban advisers, and signed friendship agreements and arms deals with the USSR and other Warsaw Pact nations. In late July 1979 Carter signed a presidential intelligence finding (a statement required by law in which the president identifies the compelling national security reasons for covert action by the CIA) authorizing efforts to expose the nature of the new Nicaraguan government and the Cuban role in the Sandinista uprising, and in November 1979 he signed another finding authorizing non-lethal CIA actions to counter Cuban and Soviet activities throughout Latin America.[76] On the last weekend of his presidency, Carter directed his ambassador in Managua to tell the Sandinistas that the administration was temporarily suspending all U.S. aid (although the administration did not announce the suspension publicly). In ways not always recognized at the time or later, the Carter administration's growing alarm laid a foundation for U.S. policy and actions in Latin America in the 1980s.

Reagan built on Carter's foundation and at first attempted to deal with the Sandinistas in a similar fashion, albeit using less carrot and more stick. The administration opened negotiations with the Nicaraguan government, but after several fruitless months announced that Carter's temporary suspension of aid would be made permanent. As the Sandinista government assumed an openly radical character, it was the fears, not the hopes, of U.S. policymakers that were realized. Nicaraguan defense minister Humberto Ortega observed in August 1981: "Our revolution has a profoundly anti-imperialistic character, profoundly revolutionary, profoundly classist; we are anti-Yankee, we are against the bourgeoisie . . . we are guided by the scientific doctrine of the revolution, by Marxism-Leninism."[77] Reagan and his advisers saw in such remarks little grounds for optimism regarding political liberties, the institution of private property, free elections, or the emergence of a pluralistic political system. Nicaragua appeared to them a "lost" cause, but one, they reasoned politically, that had slipped away on Carter's watch. Reagan's chief concern in 1981 became the fact—disputed by critics at the time but subsequently well established—that the Sandinistas were trying to export their revolution to neighboring El Salvador by supplying arms to left-wing rebels there.

The Reagan administration saw the political situation in El Salvador, the tiniest of the Latin American states, as salvageable, and sought there to reverse what they saw as a rising tide of communist influence that threatened to envelop the entire region, perhaps even touching Mexico and the U.S. border if left unchecked. The administration increased its aid to El Salvador—a small number of military advisers and large amounts of military and economic assistance, conditioned by Congress on carefully monitored progress in the area of human rights—and supported the centrist Jose Napoleon Duarte, a genuine democrat who was walking a difficult line between murderous right-wing military death squads and similarly brutal left-wing guerrillas intent on overthrowing the government. In the final months of 1981 Reagan authorized the CIA to conduct paramilitary operations against Nicaragua, using forces that soon came to be known as the Contras, with the express purpose of disrupting the flow of arms from the Sandinistas to El Salvador. The situation in El Salvador gradually stabilized with Duarte's 1984 victory in a free election validated by international observers, but by then the Contras had taken on a life of their own and, with the support of the Reagan administration, continued their struggle to overthrow the Nicaraguan government.

The Contras (short for counter-revolutionaries) soon became the focus of U.S. efforts in the region and of the controversy surrounding U.S. policy. The Contras were a mixed bag from the beginning. They included former Somoza national guardsmen, a particularly thuggish lot; various anti-Somoza fighters who had turned against the Sandinistas (the MILPAS); Miskito Indians and black Creoles from Nicaragua's Atlantic Coast region, who had suffered the wrath of a Sandinista regime intent on forcing them into allegiance to the central government in Managua; large numbers of Indian peasants from the north-central highlands of Nicaragua, whose opposition to the Sandinistas continued a thousand-year-old struggle against subjugation by outsiders; and in time a number of prominent disillusioned former Sandinistas, including Eden Pastora (a military hero of the overthrow of Somoza, known internationally as "Comandante Zero"), Alfonso Robelo (a member of the original Sandinista ruling junta), and Arturo Cruz, who had served as the Sandinista ambassador to the United States.[78]

The controversy that raged around the Contras for the remainder of the 1980s was both ideological and partisan, and it ran bitter and deep. To the administration the Contras were freedom fighters who breathed life and meaning into the inchoate Reagan Doctrine. To critics, including many Democrats in Congress, they were they were the catspaws of a new Yankee imperialism, acting out, as one activist opponent put it, "the obscene arrogance and thoughtlessness of U.S, policy."[79] To Reagan, the immediate problem in Central America was the insistence of the USSR and Cuba on sponsoring revolutionary movements that meant to transform the region by force of arms; his critics focused on the indigenous poverty and oppression that bred discontent and despair and made political turmoil inevitable. Reagan feared the historical ghost of appeasement, his critics the historical ghost of Vietnam.

In Congress, criticism of the administration's actions in Central America grew stronger with time, in part because of the administration's own miscues. In the judgment of Robert Gates, Casey's deputy at the CIA, "too many associated with the Central American effort, both in and out of CIA, were zealots."[80] And on the matter of Central America, Gates asserts, Casey was the truest of true believers, pushing the CIA harder and farther regarding Nicaragua than many of the agency's own professionals wanted to go. In 1983 the CIA used fast cigarette boats of the kind made familiar by the hit TV series *Miami Vice* to mine several Nicaraguan ports. The mines themselves, so-called limpet mines, were designed to do a minimum of damage with a maximum of hoopla; the intent was not to sink vessels but to cause the sort of uproar that would force insurers to raise rates and scare off merchant shipping bringing in supplies for the Sandinista regime. A Soviet vessel was among the ships damaged. When Congress found out that the operation had been a CIA affair, all hell broke loose. The resulting firestorm of criticism brought widespread opprobrium down on the intelligence agency and turned influential senators such as Daniel Patrick Moynihan (a Democrat from New York) and Barry Goldwater (an Arizona Republican) into outright foes of the administration's Central America covert war. A year later, the revelation of a CIA manual on psychological warfare prepared for Contra use by a low-level contract employee, which spoke of "neutralizing" officials and the uses of terror and blackmail, created yet another public relations nightmare.

From the administration's perspective, there were also actions on the opposition side that contributed to the volatility of the Central America debate. In 1984 ten prominent House Democrats, including the majority leader, sent a letter to Nicaragua's president Daniel Ortega ("Dear Comandante") commending the Sandinistas for moving toward open elections and greater political rights and counseling that further movement in that direction would frustrate "those responsible for supporting violence against your government . . . and for obstructing serious negotiations." Republicans, not unfairly, interpreted the latter characterization as referring to the House members' own government, and saw in the letter both a gratuitous slur and a questionable interference with the executive branch's constitutionally mandated conduct of the nation's foreign policy.[81]

As a result of both administration missteps and growing doubt about the essential wisdom and righteousness of the Contra policy, Congress passed a series of three so-called Boland amendments (named for the chair of the House Intelligence Committee, Edward Boland, a Democrat from Massachusetts) over the period 1982–1984. Those loosely worded directives at first limited and qualified aid to the Contras and finally cut it off entirely in 1984. Congress then reversed itself once again to approve humanitarian aid to the Contras, lest they be left high and dry after doing America's bidding (in the manner of the anti-Communists in South Vietnam and Cambodia). Colin Powell, at the time deputy assistant to the president for national security affairs, told Congress, "We're talking about whether men who placed their trust in the United States are going to live or be left to die."[82] By the mid-1980s the Contra war was limping along, with even its champions despairing of success. Some of Reagan's more fire-breathing supporters called for decisive, perhaps direct, American intervention to save the day, but Reagan, although he identified emotionally and ideologically with the Contras, was realistic enough to see that as a formula for irretrievable disaster. In 1988 the president told his chief of staff Kenneth Duberstein, "Those sonsofbitches won't be happy until we have 25,000 troops in Managua, and I'm not going to do it."[83]

On the ground in Nicaragua things looked somewhat different, however. The Contra war sapped the strength of the Sandinista regime and that, together with a drastic winding down of communist support as the Soviet empire itself imploded, helped induce the Sandinistas at the end of the 1980s to agree, under a peace plan cobbled together by Costa Rica's president Oscar Arias, to relatively free elections in return for an end to U.S. encouragement of the Contras' twilight struggle. In 1990, the Sandinistas' political gamble came a cropper. Although the administration's critics, such as the left-leaning *Nation* magazine, after years of criticizing U.S. Central American policy, claimed that "the Sandinistas have no credible opposition," a right-center coalition headed by Violeta Chamorro upended Daniel Ortega in a landslide (the official results held the margin to be 55–41 percent) and made Nicaragua into a noncommunist, albeit struggling, democracy.[84] In the election's aftermath, the Mexican writer Octavio Paz observed, "The Nicaraguan election has dealt the all-but-final blow to Marxist-Leninist revolution as an alternative in this hemisphere."[85] The Nicaraguan experience had not been pretty from any angle and had been extremely costly to the administration in a myriad of ways, but in the end Reagan's hope for Nicaragua was fulfilled.

By comparison with the tortuous, often subterranean course of events in El Salvador and Nicaragua, the administration's actions in 1983 regarding the tiny island of Grenada, some hundred miles off the Venezuelan coast, represented the most direct application of U.S. military power in support of the Reagan Doctrine. Grenada had been on the U.S. policymakers' radar screen since the late 1970s, when the pro-Cuban Marxist Maurice Bishop seized power. Once Cuban advisers and weaponry began to arrive on the island, Carter attempted to undertake covert action against the Bishop government, but was blocked by the opposition of the Senate Intelligence Committee. The situation deteriorated suddenly in 1983 when a bloody coup took Bishop's life and installed an even more radical regime. Of particular concern to Reagan, with the Iranian hostage crisis clearly on his mind, was the presence of eight hundred Americans attending the St. George's University Medical School on the island.

The administration decided to act decisively, and on October 25 a combined force of Army paratroopers, Marines, and Navy SEALs, together with military units from six Caribbean states, invaded Grenada. The resistance offered by the island's poorly armed militia and a Cuban construction battalion was stiffer than anticipated and it took almost a week to secure the island, with losses of nineteen Americans killed and more than a hundred wounded. It was, Colin Powell has observed, "a sloppy success," marred by poor coordination among the inter-service groups constituting the attack force.[86] British prime minister and Reagan ally Margaret Thatcher opposed the operation from the start. The *New York Times* promptly condemned Reagan's use of force, asserting that "the cost is loss of the moral high ground."[87] But the invasion was the first significant and successful use of American military might since the 1960s, and in an outburst of long-suppressed martial patriotism, American public opinion treated it kindly, choosing to accentuate the positive. That inclination was helped mightily when the medical students airlifted back to the United States emotionally expressed their thanks, some falling to their knees on the tarmac to kiss the ground.

Although the implementation of the Reagan Doctrine in Afghanistan and Latin America garnered the most attention, the United States also worked to support anti-Communist resistance fighters in Africa. In 1985 Congress repealed its decade-old prohibition of support to Jonas Savimbi's anti-Communist UNITA faction in its long-running struggle against the Soviet and Cuban-backed government of Angola (there were some fifty thousand Cubans fighting in Angola in the mid-1980s, while South Africa intervened on a lesser scale on the other side). The CIA promptly began supplying UNITA with Stinger anti-aircraft and TOW anti-armor missiles, which helped keep the anti-Communist resistance alive long enough for a diplomatic settlement acceptable to the United States to be worked out. In 1988 the United States brokered a deal that set a schedule for the total withdrawal of Cuban forces and the departure of the South Africans. The Angola civil war dragged on tragically, but now removed from its Cold War context. As the chief of Reagan's State Department policy planning staff has written, "For better or worse, this tragic country [Angola] was now reduced to its own historical dimensions."[88]

Taken together, Reagan's military buildup, reassertion of the West's moral superiority, campaign of economic warfare, and global geopolitical assault profoundly affected what the Soviets were fond of calling "the correlation of forces." Driving forward his multifaceted campaign, Reagan turned the tide of affairs against the Soviet Union. But his actions also contributed to a ratcheting up of Cold War tension and danger, to a point last seen at the time of the Cuban Missile Crisis in the early 1960s.

Chapter 9

WINNING THE COLD WAR

Reagan's efforts to win it caused the Cold War to heat up dramatically. It is no exaggeration to say that some of the most dangerous moments in recent world history followed. Arms control negotiations between the two superpowers came to a halt when the Soviets walked out in protest of the Euromissile deployment in the fall of 1983. "We have come to the conclusion that nothing will come from dealing with Reagan," Soviet spokesman Georgi Arbatov explained to *Time* magazine, which reported that "the deterioration of U.S.–Soviet relations to . . . frozen impasse" overshadowed all other events in 1983.[1] The *Bulletin of the Atomic Scientists*, which since 1947 had displayed on its cover the so-called Doomsday Clock that measured humankind's proximity to a nuclear holocaust, reported glumly:

> As the arms race — a sort of dialogue between weapons — has intensified, other forms of discourse between the superpowers have all but ceased. There has been a virtual suspension of meaningful contacts and serious discussions. Every channel of communications has been constricted or shut down; every form of contact has been attenuated or cut off. And arms control negotiations have been reduced to a species of propaganda.

Accordingly, in January 1984 the editors adjusted the Doomsday Clock's minute hand, which before Reagan's election had stood at seven minutes to midnight, to a scant three minutes from cataclysmic disaster.[2]

THE REAGAN PIVOT, 1983–1984

The events of 1983 were sobering at best, and, as the historian Beth A. Fischer has argued, even Ronald Reagan was affected by their impact. The fall of the year saw a particularly ominous series of developments. In September the Soviets shot down a South Korean airliner, KAL Flight 007 en route from Alaska to Seoul, after it accidentally strayed into Soviet airspace. All 269 passengers aboard, including 61 Americans, among them a member of Congress, were killed. Although the administration presented the incident as a case of cold-blooded murder (which, in reality, it was), it became apparent that the horrible outcome was also the result of monumental incompetence on the Soviet side. "If anything, the KAL incident demonstrated how close the world had come to the precipice," Reagan later wrote: "If . . . the Soviet pilots simply mistook the airliner for a military plane, what kind of imagination did it take to think of a Soviet military man with his finger close to a nuclear push button making an even more tragic mistake?"[3]

Other events added to the president's disquiet. Weeks later, in mid-October, came a private advanced screening of ABC's television movie *The Day After*. Reagan described it in his private diary as "powerfully done" and "very effective," and recorded that it "left me greatly depressed." At the end of October, the secretary of defense and chairman of the Joint Chiefs of Staff gave Reagan his first presidential briefing on the Pentagon's actual plan for nuclear war, the so-called Single Integrated Operational Plan, which detailed how the U.S. nuclear arsenal would be unleashed against some fifty thousand Soviet targets in case of full-scale war. It was, he told his diary, "a most sobering experience."[4]

In December, the director of the CIA briefed the president with the news that recent intelligence "seems to reflect a Soviet perception of an increased threat of war."[5] The Soviet fear of war had been growing since 1981, when the KGB began its operation RYAN—the Russian acronym for Nuclear Missile Attack—to carefully monitor Western activities for hints of preparation for a nuclear first-strike. The fear mushroomed dangerously when NATO forces in November 1983 conducted a nine-day war-game exercise known as "Able Archer 83," which for training purposes mimicked a nuclear war scenario. Both the KGB (the modern Soviet counterpart of the CIA) and the GRU (Soviet military intelligence) feared that Able Archer 83 might be a cover for the beginning of a real attack. Now Reagan learned that the other side was apparently already inclined toward the very sort of miscalculation he most feared. Perhaps the tension of the Cold War needed to be turned down a notch.

Certainly the pragmatists among Reagan's advisers thought so. Nancy Reagan was particularly concerned that her husband not be viewed by history as a warmonger who single-handedly reignited the Cold War. "With the world so dangerous," she later recalled, "I felt it was ridiculous for these two heavily armed superpowers to be sitting there and not talking to each other."[6] The pragmatists on the White House staff—James Baker, Richard Darman, and Michael Deaver—worried about the political cost of Reagan's Cold War activism in the run-up to the presidential election of 1984. Reagan's pollster, Richard Wirthlin, reported that the president's chief area of vulnerability was foreign affairs, an area where, according to White House's own polls, a plurality of Americans believed that Reagan was increasing, rather than decreasing, the chance of war.[7]

The administration also had to deal with the gradual insinuation of the idea of convergence into the broader culture. In early 1984, Theodor Geisel, writing as the acclaimed children's author Dr. Seuss, published a scathing satire of the superpower nuclear standoff that quickly shot to the top of the bestseller list. *The Butter Battle Book*, nominally a children's book, told the story, in Seuss's typically irrepressible style and colorful illustrations, of the arms race between the Yooks and the Zooks, two feuding groups who get locked into an escalating spiral as they arm themselves first with switches and slingshots and ultimately with the highly destructive bomb known as "the Bitsy Big-Boy Boomeroo," which is filled with "mysterious Moo-Lacka-Moo" and is capable of blowing the entire fictional world to "Sala-ma-goo." Most tragic, their disagreement is based on . . . nothing. Or, rather, virtually nothing. Indeed, perhaps worse than nothing. The illustrations make clear that the Yooks and the Zooks look exactly alike, except that one group dresses in blue, the other in orange. The telling difference between the two warring tribes is that the Yooks butter their bread on top while the Zooks butter theirs on the bottom, and on such a meaningless distinction hangs the fate of the world. The book quickly shot to the top of the best-seller list, attracting the attention of administration critics such as New York governor Mario Cuomo, who recommended that everyone read the book for a better understanding of the U.S.–Soviet confrontation.[8]

Secretary of State George Shultz quickly emerged as a key pragmatist helping to reorient U.S.–Soviet policy, replacing the hardliner Richard Pipes as the embodiment of U.S. policy inclinations. (Pipes, meanwhile, left the National Security Council, and was replaced on the NSC in the spring 1983 by Jack Matlock, a career diplomat of relatively more moderate inclinations.) Shultz, whose father worked on Wall Street, was born in Manhattan and raised in New Jersey in comfortable and nurturing surroundings. He majored in economics and played football at Princeton University—the press would later be much amused by the fact that the phlegmatic, physically imposing U.S. secretary of state had a Princeton tiger tattooed on his buttock—and during World War II saw combat in the Pacific theater as a Marine Corps officer. After the war Shultz received a Ph.D. in industrial economics from MIT, where he then taught before moving on to become dean of the Graduate School of

Business at the University of Chicago. In addition to his various academic appointments, he worked on the side as a labor-management mediator. It was during the Nixon administration that Shultz entered high-level public life, serving as secretary of labor, budget director, and secretary of the treasury. When approached by Reagan to replace Al Haig as secretary of state in 1982, Shultz was living in a faculty house on the campus of Stanford University, where he had tenure and taught part-time, while serving as president of the Bechtel Corporation, a worldwide construction firm. He was clearly a rare bird, fully at home in the worlds of both intellect and action.

Shultz brought to his job remarkable energy, tenacity, and an appreciation of the uses of persuasion and negotiation. At his Senate confirmation hearing in 1982, he told his interlocutors, "It is critical to the overall success of our foreign policy that we persevere in the restoration of our strength; but it is also true that the willingness to negotiate from that strength is a fundamental element of strength itself." As he later wrote in his memoirs, Shultz believed that "from a military standpoint, the United States was back in business" and that as a consequence the time had arrived when "power and diplomacy work *together*."⁹ He saw it as his mission to rescue the president from the thrall of his hardline advisers—"the task before me was to make them irrelevant"—and help reorient U.S. policy along the lines of his own more subtle approach of dialogue and negotiation.¹⁰

It is a mistake, however, to overestimate the impact of sudden, disquieting events or the influence of administration moderates. It is true that Reagan was spooked by the fear of accidental war as the Cold War heated up in 1983. And it is true that the pragmatists worked hard to win Reagan's ear for a more moderate approach to U.S.–Soviet relations. But in reality, Shultz and the other pragmatists were pushing on a leader already moving toward where they wanted him to go. Shultz was less the catalyst in skillfully and purposefully turning Reagan around than the highly effective vehicle for Reagan's own ends, which the president had made clear from the beginning.

Reagan had from the outset insisted on a two-track approach to the Soviets—pressure and negotiate. "Our number one goal," the president wrote in a June 1982 personal letter, "is to achieve a meaningful reduction in armaments from strategic nuclear to conventional." But he also believed, he told another correspondent at the time, that "to have any chance of getting their agreement to a reduction we must convince them we will do what we have to do to match their strength."¹¹ By 1983 Reagan judged that he had conveyed that message in a sufficiently convincing fashion. As deputy national security adviser Robert McFarlane explained to Jack Matlock, who was being recruited by the administration in the spring of 1983 to replace Pipes as the chief Soviet expert at the National Security Council: "When the president came into office, . . . he felt that we were too weak to negotiate effectively with the Soviets. Therefore, his first priority was to restore our strength. There is still a lot to do, but the president is satisfied that he has restored enough momentum to our defense programs to deal with the Soviets effectively. In fact, he feels it is time to pursue negotiations aggressively."[12]

Having gotten to where he always wanted to be, Reagan now stood ready to open a dialogue with the USSR and negotiate from strength. A memo from Herb Meyer of the CIA's National Intelligence Council that crossed the president's desk in late 1983 spoke of a "new stage in the global struggle between the Free World and the Soviet Union" and declared boldly that "if present trends continue, we're going to win the Cold War." Now that the USSR was in a "terminal stage," with an economy "heading toward calamity," Meyer cautioned, the trick would be to avoid having the fatally wounded adversary lash out in a desperate attempt to find a military "solution" to Moscow's irresolvable problems.[13] The memo captured perfectly Reagan's own thinking. There would be a turn in U.S. policy, but one driven fully as much by optimism as by fear, the two now inextricably intertwined over the course of the pivotal year 1983.

Reagan signaled the administration's new approach in a White House address on U.S.–Soviet relations on January 16, 1984, which was telecast live to Western Europe. The president reported with obvious satisfaction that "we have halted America's decline. Our economy is now in the midst of the best recovery since the sixties. Our defenses are being rebuilt, our alliances are solid, and our commitment to defend our values has never been more clear." But replacing the evil empire rhetoric of the earlier phase of Reagan's Cold War were notes of the reawakened nuclear anxiety: "Reducing the risk of war—and especially nuclear war—is priority number one," Reagan acknowledged. And there was a new, more positive agenda: The United States and USSR needed "to establish a better working relationship, one marked by greater cooperation and understanding." "We must and will engage the Soviets in a dialogue as serious and constructive as possible," he announced.[14]

Most striking was Reagan's peroration. He had long since established his ability to capture an audience through the use of simple, highly personalized homilies. Now he personally drafted the story of Jim and Sally, average Americans, and their Soviet counterparts, Ivan and Anya, thrown together by circumstance in a waiting room or just getting out of the rain. They would not, Reagan said, debate ideology but rather would compare notes on the everyday reality of their lives, finding that they had much in common. "Above all," Reagan concluded, "they would have proven that people don't make wars. People want to raise their children in a world without fear and without war. . . . Their common interests cross all borders."[15] Ronald Reagan, the arch-Cold Warrior, embraced the most common trope of the convergence crowd—a child is a child is a child—for his own pragmatic purposes. One can only wonder what Richard Pipes must have thought as he listened to the speech.

Though the turn in the Reagan administration's approach to the USSR—
the wedding of diplomacy to power—was real, there remained moments of tension. In August 1984, Reagan was warming up for his weekly radio address and
in the process of testing his microphone announced, "My fellow Americans, I
am pleased to tell you today that I've signed legislation that will outlaw Russia
forever. We begin bombing in five minutes."[16] Aides struggled to explain it as
a joke gone wrong, but the gaffe outraged both the Soviets and the president's
domestic critics. In March 1985, Major Arthur D. Nicholson Jr., a member of
the U.S. military liaison mission in Potsdam, East Germany, was shot by a Soviet sentry and left to bleed to death when Soviet authorities prevented medical
aid from reaching him.

Moreover, the administration continued to keep the pressure on in its multifaceted Cold War campaigns. Spending for SDI research doubled in 1986. In
the mid-1980s the CIA was helping to smuggle Islamic religious materials and
related anti-Soviet propaganda into the regions of the USSR with large Muslim
populations, and Afghan mujahidin trained and equipped by the CIA were
striking across the border into the Soviet Union itself, attacking infrastructure
such as power stations and setting up ambushes—activities that would appear
in a rather more ominous light for Americans after September 11, 2001. Reagan
also kept the rhetorical pressure on, as in a 1987 speech in West Berlin when he
famously demanded, "Mr. Gorbachev, tear down this wall."[17]

Nevertheless, Reagan's pivot turn of 1983–84, undertaken *before* Mikhail
Gorbachev came to power in the USSR, initiated a tide in world affairs that
first redefined and then, ultimately, decided the Cold War. The conjunction
of Reagan's new readiness to negotiate with the rise on the Soviet side of a
dynamic leader who shared that predisposition, led to a dramatic series of bi-
lateral U.S.–Soviet summit meetings: Geneva in November 1985; Reykjavik,
Iceland, in October 1986; Washington in December 1987; and Moscow in May
1988. Jack Matlock, who headed the Soviet desk at NSC from 1983 to 1987 and
then served as ambassador to Moscow from 1987 through 1991, has observed,
"Many in his administration, particularly in the Department of Defense and
the Central Intelligence Agency, doubted that the Soviet leaders would conduct negotiations in good faith, but Reagan was an optimist. For all his distaste
of the Soviet system, he nevertheless believed that it could change if subjected
to sufficient pressure and his personal negotiating skill."[18]

The summits allowed Reagan and Gorbachev to build a personal chemistry
that made for mutual trust. As the two leaders prepared to sign the official statements issued on the last day of their first summit in Geneva, Reagan leaned
over and whispered into his counterpart's ear, "I bet the hardliners in both our
countries are squirming."[19] Shortly thereafter, he wrote privately to Suzanne
Massie, an informal adviser on the Soviet Union, that he sensed "something of

a chemistry" between himself and Gorbachev: "I'm not going to let myself get euphoric but still I have a feeling we might be at a point of beginning."[20]

In the course of their summit meetings Reagan and Gorbachev achieved notable concrete results. The precedent-setting Intermediate Nuclear Forces Treaty, formally signed in Washington in December 1987, was the first agreement in the long history of the Cold War to actually eliminate an entire existing class of nuclear missiles. The White House saw the INF accord, in the words of an internal National Security Decision Directive, as "a triumph and vindication for the policy that this Administration has followed toward the Soviet Union from the start."[21] Moreover, the INF deal demonstrated that the two superpowers could, in fact, conclude complicated and far-reaching arms reduction agreements. Further progress followed. In 1991, after nearly a decade of negotiations first begun by Reagan, the United States and the USSR signed the START I Treaty, which cut back the American strategic nuclear arsenal by 25 percent and the Soviet by 35 percent. (In 1992 President George H. W. Bush and President Boris Yeltsin of the post-USSR Russian Federation signed the START II Treaty, which reduced the strategic arsenals by a further 50 percent and abolished the particularly destabilizing land-based Multiple Independently Targeted Reentry Vehicles—so-called MIRVs. The U.S. senate ratified the treaty in 1997, and the Russian Duma followed suit in 2000.)

By the end of Reagan's second presidential term, the world was becoming a safer place and the Cold War was coming to an end. Democracy, not communism, was at flood tide. The Soviets were in retreat around the world, increasingly unable or unwilling to bear the economic costs of further competition with the West. Under seemingly relentless U.S. pressure, the Soviet system now suffered *its* crisis of confidence. Gorbachev found himself struggling to keep communism alive in his own country. Forced to choose between his domestic reform agenda of *Perestroika* (economic and political restructuring) and *Glasnost* (governmental transparency) on the one hand and the maintenance of the Soviet empire and prosecution of the Cold War on the other, Gorbachev chose reform and retrenchment at home. The resultant change in world affairs was palpable. When, during Reagan's final summit in Moscow in May 1988, a reporter asked the president if he still considered the Soviet Union an "evil empire," he replied, "I was talking about another time, another era." During an official visit to Washington that November, Margaret Thatcher observed to American journalists, "We're not in a Cold War now."[22]

The Cold War had settled over Europe like a fog at the end of World War II, initially difficult to discern even as it gradually blotted out the sun. In the sunrise year of 1989, the fog lifted with surprising suddenness. In January, Hungary allowed pluralistic parties and open demonstrations for the first time in decades; Estonia and Lithuania made their own languages official, loosening the

strings of Soviet hegemony over the Baltic states. In February the last Soviet sol-
dier left Afghanistan. In May, Gorbachev informed the Nicaraguan Sandinistas
that the USSR could no longer afford its massive aid to their cause. In August,
Poland became the first Warsaw Pact nation to install a noncommunist government. In November, the wall in Berlin that Reagan had demanded Gorbachev
tear down actually did fall to the sledgehammers of ecstatic West and East
German crowds. By the end of 1989, every communist government in Eastern
Europe except Albania's had been forced from office. Vaclav Havel, the Czech
intellectual and political reformer who had been arrested by the communists
in February and then elected president of Czechoslovakia in December, called
it a "Velvet Revolution." In 1990 the Communist Party lost its monopoly on political power in the USSR, and in December of the next year the Soviet Union
came apart, separating into its numerous constituent republics.

The United States and the West won the Cold War. The Soviet Union lost,
and then expired. How much credit Reagan deserved for those developments
has been debated ever since. Margaret Thatcher's oft-quoted tribute that Reagan won the Cold War without firing a shot is viewed by many as rather too
pat. But even more mistaken are those interpretations that refuse Reagan any
credit, attributing the outcome entirely to Gorbachev's visionary leadership or
to deep-running social, economic, and technological forces beyond the influence of any individual.

Gorbachev undoubtedly deserves much credit for, in the end, letting the
Soviet imperium slip away peacefully. For that alone he deserved the Nobel
Peace Prize he was awarded in 1990. And his personal qualities left an im-
portant imprint on his times. Gorbachev's assistant Anatoly Chernyaev wrote
in his diary after a 1988 meeting between his boss and German Chancellor
Helmut Kohl:

> I came to realize how brave and far-sighted M. S. [Gorbachev] is. His ideas are:
> freedom of choice, mutual respect of each other's values, balance of interest,
> renunciation of force in politics, all-European house, liquidation of nuclear ar-
> maments etc. All this, each by itself, is not original or new. What is new is that a
> person—who came out of Soviet Marxism-Leninism, Soviet society conditioned
> from top to bottom by Stalinism—began to carry out these ideas.[23]

But while it is impossible not to admire Gorbachev's performance on the world
stage, it should be remembered that much of what happened was, on his part,
entirely unintended—the massively gifted leader had set out to save Soviet
Communism and its empire, not preside over their demise.

On the issue of responsibility for the momentous changes at the end of the
1980s, a commentator who makes particularly good sense is Jack Matlock, who
advised Reagan in Washington and then observed the end of the Cold War
and the breakup of the Soviet Union first-hand as U.S. ambassador to Moscow.

Combining firsthand knowledge with scholarly perspective, Matlock argues that Gorbachev was the most important influence in ending Communist rule in the USSR, but credits Reagan with playing the major role in ending the Cold War. In Matlock's eyes, what set Reagan apart were his "instinctive confidence" and his assumption that "there could be changes for the better and that he could influence them." So armed, he was able to set out a strategy incorporating both the use of power and the willingness to negotiate, and able to hold to both elements despite assaults from both the left (upset with the self-confident wielding of U.S. power) and the right (fearful of weak-kneed diplomatic compromise).[24]

The Cold War ended on American terms, according to a script written in Washington, not Moscow. Back in 1978, Ronald Reagan—then a private citizen well past retirement age, with political ambitions but less than shining electoral prospects—had lightheartedly informed his foreign policy adviser, Richard Allen, that he had a simple idea for U.S. policy toward the Soviet Union: " It is this: We win and they lose. What do you think of that?"[25] To the surprise of learned experts and ordinary people around the world, what sounded slightly daft at the end of the 1970s had by the end of the 1980s become history.

BALANCING THE BOOKS:
THE UNDERSIDE OF REAGAN'S COLD WAR

Winning the long twilight struggle against the Soviet Union occasioned justifiable self-congratulation in the West, but an honest balancing of the historical books requires taking note as well of the inevitable costs of victory. On Reagan's watch, some of the costs were immediately visible and registered at the time, while others lingered beneath the surface and were delayed in their impact; either way, they were not inconsiderable. Hindsight now allows us to see that the costs that seemed most significant at the time were not, and that matters that went unrecognized, or nearly so, at the time would loom very large indeed in succeeding decades.

The most dramatic short-term cost of Reagan's Cold War was the scandal that in 1986–87 threatened to eventuate in the sort of constitutional crisis that had toppled Richard Nixon's presidency. In November 1986 the news broke that the Reagan administration had been bargaining with so-called moderates in Iran for help in gaining the freedom of American citizens held hostage by terrorists in Lebanon. (Policymakers also acted in the hope of reestablishing U.S. influence in a critical part of the world threatened by the Soviet Union.) To grease the skids, the administration, using Israel as an intermediary, sold TOW antitank missiles and Hawk anti-aircraft missiles to Iran, which contravened both U.S. arms export statutes and the administration's own Operation Staunch, a campaign to get the international community to stop providing arms to Iran. Details of the story sounded like the script for a very bad movie. At one point the administration's chief agents in the affair, NSC staffer Marine Lieutenant Colonel Oliver North and former national security adviser Bud McFarland, had secretly flown to Tehran under assumed names with phony passports. They were bearing a chocolate cake and several pistols in presentation cases as gifts for the Iranian moderates with whom they planned to meet, while carrying CIA-issue suicide pills just in case things turned bad.

Still worse, it quickly came to light that North had diverted some of the profits from the Iranian arms sales through a Swiss bank account to the Nicaraguan Contras for use in their struggle against the Sandinista government. Here, too, it appeared that laws had been broken and both the letter and spirit of congressional directives circumvented. In the eyes of many, the Contra connection raised even more troubling issues than the arms-for-hostages aspect of the affair—serious constitutional issues. Was the National Security Council secretly bankrolling a covert war presided over by a gung-ho Marine Corps lieutenant colonel (North) operating out of a ramshackle NSC office in the Old Executive Office Building across a narrow street from the White House with virtually no supervision? When the two halves of the controversy—the dealings with Iran and the diversion to the Contras—came together, all hell broke loose.

The Iran-Contra Affair took an immediate toll on the administration. In the month after the first reports of a hostage deal surfaced in November 1986, the president's approval rating fell from 67 percent to 46 percent, a precipitous drop of 21 points. Polls in May 1987 indicated that 62 percent of respondents believed Reagan lied when he disavowed any knowledge of the diversion of funds to the Contras.[26] Clearly, the Iran-Contra affair caused the American people to lose trust in the president and his administration. Moreover, the impact was prolonged by the White House's inability convincingly to defend itself in the scandal's first months and by the host of investigations that were launched to get at the truth of what had happened—an internal administration investigation by Attorney General Ed Meese; two congressional select committee inquiries; a presidential review board headed by the retired Republican senator from Texas, John Tower; and an independent counsel investigation presided over by Lawrence Walsh, who issued his final report in 1994.

Although investigated to a fare-thee-well, many details regarding both the arms-for-hostages and Contra diversion operations remained shrouded in a fog of legal complexity and contradictory or incomplete recollection. The president's counsel during the scandal, Peter J. Wallison, makes clear in his account of Iran-Contra just how hard it was for even the president and his lawyers to ascertain exactly what administration underlings had done in trading arms and diverting profits.[27] The dealings were poorly documented, either purposely for easy deniability or out of sheer bureaucratic ineptitude. Moreover, several of the chief protagonists—especially North, who was engaged in both the Iran and Contra ends of the operation, and his boss, national security adviser Admiral John Poindexter—attempted to cover their tracks by destroying what little documentation there was, adding the danger of a classic Watergate-style cover-up to the White House's other woes.

As the scandal unfolded, the political stakes rose dramatically. Some critics argued that Reagan's actions and omissions approached the level of high crimes and misdemeanors that called for impeachment. In truth, there was no doubt that laws had been broken, but the president's lawyers maintained that the violations were technical in nature, *malum prohibitum* (wrong because prohibited) rather than *malum in se* (wrong in themselves), a lower level of legal transgression.[28] (Reagan's legal advisers did not appear ready to concede that some rules violations might be both *malum prohibitum* and *malum in se* at the same time.) The president's champions also argued that the scandal was being blown out of proportion by a press-corps feeding frenzy—*Washington Post* editor Ben Bradlee was prominently reported as saying that Iran-Contra was the most fun he had had since Watergate. Moreover, the Reagan camp believed that the entire brouhaha was driven by the tendency of the opposition party to criminalize what were in reality policy disputes about the Contra war in Nicaragua.[29] In the end, the talk of impeachment remained just that, in no small part because the American public was unwilling to suffer the removal of another president so soon after the trauma of Watergate. They were particularly hesitant to remove a sitting president over issues involving foreign policy and national security, areas where the executive branch in the Cold War era traditionally enjoyed a wide margin of latitude.

Reagan survived Iran-Contra also because of what appears in hindsight to have been excellent, if belated, damage control. The president waived both executive and attorney–client privilege and made all relevant documents available to congressional investigators. Most important, after an initial temporizing delay, he accepted responsibility for what had happened. He publicly admitted, albeit still somewhat grudgingly, that it could fairly be construed that he had traded arms for hostages, although he continued to insist that had not been his intention; meanwhile, he steadfastly denied any prior knowledge of the Contra diversion. In a nationally televised address on March 4, 1987, the president declared, "First, let me say I take full responsibility for my own actions and for those of my administration. As angry as I may be about activities undertaken without my knowledge, I am still accountable for those activities."[30]

Accepting responsibility while neatly slipping much of the blame for what had happened, Reagan reasserted his control of his presidency by undertaking a thorough housecleaning. The administration implemented new procedural and operational reforms at the NSC. The president fired North from the NSC for his central role in the illegal funneling of funds to the Contras (which the

White House never in any way sought to defend) and accepted Poindexter's resignation as national security adviser for approving North's shenanigans. Frank Carlucci replaced Poindexter and brought with him as his deputy the up-and-coming Colin Powell. Former senator Howard Baker replaced White House chief of staff Don Regan, who had lost favor, especially with Nancy Reagan, for having somehow failed to protect his detail-challenged boss; Baker had fewer hard edges and much better Washington contacts than his predecessor and played an important role in rehabilitating the Reagan White House. "By meeting the crisis head-on, especially in the press," writes David Gergen, a veteran of both Republican and Democratic administrations afflicted by scandal, "Reagan gradually rearranged the political landscape so he could govern again."[31]

The revelations of Iran-Contra exposed a number of mistakes in judgment. Topping the list was the president's atrocious decision to approve arms sales to Iran in the first place. It is difficult, even in retrospect, not to feel some sympathy with Reagan's good intentions. As he wrote in his memoirs, "What American trapped in such circumstances wouldn't have wanted me to do everything I possibly could to set them free? What Americans *not* held captive under such circumstances would not want me to do my utmost to get the hostages home?"[32] But Reagan had forged his own political appeal, and career, in large part on the recognition that good intentions on the part of government were simply not enough. Iran-Contra more than confirmed the essential wisdom of his insight.

In the end, the American public interpreted Reagan's personal involvement in the arms-for-hostages machinations to be not sinful or criminal so much as wrongheaded, a blunder rather than an impeachable offense. Even the zealous independent counsel Lawrence E. Walsh had to conclude in his 1994 final report that the president's actions "fell well short of criminality which could be successfully prosecuted."[33] Beneath the presidency, however, heads rolled—Walsh ended up charging fourteen people with criminal violations and winning eleven convictions. Most of those found guilty were secondary figures. North was convicted on three counts for aiding and abetting false congressional testimony by others, destroying NSC documents, and accepting an illegal gratuity (a security system for his home). Poindexter was convicted on various counts related to false statements he made to Congress regarding what had happened in Iran-Contra. Both North's and Poindexter's convictions were ultimately overturned on appeal for technical reasons. The extent of such collateral damage, the wounding of a presidency at the height of its popularity, and the dismal fact that the Muslim radicals in Beirut actually held more hostages at the end of the Iran-Contra saga than before it began, all combined to make Reagan's arms-for-hostages decision the worst blunder of his political career.

The diversion of funds from the Iranian arms sales into the hands of the Nicaraguan Contras—which Reagan persuasively claimed to have known nothing about—revealed the dangers inherent when a relaxed and trusting management style and a loosely structured but exceedingly powerful national security apparatus came together. The resultant lack of oversight allowed underlings like Poindexter and North to conduct their own foreign policy out of the NSC. Reagan's management philosophy of setting forth the broad outlines of policy and then trusting his subordinates to follow his general directions and fill in the details, which had previously worked well in both California and Washington, in this instance failed him, and the nation, badly. In the case of North, Reagan unwittingly relied on a hyperactive workaholic with a flair for drama and self-promotion and a penchant for trouble, in Michael Deaver's words a mixture of Huck Finn and Clint Eastwood; Reagan speechwriter Peggy Noonan, upon first observing the boyish North in a White House meeting, leaned over and whispered to a compatriot: "Who's Peck's bad boy?"[34] In Poindexter's case, Reagan trusted a subordinate who combined the genuine brilliance of a first-rate scientist with the nearly complete political tone-deafness of a first-rate scientist; the national security adviser did not want for mental amperage, but lacked the more elusive quality of sound political judgment.

Finally, Iran-Contra was withal a Cold War phenomenon. Both North and his boss Poindexter made their operational home in the NSC, and there used operational powers that had grown to gargantuan proportions because so much of Reagan's Cold War had been coordinated through a working nexus of the NSC and the CIA. Their interest in funneling the arms-for-hostages funds to help the Contras was merely an extension, in the face of continuing congressional disapproval, of the administration's efforts to topple the Nicaragua's Sandinista government. The controversy that accompanied the Contra side of the scandal was particularly fierce precisely because it reopened old wounds from the lingering dispute between the administration and its congressional critics over Reagan's Central America policies. In this regard, Iran-Contra was, as Peter Rodman has observed, the bastard child of the Reagan Doctrine, and, as well, of Reagan's victorious prosecution of the Cold War.

Ironically, the messy scandal came to matter less than many observers at the time predicted precisely because Reagan recovered sufficiently to bring the Cold War to a successful conclusion during his final years in office. In the end, that achievement, rather than his Iran-Contra blunders, served to define his presidency.

Fighting the Cold War in the 1980s also entailed other, less concrete costs. The Reagan Doctrine in particular took the United States ever further into uncomfortably murky moral waters where the choices were often between a highly imperfect anticommunist status quo or change in the direction of a predictably worse revolutionary and communist alternative, between, as it were, bad thugs and worse thugs. Having to choose between bad and worse alternatives entailed a loss of innocence and induced a note of cognitive dissonance that made Americans profoundly uneasy. Perhaps the resultant anxiety was inevitable, for the national moral compass had been historically habituated to distinguishing between gradations of good and only occasionally making obvious choices between good and evil. Having to choose between bad and worse both unsettled and chafed. It was precisely such discomfort that New York senator Daniel Patrick Moynihan articulated when he complained in connection with the campaign against Nicaragua's Sandinista regime that the United States was "debasing our own conduct in the course of resisting theirs."[35]

Reagan's Cold War abounded in the sort of moral compromises Americans found troubling. Early on, the administration decided that Argentina, a particularly notorious human rights abuser, would no longer be subjected to American lectures on the subject. "The practice of publicly denouncing our friends while minimizing the abuse of those rights in the Soviet Union and other totalitarian countries was at an end," Haig later explained. To drive home the point, the United States voted for Argentina to join the United Nations Human Rights Commission.[36]

Even more disturbing, the United States decided for what Haig labeled "overriding political and strategic reasons" to support the Khmer resistance movement against the Vietnamese occupation of Kampuchea (the former Cambodia). That resistance was led by a triumvirate of leaders—two noncommunists, Prince Sihanouk and Son Sann, and the infamous butcher Pol Pot, who had overseen the deaths of millions at the hands of the Khmer Rouge during the original communization of Cambodia that followed the Vietnam War. Regarding Pol Pot, Haig wrote, "It was with considerable anguish that we agreed to support . . . this charnel figure."[37] In reality, that tilt had begun in the Carter administration, when national security adviser Zbigniew Brzezinski, in his own words, "encouraged the Chinese to encourage Pol Pot [to resist the Vietnamese]," and it continued throughout the Reagan years.[38] The Reagan administration publicly provided the noncommunist resistance factions with $5 million a year in humanitarian aid (tents, medicine, etc.) throughout the 1980s, and by the end of the decade the CIA covertly was supplying another $20–25 million a year for "non-lethal" purposes such as training, uniforms, vehicles, and radio transmitters.[39]

The rub was that the noncommunist resistance factions were tied together in coalition with Pol Pot's Khmer Rouge, which constituted the strongest military force fighting against the Vietnamese occupiers. Direct aid to the noncommunist factions inevitably constituted indirect aid to those responsible for one of the worst auto-genocides of the twentieth century, the mass murder of Cambodians by Cambodians. Critics on both sides of the political aisle were distressed by the moral consequences of such realpolitik. Representative Chet

Atkins, a Massachusetts Democrat, complained, "We are still playing games with [the Khmer Rouge]. It's a goddamn outrage."[40] "The U.S.," declared Rep. Jim Leach, an Iowa Republican, "cannot pursue policies that violate basic moral precepts. Pol Pot should be tried as one of the great criminals of the 20th century, not countenanced as the eminence grise behind a new Cambodian government."[41] A nadir of sorts was reached at the 1989 Paris Conference on Cambodia, when for pragmatic reasons of state the United States balked at a proposed formal condemnation of the Khmer Rouge's record of genocide (verbal condemnations were something else, and were frequently made). As Peter W. Rodman, a high-ranking U.S. diplomat throughout the 1980s, has written, American policy in Cambodia in the 1980s was "another painful and protracted effort to reconcile our geopolitical and moral imperatives."[42]

More significant than the moral anguish engendered by the Reagan's Cold War actions of the 1980s, because it was more concrete in the damage it ultimately contributed to, was the matter of blowback. Borrowed from the argot of the intelligence community, the term denotes the adverse unintended consequences that sometimes result from initial actions or policies. American aid to the mujahidin fighting against the Soviets in Afghanistan during the 1980s served as a disastrously vivid example of the phenomenon. For defensible reasons rooted in short-term Cold War considerations and without foreseeing the possible larger ramifications of its actions, the United States stoked a pan-Islamic fundamentalist movement and directed it against the Cold War adversary. At one point, the CIA collaborated with Pakistan's Interservices Intelligence Agency (ISI) to turn the mujahidin holy war against the Soviets in Afghanistan against the USSR itself by encouraging attacks on Tajikistan, a nearby Soviet constituent republic with a sizable Muslim population.[43]

Unfortunately, policymakers failed to think through what would happen to the Afghanistan jihad once its Cold War usefulness ended. After the Soviet retreat from Afghanistan in 1989, the CIA hung around long enough to buy back, at $200,000 a pop, all the Stinger anti-aircraft missiles that could be located, but then left the Afghans to their own devices. The insurgency training camps created and funded by the United States, Saudi Arabia, and other states fell into the hands of Islamic fundamentalists known as the Taliban. Of the large number of non-Afghan Islamic militants who had come to Afghanistan to fight in the holy war there, a Western diplomat in Peshwar could only observe, "They're a real disposal problem."[44] The world-wide recruitment and support network that had been set up to sustain the anti-Soviet jihad in Afghanistan soon fell under the control of the Islamic terrorist organization known as al-Qaeda ("the Base" in Arabic) led by Osama bin Laden.

The concept of blowback has been invoked by some commentators to suggest that al-Qaeda's deadly attacks of September 11, 2001, on New York City's Twin Towers and the Pentagon in Washington were the ineluctable result of earlier American actions in sponsoring the anti-Soviet resistance in Afghanistan. That is an argument that blames the victim in a particularly perverse fashion by mistaking a historical convergence for a fundamental historical cause. The United Sates did not create pan-Islamic fundamentalism, or Osama bin Laden, for the purposes of the Cold War. The CIA had no known dealings with bin Laden during the Afghanistan conflict.[45] But the United States did nurture and attempt to use for its own transitory Cold War purposes a volatile and malignant force that could not be extinguished or controlled when its usefulness in the Cold War struggle came to an end.[46] That was a truth about the Cold War that Americans would have to live with.

Finally, putting America's Cold War triumph into perspective requires also an admission of the awful dangers courted and risks run in the pursuit of victory. The threatening events of 1983, the all-too-real possibility of misunderstanding and fear combining with cocked nuclear arsenals to create a true Armageddon, spooked even the preternaturally sanguine Ronald Reagan. The dangers were in their horror difficult even fully to imagine. Should Reagan be blamed for running such risks or in the final analysis lauded for managing them so adroitly with his pragmatic blend of power and diplomacy? Blamed for the fact that the Doomsday Clock was moved to three minutes to midnight in 1984, or lauded for the fact that it was moved back to seventeen minutes to midnight in 1991, the most favorable setting since the advent of the nuclear age? On those questions, historians will likely continue to divide.

Perhaps the final accounting on the Cold War triumph is too important to be left entirely to historians, however. Looking back after it was over, Paul Nitze, a participant who had fought the Cold War from both inside and outside the U.S. government from the 1940s through the 1980s, remarked, "We did a goddamn good job." Believing that Soviet Communism was in truth "a darkness that could be touched," a modern evil of biblical proportions, most Americans agreed with Nitze's assessment. Many of the victims of what the playwright and Czech president Vaclav Havel described as "the communist type of totalitarian system" agreed as well. As Havel told a joint meeting of the U.S. Congress in 1990, communism had "left both . . . Czechs and Slovaks, as it has all the nations of the Soviet Union and the other countries the Soviet Union subjugated in its time, a legacy of countless dead, an infinite spectrum of human suffering, profound economic decline and, above all, enormous human humiliation."[47] The defeat of Soviet communism, and the undoing of so many of its acolytes and surrogates, left the world still imperfect, but immensely improved. If the sacrifices made and the risks run were considerable, even in retrospect, so too, and honorable, was the achievement.

Chapter 10

THE EIGHTIES LEGACY

The Recentering of Politics and Culture

As he was leaving the presidency, Ronald Reagan spoke one last time to the American public from the Oval Office. His farewell address on January 11, 1989, was the opportunity designated by precedent for him to play his own historian, to make the pitch for what he had accomplished and why it mattered. His former speechwriter Peggy Noonan, who had helped write many of his finest speeches but had since left his staff, came back to help in the final effort. But they tussled, and the speech that emerged was in significant ways more his than hers. She felt it too self-assertive and self-serving; she wanted some mention of regret, of good and necessary things desired but not achieved. But Reagan had not traveled from Dixon to the Oval Office by trading in what-might-have-been's. "Well, you are the president, sir, and this is your speech."

"That's right," he replied good-naturedly. As always, he preferred to speak plainly and in his own voice.

"There was," she recalled without rancor, "a childlike quality to his robust self-regard, an innocence even to his sin."[1]

As it turned out, Reagan's farewell was an adequate speech but not a great one. He noted in passing that he had won the nickname "the Great Communicator," then added, "But I never thought it was my style or the words I used that made a difference: It was the content. I wasn't a great communicator, but I communicated great things." Those great things had enabled Americans to rediscover their values and their common sense and to reclaim their place in the world. The changes, Reagan asserted, had rippled outward: "We meant to change a nation, and instead, we changed a world." Following the American example, democracy, "profoundly good" and "profoundly productive," was on the march around the globe.

It was only in closing that Reagan finally achieved the eloquence for which he was so noted. He reminded his audience that he had often spoken of America as the "shining city upon a hill." "And how stands the city on this winter night?" he asked. "She still stands strong and true on the granite ridge, and her glow has held steady no matter what storm. And she's still a beacon, still a magnet for all who must have freedom, for all the pilgrims from all the lost places who are hurtling through the darkness, toward home." Speaking intimately to an audience he could not see, Reagan concluded: "My friends: We did it. . . . We made a difference. We made the city stronger. We made the city freer, and we left her in good hands. All in all, not bad, not bad at all. And so, good-bye."[2]

RATING REAGAN

What could Reagan fairly claim to have accomplished during his two terms in the White House? Four significant achievements stand out. First, he helped engineer an economic recovery that would, with but one brief stutter, a short-lived recession in 1990–91, continue for nearly two decades. Reagan's fiscal, de-regulatory, and antitrust policies all played a role in facilitating the emergence of a new entrepreneurial economy. But nothing he did was more important for the long-term health of the economy than helping to defeat inflation. Finally getting inflation under control required that the administration support the Federal Reserve in its determination to "wring out of the system" the stubborn and strong inflationary pressures that had brought the economy to grief in the 1970s, even while the Fed's tight money policy to do so was, in the process, causing the sharpest economic downtown of the postwar era. In staying the course in the battle against inflation, in supporting the Fed even when some of his advisers began to lose their stomach for the fight, Reagan risked his short-term political capital, his popularity, and his chances for reelection. The gamble paid off, both politically and economically. Anything less almost certainly would have failed. Although the immediate pain of the 1981–82 recession was considerable, the long-term prosperity that followed proved Reagan right. As Samuel C. Hayes of the Harvard Business School later put it, "I credit the '80s for giving a foundation to the economy of the '90s."[3]

Reagan's second major achievement was bringing the Cold War to a successful conclusion on Western terms. The issue remains a matter of contention. There is no gainsaying that Reagan shared the stage with a person of world-historical significance, Mikhail Gorbachev. At the same time, it is hard to overlook the fact that what happened as the Cold War played out in the 1980s usually followed an American script that Reagan had personally written. It was Reagan who undertook the multifaceted military, economic, diplomatic, and rhetorical offensive that rocked the Kremlin back on its heels. It was Reagan who initiated the negotiation from strength that brought about the first real arms reductions in the history of the Cold War. The treaties of the late 1980s were concluded on American terms. It is not necessarily gloating to remark all this; it is simply true. It is impossible to realistically imagine the Cold War ending as it did, when it did, absent Ronald Reagan.

Reagan's third large achievement was his most intangible. In his farewell address, he called it "the recovery of our morale" and counted it among his great triumphs. In a sense, it may well have been the greatest, or at least the most fundamental, for it undergirded and made possible all the others. Reagan wrote to James Baker in 1985, "Americans are a people who look forward to the future with optimism. That sense of optimism is the most important thing we have tried to restore in America during the past four years." Without the restoration and reinvigoration of the native optimism of the American people, the United States neither could have recovered economically to become the locomotive of the global premillennial boom nor prevailed in the Cold War. According to polling data, Americans in the 1970s saw their immediate past as brighter than the future before them. Indeed, in 1979 President Carter told the national television audience in his "Crisis of Confidence" speech that "a majority of our people believe that the next five years will be worse than the past five years." By 1988 Reagan had reversed that pattern. Americans were both more satisfied with their present quality of life and more hopeful that it would improve in the foreseeable future.[4] Reagan told Americans it was "morning again in America" and by his rhetorical and substantive leadership helped them believe just that.

In no small irony, Reagan also reinvigorated the belief that government was capable of running the country. While seeking to minimize government's role and scale, he inadvertently made governance credible again. He said he would do a limited number of things, and some of the biggest of those actually seemed to get done. To be sure, the continued inability to rein in the deficit and the gradual public recognition of the scope of the S&L debacle undercut the new message of governmental competency. But despite stupid gaffes and serious mistakes, Washington no longer seemed quite as hapless as it had in the disheartening 1970s.

At the same time, Reagan renewed faith in the presidency as an institution. He demonstrated that the presidency remained a powerful political instrument and that the office did not necessarily destroy or overwhelm its occupant. Lyndon B. Johnson had been broken in office, Nixon besieged, Ford befuddled, and Carter overwhelmed. Perhaps, thought some, the job had just gotten too big, the challenges too daunting, the times too complex. Reagan proved all that wrong. He managed to do the job while appearing to enjoy it. He could even quip about not working all that hard at it. Some of the jokes were old and tired—"A hard day's work never killed anybody, but I figure why take the chance." Others were wickedly funny, as when toward the end of his presidency Reagan publicly contemplated retirement—"I'm looking forward to going home at last, putting my feet up and taking a good long nap. [Pause.] I guess it won't be that much different after all."[5] Lame or clever, such jokes had a self-deprecating charm and conveyed a significant message—I am in charge here. This is doable. Man is in the saddle, not events. Harvard's Richard Neustadt, the dean of presidential scholars in the discipline of political science, updated his classic study of the executive office, *Presidential Power*, to observe that Reagan restored the public image of the presidency to a "fair (if perhaps rickety) approximation of its Rooseveltian mold: a place of popularity, influence, and initiative, a source of programmatic and symbolic leadership, both pacesetter and tonesetter, the nation's voice to both the world and us, and—like or hate the policies—a presence many of us loved to see as Chief of State."[6]

Tellingly, it was intellectuals who were most spectacularly immune to Reagan's cultivation of national optimism. The mid-to-late 1980s saw an epidemic of despair, with the publication of a number of much-talked-about books on the theme of American decline. On some of the nation's most prestigious university campuses, it was not morning in America but rather twilight. The highly regarded historian Paul Kennedy of Yale garnered the most acclaim with his book *The Rise and Fall of the Great Powers*, which looked at Britain as the latest empire to expire from imperial overstretch and America as the next in line to suffer that fate. Kennedy's book, a serious and intellectually impressive work of historical scholarship, rose to the top of the best-seller list, and for a season the author found himself the center of media attention. Senator Timothy E. Wirth, a Colorado Democrat, reported that Kennedy's ideas were "circulating everywhere in Congress; they are referred to in hearings on and off the floor."[7] Others scholars advanced similar arguments. Mancur Olson of the University of Maryland focused on the theme of domestic decline in his 1982 book *The Rise and Decline of Nations*; David Calleo of Johns Hopkins contributed a 1987 study entitled *Beyond American Hegemony*; and Walter Russell Mead in his book *Mortal Splendor* indicted the excesses of both the LBJ years and the Reagan era for causing the loss of American preeminence. The passage of time, however, has proven the so-called declinists, in their learned pessimism, quite wrong. In his plainspoken, sunny optimism, Reagan had it right.

Reagan's final major achievement was slowing the growth of the federal government. He was not able to roll back the American welfare state, but he was able to arrest its movement—seemingly inexorable until 1980—in the direction of the more thoroughgoing European welfare-state model. Milton Friedman, the high priest of the free-market political economy, later joked that Reagan had replaced galloping socialism with creeping socialism. In other words, for conservatives, Reagan's holding steady of the federal government's share of national economic activity was not a total victory, but it was a genuine achievement. Liberals saw the matter differently. In their eyes, holding the size of government steady in the face of an increasing population and unmet needs was a failure of both governance and moral imagination.

As for the noteworthy regrets of his presidency, Reagan mentioned only one in passing in his farewell address—the deficit. Despite the accusation and the appearance of having purposely engineered the trebling of the national debt from $1 trillion to nearly $3 trillion over the course of his presidency, Reagan truly did bemoan his inability to bring the problem under some semblance of control. As we have seen, the negative impact of the deficit overhang never proved to be quite as large or as certain as contemporary critics suggested; but the deficit did continue to serve as a significant and lingering drag (partly substantive, largely psychological) on future economic growth, and a significant problem for Reagan's successors to resolve. When those successors finally solved the deficit problem in the early 1990s, they did so, it should be noted, in part because Reagan's Cold War victory produced a large peace dividend in the form of dramatically reduced defense outlays.

One significant shortcoming went unmentioned in Reagan's final summing up: the failure to make progress in healing the nation's longstanding racial wounds. Although the number of affluent black families doubled in the 1980s, the president and his administration were widely reviled by the nation's black leadership.[8] Civil-rights leaders accused Reagan of being a racist or allowing himself to be manipulated by racists. The chairman of the board of the NAACP said Reagan was "basically a reactionary and a racist." Benjamin Hooks, the executive director of the group, observed, "If he doesn't have a discriminatory bone in his body, somebody round him does." Roger Wilkins complained that Reagan had "found a way to make racism palatable and politically potent again." There is little doubt that many African Americans shared those attitudes. A *Washington Post* poll in 1986 reported that 56 percent of blacks considered Reagan to be a racist.[9]

The accusation of personal racism was mistaken. Reagan had heard it before in his political career, and it was the one line of attack that could shatter his usual equanimity. Reagan's parents went out of their way to instill in their two sons an abhorrence of prejudice, and the president's biographers agree that Reagan internalized those lessons fully in his personal affairs. In one oft-recounted incident, the young Reagan took two black Eureka College football teammates, who had been denied a hotel room because of their race, home to stay with him and his parents while the team was on the road. But a lack of personal prejudice did not translate into complete, or even noteworthy, support for the political preferences of blacks.

Reagan opposed important elements of the mainstream civil-rights movement's agenda throughout his political career. At the outset, he opposed the Voting Rights Act of 1965 on Constitutional grounds. In time, he came to believe that affirmative action, especially as its focus shifted from outreach to outcomes, was itself racially discriminatory. As the historian Raymond Wolters has made clear, Reagan sought to reorient the federal government's approach in civil rights policy. His administration moved away from the support for color consciousness, affirmative action, and group rights that had become the norm, into outright opposition to quotas, forced busing, and the use of race in drawing electoral boundaries.

Edwin Meese, Reagan's longtime adviser and the attorney general from 1984 to 1988, and William Bradford Reynolds, the assistant attorney general who headed the Civil Rights Division of the Justice Department, together led the charge to the right. Their efforts appeared to pay off when the Supreme Court in a series of decisions in the late 1980s and early 1990s chipped away at the foundations of affirmative action, which had by default become the virtual centerpiece of the civil rights agenda. "I think our effort succeeded," Reynolds maintained. "We wanted to get rid of group entitlement and equal results and move toward equal opportunity. I think that's been accomplished."[10] That verdict was, however, premature.

In fact, affirmative action withstood the assaults of the Reagan conservatives and an increasingly hostile public opinion. It was saved ultimately by resort to a new rationale—the need for "diversity" on college campuses and in the workplace—which enjoyed the support of the broader culture (especially after the infusion of multiculturalism in the 1980s), the educational establishment, and, not least, the U.S. corporate elite. By the beginning of the 1990s Americans increasingly viewed affirmative action as an attempt to accommodate changing demographic realities—an increasingly multicultural society. Affirmative action's original rationale of attempting to redress old injuries remained, of course, but it was bolstered substantially by the appeal to the emergent cultural goal and ideal of "diversity." By the turn of the century, it was not just the federal government but increasingly also the "diversity officers" of large educational and business institutions who drove affirmative action as a policy.[11]

What, then, to make of Reagan's record on race? To condemn his intentions (especially remembering that issues of race relations were never at the top of his tightly focused personal political agenda and that he usually left the heavy-lifting in matters external to that agenda to others) or the outcomes of those intentions in starkly moralistic terms implies that there was only one morally correct and practically wise course open to policymakers in this most vexed and vexing policy area. That contention would strike many thoughtful

Americans, and certainly most conservatives, as highly dubious. Instead, it seems likely that liberals and conservatives will continue to differ in their assessment of Reagan's record on race.

Still, the liberal complaint that Reagan should have done more, paid more attention, is not wholly unpersuasive. Even the black appointees within the administration, led by Clarence Thomas, complained directly to the president that the administration had "no positive or coherent policy" to put alongside its opposition to quotas and bussing.[12] Once again, as in the matter of the AIDS epidemic, Reagan, the master of symbolic politics, could have tried harder to communicate to African Americans that they were not, as the writer Tamar Jacoby put it in a superb study of race relations, dwellers in "someone else's house."[13] To convey powerfully that he was the president of *all* Americans, even while opposing on principled grounds the mainstream civil-rights agenda of the day, would have been a daunting undertaking, open to charges of insincerity and hypocrisy, fraught with political costs, and likely without political payoff. Nevertheless, it was a challenge Reagan should have accepted.

One is again reminded of Hugh Heclo's point about the limits of Reagan's underlying sacramental vision of America as a land and an experience existing providentially outside of history, a city upon a hill. In Reagan's vision, Heclo writes, "one finds an unqualified assertion of American goodness with only the barest sense of judgment looming in the background."[14] That perspective, reinforced by his inexhaustible personal optimism, caused in Reagan a certain fuzziness of vision regarding aspects of American life that might fairly be viewed by others as systemically flawed or problematic. Race was one of those blurry spots. Reagan was temperamentally and philosophically indisposed to look there, certainly not relentlessly enough to discern the full outlines of what was a continuing American dilemma, one so troubled as to lie beyond presidential solution but one perhaps nevertheless open to some modicum of presidential amelioration.

How historians have come to grips with Reagan's overall record is an illuminating story in its own right. Reagan left Washington with the highest popular approval rating of any retiring president in the postwar era, but that did not translate into critical approval by either commentators or scholars. At the end of the Reagan presidency the television journalist Lesley Stahl commented, "I predict historians are going to be totally baffled by how the American people fell in love with this man and followed him the way they did."[15] The casual quality of Stahl's assumption that Reagan did not deserve such popular approval is itself arresting, but her implicitly negative judgment was initially widely shared by scholars. A 1994 poll of 481 historians placed Reagan in the "below average" category of presidents, rating him twenty-eighth in a field of thirty-seven. Two years later, Arthur M. Schlesinger Jr. conducted a poll of thirty elite historians and two prominent, strongly liberal politicians, which rated Reagan only marginally higher—twenty-fifth in a field of thirty-nine, in the "low average" category. In 2000, the *Wall Street Journal* joined with the Federalist Society to conduct a poll purposely designed to probe a more ideologically diverse body of expert opinion. They selected their 78 experts so as to create a rough balance between left-leaning and right-leaning individuals, and they broadened their panel's range of expertise by including professors of law and political science in additional to the usual historians. Reagan fared considerably better after such adjustments and with the further passage of time, ranking eighth overall, in the middle of the "near great" category. Here, too, however, Reagan's leadership remained a matter of dispute and controversy, with the experts ranking him both the single most underrated and the second most overrated president of all time. The historians were notably less generous in their evaluations than the professors of law and political science.[16]

One can fairly conclude from these early results that polls of scholars seeking to measure presidential greatness are blunt instruments, much influenced by the ideological predilections of the individuals doing the judging and, in the case of recent presidents, by lingering partisan passions. It is likely that the gradual waning of those passions with the passage of time will cause Reagan's ranking to rise in future evaluations of presidential greatness, but just how high is uncertain. In the meantime there is available a different but powerfully illuminating way to gauge the impact of Reagan's presidential leadership, a way to assess that leadership in a large analytical frame using the theoretical model of presidential politics developed in the recent scholarship of the Yale political scientist Stephen Skowronek.

REDEFINING THE POLITICAL MAINSTREAM: REAGAN AS A RECONSTRUCTIVE PRESIDENT

According to Skowronek's typology of political leadership, Reagan stands as a president of the reconstructive sort, historically the most consequential of all presidential types. Reconstructive presidents tend to appear on the scene when the previous political regime has been thoroughly discredited by an inability to respond relevantly and successfully to the pressing problems of the day and appears, in a word, exhausted. (Think of Jimmy Carter and the malaise of the 1970s.) That background of failure, according to Skowronek, opens up the opportunity for reconstructive presidents "to remake the government wholesale" and "reset the very terms and conditions of constitutional government." They "reformulate the nation's political agenda altogether, to galvanize support for the release of governmental power on new terms, and to move the nation past the old problems, eyeing a different set of possibilities altogether."[17]

Reagan met the specifications of the reconstructive type in a nearly perfect fit. As Skowronek, not himself an uncritical admirer of Reagan or his achievements, writes, "No president in recent times has so radically altered the terms in which prior governmental commitments are now dealt with or the conditions under which previously established interests are served."[18] Reagan cast an exceedingly long shadow. He ushered in the longest period of prosperity in U.S. history, led the West to victory in the Cold War while reestablishing an international preeminence that many feared had been permanently lost, and changed significantly the way Americans thought about themselves, their government, and their country. He orchestrated the most consequential presidency since that of the twentieth century's other reconstructive leader, young Dutch Reagan's early political idol, Franklin D. Roosevelt.

Reagan shifted the American political mainstream to the right in part by forcing his opponents to move in that direction in order to counter his electoral and programmatic success. A sometimes overlooked but compelling example occurred in the area of economic policymaking. In the early 1980s Reagan's economic policy prescriptions were commonly denounced as "voodoo economics" and casually dismissed as Reaganomics—a term often used to suggest an idiosyncratic and loopy brand of economic preference rather than economic analysis. But as the decade unfolded more than a few Democrats found themselves gravitating in the direction of supply-side economics. "Democrats have been concerned for too long with the distribution of golden eggs," said Paul Tsongas, a Massachusetts Democrat, in 1984. "Now it's time to worry about the health of the goose."[19]

Even hardcore Keynesians found themselves pulled (or was it pushed?) to the right during the Reagan years. Just how far so was inadvertently illustrated by the publication in 1987 of a new Keynesian manifesto, *Hard Heads, Soft Hearts: Tough-Minded Economics for a Just Society*, written by the distinguished Princeton economist Alan Blinder. A chastened but still resolute Keynesian, Blinder set out to sketch the main features of the "matured, battle-scarred Keynesianism of the 1980s" that had succeeded the "naive, optimistic Keynesianism of the 1960s," which itself had failed so dramatically both as analysis and as policy prescription in the era of stagflation. First, he reported, the new improved 1980s-style Keynesianism had lost its innocence; thoroughly modern Keynesians no longer believed that the economy could be fine-tuned by the careful application of macroeconomic theory. Second, he admitted that "the 1960s view that stabilization policy can push the economy toward permanently lower unemployment, albeit at the cost of permanently higher inflation, is gone forever." In other words, Keynesians had surrendered their belief in a permanent tradeoff between inflation and unemployment. Third, Blinder acknowledged that the failures of the 1970s "taught Keynesians that aggregate demand fluctuations are not always the dominant influence on the economy. . . . Now, of course, we know that supply fluctuations can, and sometimes do it, dominate demand fluctuations." Fourth, even Keynesians now admitted that the rational expectationists had raised important questions about the efficacy of state interventions in the economy. Finally, Blinder confessed that the Keynesian belief that only fiscal policy really mattered was "long since gone." "In that limited respect," he wrote in an understated concession, "monetarism has been victorious." Blinder insisted that the central tenets of Keynesian economics remained intact, but it is impossible not to be impressed by how much ground the new chastened Keynesianism had been forced to concede. Clearly, the combination of historical adversity in the 1970s and Reaganomics in the 1980s moved the discussion of economic analysis and policy discernibly to the right.[20]

The effects of Reagan's powerful gravitational pull could also be seen in the emergence within the opposition party of the so-called New Democrats. Reagan's significant electoral victory in 1980, together with the accompanying Republican capture of the Senate for the first time since 1952, prompted predictable soul-searching on the part of Democrats. Reagan's success in dominating the national agenda, his early steamroller legislative victories, and especially his overwhelming victory in the 1984 election lent increasing urgency to the task of formulating a credible response to his leadership. In 1985, the efforts of Democratic moderates and conservatives to forge a coherent and compelling alternative to Reagan's initiatives led to the creation of the Democratic Leadership Council (DLC). The DLC aimed to reorient the larger party away from its post-1960s focus on redistribution, toward a more Reaganesque emphasis on growth and opportunity. One of the DLC's founding spokesmen, Georgia's Senator Sam Nunn, announced, "We are going to try to move the party—both in substance and perception—back into the mainstream of American political life."[21]

The political mainstream Nunn referred to was the one that Reagan's reconstructive presidency had shifted rightward. In transforming the national political discussion, Reagan redefined and reenergized conservatism and also delegitimated the liberalism that had defined the previous New-Deal-and-postwar political regime. It was Reagan who defined the contours and direction of the new political mainstream, as well as the pace of its flow. His successors had little choice but to accommodate to the new political reality he created, to consolidate the gains, polish the rough edges, and attempt to solve some of the new problems caused by the Reagan reconstruction itself.

George H. W. Bush's single presidential term illustrated just how difficult it could be to play the role of the faithful son following in the footsteps of a reconstructive leader. When running for the presidency in his own right in 1988, Bush promised to extend the Reagan reconstruction by rounding off its roughest edges, by achieving a "kinder, gentler" America through the voluntary energy of "a thousand points of light." At the same time, the former vice president predictably wrapped himself in the mantle of the Reagan reconstruction and vowed to continue to pursue its fundamental agenda, asking, "Who can you most trust to continue the Reagan revolution?" And it was the need to pay homage to the Reagan record that lured Bush into making his disastrous pledge to continue the new orthodoxy no matter what. "The Congress," he told the 1988 Republican nominating convention, "will push me to raise taxes, and I'll say no, they'll push, and I'll say no, and they'll push again. And all I can say to them is: Read my lips: no new taxes."[22]

A year and a half later Bush derailed his presidency when he broke his "Read My Lips" pledge and negotiated a tax hike-spending control deal with congressional Democrats. The arrangement was a reasonable policy response to Reagan's self-admitted deficit failure, but it touched off a firestorm of opposition from the Republican right wing, which had never fully trusted Bush's commitment to Reaganism in the first place. In response to heated charges of betrayal and heresy, Bush then flip-flopped and denounced the tax increase he had agreed to. In a risky effort to heal the breach within the party, he also allowed the Republican right wing to dominate the 1992 convention, which enabled the Clinton campaign to paint the Republicans, including the moderate Bush, as the party of divisive extremism. Reagan's shadow did not destroy George H. W. Bush's presidency, but it did vastly complicate his leadership and weaken him in ways that left him dangerously vulnerable when other things, such as the mild 1990–91 recession, went wrong. For Republicans, even the appearance of drifting out of Reagan's newly redefined political mainstream carried serious political risk. The experiences of the DLC on the Democratic side and George H. W. Bush on the Republican make it clear how necessary it was for those seeking or holding the presidency after Reagan to "get right" with the reorientation of American politics he had presided over.

REDEFINING THE CULTURAL MAINSTREAM

While politics turned right in the 1980s, American culture accelerated its movement, already under way since the 1960s, in a leftward direction away from the sway of bourgeois values, mores, and institutions. "The great contradiction of the decade," Gilbert T. Sewall has observed acutely, "remains the consolidation of progressive power in culture and society despite the solid Reagan Majority."[23] As a result of that consolidation, the cultural mainstream shifted, much as did the political mainstream, except in the opposite direction.

The cultural reorientation away from the traditional middle-class moral order that had long dominated American culture constituted a second overarching change in American life in the 1980s. The bourgeois ethos exalted the values and habits of work, thrift, delayed gratification, temperance, fidelity, reticence, self-reliance, and self-discipline; rested upon such fundamental institutions as the traditional family (two heterosexual parents, with offspring) and the Judeo-Christian religious tradition; and acknowledged the existence of moral authority and standards external to the self. One could see the weakening of the middle-class cultural regime occurring in small, discrete, and seemingly isolated particulars, but it was difficult at the time to discern the larger pattern of change and its underlying dynamic. In the early 1990s, however, two of the nation's most astute cultural observers offered a compelling interpretation of the decline of the bourgeois cultural order.

In a famous and much-discussed essay, Daniel Patrick Moynihan, the senior Democratic senator from New York, explained how the bourgeois moral order had been progressively weakened by the tendency of social workers, intellectuals, and the mass media to redefine as "normal" kinds of behavior that had previously been considered aberrant. Moynihan called the phenomenon "defining deviancy down," and pointed as an example to the normalizing of the bizarre behavior of the de-institutionalized mentally ill, who were often viewed in the 1980s simply as homeless people in need of affordable shelter rather than as, in all too many cases, the seriously psychotic in dire need of medical help and supervision. The process of normalizing also occurred in the matter of escalating crime and violence, both of which reached epidemic proportions in the 1980s. The pace of violence so outran the capacity for outrage that Americans became inured to levels of criminal activity that would have provoked national disbelief and outrage only a generation before. Finally, Moynihan pointed to the skyrocketing increase in out-of-wedlock births, which, despite mountainous evidence of a causal connection between fatherlessness and poverty, welfare dependency, and educational failure, was increasingly defined as a viable and worthy lifestyle choice rather than as a socially very risky one. In all these cases, the redefinition as normal or unexceptional of kinds and levels of behavior that just a generation earlier had been considered troubling breaches of the bourgeois order tended to make that order increasingly irrelevant.[24]

At the same time, argued Charles Krauthammer, a Pulitzer-Prize winner for journalistic commentary and one of the nation's most acute pundits, a related process of "defining deviancy up" was undermining the bourgeois order's most hallowed institutions. "As part of the vast social project of moral leveling, it is not enough for the deviant to be normalized," he explained. "The normal must be found to be deviant. . . . Normal middle-class life then stands exposed as the true home of violence and abuse and a whole catalog of aberrant acting and thinking."

Among the bourgeois institutions called into question by defining deviancy up was the traditional two-heterosexual-parent family. Throughout the 1980s, feminists joined with therapeutic professionals (social workers, psychologists, and psychiatrists) and the media in the discovery of what was perceived to be a virtual national epidemic of childhood sexual abuse. Suspecting (no doubt correctly) that child sexual abuse was, by its very nature, an under-reported criminal offense, the coalition of the concerned was determined to uncover the offense wherever it might lie hidden, even (or especially) if nestled in the bosom of the family and secreted in the darkest recesses of the victim's psyche. The contemporaneous development among therapists of a new emphasis on so-called repressed memories, which, it was claimed, could be retrieved with the help of recovered-memory specialists, provided further impetus to what quickly became a national crusade against child sexual abuse. As the radical feminist authors of *The Courage to Heal: A Guide for Women Survivors of Child Sexual Abuse*, a particularly popular and influential self-help book published in 1988, explained, "If you are unable to remember any specific instances [of childhood sexual abuse] . . . but still have a feeling that something abusive happened to you, it probably did." One result of the crusade against sexual abuse was a proliferation of long-after-the-alleged-fact accusations of fathers having sexually abused their daughters, charges often based on memories "recovered" under the careful guidance of therapeutic experts. Another result of the crusade was the delegitimization of the bourgeois family. Over the course of the next decade, the scientific community thoroughly discredited the recovered memory movement, but only after it had caused immense personal harm to both accusers and accused, and serious collateral damage to the notion of the bourgeois family as a vital, irreplaceable cultural institution, society's haven in a heartless world.[25]

Krauthammer argued that other pillars of everyday bourgeois life suffered similarly. The redefining of rape to include varieties of what was called date rape, which by some definitions involved not the use of force but such intangibles as male verbal insistence and persistent cajoling, made rape appear endemic and also called into question (and threatened to criminalize) traditional heterosexual mating rituals. Accordingly, the feminist writer Naomi Wolf could write in 1991 that there existed "a situation among the young in which boys rape and girls get raped *as a normal course of events* [emphasis in the original]."[26] A final example of putative bourgeois iniquity involved the undeniably judgmental (and inevitably hypocritical) nature of middle-class morality, which opened traditionalists to charges of intolerance and insensitivity, among the worst of cultural offenses according to the newly minted standards of diversity and multiculturalism. In this sense, asserted Krauthammer, defining deviancy up served as "the perfect vehicle for exposing the rottenness of bourgeois life." And a rotten value system invited its own replacement.

The calling into question of the bourgeois ethos coincided with the ascendancy in the 1980s of a competing value system and cultural order based on the emergent values of postmodernism and the highly individualistic therapeutic culture, inevitably colored by the increasing materialism of American life and often strained through the ideological sieves of diversity and multiculturalism.

The end product was a largely secular cultural system noteworthy for its unwillingness to judge the actions of its adherents by fixed and objective standards of good or bad, right or wrong; for its tolerance; for its elevation of the self as the lodestar for life; and for its emphasis on personal self-actualization and self-fulfillment. The collision of these two competing cultural orientations constituted the essence of the culture war of the 1980s.

Observers of the 1980s culture war, a clash of value systems that continued through the following decade, have interpreted its outcome in a number of different ways. A number of conservative commentators saw the results as a rather complete victory for the progressivist cultural worldview. Writing in 1998, Roger Kimball asserted that "the radical trends that seemed startling in 1990 have by now thoroughly established themselves. They're part of the ambient cultural poison surrounding us: so familiar as to be barely detectable, but progressively damaging nevertheless." George Gilder in 1995 reported that "Bohemian values have come to prevail over bourgeois virtue in sexual morals and family roles, arts and letters, bureaucracies and universities, popular culture and public life. As a result, culture and family life are widely in chaos, cities seethe with venereal plagues, schools and colleges fall to obscurantism and propaganda, the courts are a carnival of pettifoggery." Robert H. Bork, whose rejection as a nominee to the U.S. Supreme Court in 1988 constituted a notable defeat for the old order in the culture war, wrote in 1995 of a society and culture "slouching towards Gomorrah," and warned that "for the moment our trajectory continues downward." William J. Bennett, the head of the National Endowment for the Humanities and secretary of education under Reagan, urged conservatives to struggle against the "de-valuing of America," but spoke of the effort as a "cultural and institutional reclamation project," the term reclamation seeming to imply a taking back of that which had been lost.[27]

Other commentators have taken a slightly different tack, viewing the outcome of the culture war not in terms of victory or defeat but rather of its having created a new cultural amalgam. The sociologist Alan Wolfe suggested that "the two sides presumed to be fighting the culture war do not so much represent a divide between one group of Americans and another as a divide between sets of values important to everyone. . . . It is a basic truth of American society that no one is a traditionalist or a modernist, but that everyone lives with varying degrees of both." The journalist David Brooks, perhaps the most widely read proponent of the amalgam interpretation, maintained that the cultural struggles in the decades since the 1960s had created a new cultural type that combined elements of both bourgeois and bohemian culture, which he labeled the "Bobo." "The truth is," he wrote, "that Bobos have constructed new social codes that characteristically synthesize bourgeois self-control and bohemian emancipation." Bobos fused "the bourgeois imperative to strive and succeed" and "the bohemian impulse to experience new sensations." But both Wolfe and Brooks treated the culture war as superficial friction rather than fundamental disagreement, and in that they erred.[28] Although some cultural blending has undoubtedly occurred, chiefly in the upper middle class, it has resembled a hostile takeover more than a friendly merger, with the bohemian ethos gaining its influence from the retreat of the bourgeois order.[29]

In reality, the culture war continues, with postmodern America in the twenty-first century more nearly resembling the "one nation, two cultures" model articulated by the historian Gertrude Himmelfarb. In her 1999 book of that name, Himmelfarb declared that the progressivist, aggressively secular, postmodern ethos of the 1980s had, by the end of the century, become the dominant American culture. The older bourgeois order had in the meantime been reduced to the status of a dissident subculture, still influential but clearly no longer hegemonic in the way it had been a generation or two earlier. The two cultural regimes coexisted uneasily, with much continuing friction between them.[30]

By the end of the nineties a number of prominent cultural conservatives from the religious right voiced agreement with the two-cultures analysis and publicly accepted their newly subordinate cultural status. Paul Weyrich, the conservative Christian activist who suggested to Jerry Falwell back in the late 1970s that he name his organization the Moral Majority, announced in a 1999 open letter to Christian traditionalists that "we probably have lost the culture war. That doesn't mean the war is not going to continue and that it isn't going to be fought on other fronts. But in terms of society in general, we have lost." As proof, he observed that "what Americans would have found absolutely intolerable only a few years ago, a majority now not only tolerates but celebrates." The way to respond to that state of affairs was not to further contest the matter in the political realm, Weyrich asserted, because "while we have been fighting and winning in politics, our culture has decayed into something approaching barbarism." Instead, he called upon politically conservative Christians "to look at ways to separate ourselves from the institutions that have been captured by the ideology of Political Correctness, or by other enemies of our traditional culture." Cal Thomas and Ed Dobson, two other veterans of Falwell's Moral Majority, published a similar analysis and summoned their fellows to cultivate the dissident, traditionalist subculture. "The Left, securely in control of all cultural and educational institutions, has won the culture wars," commented the Godfather of neoconservatism, Irving Kristol, "and the Right has left the major battlefields—but not to sulk, instead to 'do it their way.'"[31]

Even the happy warrior of the Kulturkampf, Pat Buchanan, eventually despaired. Some thirteen years after his call to arms at the 1992 Republican convention, Buchanan described American culture as "toxic and poisonous" and remarked, "I can't say we won the culture war, and it's more likely we lost it."

Not even the defeat of gay marriage in eleven state-ballot referenda in 2004 could cheer him up. "I think in the long run," he observed, "that will be seen as a victory in defense of a citadel that eventually fell." He blamed not only his cultural adversaries, but also the Republican Party, for failing to commit itself to the sort of all-out cultural struggle he had called for earlier. The Republicans had "abdicated from the cultural war." "They've stacked arms" he complained, in large part because they correctly saw the traditionalist moral agenda "as no longer popular, no longer the majority positions they used to be."[32]

Thus, while U.S. politics took a right turn in the 1980s, American culture accelerated its movement in a nominally leftward direction away from the sway of bourgeois values, mores, and institutions. The cultural mainstream shifted, much as did the political mainstream, except in a nearly opposite direction. The result was a seeming disjunction in American life, but one that could, in fact, be bridged, as President Bill Clinton and hosts of ordinary Americans have proven.

BILL CLINTON AND
THE LONG SHADOW OF THE EIGHTIES

The shadow cast by the changes of the 1980s was a long one. No public figure better exemplified the pervasive and long-lasting influence of the 1980s on both American politics and culture than Bill Clinton. Indeed, in Clinton the political and cultural aftereffects of the 1980s became inextricably intertwined. His person, politics, and presidency all reflected clearly both Reagan's rightward reorientation of politics and the longer-running leftward movement of culture that was powerfully underway in the 1980s.

Clinton joined the Democratic Leadership Council in its early days, used the organization as a vehicle for his political rise, and thus played a key role in moving the so-called New Democrats into the reoriented Reagan mainstream. He served as the DLC's chairman in 1990–91, articulating its call for greater personal social responsibility and increased governmental fiscal responsibility, for more efficient and innovative government, and for a strong national defense, while at the same time advancing his own prospects for national office. In 1992 Clinton won the Democratic nomination and then the presidency on a platform that incorporated the main elements of the DLC's New Democrat approach.[33]

Clinton's presidency temporarily transformed the Democratic Party. As the historian Kenneth S. Baer has written, "A party that for the past thirty years had been seen as profligate 'tax-and-spenders,' reflexive defenders of federal governmental programs, pacifist isolationists, and advocates of an active social liberalism now had a president who championed the reinvention of government, welfare reform, fiscal restraint, economic growth, free trade, mainstream values, and an internationalist foreign policy."[34] In order to effect those changes, Clinton, his DLC allies, and their supporters had to wrest control of the Democratic Party from its left wing—Jesse Jackson, his Rainbow Coalition faction, and such wheelhorse liberals as Ohio's senator Howard Metzenbaum, New York's governor Mario Cuomo, and the omnipresent Ted Kennedy. The internecine struggle was hard-fought and occasionally nasty, with charges of DLC racism and the accusation that the DLC was nothing more than the "southern white boys' caucus."[35] In 1992 the centrists won, at least for a season. "We are all 'New' Democrats now," commented the liberal congressman Richard Gephardt (D-Missouri) in 1996.[36]

Clinton's presidency looked from a distance to be a fulfillment of the Reagan presidency. To be sure, significant differences appeared when one tightened the focus (Clinton hit wealthy Americans with a large tax increase and redistributed wealth to the working poor by doubling the Earned Income Tax Credit during his time in office), but to overlook the several broad continuities is to miss an important point. Clinton carried his party away from its protectionist past, away from the infatuation with so-called strategic trade policy, into a new era of global free trade. After a tough fight and over bitter opposition, Clinton in 1993 signed into law the North American Free Trade Act (NAFTA), which had been negotiated under Bush, bringing to fruition a vision Reagan first expressed in his speech announcing his candidacy for president in 1979. Perhaps even more striking, in a symbolic sense, Clinton boldly announced in his 1996 state of the union address that "the era of Big Government is over." As if to prove that he really meant it, Clinton cooperated with House Republicans to achieve the most dramatic restructuring of social welfare policy since the advent of the New Deal. As the governor of California in the early 1970s, Reagan had opposed a proposal presented at a meeting of the National Governors' Association to have Washington wholly federalize the welfare entitlement embodied primarily in the Aid to Families with Dependent Children (AFDC) program; the vote went against him 49–1. A quarter-century later, in 1996, Clinton signed into law the Temporary Assistance for Needy Families Act, which ended the legal entitlement to welfare benefits, required a large proportion of recipients to work or undergo employment-related training, and imposed a five-year limit for the receipt of federal welfare funds. The new law terminated AFDC, the old mainstay of the New Deal–Great Society welfare regime. It was the biggest rollback of the federal welfare-state apparatus in the modern era and the attainment of a longtime Reagan goal. That it happened under a Democratic president was compelling evidence of the rightward shift of the political system's center of gravity under Reagan.

Clinton embodied the cultural changes of the 1980s as well as that era's political shift. His pledge to put together a cabinet "that looked like America" represented a triumph of multiculturalism and diversity, in both its idealistic and problematic aspects. He was the first American president fundamentally shaped by, and fully at home in, the postmodern, therapeutic culture; he personified its values, both the good and the dubious. The cultural predilections of Clinton (and his vice presidential running mate Albert Gore) quickly became fodder for an increasingly postmodern style of journalistic commentary that often seemed to adopt the same therapeutic sensibility that it so archly described. On the eve of his inauguration, the White House correspondents for the New York Times wrote acidly about what they saw as the upcoming "Co-Dependent White House." "The President," they elaborated, "likes to talk of his family's two generations of compulsions (stepfather an abusive alcoholic, mother a gambler, brother a recovering cocaine addict, himself a fast-food addict). He has admitted to marital problems and has been through family therapy for his brother's addiction."[37] Cut from the same cultural cloth, Gore, too, was at home with the therapeutic approach. He was fluent in the language of dysfunctional families and psychic numbing, and able to quote from memory from the work of John Bradshaw, author of the popular therapeutic text *Healing the Shame That Binds You*.

The therapeutic sensibility surfaced again a month after the inauguration, when the newly installed president took forty top officials on a weekend retreat to Camp David, along with two outside facilitators. In an effort to help build up trust among the attendees, the facilitators asked each person to share a personal secret with the others. The president informed his staff and advisers that his life had been profoundly affected by the fact that he had been a chubby youngster and was often taunted by others, with enough injury to his self-esteem to make the matter memorable. Most of the participants took the retreat in stride. Donna Shalala, Clinton's health and human services secretary and the veteran of a career in the postmodern university, commented off-handedly that "all of us have been on 5,000 retreats." The enforced intimacy and sharing was too much, however, for seventy-two-year-old Lloyd Bentsen, the Treasury secretary, who thought the entire exercise bizarre. "Afterwards," reported James Adams of London's *Sunday Times*, "whenever anyone asked [Bentsen] . . . about the culture of the Clinton government, his eyes would move heavenward and he would shake his head in sorrow."[38]

In national politics as in personal affairs, the therapeutic approach held out special promise when the going got tough. The off-year election of 1994, when the Republicans gained control of both the House of Representatives and the Senate for the first time since 1946, stunned the Clinton family and administration and prompted a searching psychic re-assessment. One day in late December 1994, Clinton invited to the White House three of the best-known gurus of the therapeutic culture: Stephen R. Covey, the author of the best-selling book *The Seven Habits of Highly Effective People* (and creator of the Seven Habits

Executive Organizer, the Seven Habits Pocket Organizer, and the Seven Habits Effectiveness Profile); Marianne Williamson, the lay minister who presided at Elizabeth Taylor's eighth wedding and was known in the celebrity press as "the guru to the glitterati"; and the indefatigable "peak performance" coach Tony Robbins. The White House refused to discuss what transpired that day, but the cast of characters pretty much gave the game away. The president was obviously energizing his inner resources in order to bounce back after political defeat. A British journalist commented skeptically: "All the 'touchy feely' talk is simply another excuse to avoid taking any responsibility in a society that encourages people to blame everyone else for anything that goes wrong." "The first couple's self-pity and stress," sniffed an American editorialist, "are beginning to show in ways that diminish them."[39]

Clinton's therapeutic sensibility was often dismissed as a wholly idiosyncratic quirk or misunderstood as simply the generational consequence of having come of age in the 1960s. To hardcore conservatives, it was proof of serious spiritual impairment — "The President as Navel-Gazer-in-Chief, the National Narcissus," the Conservative Book club warned its clientele.[40] But Clinton's fascination with feelings, both his own and those of others, could endear as well as enrage. While Clinton's detractors mocked his self-proclaimed ability to feel the pain of others, many Americans found his vaunted empathetic powers and therapeutic vulnerabilities both seductive and soothing. At the 1992 Democratic national convention, Clinton won over his audience with an empathetic discussion of family values. "And I want to say to every child in America tonight who's out there trying to grow up without a father or a mother; I know how you feel. You're special, too. You matter to America. . . . And if other politicians make you feel like you're not a part of their family, come on and be part of ours."[41] What was striking about Clinton's reliance on the language of feelings was not that it was slick and manipulative, which it was, but rather that it was at the same time paradoxically heartfelt and real.

Clinton personified the triumph of the therapeutic culture with a special clarity in the mid-1990s, but the therapeutic sensibility was in evidence elsewhere in the political culture as well. The self-help guru Stephen Covey advised the Republican Speaker of the House Newt Gingrich as well as the president. Morris Shechtman, a managerial consultant and psychotherapist, met with congressional Republicans but brought with him a tougher therapeutic approach — he skipped the talk about sharing and empowerment to focus on such sharper-edged topics as the racism that he alleged was inherent in liberal Democrats' vision of the welfare state. And just weeks after the guru pilgrimage to the White House, the Republican House budget committee chairman, John Kasich of Ohio, invited Doug Hall, the author of *Jump Start Your Brain*, to run a seminar for his committee staff members. Hall blasted the 1960s Sam the Sham hit song "Wooly Bully" while the staff members got in touch with their inner-gunslingers by participating in an empowering Nerf-gun shoot-out among themselves.[42] America had, indeed, changed.

The complaints of outraged liberals about the political outcomes of the 1980s and of sour conservatives about the cultural ones have become the staples of America's national conversation in the earliest years of the twenty-first century. Indeed, the combination of a rightward political shift and a leftward cultural tilt helps mightily to explain the increasingly shrill tenor and brittle nature of American public life at the dawn of the new century—in the aftermath of the Long Eighties the right felt frustrated by the fact that it had triumphed politically but continued to lose ground in the cultural struggles of the day, while the left was similarly disappointed at its inability to translate its cultural influence into political victory. Moreover, beginning in the 1980s and accelerating thereafter, political and cultural conflict began to overlap as the two main political parties became increasingly polarized along cultural and religious lines.[43] One result is the political and cultural intertwining that gives meaning to the popular concept of a Red State–Blue State division in American life.

Although it is sometimes said that the debates dominating American life early in the twenty-first century are really the continuation of an interminable argument about the 1960s, both the right and the left agree that the 1980s constituted a tipping point when the United States went seriously wrong. Their political and cultural critiques are persuasive in many of their particulars. The U.S. economy and public policy did become more rigorous and demanding, harsher if you will. American culture did become coarser, more vulgar, and more fragmented. As always, there was much to worry a decent people, mistakes of commission to rectify and of omission to address. But the critics of left and right are hard-pressed to convincingly portray the changes they decry as anything other than the free choices of a free people.

The American people got in the 1980s pretty much what they wanted—a country at once more competitive and efficient *and* more tolerant and inclusive; a country that worked hard and well *and* that allowed its citizens the freedom, within the broadest of boundaries, to be themselves. That combination was unusual, both in the contemporary world and, most certainly, in human history. America continued to fall short of its ideals, but also came sufficiently close to them still to play the role Reagan described movingly in his farewell address: As the new millennium began, the United States remained "still a magnet for all who must have freedom, for all the pilgrims from all the lost places who are hurtling through the darkness, toward home."

In November 1994 Reagan wrote his last letter to the American people. He had recently learned that he had Alzheimer's Disease, a condition that gradually but inexorably erases the victim's memory. As he had so many times before over the course of his long career, he went off by himself to commit his thoughts to paper. In longhand he wrote out a final goodbye. Despite his illness, the prose was as it had been—straightforward and sinewy, its elegance achieved through simplicity and sincerity of expression. He did not complain about his fate, and he wrote, as always, of the future. "I now begin the journey that will lead me into the sunset of my life," he concluded. "I know that for America there will always be a bright dawn ahead." Because of both the political and cultural changes of the 1980s, it remained possible for most Americans to believe Reagan still had it right. All in all, not bad, not bad at all.

NOTES

INTRODUCTION

1. Jon Meacham, "American Dreamer," *Newsweek*, June 14, 2004, 28.

2. Edmund Morris, "The Unknowable," *The New Yorker*, June 28, 2004, 50.

3. George F. Will, "Reagan's Echo in History," *Newsweek*, June 14, 2004, 70; Michael Barone, "Where He Stands in History," *U.S. News and World Report*, June 21, 2004, 59; Charles Krauthammer, "Reagan Revisionism," *Washington Post*, June 11, 2004.

4. Marilyn Berger, "Ronald Reagan Dies at 93," *New York Times*, June 6, 2004.

5. Arthur Schlesinger Jr., "He Knew How to Lead a People," *Newsweek*, June 14, 2004, 44.

6. Christopher Hitchens, "Neither Icon nor Hero," *Ottawa Citizen* [Canada], June 9, 2004; Larry Kramer, "Adolf Reagan," *The Advocate*, July 6, 2004, 32–33.

7. Robert Brustein, "Forty Million Frenchmen," *New Republic*, July 5 and 12, 2004, 27.

8. Peter Yronwood, "Reagan Administration Was a Preview for Bush Fascism," *Columbia Daily Tribune*, July 8, 2004 (letter to editor).

9. Sidney Hook, *The Hero in History: A Study in Limitation and Possibility* (New York: The John Day Company, 1943).

1. MALAISE

1. Lyn Nofziger, *Nofziger* (Washington: Regnery Gateway, 1992), 207.

2. The discussion of the economic woes of the 1970s draws heavily from "Person of the Year 1974: Faisal and Oil," *Time*, January 6, 1975, 8–32; the several essays in "The Reindustrialization of America," *Business Week*, June 30, 1980; and the analytical papers from a January 1980 National Bureau of Economic Research conference on recent economic developments gathered together in *The American Economy in Transition*, ed. Martin Feldstein (Chicago: University of Chicago Press, 1980).

3. Quoted in James R. Schlesinger, "Whither American Industry?" in *Economy in Transition*, ed. Feldstein, 557.

4. Quoted in David Halberstam, *The Reckoning* (New York: Avon, 1986), 518.

5. The impact of imports on the U.S. auto industry is treated in Peter H. Lindert, "U.S. Foreign Trade and Trade Policy in the Twentieth Century," in *The Cambridge Economic History of the United States*, vol. 3, *The Twentieth Century*, ed. Stanley L. Engerman and Robert E. Gallman (New York: Cambridge University Press, 2000), 432–39.

6. Ibid., 438.

7. Lee Iacocca, *Iacocca: An Autobiography* (New York: Bantam Books, 1984), 172.

8. David Hounshell, "Why Corporations Don't Learn Continuously: Waves of Innovation and Desperation at Ford Motor Company, 1903–2003," unpublished paper presented at "Organizing for Innovation: Conference in Honor of Louis P. Galambos," Baltimore, Md., October 25–26, 2002.

9. Ezra Vogel, *Japan as Number One: Lessons for America* (Cambridge: Harvard University Press, 1979).

10. Edwin Mansfield, "Technology and Productivity in the United States," in *American Economy in Transition*, ed. Feldstein, 564–65.

11. Ibid., 564 ff.

12. Seymour Martin Lipset and William Schneider, *The Confidence Gap: Business, Labor, and Government in the Public Mind* (New York: The Free Press, 1983), 408: Lance Morrow, "Epitaph for a Decade," *Time*, January 7, 1980, 38.

13. See, for example, Michael Schudson, *Watergate in History and Memory* (New York: Basic Books, 1992); and Stanley Kutler, *The Wars of Watergate; The Last Crisis of Richard Nixon* (New York: Knopf, 1990).

14. John Robert Greene, *The Presidency of Gerald R. Ford* (Lawrence: University Press of Kansas, 1995), 53.

15. Elizabeth Drew, *American Journal: The Events of 1976* (New York: Random House, 1977), 3.

16. Quoted in Henry Kissinger, *Ending the Vietnam War: A History of America's Involvement in and Extrication from the Vietnam War* (New York: Simon and Schuster, 2003), 529–30.

17. Lewis, "Avoiding a Bloodbath," *New York Times*, March 17; and Schanberg, "Indochina without Americans: For Most, a Better Life," *New York Times*, April 13, 1975.

18. Stephane Courtois et al., *The Black Book of Communism: Crimes, Terror, Repression* (Cambridge: Harvard University Press, 1999), 588–91.

19. The following on the final American departure from Vietnam draws on Larry Berman, *No Peace, No Honor: Nixon, Kissinger, and Betrayal in Vietnam* (New York: Free Press, 2001).

20. A. J. Langguth, *Our Vietnam War, 1954–1975* (New York: Simon and Schuster, 2000), 658, 665.

21. Van Tien Dung, *Our Great Spring Victory: An Account of the Liberation of South Vietnam* (New York: Monthly Review Press, 1977), 236.

22. Quoted in Berman, *No Peace, No Honor*, 4–5.

23. U.S., President, *Public Papers, Carter, 1977*, 1:957.

24. George C. Herring, *America's Longest War: The United States and Vietnam, 1950–1975*, 3rd ed. (New York: McGraw-Hill, 1996), 304–5.

25. Quoted in Lipset and Schneider, *Confidence Gap*, 15.

26. Ibid., 137, 132.

27. Kevin Phillips, *Post-Conservative America: People, Politics, and Ideology in a Time of Crisis* (New York: Random House, 1982), 74.

28. Ibid., 74–76; Bruce J. Schulman, *The Seventies: The Great Shift in American Culture, Society, and Politics* (New York: The Free Press, 2001), 106.

29. Schulman, *Seventies*, 62.

30. Ibid., 170–76, 295.

31. Quoted in Michael Lind, *The Next American Nation: The New Nationalism and the Fourth American Revolution* (New York: The Free Press, 1995), 115. On the categorization of minorities in the 1970s, see also Philip Gleason, *Speaking of Diversity: Language and Ethnicity in Twentieth-Century America* (Baltimore: The Johns Hopkins University Press, 1992), 102–5.

32. "Person of the Year 1976: Jimmy Carter," *Time*, January 23, 1977, 11–22.

33. Ibid.; James Fallows, "The Passionless Presidency," *Atlantic Monthly*, May 1979, 34; James Wooten, *Dasher: The Roots and Rising of Jimmy Carter* (New York: Warner Books, 1979); and Kenneth E. Morris, *Jimmy Carter: American Moralist* (Athens: University of Georgia Press, 1996).

34. Thomas P. O'Neill Jr., *Man of the House: The Life and Political Memoirs of Speaker Tip O'Neill* (New York: Random House, 1987), 310–11; and John A. Farrell, *Tip O'Neill and the Democratic Century* (Boston: Little, Brown and Company, 2001), 450–52.

35. Farrell, *O'Neill and the Democratic Century*, 446.

36. Ibid., 458.

37. Jimmy Carter, *Keeping Faith: Memoirs of a President* (Fayetteville: University of Arkansas Press, 1995), 69.

38. Fallows, "Passionless Presidency," 42.

39. Farrell, O'Neill and the Democratic Century, 457.

40. Quoted in Steven F. Hayward, The Age of Reagan: The Fall of the Old Liberal Order, 1964–1980 (New York: Forum, 2001), 514–15.

41. Don Richardson, ed., Conversations with Carter (Boulder, Col.: Lynne Rienner Publishers, 1998), 146.

42. "The Mystic Who Lit the Fires of Hatred," Time, January 7, 1980, 9–21.

43. Quoted in J. William Holland, "The Great Gamble: Jimmy Carter and the 1979 Energy Crisis," Prologue 22 (Spring 1990): 64–65.

44. Richard Cohen, "Carter's New Theme No Sudden Inspiration," Washington Post, July 19, 1979.

45. The Eizenstat memo was published in its entirety in "Nothing Else Has So Frustrated the American People," Washington Post, July 7, 1979; oil price datum from John M. Berry, "Carter Sees Need to Do Better Job, Counter 'Malaise,'" Washington Post, July 10, 1979.

46. Quoted in Edward Walsh, "8 Governors Join Carter at Retreat," Washington Post, July 7, 1979. The single most useful treatment of Carter's presidential leadership in the summer of 1979 is Daniel Horowitz, Jimmy Carter and the Energy Crisis of the 1970s: The "Crisis of Confidence" Speech of July 15, 1979: A Brief History with Documents (Boston: Bedford/St. Martins, 2005).

47. Carter, Keeping Faith, 123.

48. Ibid., 126.

49. U.S., President, Public Papers, Carter, 1979, 2:1235–47.

50. Grunwald, "American Renewal," Time, February 23, 1981, 3.

51. Quoted in Steven M. Gillon, The Democrats' Dilemma: Walter F. Mondale and the Liberal Legacy (New York: Columbia University Press, 1992), 262.

52. H. M. Zullow and M. Seligman, "Pessimistic Rumination Predicts Defeat of Presidential Candidates: 1900–1984," Psychological Inquiry 1 (1990): 52–61; and Martin E. P. Seligman, Learned Optimism (New York: Knopf, 1991), 187–98.

53. Carter, Keeping Faith, 21. For a thoughtful discussion of the theme of limits in the Carter presidency, see W. Carl Biven, Jimmy Carter's Economy: Policy in an Age of Limits (Chapel Hill: University of North Carolina Press, 2002), 253–63.

54. U.S., President, Public Papers, Carter, 1977, 1:2; U.S., President, Public Papers, Carter 1979, 2:1981.

55. Gillon, Democrats' Dilemma, 264–65.

56. Haynes Johnson, In the Absence of Power: Governing America (New York: Viking Press, 1980), 314.

57. Peter G. Bourne, Jimmy Carter: A Comprehensive Biography from Plains to Postpresidency (New York: Scribner's, 1997), 455.

58. David Broder et al., The Pursuit of the Presidency 1980 (New York: Berkeley Books, 1980), 43.

59. Quoted in Hayward, *Collapse of the Old Liberal Order*, 604.

60. William Kowinski, "The Squeeze on the Middle Class," *New York Times Magazine*, July 13, 1980.

2. ENTER RONALD REAGAN, PRAGMATIC IDEOLOGUE

1. Ronald W. Reagan, *An American Life* (New York: Simon and Schuster, 1990), 23.

2. Anne Edwards, *Early Reagan* (New York: William Morrow, 1987), 23–112.

3. Reagan, *American Life*, 27.

4. Ibid., 35, 31.

5. Edwards, *Early Reagan*, 53

6. Peggy Noonan, *What I Saw at the Revolution: A Political Life in the Reagan Era* (New York: Random House, 1990), 150–54 (quote from p. 154).

7. Marvin Zuckerman, "Optimism and Pessimism: Biological Foundations," in *Optimism & Pessimism: Implications for Theory, Research, and Practice*, ed. Edward C. Chang (Washington: American Psychological Association, 2001), 177.

8. Reagan, *American Life*, 22.

9. William N. Dember, "The Optimism-Pessimism Instrument: Personal and Social Correlates," in *Optimism & Pessimism*, 284–85. See also Lisa Miller, "Intergenerational Transmission of Religion"; and Rabbi Yechiel Eckstein, "The Role of Faith in Shaping Optimism," both in *The Science of Optimism & Hope: Research Essays in Honor of Martin E. P. Seligman*, ed. Jane E. Gillham (Philadelphia: Templeton Foundation Press, 2000), 337–45.

10. Reagan, *American Life*, 56.

11. Martin P. Seligman, *Learned Optimism: How to Change Your Mind and Your Life* (New York: Knopf, 1991), ch. 7.

12. Reagan, *American Life*, 21, 76.

13. Ibid., 44.

14. Ibid., 71.

15. Ibid., 60.

16. Ibid., 81, 84.

17. Ibid., 89.

18. Quoted in Edwards, *Early Reagan*, 214.

19. Regarding *Kings Row*, see Stephen Vaughn, *Ronald Reagan in Hollywood: Movies and Politics* (New York: Cambridge University Press, 1994), 63–66; Garry Wills, *Reagan's America: Innocents at Home* (Garden City, N.Y.: Doubleday & Company, 1987), 173–79; and Reagan, *American Life*, 95–96.

20. Vaughn, *Reagan in Hollywood*, 37.

21. Edwards, *Early Reagan*, 255.

22. Ibid., 229.

23. Reagan, *American Life*, 105–6. .

24. Ronald Reagan and Richard Hubler, *Where's the Rest of Me?* (New York: Dell, 1965), 155.

25. There seems to be a reluctance to give Reagan proper credit for the winning of residuals, by any reasonable measure a signal victory on behalf of labor in the entertainment industry. An exception is Lou Cannon, *Governor Reagan: His Rise to Power* (New York: Public Affairs, 2003), 112; more typical is Wills, *Reagan's America*, 261–70.

26. Reagan, *American Life*, 110.

27. Quoted in Lou Cannon, *Governor Reagan*, 87–88. On Communists in Hollywood, see Ronald and Allis Radosh, *Red Star Over Hollywood: The Film Colony's Long Romance with the Left* (San Francisco: Encounter Books, 2005).

28. Ibid., 115.

29. See Wills, *Reagan's America*, 249–50.

30. Edwards, *Early Reagan*, 396.

31. Edwin Meese, *With Reagan: The Inside Story* (Washington: Regnery Gateway, 1992), 26.

32. Reagan, *American Life*, 129.

33. Quoted in Rick Perlstein, *Before the Storm: Barry Goldwater and the Unmaking of the American Consensus* (New York: Hill and Wang, 2001), 504.

34. Quoted in Noonan, *What I Saw at the Revolution*, 288–89.

35. Quoted in Matthew Dallek, *The Right Moment: Ronald Reagan's First Victory and the Decisive Turning Point in American Politics* (New York: The Free Press, 2000), 195.

36. Quoted in William Pemberton, *Exit with Honor: The Life and Presidency of Ronald Reagan* (Armonk, N.Y.: M. E. Sharpe, 1998), 69.

37. Quoted in Dallek, *The Right Moment*, 174.

38. Quoted in Pemberton, *Exit with Honor*, 67.

39. Quoted in Lou Cannon, *Ronald Reagan: The Presidential Portfolio* (New York: Public Affairs, 2001). 46.

40. Cannon, *Governor Reagan*, 4.

41. Ibid., 199.

42. Quoted in ibid., 197.

43. Ibid., 213.

44. Quoted in ibid., 334.

45. Quoted in ibid., 319.

46. On Reagan as a welfare reformer, see ibid., 348–62.

47. Quoted in ibid., 377. Regarding Prop 1, I have been guided by the discussion in ibid., 368–79; William Roberts, "Ronald Reagan's Prelude to the Tax Revolt: The Campaign for California Proposition One and Its Aftermath," History Undergraduate Honors Thesis, University of Missouri—Columbia, May 2001; Ronald Reagan,

"Reflections on the Failure of Proposition #1: On Spending and the Nature of Government," *National Review*, December 7, 1973, 1358 ff.; and Milton and Rose Friedman, *Two Lucky People: Memoirs* (Chicago: University of Chicago Press, 1998), 388–89.

48. Quoted in Robert M. Collins, *More: The Politics of Economic Growth in Postwar America* (New York: Oxford University Press, 2000), 207.

49. James Adams, *Secrets of the Tax Revolt* (New York: Harcourt, 1984), 156.

50. Lou Cannon, *President Reagan: The Role of a Lifetime* (New York: Public Affairs, 2000), 31.

51. "Ronald for Real," *Time*, October 7, 1966, 31–35.

52. Quoted in Steven F. Hayward, *The Age of Reagan: The Fall of the Old Liberal Order, 1964–1980* (Roseville, Calif.: Prima Publishing, 2001), 165.

53. Reagan, *American Life*, 178.

54. Quoted in Cannon, *Governor Reagan*, 407.

55. Craig Shirley, *Reagan's Revolution: The Untold Story of the Campaign That Started It All* (Nashville, Tenn.: Nelson Current, 2005), vii.

56. Quoted in Cannon, *Governor Reagan*, 432–33. See also Martin Anderson, *Revolution* (New York: Harcourt Brace Jovanovich, 1988), 68–72.

57. Lyn Nofziger, *Nofziger* (Washington: Regnery Gateway, 1992), 215; *Reagan: A Life in Letters*, ed. Kiron K. Skinner, Annelise Anderson, and Martin Anderson (New York; Free Press, 2003), 220, 709.

58. Jerome L. Himmelstein, *To the Right: The Transformation of American Conservatism* (Berkeley: University of California Press, 1990), 129–64; Leonard and Mark Silk, *The American Establishment* (New York: Basic Books, 1980), 252–58; Kim McQuaid, *Big Business and Presidential Power: From FDR to Reagan* (New York: William Morrow, 1982); John Micklethwait and Adrian Wooldridge, *The Right Nation: Conservative Power in America* (New York: Penguin, 2004), 76–80.

59. Peter Steinfels, *The Neoconservatives: The Men Who Are Changing America's Politics* (New York: Simon and Schuster, 1979); John Ehrman, *The Rise of Neoconservatism: Intellectuals and Foreign Affairs, 1945–1994* (New Haven: Yale University Press, 1995); Mark Gerson, *The Neoconservative Vision: From the Cold War to the Culture Wars* (Lanham, Md.: Madison Books, 1997); Irving Kristol, *Neoconservatism: The Autobiography of an Idea* (New York: The Free Press, 1995); Lewis Coser and Irving Howe, eds., *The New Conservatives: A Critique from the Left* (New York: Meridian Books, 1977).

60. Donald T. Critchlow, "Mobilizing Women: The 'Social' Issues," in *The Reagan Presidency: Pragmatic Conservatism and Its Legacies*, ed. W. Elliot Brownlee and Hugh Davis Graham (Lawrence: University Press of Kansas, 2003), 299–301. Also insightful is Ted V. McAllister, "Reagan and the Transformation of American Conservatism," in ibid., 40–60. On conservatism's overall modern evolution, see Gregory Schneider, *Conservatism in America since 1930: A Reader* (New York: New

York University Press, 2003). Schlafly's singularly significant role in the emergence of modern conservatism is insightfully examined in Donald T. Critchlow, *Phyllis Schlafly and Grassroots Conservatism: A Woman's Crusade* (Princeton: Princeton University Press, 2005).

61. The discussion of the 1980 campaign that follows is based on Cannon, *Governor Reagan*, 451–511; Gerald Pomper et al., *The Election of 1980: Reports and Interpretations* (Chatham, N.J.: Chatham House Publishers, 1981); Steven F. Hayward, *Age of Reagan*, 609–717; Jack W. Germond and Jules Witcover, *Blue Smoke and Mirrors: How Reagan Won and Why Carter Lost the Election of 1980* (New York: Viking Press, 1981); and Andrew E. Busch, *Reagan's Victory: The Presidential Election of 1980 and the Rise of the Right* (Lawrence: University Press of Kansas, 2005).

62. Cannon, *Governor Reagan*, 496–97.

63. Hayward, *Age of Reagan*, 700–701; Richard L. Berke, "A Political Rarity: Seven Weeks of Maybe," *New York Times*, September 17, 2000.

64. On the 1980 presidential debate, see Edward A. Hinck, *Enacting the Presidency: Political Argument, Presidential Debates, and Presidential Character* (Westport, Conn.: Praeger, 1993), 99–124.

65. Quoted in Wills, *Reagan's America*, 385; and David Shi, *The Simple Life: Plain Living and High Thinking in American Culture* (New York: Oxford University Press, 1985), 273.

66. U.S., President, *Public Papers, Reagan, 1981*, 4.

67. Clifford, Broder, and Noonan quotes from Peggy Noonan, *When Character Was King: A Story of Ronald Reagan* (New York: Viking, 2001), 248–49; Jack Beatty, "The President's Mind," *New Republic*, April 7, 1982, 13.

68. Richard Darman, *Who's in Control? Polar Politics and the Sensible Center* (New York: Simon and Schuster, 1996), 39–40; Edmund Morris, "The Unknowable," *The New Yorker*, June 28, 2004, 50.

69. Darman, *Who's in Control?*, 39–40.

70. Kiron K. Skinner, Annelise Anderson, and Martin Anderson, eds., *Reagan in His Own Hand: The Writings of Ronald Reagan That Reveal His Revolutionary Vision for America* (New York: Free Press, 2001) and *Reagan's Path to Victory: The Shaping of Ronald Reagan's Vision: Selected Writings* (New York: Free Press, 2004).

71. Lawrence W. Levine and Cornelia R. Levine, *The People and the President: America's Conversation with FDR* (Boston: Beacon Press, 2002), 8.

72. Kiron K. Skinner, Annelise Anderson, and Martin Anderson, eds., *Reagan: A Life in Letters* (New York: Free Press, 2003); and Presidential Handwriting File, Ronald Reagan Presidential Library, Simi Valley, California.

73. Nancy Reagan, *My Turn: The Memoirs of Nancy Reagan* (New York: Random House, 1989), 114; Helene von Damm, *At Reagan's Side* (New York: Doubleday, 1989), 182; Darman, *Who's in Control?*, 40; Rollins quoted in Ann Reilly Dowd, "What Managers Can Learn from Manager Reagan," *Fortune*, September 15, 1986, 38.

74. See, for example, Haynes Johnson, *Sleepwalking Through History: America in the Reagan Years* (New York: Doubleday, 1992).

75. Cannon, *President Reagan*, 142.

76. Dowd, "Manager Reagan," 36.

77. Anderson, *Revolution*, 290.

78. Alexander M. Haig, Jr., *Caveat: Realism, Reagan, and Foreign Policy* (New York: Macmillan, 1984), 85; Donald Regan, *For the Record: From Wall Street to Washington* (New York: Harcourt Brace Jovanovich, 1988), 142.

79. Reagan to Clymer Wright, May 18, 1982, in Skinner et al., *Reagan: A Life in Letters*, 555. Reagan's active engagement as president is an important theme in Richard Reeves, *President Reagan: The Triumph of Imagination* (New York: Simon and Schuster, 2005).

80. George Will, "How Reagan Changed America," *Newsweek*, January 9, 1989, 12–17; David Gergen, *Eyewitness to Power: The Essence of Leadership, Nixon to Clinton* (New York: Simon and Schuster, 2000), 202–3; George Shultz, *Turmoil and Triumph: My Years as Secretary of State* (New York: Scribner's, 1993), 1135.

81. Regarding the pony story, see Michael K. Deaver, *Different Drummer: My Thirty Years with Ronald Reagan* (New York: HarperCollins, 2001), 212–14; and Laurence I. Barrett, *Gambling with History: Reagan in the White House* (New York: Penguin Books, 1984), 174.

82. Regarding the relation between pessimism and realism, see Seligman, *Learned Optimism*, 107–15; L. B. Alloy and L. Y. Abramson, "Judgment of Contingency in Depressed and Non-Depressed Students: Sadder but Wiser," *Journal of Experimental Psychology: General*, 108 (1979), 441–85; P. Lewinsohn, W. Mischel, W. Chaplin, and R. Barton, "Social Competence and Depression: The Role of Illusory Self-Perceptions," *Journal of Abnormal Psychology*, 89 (1980), 203–12.

83. Nancy Reagan, *My Turn*, 273.

84. Cannon, *President Reagan*, 153; U.S., President, *Public Papers, Reagan, 1981*, 275, 278.

85. Noonan, *What I Saw at the Revolution*, 268; David Stockman, *The Triumph of Politics: Why the Reagan Revolution Failed* (New York: Harper and Row, 1986), 9; Darman, *Who's in Control?*, 115.

86. Skinner et al., *Reagan: A Life in Letters*, 428.

87. Larry Speakes, *Speaking Out: The Reagan Presidency from Inside the Reagan White House* (New York: Scribner's, 1988), 144; Deaver, *Different Drummer*, 63.

88. Meese, *With Reagan*, 101; Michael K. Deaver, *Behind the Scenes* (New York: William Morrow, 1987), 170.

89. Quoted in Shultz, *Turmoil and Triumph*, 508; Gergen, *Eyewitness to Power*, 183.

90. Meese, *With Reagan*, 102.

91. Gergen, *Eyewitness to Power*, 183; Shultz, *Turmoil and Triumph*, 269–70, 726; Haig, *Caveat*, 82–88.

3. REAGANOMICS

1. Lawrence B. Lindsey, "The Seventeen-Year Boom," *Wall Street Journal*, January 27, 2000.

2. Daniel Patrick Moynihan, *Miles to Go: A Personal History of Social Policy* (Cambridge: Harvard University Press, 1996), 10.

3. Quoted in Alessandra Stanley, "The Quarterback of Supply Side," *Time*, April 13, 1987, 25.

4. Quoted in David E. Rosenbaum, "A Passion for Ideas," *New York Times*, August 11, 1996.

5. Jack Kemp, *An American Renaissance: A Strategy for the 1980s* (New York: Harper and Row, 1979), 49, 185.

6. Ibid., 49.

7. Bruce R. Bartlett, *Reaganomics: Supply Side Economics in Action* (Westport, Conn.: Arlington House, 1981), 150–58. Quoted material from 153.

8. Milton Friedman, "The Role of Monetary Policy," *American Economic Review* 58 (March 1968): 11.

9. Franco Modigliani, "The Monetarist Controversy, or Should We Forsake Stabilization Policies?" *American Economic Review* 67 (March 1977): 5.

10. Paul Krugman, *Peddling Prosperity: Economic Sense and Nonsense in the Age of Diminished Expectations* (New York: Norton, 1994), 72. See, for example, the essays by Feldstein, Summers, and Boskin in Martin S. Feldstein, ed., *Taxes and Capital Formation* (Chicago: University of Chicago, 1987).

11. Alan S. Blinder, "The Rise and Fall of Keynesian Economics," *The Economic Record* (December 1988): 278.

12. Robert Lucas, "Tobin and Monetarism: A Review Article," *Journal of Economic Literature* 19 (June 1981): 559.

13. Quoted in William R. Neikirk, *Volcker: Portrait of the Money Man* (Chicago: Congdon and Weed, 1987), 78.

14. This distillation of supply-side doctrine is based on Paul Craig Roberts, *The Supply-Side Revolution: An Insider's Account of Policymaking in Washington* (Cambridge: Harvard University Press, 1984); Bartley, *Seven Fat Years: And How to Do It Again* (New York: The Free Press, 1995); Michael K. Evans, *The Truth About Supply-Side Economics* (New York: Basic Books, 1983); and Herbert Stein, "Some 'Supply-Side' Propositions," *Wall Street Journal*, March 19, 1980. For a useful supply-side bibliography, see Bruce Bartlett, "Supply-side Economics: 'Voodoo Economics' or Lasting Contribution?" *Laffer Associates Supply-Side Investment Research*, November 11, 2003.

15. Regarding Say's ideas, see Thomas Sowell, *Say's Law: An Historical Analysis* (Princeton: Princeton University Press, 1972).

16. Martin Anderson, *Revolution* (New York: Harcourt Brace Jovanovich, 1988), 147. On the creation of the Laffer curve, see Bartley, *Seven Fat Years*, 57–58. The role

of Laffer and Mundell is sketched acerbically but compellingly in Krugman, *Peddling Prosperity*, ch. 3. See also Jude Wanneski, "The Mundell-Laffer Hypothesis—A New View of the World Economy," *The Public Interest* 39 (Spring 1975): 31–52; and, on Mundell, Robert A. Bennett, "Supply-Side's Intellectual Guru," *New York Times Magazine*, January 12, 1986.

17. Robert Bartley, "Jack Kemp's Intellectual Blitz," *Wall Street Journal*, November 29, 1979; Roberts, *Supply-Side Revolution*, 7–33.

18. Herbert Stein, *Presidential Economics: The Making of Economic Policy from Roosevelt to Reagan and Beyond* (New York: Simon and Schuster, 1984), 241; Robert Bartley, "Introduction to the Third Edition," in Jude Wanniski, *The Way the World Works*, 3rd ed. (Morristown, N.J.: Polyconomics, 1989), xii.

19. Klein quoted in John Greenwald, "Where Have All the Answers Gone," *Time*, January 17, 1983, 36; Krugman, *Peddling Prosperity*, 89–92; Herbert Stein, "Some 'Supply-Side' Propositions," *Wall Street Journal*, March 19, 1980; Stein, "My Life as a Dee-cline," in *On the Other Hand: Essays on Economics, Economists, and Politics* (Washington: AEI Press, 1995), 18; Stein, "Changes in Macroeconomic Conditions," in *American Economy in Transition*, ed. Martin Feldstein (Chicago: University of Chicago Press, 1980), 172–73.

20. Congress of the United States, Joint Economic Committee, *Joint Economic Committee Report*, 1979, Senate Report No. 96–44, 96th Cong., 1st sess. (Washington, 1979), 3; Bentsen press release, quoted in Bartley, *Seven Fat Years*, 87; and Congress of the United States, Joint Economic Committee, *Joint Economic Committee Report*, 1980, Senate Report No. 96–618, 96th Cong., 2nd sess. (Washington, 1980), 1.

21. Feldstein, "Introduction," in *American Economy in Transition*, ed. Feldstein, 6. See also A. F. Ehrbar, "Martin Feldstein's Electric-Blue Economic Prescriptions," *Fortune*, February 27, 1978, 54–58; and Soma Golden, "Superstar of the New Economists," *New York Times Magazine*, March 23, 1980, 30 ff.

22. Wanniski, "Introduction to the Revised and Updated Edition," in *Way the World Works*, 345.

23. Kemp, *American Renaissance*, 10, 13.

24. Anderson, *Revolution*, 114–21, 126; "White House Report on the Program for Economic Recovery, February 18, 1981," in U.S., President, *Public Papers, Reagan, 1981*, 116–32.

25. William Niskanen, William Poole, and Murray Weidenbaum, "Introduction," in *Two Revolutions in Economic Policy: The First Economic Reports of Presidents Kennedy and Reagan*, ed. James Tobin and Murray Weidenbaum (Cambridge: MIT Press, 1988), 279.

26. Ronald Reagan, *An American Life* (New York, 1990), 231; Reagan speech to the Phoenix, Arizona, Chamber of Commerce, March 30, 1961, in *A Time for Choosing: The Speeches of Ronald Reagan, 1961–1982* (Chicago: Regnery Gateway, 1983).

27. Meese, *With Reagan: The Inside Story* (Washington, D.C.: Regnery Gateway, 1992), 123, 121; Reagan, *An American Life*, 232.

28. Anderson, *Revolution*, 140–63 (quote from 163).

29. Niskanen, Poole, and Weidenbaum, "Introduction," 287. On the rejection of "the simple-minded supply side approach," see Weidenbaum's comments in Kenneth W. Thompson, ed., *Reagan and the Economy: Nine Intimate Perspectives* (Lanham, Md.: University Press of America, 1995), 13.

30. Brock quoted in Kenneth W. Thompson, ed., *The Reagan Presidency: Ten Intimate Perspectives of Ronald Reagan* (Lanham, Md.: University Press of America, 1997), 114; Kemp quoted in *Recollections of Reagan: A Portrait of Ronald Reagan*, ed. Peter Hannaford (New York: William Morrow, 1997), 74; the Chicago speech is discussed in Anderson, *Revolution*, 122–39; U.S., President, *Public Papers, Reagan, 1981*, 83.

31. U.S., President, *Public Papers, Reagan, 1984*, 2:1174.

32. Reagan, *An American Life*, 316, 232.

33. Larry Speakes, *Speaking Out: The Reagan Presidency from Inside the White House* (New York: Scribner's, 1988), 6. See also Philip Taubman, "Explosive Bullet Struck Reagan, F.B.I. Discovers," *New York Times*, April 2, 1981.

34. Quoted in Lyn Nofziger, *Nofziger* (Washington: Regnery Gateway, 1992), 293, 295.

35. Peter Goldman, "American Nightmare," *Newsweek*, April 13, 1981; O'Neill quoted in John A. Farrell, *Tip O'Neill and the Democratic Century* (Boston: Little, Brown, 2001), 556.

36. William A. Niskanen, *Reaganomics: An Insider's Account of the Policies and the People* (New York: Oxford University Press, 1988), 73–76; Don Fullerton, "Inputs to Tax Policy-Making: The Supply-Side, the Deficit, and the Level Playing Field," in *American Economic Policy in the 1980s*, ed. Martin Feldstein (Chicago: University of Chicago Press, 1994) 165–85.

37. Meese, *With Reagan*, 156; Volcker quoted in Neikirk, *Volcker: Portrait of the Money Man*, 110; Michael Mussa, "U.S. Monetary Policy in the 1980s," in *American Economic Policy in the 1980s*, ed. Feldstein, 111.

38. Quoted in James M. Poterba, "Federal Budget Policy in the 1980s," in *American Economic Policy in the 1980s*, ed. Feldstein, 246.

39. Anderson, *Revolution*, 245; Donald T. Regan, *For the Record: From Wall Street to Washington* (San Diego: Harcourt Brace Jovanovich, 1988), 156; David A. Stockman, *The Triumph of Politics: Why the Reagan Revolution Failed* (New York: Harper and Row, 1986), 271.

40. Joseph White and Aaron Wildavsky, *The Deficit and the Public Interest: The Search for Responsible Budgeting in the 1980s* (Berkeley: University of California Press, 1989), ch. 8.

41. Regarding the Rosy Scenario, the fundamental underpinnings of the revenue hemorrhage, and the problem of income tax indexation, see Murray L. Weidenbaum, *Confessions of a One-Armed Economist* (St. Louis: Center for the Study of American Business, Washington University, 1983), 9–11, 14–18.

42. Stockman, *Triumph of Politics*, 8, 11; liberal complaints are quoted in Dinesh D'Souza, *Ronald Reagan: How an Ordinary Man Became an Extraordinary Leader* (New York: Free Press, 1997), 102; Benjamin Friedman, *Day of Reckoning: The Consequences of American Economic Policy Under Reagan and After* (New York: Random House, 1988), 272–73.

43. Stockman, *Triumph of Politics*, 11; Niskanen, *Reaganomics*, 39.

44. Stockman, *Triumph of Politics*, 136–38.

45. Stockman, *Triumph of Politics*, 106, 278, 297; Niskanen, *Reaganomics*, 33.

46. Stockman, *Triumph of Politics*, 356; Iwan W. Morgan, *Deficit Government: Taxing and Spending in Modern America* (Chicago: Ivan R. Dee, 1995), 148–49; Poterba, "Federal Budget Policy in the 1980s," 238–39. Experts continue to disagree how much responsibility the Reagan tax cuts bear for the subsequent deficits of the 1980s. Lawrence Lindsey, *The Growth Experiment: How the New Tax Policy Is Transforming the U.S. Economy* (New York: Basic Books, 1990), 98, argues that tax reductions account for only a quarter of the rise in the deficits of the 1980s; Paul Krugman, *Peddling Prosperity*, 154, estimates that over 70 percent of the increase in the deficit results from tax changes.

47. Carter and Ford joint statement in *American Agenda: Report to the Forty-First President of the United States* (n.p., n.d.), 8; White and Wildavsky, *The Deficit and the Public Interest*, xv; Moynihan, *Miles to Go*, 95 (quote), 11, 126.

48. Alan Brinkley, "Reagan's Revenge," *New York Times Magazine*, June 19, 1994, 37; Griscom quote from *The Reagan Presidency: Ten Intimate Perspectives*, ed. Kenneth W. Thompson, 43. See also Charles L. Schultze, "Paying the Bills," in *Setting Domestic Priorities: What Can Government Do?*, ed. Henry J. Aaron and Charles L. Schultze (Washington: The Brookings Institution, 1992), 295; Theda Skocpol, *Boomerang: Clinton's Health Security Effort and the Turn Against Government in U.S. Politics* (New York: Norton, 1996); and Paul Pierson, *Dismantling the Welfare State? Reagan, Thatcher, and the Politics of Retrenchment* (New York: Cambridge University Press, 1994), 149–55, 162–64.

49. Daniel Patrick Moynihan, *Came the Revolution: Argument in the Reagan Era* (San Diego: Harcourt Brace Jovanovich, 1988), 21, 31, 34 (quote).

50. Ibid., 151, 153.

51. Stockman's comments are in "Summary of Discussion," *American Economic Policy in the 1980s*, ed. Feldstein, 287; Richard Darman *Who's in Control?: Polar Politics and the Sensible Center* (New York: Simon and Schuster, 1996), 80.

52. *Newsweek*, August 7, 1967, 68; February 23, 1981, 70. See also Friedman, "The Kemp-Roth Free Lunch," *Newsweek*, August 7, 1978, 59; Elton Rayack, *Not So Free to Choose: The Political Economy of Milton Friedman and Ronald Reagan* (New York: Praeger, 1987), 188–89; Milton and Rose D. Friedman, *Two Lucky People: Memoirs* (Chicago: University of Chicago Press, 1998), 388–92; Jude Wanniski, "The Two Santa Claus Theory," *The National Observer*, March 6, 1976;

George Will, "Reining In the Federal Spending Urge," *Washington Post*, July 27, 1978.

53. Stockman, *Triumph of Politics*, 133.

54. U.S., President, *Public Papers, Reagan, 1982,* 1:328.

55. Stockman's self-characterization is in Stockman, "Budget Policy," in *American Economic Policy in the 1980s,* ed. Feldstein, 275; Wanniski, "Introduction to the Second Edition," in *Way the World Works,* 360; Meese, *With Reagan,* 138.

56. Reagan quoted in Darman, *Who's In Control?,* 118.

57. U.S., President, *Public Papers, Reagan, 1983,* 1:105; Reagan, *An American Life,* 325.

58. Regan, *For the Record,* 327.

59. Stockman, *Triumph of Politics,* 272.

60. William Greider, *The Education of David Stockman and Other Americans* (New York: Dutton, 1982), 100–101.

61. U.S., President, *Public Papers, Reagan, 1981,* 139. For other examples, see ibid., *1981,* 178, 200, 468, 510, 557–58, 567; and ibid., *1982,* 1:182. Martin Anderson has argued that no one in the administration actually said that massive tax reductions would yield increased revenues, merely that the loss would be offset to a substantial degree by increased growth. On this count, he is quite simply wrong, as the above citations indicate. See Anderson, *Revolution,* 152–57.

62. Reagan quoted in Barrett, *Gambling With History: Reagan in the White House* (New York: Penguin Books, 1984), 341; Martin Feldstein, "American Economic Policy in the 1980s: A Personal View," in *American Economic Policy in the 1980s,* ed. Feldstein, 59.

63. Weidenbaum in *Reagan and the Economy,* ed. Thompson, 7.

64. Ibid., 9.

65. Christopher deMuth, "Comments: Health and Safety Regulation," in *American Economic Policy in the 1980s,* ed. Feldstein, 508.

66. Richard H.K. Vietor, "Government Regulation of Business," in *The Cambridge Economic History of the United States,* vol. 3, *The Twentieth Century,* ed. Stanley L. Engerman and Robert E. Gallman (New York: Cambridge University Press, 2000), 1009–10.

67. Ibid., 1009.

68. The following discussion of the S&L crisis is based on Michael A. Bernstein, "The Contemporary American Banking Crisis in Historical Perspective," *Journal of American History* 80 (March 1994): 1382–96. In addition to the works cited in that essay, insightful accounts include Banning K. Lary, "Insolvent Thrifts: A National Crisis," *Management Review* 78 (March 1989): 29–33; John J. Curran, "Does Deregulation Make Sense? Freeing Banks, Brokers, and Thrifts to Compete Promised Big Benefits for Consumers," *Fortune,* June 5, 1989, 181–87; Alan Reinstein and Paul W. Steih, "Implications of the Savings and Loan Debacle: Lessons for the Banking Industry," *Review of Business* 17 (Fall 1995): 16–22; Steven V. Roberts, "Villains of the

S&L Crisis: Since the Mid-1970s, Many Officials Have Been Part of the Cover-up," *U.S. News and World Report*, October 1, 1990, 53–58; Amy Waldman, "Move Over, Charles Keating," *Washington Monthly*, May 1995, 26–33; James K. Glassman, "The Great Banks Robbery: Deconstructing the S&L Crisis," *New Republic*, October 8, 1990, 16–22; and Kathleen Day, "When Hell Sleazes Over: Judgment Day for S&L Slimeballs," *New Republic*, March 20, 1989, 26–31.

69. Particularly useful for thinking about the S&L crisis of the 1980s as a textbook case of unintended consequences are Robert K. Merton, "The Unanticipated Consequences of Purposive Social Action," *American Sociological Review* 1 (December 1936): 894–904; and Steven M. Gillon, *"That's Not What We Meant to Do": Reform and Its Unintended Consequences in Twentieth-Century America* (New York: Norton, 2000).

70. "Sacked & Looted," *The Nation*, May 7, 1990, 619; John J. Curran, "Does Deregulation Make Sense?" *Fortune*, June 5, 1989, 188.

71. David Gergen, "The Lessons of the HUD Scandal," *U.S. News and World Report*, August 7, 1989.

72. Lou Cannon, *President Reagan: The Role of a Lifetime* (New York: Public Affairs, 2000), 758.

73. See, for example, Robert Bartley, *The Seven Fat Years*; Richard B. McKenzie, *What Went Right in the 1980s* (San Francisco: Pacific Research Institute for Public Policy, 1994); and Donald L. Barlett and James B. Steele, *America: What Went Wrong?* (Kansas City, Missouri: Universal Press Syndicate, 1992).

74. Robert J. Barro, "Reagan vs. Clinton: Who's the Economic Champ?" *Business Week*, February 22, 1999, 22.

75. Schultze quote is from Herbert D. Rosenbaum and Alexej Ugrinsky, eds., *The Presidency and Domestic Policies of Jimmy Carter* (Westport, Conn.: Greenwood, 1994), 671.

76. David H. Vance, "Long-Run Oil Prices and U.S. Energy Security," in *After the Oil Price Collapse: OPEC, the United States, and the World Oil Market*, ed. Wilfrid L. Kohl (Baltimore: The Johns Hopkins University Press, 1991), 80.

77. Quoted in U.S., Congress, Joint Economic Committee, *The Great Expansion: How It Was Achieved and How It Can Be Sustained*, Growth and Prosperity Series, Vol. 4, 106th Cong., 2nd Sess., April 2000, 5.

78. Darman, *Who's in Control?*, 64

79. William Pemberton, *Exit with Honor: The Life and Presidency of Ronald Reagan* (Armonk, N.Y.: M. E. Sharpe, 1998), 105; Meese, *With Reagan*, 160, 150.

80. McKenzie, *What Went Right in the 1980s*, 28.

81. Niskanen, *Reaganomics*, 112; Paul Krugman, *The Age of Diminished Expectations: U.S. Economic Policy in the 1990s*, rev. and updated ed. (Cambridge: MIT Press, 1994), 87. Examples of the argument (from the left and right respectively) that deficits matter little are Robert Eisner, *The Misunderstood Economy: What Counts and How to Count It* (Boston: Harvard Business School Press, 1994) and Robert J.

Barro, *Macroeconomics*, 2nd ed. (New York: Wiley, 1987). David P. Calleo provides a "road to ruin" perspective in *The Bankrupting of America: How the Federal Budget Is Impoverishing the Nation* (New York: William Morrow, 1992).

82. Friedman, *Day of Reckoning*, 164, 171–75, 185.

83. Thomas Friedman, "It's a Mad, Mad, Mad, Mad World Money Market," *New York Times*, May 8, 1994; and Krugman, *Peddling Prosperity*, 167, 128. See also Krugman, *Age of Diminished Expectations*, 85 99; White and Wildavsky, *The Deficit and the Public Interest*, 331–54; and Herbert Stein, "The Fiscal Revolution in America, Part II: 1964–1994," in *Funding the Modern American State, 1941–1995: The Rise and Fall of the Era of Easy Finance*, ed. W. Elliott Brownlee (New York: Cambridge University Press, 1996), 278–86.

84. White and Wildavsky, *The Deficit and the Public Interest*, 428

4. GREED IS GOOD?

1. Dennis B. Levine, "The Inside Story of an Inside Trader," *Fortune*, May 21, 1990, 80–89.

2. James B. Stewart, *Den of Thieves* (New York: Simon and Schuster, 1991), 318.

3. Gwen Kinkead, "Ivan Boesky, Money Machine," *Fortune*, August 6, 1984, 102–6.

4. Both quotes from Connie Bruck, "'My Master Is My Purse': Ivan Boesky Is the Biggest Winner in the Dangerous Game of Risk Arbitrage," *Atlantic*, December 1984, 3, 16.

5. Ibid., 9.

6. Stewart, *Den of Thieves*, 261.

7. Kinkead, "Ivan Boesky, Money Machine," 106.

8. Quoted in Bruck, "My Master Is My Purse," 2.

9. Gwen Kinkead, "Crook of the Year: Ivan Boesky," *Fortune*, January 5, 1987, 48.

10. "The Predators' Ball," *The Economist* (U.S.), July 9, 1988, 81; Andrew Evan Serwer, "Mystery Man of Mergers: Michael Milken," *Fortune*, January 5, 1987, 50; "Wall Street's Hottest Hands," *Forbes*, January 26, 1987, 87.

11. The standard account of Milken's rise and fall is Stewart, *Den of Thieves*.

12. Brad Darrach, "Michael Milken," 20 Who Defined the Decade, *People Weekly*, Fall 1989, v.32 Special Issue.

13. James Gibney, "The Last Temptation of Santa," *New Republic*, October 31, 1988, 42.

14. Cohen quoted in Dan Rottenberg, "A Few Kind Words about Mike Milken," *The Quill*, July-August 1989.

15. Quoted in George P. Brockway, "Bunk the Junk," *The New Leader*, April 30, 1990, 14. For a powerful defense of Milken, see Jude Wanniski, "Insider Reporting," *National Review*, December 2, 1991, 26–31.

16. Robert Lindsey, "Reagan Declares Candidacy," *New York Times*, November 14, 1979; Ira C. Magaziner and Robert B. Reich, *Minding America's Business: The*

Decline and Rise of the American Economy (New York; Random House, 1982); quoted in Henry C. Dethloff, *The United States and the Global Economy Since 1945* (Fort Worth, Texas: Harcourt Brace, 1997), 123.

17. "Globalization in Historical Perspective," *World Economic Outlook*, May 1997, 112.

18. Ibid.; Jeffrey G. Williamson, "Globalization, Convergence, and History," *Journal of Economic History* 56 (June 1996): 277–306; and David Hale, "A Second Chance: Globalization and Its Many Benefits Are Not Just Latter-day Blessings," *Fortune*, November 22, 1999, 189–90.

19. Tamim Bayoumi, "The Postwar Economic Achievement," *Finance and Development: A Quarterly Magazine of the IMF* 32 (June 1995): 48.

20. Dethloff, *United States and the Global Economy*, 107–8

21. Deborah Rawson with Jennifer Ash and S. Chang, "Foreign Exchange: One Family's Shopping in the International Mall," *Life*, Fall 1989 (Special Issue).

22. Bayoumi, "The Postwar Economic Achievement," 48.

23. "Business This Decade," *The Economist* (U.S.), December 23, 1989.

24. Bruce G. Resnick, "The Globalization of World Financial Markets," *Business Horizons*, November–December 1989, 34–42.

25. See, for example, James M. Boughton, "Globalization and the Silent Revolution of the 1980s," *Finance and Development: A Quarterly Magazine of the IMF* 39 (March 2002): 40–43. The literature on globalization is suitably immense. For a good introduction to the issues and debates, see Thomas L. Friedman, *The Lexus and the Olive Tree* (New York: Anchor Books, 2000); and Joseph E. Stiglitz, *Globalization and Its Discontents* (New York: Norton, 2002).

26. Martin Campbell-Kelly and William Aspray, *Computer: A History of the Information Machine* (New York: Basic Books, 1996), 236. See also T. R. Reid, *The Chip* (New York: Simon and Schuster, 1984).

27. Quoted in Paul Freiberger and Michael Swaine, *Fire in the Valley: The Making of the Personal Computer* (Berkeley, Calif.: Osborne/McGraw-Hill, 1984), 37.

28. Ibid., 108.

29. Ibid., 211.

30. Ibid., 223.

31. "The Hottest-Selling Hardware," *Time*, January 3, 1983, 37. On the role of the IBM PC in the business history of the microcomputer revolution, see Alfred D. Chandler, Jr., *Inventing the Electronic Century: The Epic Story of the Consumer Electronics and Computer Industries* (Cambridge: Harvard University Press, 2005), 132–76.

32. Otto Friedrich, "The Computer Moves In," *Time*, January 3, 1983, 14–24.

33. So named by *TV Guide*. *Advertising Age* named it the most influential commercial of the decade of the 1980s. See Ted Friedman, "Apple's *1984*: The Introduction of the Macintosh in the Cultural History of Personal Computers" (paper presented at Society for the History of Technology meeting, October 1997).

34. Campbell-Kelly and Aspray, *Computer: A History of the Information Machine*, 280.

35. Ibid., 283.

36. Stratford Sherman, "The New Computer Revolution," *Fortune*, June 14, 1993, 56–81; David Mowery and Nathan Rosenberg, "Twentieth-Century Technological Change," in *Cambridge Economic History of the United States*, vol. 3, *The Twentieth Century*, ed. Engerman and Gallman, 896.

37. Harley Shaiken, *Work Transformed: Automation and Labor in the Computer Age* (New York: Holt, Rinehart and Winston, 1985), xi.

38. Shoshana Zuboff, *In the Age of the Smart Machine: The Future of Work and Power* (New York: Basic Books, 1988), 415.

39. Richard B. McKenzie and Dwight R. Lee, *Quicksilver Capital: How the Rapid Movement of Wealth Has Changed the World* (New York: The Free Press, 1991), 45.

40. U.S. Bureau of Census, *Statistical Brief: The Growing Use of Computers*, 1991.

41. Craig Brod, *Technostress: The Human Cost of the Computer Revolution* (Reading, Mass.: Addison-Wesley, 1984).

42. Louis Galambos, "The Monopoly Enigma, the Reagan Administration's Antitrust Experiment, and the Global Economy," unpublished paper, in possession of the author.

43. Louis Galambos and Joseph Pratt, *The Rise of the Corporate Commonwealth: U.S. Business and Public Policy in the Twentieth Century* (New York: Basic Books, 1988), 197.

44. WHORM: Subject File, FG 010–01 (118584-end), Box 17, Restricted (P5) Materials Opened, Ronald Reagan Presidential Library.

45. William Baxter, "Antitrust Policy," in *American Economic Policy in the 1980s*, ed. Martin Feldstein (Chicago: University of Chicago Press, 1994), 610.

46. Louis Galambos, "The U.S. Corporate Economy in the Twentieth Century," in *Cambridge Economic History of the United States*, vol. 3, *The Twentieth Century*, ed. Engerman and Gallman, 960.

47. Andrei Shleifer and Robert W. Vishny, "The Takeover Wave of the 1980s," *Science*, August 17, 1990, 745–46.

48. Ibid., 745.

49. Thomas J. Peters and Robert H. Waterman, Jr., *In Search of Excellence: Lessons from America's Best-Run Companies* (New York: Harper & Row, 1982), 305.

50. Ibid., 299.

51. My discussion of Ford in the 1980s relies heavily on David Hounshell, "Why Corporations Don't Learn Continuously: Waves of Innovation and Desperation at Ford Motor Company, 1903–2003," unpublished paper presented at "Organizing for Innovation: Conference in Honor of Louis P. Galambos," Baltimore, Md., October 25–26, 2002.

52. On Deming and his influence, see David Halberstam, *The Reckoning* (New York: Avon Books, 1986), 312–20.

53. John Fernald, "Information Technology and the U.S. Productivity Accelera-tion," *Chicago Fed Letter* (Federal Reserve Bank of Chicago), September 2003. For an insightful study illustrating how deregulation, technological change, globaliza-tion, and corporate restructuring could come together with striking results, see Louis Galambos and Eric John Abrahamson, *Anytime, Anywhere: Entrepreneurship and the Creation of a Wireless World* (New York: Cambridge University Press, 2002).

54. Sylvia Nasar, "U.S. Rate of Output Called Best," *New York Times*, October 13, 1992.

55. Margaret M. McConnell, Patricia C. Mosser, and Gabriel Perez Quiros, "A Decomposition of the Increased Stability of GDP Growth," *Current Issues in Eco-nomics and Finance*, Federal Reserve Bank of New York, September 1999.

5. SOCIAL PROBLEMS, SOCIETAL ISSUES

1. For vivid accounts of life on the street, see Scott Shuger, "Who Are the Home-less?" *Washington Monthly*, March 1990; Jon D. Hull, "Slow Descent into Hell," *Time*, February 2, 1987, 26–28; and Elliott Liebow, *Tell Them Who I Am* (New York: Free Press, 1993).

2. TRB (Dorothy Wickenden), "Let Them Eat Tarts," *New Republic*, February 10, 1986, 4.

3. Charles E. Cohen, "Mitch Snyder Saved Many Lives But Finally Took His Own," *People Weekly*, July 23, 1990, 36–37.

4. Dorothy Wickenden, "Abandoned Americans," *New Republic*, March 18, 1985, 19–25.

5. Carl Horowitz, "Phony Numbers: The Fiction of Three Million Homeless," *Policy Review* (Summer 1989).

6. Quoted in Christopher Jencks, *The Homeless* (Cambridge: Harvard University Press, 1994), 2.

7. "I Give to People Who Are Suffering," *Newsweek*, July 16, 1990, 25.

8. Jencks, *The Homeless*, 17.

9. Ibid., 46.

10. *New York Times*, May 22, 1989.

11. John Carmody, "The TV Column," *Washington Post*, April 19, 1989.

12. Jencks, *The Homeless*, 22, 24, 41, 43.

13. Quoted in David Whitman, "The Unsettling Power of a Contentious Zealot," *U.S. News and World Report*, July 16, 1990, 10–11.

14. Quoted in Myron Magnet, "The Homeless," *Fortune*, November 23, 1987, 172.

15. Jencks, *The Homeless*, vi. A particularly lucid treatment of how the deinstitu-tionalization of the mentally ill, a reform with broad initial political support, went awry is Steven M. Gillon, *"That's Not What We Meant to Do": Reform and Its Un-intended Consequences in Twentieth-Century America* (New York: Norton, 2000), ch. 2.

16. Robert Hayes, quoted in David Whitman, "Shattering Myths About the Homeless," *U.S. News and World Report*, March 20, 1989.

17. Jencks, *The Homeless*, 96–97; and Robert C. Ellickson, "The Homelessness Muddle," *Public Interest* (Spring 1990), 45–60.

18. Heather Mac Donald, *The Burden of Bad Ideas: How Modern Intellectuals Misshape Our Society* (Chicago: Ivan R. Dee, 2000), 144–54.

19. Cohen, "Mitch Snyder Saved Many Lives But Finally Took His Own," 36–37.

20. Fox Butterfield, "New Yorkers Growing Angry Over Aggressive Panhandlers," *New York Times*, July 29, 1988.

21. Quoted in Jason DeParle, "Service for Snyder Brings Celebrities," *New York Times*, July 11, 1990.

22. Whitman, "The Unsettling Power of a Contentious Zealot," *U.S. News and World Report*, July 16, 1990.

23. Quoted in DeParle, "Service for Snyder Brings Celebrities."

24. Ken Auletta, *The Underclass* (New York: Random House, 1982), 26.

25. "The American Underclass," *Time*, August 29, 1977, 14–27.

26. Auletta, *The Underclass*, 27–30; Myron Magnet, "America's Underclass: What to Do?" *Fortune*, May 11, 1987, 130–50; Isabel Wilkerson, "Growth of the Very Poor Is Focus of New Studies," *New York Times*, December 20, 1987.

27. Wilkerson, "Growth of the Very Poor."

28. Charles Murray, *Losing Ground: American Social Policy, 1950–1980* (New York: Basic Books, 1984), x.

29. Quotes from ibid., 9, 189, 228.

30. See, for example, John E. Schwarz, *America's Hidden Success: A Reassessment of Public Policy from Kennedy to Reagan*, rev. ed. (New York: Norton, 1988), 157–61.

31. See Brendon O'Connor, "The Intellectual Origins of 'Welfare Dependency,'" *Australian Journal of Social Issues* 36 (August 2001):221–33.

32. (Chicago: University of Chicago Press, 1987).

33. Quoted in Diane Lewis, "The Great Divide," *Boston Globe Magazine*, June 22, 1997.

34. The full text of Moynihan's report, *The Negro Family: The Case for National Action*, is found in Lee Rainwater and William L. Yancey, *The Moynihan Report and the Politics of Controversy* (Cambridge: MIT Press, 1967), 39–124.

35. Quoted in Godfrey Hodgson, *The Gentleman from New York: Daniel Patrick Moynihan: A Biography* (Boston: Houghton Mifflin, 2000), 118.

36. Wilson, *The Truly Disadvantaged*, 21.

37. Adolph Reed, Jr., "The Liberal Technocrat," *Nation*, February 6, 1988, 167–70.

38. Nicholas Lemann, "The Origins of the Underclass," *Atlantic Monthly*, June, 54–69; and July, 1986, 31–53.

39. Magnet, "America's Underclass," 132.

40. Roger Waldinger, *Still the Promised City?: African Americans and New Immigrants in Post-Industrial New York* (Cambridge: Harvard University Press, 1996).

41. "Special Report: Poverty in America," *Business Week*, October 18, 1999, 156–66; Michael M. Weinstein, "Trickle-Down Prosperity; How Low the Boom Can Go," *New York Times*, June 13, 1999.

42. G. Thomas Kingsley and Kathryn L.S. Pettit, "Concentrated Poverty: A Change in Course," Urban Institute, May 2003. See also Jodie T. Allen, "Exit the Underclass," *U.S. News and World Report*, November 15, 1999, 32.

43. "America's Great Achievement," *The Economist*, August 25, 2001, 25–27.

44. Charles Murray, "Prole Models," *Wall Street Journal*, February 6, 2001.

45. David Finkel, "In the Shadows of Prosperity," *Washington Post*, January 17, 2000.

46. Mortimer B. Zuckerman, "Our Rainbow Underclass," *U.S. News and World Report*, September 23, 2002, 118.

47. *Democracy in America* (Garden City, N.Y.: Anchor Books, 1969), 9.

48. Claudia Goldin and Robert A. Margo, "The Great Compression: The Wage Structure in the United States at Mid-Century," *The Quarterly Journal of Economics* 107 (February 1992): 1–34.

49. U.S., President, *Presidential Papers, Truman, 1952–1953*, 1202.

50. Henry J. Aaron, *Politics and Professors: The Great Society in Perspective* (Washington: The Brookings Institution, 1978), 17.

51. See, for example, John H. Hinderaker and Scott W. Johnson, "The Truth About Income Inequality," Center of the American Experiment, Minneapolis, Minnesota, December 1995.

52. Kevin M. Murphy and Finis Welch, "Wage Differentials in the 1990s: Is the Glass Half-Full or Half-Empty?" in *The Causes and Consequences of Increasing Inequality*, ed. Finis Welch (Chicago: University of Chicago Press, 2001), 342.

53. Richard B. Freeman, "Unequal Incomes," *Harvard Magazine*, January–February 1998, 62.

54. Robert D. Plotnick et al., "The Twentieth-Century Record of Inequality and Poverty in the United States," in *The Cambridge Economic History Of the United States* vol. 3, *The Twentieth Century*, ed. Engerman and Gallman, 292–94.

55. James P. Smith, "Why Is Wealth Inequality Rising?" in *The Causes and Consequences of Increasing Inequality*, ed. Finis Welch, 83–113.

56. (New York; Random House, 1990), 35. For a similar argument by two influential economists, see Bennett Harrison and Barry Bluestone, *The Great U-Turn: Corporate Restructuring and the Polarizing of America* (New York: Basic Books, 1988).

57. Phillips, *Politics of Rich and Poor*, ch. 4.

58. Frank Levy and Richard J. Murname, "U.S. Earnings Levels and Earnings Inequality: A Review of Recent Trends and Proposed Explanations," *Journal of Economic Literature* 30 (September 1992): 1333–81; and Peter Henle and Paul Ryscavage, "The Distribution of Earned Income Among Men and Women, 1958–77," *Monthly Labor Review*, April 1980, 3–10.

59. Peter Gottschalk and Timothy M. Smeeding, "Cross-National Comparisons of Earnings and Income Inequality," *Journal of Economic Literature* 35 (June 1997):

633–87; and Franco Peracchi, "Earnings Inequality in International Perspective," in *The Causes and Consequences of Increasing Inequality*, ed. Finis Welch, 117–52.

60. Marvin H. Kosters, "Government Policy and Wage Inequality: Regulation, Incentives, and Opportunities," in *The Causes and Consequences of Increasing Inequality*, ed. Finis Welch, 201–40.

61. Paul Krugman, *The Age of Diminished Expectations: U.S. Economic Policy in the 1990s*, rev. and updated ed. (Cambridge: MIT Press, 1994), 29.

62. Thomas Byrne Edsall, "The 'Reagan Revolution' as a Revolution from Above," in *The Reagan Legacy*, ed. Sydney Blumenthal and Edsall (New York: Pantheon Books, 1988).

63. George J. Borjas, "The New Economics of Immigration," *Atlantic Monthly*, November 1996, 72–80.

64. Robert E. Baldwin and Glen G. Cain, "Shifts in Relative U.S. Wages: The Role of Trade, Technology, and Factor Endowments," *Review of Economics and Statistics* 82 (November 2000): 580–95.

65. Katherine Bradbury and Jane Katz, "Are Lifetime Incomes Growing More Unequal?" *(Federal Reserve Bank of Boston) Regional Review* (Q4 2002), 3–5.

66. John-Manuel Andriote, *Victory Deferred: How AIDS Changed Gay Life in America* (Chicago: University of Chicago Press, 1999), 27.

67. Ibid., 48–49.

68. Centers for Disease Control, "Current Trends Prevention of Acquired Immune Deficiency Syndrome (AIDS): Report of Inter-Agency Recommendations," *Mortality and Morbidity Weekly Report*, March 4, 1983, 101–3.

69. Andriote, *Victory Deferred*, 80.

70. Quoted in ibid., 340.

71. Ibid., 67–68.

72. Quote in Randy Shilts, *And the Band Played On: Politics, People, and the AIDS Epidemic* (New York: St. Martin's Press, 1987), 576. See also Gerald Clarke, "The Double Life of an AIDS Victim: Rock Hudson, 1925–1985," *Time*, October 14, 1985, 106.

73. Quoted in Dirk Johnson, "Ryan White Dies of AIDS at 18," *New York Times*, April 9, 1990.

74. "Grave of Boy Who Led Fight on AIDS Bias Is Vandalized," *New York Times*, July 10, 1991.

75. Cannon, *Governor Reagan: His Rise to Power* (New York: Public Affairs, 2003), 252.

76. Deroy Murdock, "The Truth About Reagan and AIDS," *Independent Gay Forum* (First published December 3, 2003, in *National Review Online*), http://www.indegayforum.org/authors/murdock/murdock4.html.

77. See Kiron Skinner, Annelise Anderson, and Martin Anderson, eds., *Reagan: A Life in Letters*, (New York: Free Press, 2003), 366.

78. Ibid., 67.

79. Shilts, *And the Band Played On*, 297.

80. Judith Johnson, *AIDS Funding for Federal Government Programs: FY1981–FY2001* (Washington: Congressional Research Service, Library of Congress, 2000).

81. Cannon, *President Reagan: The Role of a Lifetime* (New York: Public Affairs, 2000), 731.

82. Lindsay Barnes, "Koop Reminisces on Reagan Presidency," *The Dartmouth*, July 1, 2004.

83. On household contact reports, see Shilts, *And the Band Played On*, 299–302; on the mosquito scare, see Joe Levine, "Aids: Prejudice and Progress," *Time*, September 8, 1986, 86; Silverman quoted in "Week of Adulation Chafes Critics," *Columbia [Missouri] Daily Tribune*, June 13, 2004; on the bathhouses of San Francisco, see Shilts, *And the Band Played On*; Andriote, *Victory Deferred*; and David Horowitz, *Radical Son: A Generational Odyssey* (New York: The Free Press, 1997), 337–49.

84. Andrew Sullivan, "Reagan Did Not Give Me HIV," *The Advocate*, June 18, 2004.

85. I have profited particularly from the unpublished scholarship of Professor William B. Turner on this point.

86. Ronald Mark Kraft, "Hetero Heroes: Mathilde Krim," *The Advocate*, November 16, 1993; *Ms.*, January 1986.

87. Quoted in "Mathilde Krim," *Current Biography Yearbook*, 1987.

88. Quotes from George Johnson, "Dr. Krim's Crusade," *New York Times Magazine*, February 14, 1988; and Sandra Panem, *The Interferon Crusade* (Washington: The Brookings Institution, 1984), 99.

89. Quoted in Johnson, "Dr. Krim's Crusade."

90. Quoted in Steven Epstein, *Impure Science: AIDS, Activism, and the Politics of Knowledge* (Berkeley: University of California Press, 1996), 235.

91. See Jason DeParle, "Rude, Rash, Effective, Act-Up Shifts AIDS Policy,' *New York Times*, January 3, 1990.

92. Quoted in Janice C. Simpson, "Using Rage to Fight the Plague," *Time*, February 5, 1990, 7.

93. Frank Rich, "Theater: 'The Normal Heart,'" *New York Times*, April 22, 1985.

94. Quoted in Gregory Kolovakos, "AIDS Words," *Nation*, May 1, 1989, 600–601.

95. Gloria Hochman, "In Short: Review of 'Reports from the Holocaust,'" *New York Times Book Review*, April 2, 1989.

96. Quoted in Andriote, *Victory Deferred*, 235. On the phenomenon of de-gaying, see 235–40.

97. Statistics from *www.cdc.gov/hiv/stats.htm*.

6. THE POSTMODERN MOMENT

1. Andrew Hacker, ed., *U/S: A Statistical Portrait of the American People* (New York: Penguin, 1983), 5.

2. Fredric Jameson, "Postmodernism and Consumer Society," in *The Anti-Aesthetic: Essays on Postmodern Culture*, ed. Hal Foster (Seattle, Wash.: Bay Press, 1983), 125.

3. Kenneth Gergen, "Identity Through the Ages," *U.S. News and World Report*, July 1, 1991, 59.

4. David Riesman, with Nathan Glazer and Reuel Denney, *The Lonely Crowd: A Study of Changing American Character* (New Haven: Yale University Press, 1950); Kenneth J. Gergen, *The Saturated Self: Dilemmas of Identity in Contemporary Life* (New York: Basic Books, 1991), 7.

5. Quoted in Ross Miller, "Putting on the Glitz: Architecture after Postmodernism" in *Culture in an Age of Money: The Legacy of the 1980s in America*, ed. Nicolaus Mills (Chicago: Ivan R. Dee, 1990), 56–7.

6. Christopher Jencks, *The Language of Post-Modern Architecture* (New York: Rizzoli, 1977)

7. Quoted in Gergen, *Saturated Self*, 116.

8. See Todd Gitlin, "Hip-Deep in Postmodernism," *New York Times*, November 6, 1988.

9. Steven Waldman, "The Tyranny of Choice," *New Republic*, January 27, 1992, 22–25.

10. James L. Nolan, Jr., *The Therapeutic State: Justifying Government at Century's End* (New York: New York University Press, 1998), 3.

11. Quoted in Charles J. Sykes, *A Nation of Victims: The Decay of the American Character* (New York: St. Martin's Press, 1992), 41.

12. Robert H. Bellah et al., *Habits of the Heart: Individualism and Commitment in American Life* (New York: Perennial Library, 1985), vi, 81, 138.

13. Ronald Inglehart, *The Silent Revolution: Changing Values and Political Styles Among Western Publics* (Princeton: Princeton University Press, 1977); *Culture Shift in Advanced Industrial Society* (Princeton: Princeton University Press, 1990); *Modernization and Postmodernization: Cultural, Economic, and Political Change in 43 Societies* (Princeton: Princeton University Press, 1997); and "Observations on Cultural Change and Postmodernism," in *Contemporary Political Culture: Politics in a Postmodern Age*, ed. John R. Gibbons (London: Sage Publications, 1989), 251–56.

14. Inglehart, *Culture Shift*, 96.

15. Seligman, "Boomer Blues: With Too Great Expectations, the Baby-boomers Are Sliding into Individualistic Melancholy" *Psychology Today*, October 1988, 50–55.

16. Nolan, *Therapeutic Culture*, 5.

17. Nancy Faber, "Okay, We Make Fun of California" *People Weekly*, March 2, 1987, 32.

18. Nolan, *Therapeutic State*, 155–56.

19. Ibid., 152.

20. John Leo, "The Trouble with Self-Esteem" *U.S. News and World Report*, April 2, 1990, 16.

21. Rita Kramer, "Inside the Teacher's Culture," *The Public Interest* (Winter 1997): 68.

22. Bellah, *Habits of the Heart*, 281.

23. John Leo, "Selling Strong Emotions," *Time*, May 12, 1986, 95.

24. Nolan, *Therapeutic State*, 7–8.

25. The point is powerfully made in Christina Hoff Sommers and Sally Satel, *One Nation Under Therapy: How the Helping Culture Is Eroding Self-Reliance* (New York: St. Martin's Press, 2005), 76–109.

26. Nolan, *Therapeutic State*, 11–13.

27. U.S. Department of Health, Education, and Welfare, *Smoking and Health: Report of the Advisory Committee to the Surgeon General of the Public Health Service*, U.S. Public Health Service, 1964, 350.

28. U.S. Department of Health and Human Services, *The Health Consequences of Smoking: Nicotine Addiction: A Report of the Surgeon General*, U.S. Public Health Service, Centers for Disease Control, Office on Smoking and Health, 1988, vi, Foreword.

29. Nolan, *Therapeutic State*, 10; and Sykes, *Nation of Victims*, 9.

30. Jesse Birnbaum, "Crybabies," *Time*, August 12, 1991, 18.

31. Lance Morrow, "A Nation of Finger Pointers," *Time*, August 12, 1991, 14–15; Wendy Kaminer, *I'm Dysfunctional, You're Dysfunctional: The Recovery Movement and Other Self-Help Fashions* (New York: Vintage Books, 1993), 30.

32. Myron Magnet, "The Money Society," *Fortune*, July 6, 1987, 26.

33. Tom Wolfe, "The Years of Living Prosperously," *U.S. News and World Report*, December 25, 1989.

34. De Tocqueville, *Democracy in America*, 543.

35. Quoted in Sean Wilentz, "Freedoms and Feelings: Taking Politics Out of Political History," *New Republic*, April 7, 2003.

36. Quoted in Debora Silverman, *Selling Culture: Bloomingdale's, Diana Vreeland, and the New Aristocracy of Taste in Reagan's America* (New York: Pantheon Books, 1986), 161.

37. John P. Robinson, "When the Going Gets Tough," *American Demographics*, February 1989, 50.

38. Maureen Boyle Gray, "Consumer Spending on Durables and Services in the 1980's," *Monthly Labor Review*, May 1992, 18–19.

39. William S. Kowinski, "Endless Summer at the World's Biggest Shopping Wonderland" *Smithsonian*, December 1986, 34 ff. See also Kenneth Jackson, "All the World's a Mall: Reflections on the Social and Economic Consequences of the American Shopping Center," *American Historical Review* 101 (October 1996): 1111–21.

40. Joshua Levine, "Lessons from Tysons Corner," *Forbes*, April 30, 1990, 186.

41. Eric Hubler, "Four Million Square Feet of Mall," *New York Times*, October 25, 1992; and David Guterson, "Enclosed. Encyclopedic. Endured: One Week at the Mall of America," *Harper's*, August 1993, 49 ff.

42. The discussion of Wal-Mart that follows is based on "Small-town Hit," *Time*, May 23, 1983, 43; Howard Rudnitsky, "Play It Again, Sam," *Forbes*, August 10, 1987, 48; Stephen Koepp, "Make That Sale, Mr. Sam," *Time*, May 18, 1987, 54–55; John Huey, "Wal-Mart: Will It Take Over the World?" *Fortune*, January 30, 1989, 52–59; Jim Cory, "Up Against Wal-Mart," *Chilton's Hardware Age*, February 1988, 31–40; John Dicker, *The United States of Wal-Mart* (New York: Penguin, 2005); Sharon Zukin, *Point of Purchase: How Shopping Changed American Culture* (New York: Routledge, 2004); and Sandra S. Vance and Roy V. Scott, *Wal-Mart: A History of Sam Walton's Retail Phenomenon* (New York: Twayne, 1994).

43. Nicolaus Mills, "The Culture of Triumph and the Spirit of the Times," in *Culture in an Age of Money: The Legacy of the 1980s in America*, ed. Mills (Chicago: Ivan R. Dee, 1990), 20.

44. A handy reprise of 1980s pop culture is *Pride and Prosperity: The 1980s* (Alexandria, Va.: Time-Life Books, n.d.).

45. Josephine Hendin, "Fictions of Acquisition," in *Culture in an Age of Money*, ed. Mills, 216–33.

46. Jerry Adler, "The Year of the Yuppie," *Newsweek*, December 31, 1984, 14 ff.; and Marissa Piesman and Marilee Hartley, *The Yuppie Handbook* (New York: Pocket Books, 1984). See also Hendrik Hertzberg, "The Short Happy Life of the American Yuppie," in Mills, ed., *Culture in an Age of Money*, 66–82.

47. Robert W. Pittman, "Counterpoint: Voices of the New Generation: How 'TV Babies' Learn," *New York Times*, September 30, 1990. On MTV in general, see Ed Levine, "TV Rocks with Music," *New York Times Magazine*, May 8, 1983; Serge Denisoff, *Inside MTV* (New Brunswick, N.J.: Transaction Books, 2002); and E. Ann Kaplan, *Rocking Around the Clock: Music Television, Postmodernism, and Consumer Culture* (New York: Methuen, 1987).

48. Quoted in Peter J. Boyer, "After Rebellious Youth, MTV Tries the System," *New York Times*, May 9, 1988.

49. Quotes from George Hackett, "Banding Together for Africa," *Newsweek*, July 15, 1985, 52.

50. Quoted in Eric Gelman, "Rocking Video," *Newsweek*, April 18, 1983, 96.

51. Quoted in Kathy Brown, "MTV Rejects Neil Young's Ad-Bashing Music Video," *Adweek*, July 25, 1988.

52. Quoted in Anna Mulrine, "A Daydream Nation," *U.S. News and World Report*, July 8, 2002, 64.

53. Quoted in Gelman, "Rocking Video."

54. Jon Pareles, "After Music Videos, All the World Has Become a Screen," *New York Times*, December 10, 1989.

55. Quoted in "TV Biz Boogies to Socko Rock Flock," *Variety*, November 9, 1998.

56. Lynn Goldsmith, "The Charismatic Kid: Tony Robbins, 25, Gets Rich Peddling a Hot Self-Help Program," *Life*, March 1985.

57. Ibid.

58. Edward Fox, "Sweet Smell of Success," *The Guardian* (Great Britain), October 31, 1993; and Patrick Kelly, "Tony Robbins," *Current Biography*, July 2001, 63–68.

59. Goldsmith, "Charismatic Kid."

7. CULTURE WAR

1. Pat Buchanan, "The Election Is About Who We Are: Taking Back Our Country," *Vital Speeches*, September 15, 1992, 712–15.

2. Quoted in John Robert Greene, *The Presidency of George Bush* (Lawrence: University Press of Kansas, 2000), 171.

3. Chancellor quoted in *MediaWatch*, November 1992, http://www.mediaresearch. org; Kemp quoted in John W. Mashek, "Reeling from Election, GOP Faces Dissension," *Boston Globe*, November 15, 1992.

4. Bill Clinton, *My Life* (New York: Knopf, 2004), 426.

5. John Davison Hunter, *Culture Wars: The Struggle to Define America* (New York: Basic Books, 1991), 44, 46, 50.

6. See Bruce J. Schulman, *The Seventies: The Great Shift in American Culture, Society, and Politics* (New York: The Free Press, 2001), 92–96.

7. Maurice Isserman and Michael Kazin, "The Failure and Success of the New Radicalism," in *The Rise and Fall of the New Deal Order, 1930–1980*, ed. Steve Fraser and Gary Gerstle (Princeton: Princeton University Press, 1989), 214, 229, 230, 231.

8. Quoted in Hunter, *Culture Wars*, 64.

9. Samuel G. Freedman, "Mr. Falwell Meets an Outspoken Antagonist, Yale's Giamatti," *New York Times*, November 12, 1982; Richard N. Ostling, "Power, Glory—and Politics; Right-Wing Preachers Dominate the Dial," *Time*, February 17, 1986, 62–69; Dinesh D'Souza, *Falwell, Before the Millennium: A Critical Biography* (Chicago: Regnery Gateway, 1984); and Edward B. Fiske, "College Aims to be Fundamentalism's Notre Dame," *New York Times*, October 4, 1981.

10. Quotes from Kenneth Woodward, "The Right's New Bogeyman," *Newsweek*, July 6, 1981, 48–50; and "Circuit Rider to Controversy," *U.S. News and World Report*, September 2, 1985.

11. See Alan Crawford, *Thunder on the Right: The "New Right" and the Politics of Resentment* (New York: Pantheon Books, 1980).

12. Richard N. Ostling, "A Jerry-built Coalition Regroups," *Time*, November 16, 1987, 68.

13. Quoted in Joseph Sobran, "Sorry, Sodom!" *National Review*, February 22, 1985, 41; Samuel G. Freedman, "Mr. Falwell Meets an Outspoken Antagonist, Yale's Giamatti," *New York Times*, November 12, 1982.

14. Diana and Norman Fleischman, "How We Saved the World from Nuclear War," *The Humanist*, March–April 2003, 27–29.

15. Quoted in D'Souza, *Falwell*, 144.

16. Ann Reilly Dowd, "Winning One from the Gipper," *Fortune*, November 9, 1987.

17. Roger Lewin, "Texas Repeals Antievolution Rules," *Science*, April 27, 1984, 370; Norman Colin, "A Guide to Biology Texts," *Science*, February 15, 1985, 731.

18. Robert Lindsey, "Goldwater and Jane Fonda Lead Civil Liberties Rally," *New York Times*, February 24, 1982; Robert Zoglin, "Is This Entertainment Special Promoting a Special Interest?" *New York Times*, March 21, 1982; John J. O'Connor, "Lear's 'I Love Liberty' Leads Specials," *New York Times*, March 19, 1982.

19. "Mondale's Whipping Boy," *Time*, October 22, 1984, 28.

20. "A Debate on Religious Freedom," *Harper's*, October 1984, 15–20.

21. Memorandum, Fred Fielding to Richard Darman, November 5, 1984, in Folder 136, Box 10, President's Handwriting File, Ronald W. Reagan Presidential Library, Simi Valley, California.

22. Quoted in Dinesh D'Souza, *Illiberal Education: The Politics of Race and Sex on Campus* (New York: The Free Press, 1991), 63.

23. Roger Kimball, *Tenured Radicals: How Politics Has Corrupted Our Higher Education*, rev. ed. (Chicago: Ivan R. Dee, 1998), 44.

24. William J. Bennett, "Why the West?" in *The Eighties: A Reader*, ed. Gilbert T. Sewall (Reading, Mass.: Perseus Books, 1997), 274, 278.

25. Kimball, *Tenured Radicals*, 45.

26. See, for example, such arguments advanced in Stephen R. Graubard, "Bennett Misreads Stanford's Classics," in *The Eighties: A Reader*, ed. Sewall, 281–83.

27. Joseph Berger, "U.S. Literature: Canon Under Siege," *New York Times*, January 6, 1988. See also James Atlas, "On Campus: The Battle of the Books," *New York Times Magazine*, June 5, 1988.

28. Henry Louis Gates, Jr., "Whose Canon Is It Anyway?" *New York Times*, February 26, 1989.

29. Jon Wiener, "A Tale of Two Conclaves: Campus Voices Right and Left," *Nation*, December 12, 1988, 645.

30. On the French influence, see Jonathan Culler, *On Deconstruction: Theory and Criticism after Structuralism* (Ithaca: Cornell University Press, 1982); Christopher Norris, *Deconstruction: Theory and Practice*, rev. ed. (London: Routledge, 1991); James Miller, *The Passion of Michel Foucault* (New York: Simon and Schuster, 1993); James Atlas, "The Case of Paul De Man," *New York Times Magazine*, August 28, 1988; and Roger Scruton, "What Ever Happened to Reason?" *City Journal* (Spring 1999).

31. Gerald Early, "American Education and the Postmodernist Impulse," *American Quarterly* 45 (June 1993): 221–22.

32. Andrew Grossman, *You Can't Say That* (New York: Cato Institute, 2003).

33. D'Souza, *Illiberal Education*, 9. See also Robert M. O'Neil, *Free Speech in the College Community* (Bloomington: Indiana University Press, 1997).

34. Alan Charles Kors and Harvey A. Silvergate, *The Shadow University: The Betrayal of Liberty on America's Campuses* (New York: Free Press, 1998).

35. "The Wrong Way to Reduce Campus Tensions: A Statement by the National Association of Scholars, December 1991," in Patricia Aufderheide, ed., *Beyond PC: Toward a Politics of Understanding* (St. Paul, Minn.: Greywolf Press, 1992), 10; Joseph Berger, "Scholars Attack Campus 'Radicals,'" *New York Times*, November 15, 1988; Denise K. Magner, "10 Years of Defending the Classics and Fighting Political Correctness," *Chronicle of Higher Education*, December 12, 1997.

36. Quoted in National Endowment for the Humanities, *Telling the Truth: A Report on the State of the Humanities in Higher Education* (Washington: NEH, 1992), 47.

37. Richard Bernstein, *Dictatorship of Virtue: Multiculturalism and the Battle for America's Future* (New York: Knopf, 1994), 62–63.

38. Quoted in Hunter, *Culture Wars*, 227.

39. See the references in ibid., note 3, 373.

40. Alex S. Jones, "Polls Compare Journalists' and Public Views," *New York Times*, October 30, 1985; and David Shaw, "Of Isms and Prisms," *Columbia Journalism Review* 29 (January–February 1991): 55.

41. Quoted in "AIM Claims PBS Has Double Standard," *Broadcasting*, January 27, 1986.

42. Dinesh d'Souza, "Eye on the Press: Accuracy in Media," *National Review*, November 2, 1984, 37.

43. Ibid.; Walter and Miriam Schneir, "The Right's Attack on the Press," *Nation*, March 30, 1985, 361–67; and Michael Massing, "Who's Afraid of Reed Irvine?" *Nation*, September 13, 1986, 200–214.

44. Hunter, *Culture Wars*, 227–29.

45. Quoted in ibid., 231.

46. Quoted in ibid., 231, 242.

47. Ibid., 232. On the culture war in America's foundations and museums, see Heather Mac Donald, *The Burden of Bad Ideas: How Modern Intellectuals Misshape Our Society* (Chicago: Ivan R. Dee, 2000), 3–24, 117–43.

48. Abortion statistics from the Alan Guttmacher Institute of Planned Parenthood.

49. Quoted in Richard Lacayo, "Whose Life Is It?" *Time*, May 1, 1989, 20.

50. Quoted in James Davison Hunter, *Before the Shooting Starts: Searching for Democracy in America's Culture War* (New York: The Free Press, 1994), 6–7.

51. Lacayo, "Whose Life Is It?" 21.

52. Quoted in "Randall A. Terry," *1994 Current Biography Yearbook*, 593.

53. Quoted in Hunter, *Before the Shooting Starts*, 47.

54. Garry Wills, "'Save the Babies': Operation Rescue," *Time*, May 1, 1989, 26–28.

55. "Randall A. Terry," *1994 Current Biography Yearbook*, 589–93.

56. Quoted in "Roe v. Wade at 25," *CQ Researcher*, November 28, 1997. See David Garrow, *Liberty and Sexuality* (New York: Macmillan, 1994).

57. "Abortion Clinic Protests," *CQ Researcher*, April 7, 1995; "Rescue Bails Out," *Time*, February 12, 1990, 29.

58. Quoted in Kio Stark, "Call It Pro-Death," *Nation*, August 22, 1994, 183–84.

8. COMBATING THE EVIL EMPIRE

1. Quoted in Richard Pipes, *Vixi: Memoirs of a Non-Belonger* (New Haven: Yale University Press, 2003), 160.

2. Ibid., 56.

3. Ibid., 89.

4. Ibid., 136.

5. Ibid., 149.

6. Quoted in Peter Schweizer, *Reagan's War: The Epic Story of His Forty-Year Struggle and Final Triumph over Communism* (New York: Doubleday, 2002), 156.

7. U.S., President, *Public Papers, Reagan, 1981*, 57.

8. Anatoly Dobrynin, *In Confidence: Moscow's Ambassador to America's Six Cold War Presidents* (New York: Times Books, 1995), 490–91.

9. Ibid., 492.

10. Caspar W. Weinberger, *Fighting for Peace: Seven Critical Years in the Pentagon* (New York: Warner Books, 1990), 36.

11. Robert M. Gates, *From the Shadows: The Ultimate Insider's Story of Five Presidents and How They Won the Cold War* (New York: Touchstone, 1996), 174. That the Soviets shared this assessment of their looming success in the Cold War is apparent from the evidence presented in Christopher Andrew, *The World Was Going Our Way: The KGB and the Battle for the Third World* (New York: Perseus Books, 2005).

12. Alexander M. Haig, Jr., *Caveat: Realism, Reagan, and Foreign Policy* (New York: Macmillan, 1984), 29.

13. Ibid., 27, 31.

14. Richard V. Allen, "The Man Who Changed the Game Plan," *The National Interest* (Summer 1996).

15. Reprinted in Robert C. McFarland with Zofia Smardz, *Special Trust* (New York: Cadell and Davies, 1994), Appendix B, 372–80.

16. Ibid., 372.

17. Allen, "Man Who Changed the Game Plan."

18. Quoted in Schweizer, *Reagan's War*, 140.

19. Caspar W. Weinberger, *Fighting for Peace: Seven Critical Years in the Pentagon* (New York: Warner Books, 1990), 39; Derek Leebaert, *The Fifty-Year Wound: The True Price of America's Cold War Victory* (Boston: Little, Brown, 2002), 501–2; Allen, "Man Who Changed the Game Plan." By historical Cold War standards, Reagan's defense budgets were less extraordinary than observers, both critics and champions, allowed. During the 1950s, defense spending constituted slightly over 10 percent of the yearly GNP; in the 1960s, the figure hovered around 9 percent of GNP; under Reagan, annual defense spending never exceeded 6.5 percent of GNP. See Paul Lettow, *Ronald Reagan and His Quest to Abolish Nuclear Weapons* (New York: Random House, 2005), 259.

20. Adam M. Garfinkle, *The Politics of the Nuclear Freeze* (Philadelphia: Foreign Policy Research Institute, 1984), 204, 234–38.

21. Leebaert, *Fifty-Year Wound*, 504.

22. "President Says Foes of U.S. Have Duped Arms Freeze Group," *New York Times*, October 5, 1982.

23. Dobrynin, *In Confidence*, 563.

24. Judith Miller, "Soviet Role in Freeze Movement Found Minor," *New York Times*, December 10, 1982.

25. "Reagan Calls Nuclear Freeze Dangerous," *New York Times*, April 1, 1983.

26. "An Audience of 100 Million — How ABC Built It," *U.S. News and World Report*, December 5, 1983.

27. "Intimations of Mortality," *The Economist*, November 26, 1983.

28. "After 'The Day After,' " *Newsweek*, December 5, 1983, 62.

29. See, for example, Frances FitzGerald, *Way Out There in the Blue: Reagan, Star Wars and the End of the Cold War* (New York: Simon and Schuster, 2000), 22–23.

30. Ronald Reagan, *An American Life* (New York: Pocket Books, 1990), 547. For an extended and compelling analysis of Reagan's antipathy to the doctrine of Mutually Assured Destruction, see Lettow, *Reagan and His Quest to Abolish Nuclear Weapons*.

31. George P. Shultz, *Turmoil and Triumph: My Years as Secretary of State* (New York: Scribner's, 1993), 261–62.

32. Edward Teller, *Memoirs: A Twentieth-Century Journey in Science and Politics* (Cambridge, Mass.: Perseus Publishing, 2001), 509, 525–33.

33. See Donald R. Baucom, *The Origins of SDI 1944–1983* (Lawrence: University Press of Kansas, 1992); and FitzGerald, *Way Out There*.

34. Quoted in Shultz, *Turmoil and Triumph*, 259.

35. Quoted in Leebaert, *Fifty-Year Wound*, 529.

36. Leebaert, *Fifty-Year Wound*, 528–29.

37. Colin Powell, *My American Journey* (New York: Random House, 1995), 295.

38. FitzGerald, *Way Out There*, 265–313; Shultz, *Turmoil and Triumph*, 250–51.

39. Jay Keyworth SDI Oral History, Ronald Reagan Presidential Library, Simi Valley, California.

40. U.S., President, *Public Papers, Reagan, 1983*, 1:442–43; Kiron Skinner, Annelise Anderson, and Martin Anderson, eds., *Reagan: A Life in Letters* (New York: Free Press, 2003), 425.

41. Jay Keyworth SDI Oral History, Ronald Reagan Presidential Library, Simi Valley, California.

42. Lou Cannon, *President Reagan: The Role of a Lifetime* (New York: Public Affairs, 2000), 787 (n. 122).

43. Shultz, *Turmoil and Triumph*, 263.

44. Gates, *From the Shadows*, 264.

45. Pavel Palazchenko, *My Years with Gorbachev and Shevardnadze: The Memoir of a Soviet Interpreter* (University Park: Pennsylvania State University Press, 1997), 41.

46. Mikhail Gorbachev, *Memoirs* (New York: Doubleday, 1995), 407.

47. Ibid., 444; statistics from Leebaert, *Fifty-Year Wound*, 516–17. On the Soviets' economic woes, see also Stephen G. Brooks and William C. Wohlforth, "Economic Constraints and the End of the Cold War," in William C. Wohlforth, ed., *Cold War Endgame: Oral History, Analysis, Debates* (University Park: The Pennsylvania State University Press, 2003), 273–309.

48. Quoted in Schweizer, *Reagan's War*, 242.

49. Skinner et al., eds., *Reagan: A Life in Letters*, 427.

50. U.S., President, *Public Papers, Reagan*, 1981, 1982, 1983.

51. *New York Times*, March 9, 1983.

52. Dobrynin, *In Confidence*, 533.

53. Skinner et al., eds., *Reagan: A Life in Letters*, 376.

54. Arch Puddington, *Broadcasting Freedom: The Cold War Triumph of Radio Free Europe and Radio Liberty* (Lexington: University Press of Kentucky, 2000), 224.

55. Seweryn Bialer, "Danger in Moscow," *The New York Review of Books*, February 16, 1984.

56. Reagan, *American Life*, 238.

57. McFarland with Zofia Smardz, *Special Trust*, 373

58. See Leebaert, *Fifty-Year Wound*, 518–24; Shultz, *Turmoil and Triumph*, 135–45; Schweizer, *Reagan's War*, 170–72.

59. Shultz, *Turmoil and Triumph*, 135.

60. Quoted in Schweizer, *Reagan's War*, 240.

61. Schweizer, *Reagan's War*, 239–41; Allen, "Man Who Changed the Game Plan."

62. Leebaert, *Fifty-Year Wound*, 397–400, 524–527; William Safire, "The Farewell Dossier," *New York Times*, February 2, 2004; Gus W. Weiss, "Duping the Soviets: The Farewell Dossier," *Studies in Intelligence* 39 (1996): 121–26; and Thomas C. Reed, *At the Abyss: An Insider's History of the Cold War* (New York: Random House, 2004), 266–70.

63. Quoted in Schweizer, *Reagan's War*, 164.

64. Weinberger, *In the Arena*, 280. On the alliance between Washington and Rome to help Solidarity, see Carl Bernstein, *His Holiness: John Paul II and the Hidden History of Our Time* (New York: Doubleday, 1996).

65. Charles Krauthammer, "The Reagan Doctrine," *Time*, April 1, 1985, 54–55.

66. U.S., President, *Public Papers, Reagan*, 1984, 1:811.

67. U.S., President, *Public Papers, Reagan*, 1985, 1:135; Shultz quoted in Peter W. Rodman, *More Precious than Peace: The Cold War and the Struggle for the Third World* (New York: Scribner's, 1994), 274.

68. Rodman, *More Precious than Peace*, 266.

69. Gates, *From the Shadows*, 256.

70. Quoted in Stephen F. Knott, "Reagan's Critics," *The National Interest* (Summer 1996).

71. Rodman, *More Precious than Peace*, 336–40.

72. Leebaert, *Fifty-Year Wound*, 549.

73. Rodman, *More Precious than Peace*, 356–57.

74. Reagan, *American Life*, 471.

75. Quoted in Robert Kagan, *A Twilight Struggle: American Power and Nicaragua, 1977–1990* (New York: The Free Press, 1996), 122.

76. Gates, *From the Shadows*, 151.

77. Quoted in Kagan, *Twilight Struggle*, 196–97.

78. On the indigenous peoples in the Contra War, see Timothy C. Brown, *The Real Contra War: Highlander Peasant Resistance in Nicaragua* (Norman: University of Oklahoma Press, 2001).

79. Quoted in Christian Smith, *Resisting Reagan: The U.S. Central America Peace Movement* (Chicago: University of Chicago Press, 1996), xv.

80. Gates, *From the Shadows*, 295.

81. Edwin Meese, *With Reagan: The Inside Story* (Washington: Regnery Gateway, 1992), 238–39.

82. Powell, *My American Journey*, 340.

83. Quoted in Rodman, *More Precious than Peace*, 250.

84. Ibid., 441.

85. Quoted in ibid., 447.

86. Powell, *My American Journey*, 292.

87. Quoted in Leebaert, *Fifty-Year Wound*, 544.

88. Rodman, *More Precious Than Peace*, 399.

9. WINNING THE COLD WAR

1. "Men of the Year," *Time*, January 1, 1984, 32, 18.

2. *Bulletin of the Atomic Scientists*, January 1984.

3. Ronald Reagan, *An American Life* (New York: Pocket Books, 1990), 584.

4. Quoted in ibid., 585. See also Don Oberdorfer, *From the Cold War to a New Era: The United States and the Soviet Union, 1983–1991*, updated ed. (Baltimore: The Johns Hopkins University Press, 1998), 65.

5. Quoted in Robert M. Gates, *From the Shadows: The Ultimate Insider's Story of Five Presidents and How They Won the Cold War* (New York: Touchstone, 1996), 271–72.

6. Nancy Reagan, *My Turn: The Memoirs of Nancy Reagan* (New York: Random House, 1989), 336–37.

7. Oberdorfer, *Cold War to New Era*, 70–71.

8. Dr. Seuss, *The Butter Battle Book* (New York: Random House Books for Young Readers, 1984); Michael Oreskes, "Civil Defense Planning Futile, Cuomo Says," *New York Times*, May 14, 1984.

9. George P. Shultz, *Turmoil and Triumph: My Years as Secretary of State* (New York: Scribner's, 1993), 19, 10.

10. Ibid., 274.

11. Kiron K. Skinner, Annelise Anderson, and Martin Anderson, eds., *Reagan: A Life in Letters* (New York: Free Press, 2003), 407, 402.

12. Jack F. Matlock, Jr., *Reagan and Gorbachev: How the Cold War Ended* (New York: Random House, 2004), xi.

13. Quoted in Peter Schweizer, *Reagan's War: The Epic Story of His Forty-Year Struggle and Final Triumph over Communism* (New York: Doubleday, 2002), 231–32.

14. U.S., President, *Public Papers, Reagan, 1984*, 1:40–44.

15. Ibid.

16. Quoted in Oberdorfer, *Cold War to New Era*, 85.

17. Schweizer, *Reagan's War*, 257, 234–35, 270–71.

18. Jack F. Matlock, Jr., *Autopsy on an Empire: The American Ambassador's Account of the Collapse of the Soviet Union* (New York: Random House, 1995), 77.

19. Quoted in Larry Speakes, *Speaking Out: Inside the Reagan White House* (New York: Scribner's, 1988), 138.

20. Skinner et al., eds., *Reagan: A Life in Letters*, 417.

21. Quoted in Paul Lettow, *Ronald Reagan and His Quest to Abolish Nuclear Weapons* (New York: Random House, 2005), 238.

22. Quoted in Skinner et al., eds., *Reagan: A Life in Letters*, 385–86; Shultz, *Turmoil and Triumph*, 1131.

23. Cold War International History Project Virtual Archive, New Evidence on the End of the Cold War Collection.

24. Matlock, *Autopsy*, 590–91, 667–71;

25. Quoted in Schweizer, *Reagan's War*, 106.

26. Polling numbers cited in Peter J. Wallison, *Ronald Reagan: The Power of Conviction and the Success of His Presidency* (Boulder, Col.: Westview Press, 2003), 210; Michael Deaver, *Behind the Scenes* (New York; William Morrow and Company, 1987), 13.

27. Wallison, *Ronald Reagan: The Power of Conviction*.

28. Ibid., 190.

29. On Bradlee, Peggy Noonan, *When Character Was King: A Story of Ronald Reagan* (New York: Viking, 2001), 277; Elliott Abrams, *Undue Process: A Story of How Political Differences Are Turned into Crimes* (New York: The Free Press, 1993).

30. U.S., President, *Public Papers, Reagan, 1987*, 1:209.

31. David Gergen, *Eyewitness to Power: The Essence of Leadership, Nixon to Clinton* (New York: Simon and Schuster, 2000), 188. On the fallout and recovery from Iran Contra, see David Abshire, *Saving the Reagan Presidency: Trust Is the Coin of the Realm* (College Station, Texas: Texas A&M University Press, 2005).

32. Reagan, *An American Life*, 513.

33. Quoted in William Pemberton, *Exit With Honor: The Life and Presidency of Ronald Reagan* (Armonk, N.Y.: M. E. Sharpe, 1998), 191.

34. Michael Deaver, *Behind the Scenes* (New York: William Morrow, 1988), 257; Peggy Noonan, *What I Saw at the Revolution: A Political Life in the Reagan Era* (New York: Random House, 1990), 235. For an instructive glimpse of North and Poindexter, see Robert Timberg, *The Nightingale's Song* (New York: Simon and Schuster, 1995).

35. Quoted in Peter W. Rodman, *More Precious than Peace: The Cold War and the Struggle for the Third World* (New York: Scribner's, 1994), 282.

36. Alexander M. Haig, Jr., *Caveat: Realism, Reagan, and Foreign Policy* (New York: MacMillan, 1984), 90.

37. Ibid., 91.

38. Quoted in Richard Cohen, "On the Side of Genocide," *Washington Post*, September 29, 1989.

39. Rodman, *More Precious than Peace*, 452.

40. Quoted in Rodman, *More Precious than Peace*, 460.

41. Jim Leach, "Don't Help Pol Pot. Try Him," *New York Times*, September 27, 1989.

42. Rodman, *More Precious than Peace*, 454.

43. Steve Coll, *Ghost Wars: The Secret History of the CIA, Afghanistan, and bin Laden, from the Soviet Invasion to September 10, 2001* (New York: Penguin Books, 2005), 90.

44. Quoted in Derek Leebaert, *The Fifty-Year Wound: The True Price of America's Cold War Victory* (Boston: Little, Brown, 2002),, 550.

45. Coll, *Ghost Wars*, 84–88.

46. Tim Weiner, "Blowback from the Afghan Battlefield," *New York Times Magazine*, March 13, 1994; and Mary Anne Weaver, "Blowback," *Atlantic Monthly*, May 1996, 24 ff.

47. *Washington Post*, February 22, 1990.

10. THE EIGHTIES LEGACY

1. Peggy Noonan, *What I Saw at the Revolution: A Political Life in the Reagan Era* (New York: Random House, 1990), 335.

2. U.S., President, *Public Papers, Reagan, 1989*, 2:718–23.

3. Quoted in "Thank '80s Greed for '90s Growth," *Business Week*, April 5, 1999.

4. William Ker Muir, Jr., *The Bully Pulpit: The Presidential Leadership of Ronald Reagan* (San Francisco: ICS Press, 1992), 107 -110.

5. Quoted in Andrew Sullivan, "A Mash Note: Reagan Was Right about Almost Everything," *Sunday Times* (London), February 4, 2001.

6. Richard Neustadt, *Presidential Power and the Modern Presidents*, updated ed. (New York: Free Press, 1990), 269.

7. Quoted in Peter Schmeisser, "Is America in Decline?" *New York Times Magazine*, April 17, 1988.

8. "Study Finds Gains for Black Middle Class," *New York Times*, August 10, 1991.

9. Raymond Wolters, *Right Turn: William Bradford Reynolds, the Reagan Administration, and Black Civil Rights* (New Brunswick, NJ: Transaction Publishers, 1996), 2–3.

10. Ibid., 15.

11. Erin Kelly and Frank Dobbin, "How Affirmative Action Became Diversity Management," *American Behavioral Scientist* 41 (April 1998): 960–84; and Peter W. Wood, *Diversity: The Invention of a Concept* (San Francisco: Encounter Books, 2003).

12. Thomas to Reagan, July 10, 1984, quoted in Kiron K. Skinner, Annelise Anderson, and Martin Anderson, eds., *Reagan: A Life in Letters* (New York: Free Press, 2003), 339.

13. Tamar Jacoby, *Someone Else's House: America's Unfinished Struggle for Integration* (New York: Free Press, 1998).

14. Heclo, "Ronald Reagan and the American Public Philosophy," in *The Reagan Presidency: Pragmatic Conservatism & Its Legacies*, ed. W. Elliot Brownlee and Hugh Davis Graham (Lawrence: University Press of Kansas), 35.

15. "Liberal Media's Reagan-Bashing Record," Media Research Center Report, June 2004, http://www.mediaresearch.org/realitycheck/2004/fax20040609.asp.

16. Paul Kengor, "Reagan Among the Professors," *Policy Review* 98 (December 1999–January 2000): 15–27; Arthur M. Schlesinger, Jr., "The Ultimate Approval Rating," *New York Times Magazine*, December 15, 1996; James Lindgren, "Ranking Our Presidents" (Federalist Society–Wall Street Journal Ratings), November 16, 2000; and James Tartanto and Leonard Leo, *Presidential Leadership* (New York: Wall Street Journal Books, 2004).

17. Stephen Skowronek, *The Politics Presidents Make: Leadership from John Adams to Bill Clinton* (Cambridge: Harvard University Press, 1997), 37–39.

18. Ibid., 411.

19. Quoted in John A. Farrell, *Tip O'Neill and the Democratic Century* (Boston: Little, Brown, 2001), 642.

20. Alan S. Blinder, *Hard Heads, Soft Hearts: Tough-Minded Economics for a Just Society* (Reading, Mass.: Addison-Wesley, 1987), 105–108.

21. Quoted in Jon F. Hale, "The Making of the New Democrats," *Political Science Quarterly* 110 (Summer 1995): 215. See also Kenneth S. Baer, *Reinventing Democrats: The Politics of Liberalism from Reagan to Clinton* (Lawrence: University Press of Kansas, 2000).

22. Quoted in Skowronek, *Politics Presidents Make*, 431.

23. Gilbert T. Sewall, "Revisiting the Eighties," in *The Eighties: A Reader*, ed. Sewall (Reading, Mass.: Perseus Books, 1997), xii.

24. Daniel Patrick Moynihan, "Defining Deviancy Down," *The American Scholar* (Winter 1993): 17–30.

25. Charls Krauthammer, "Defining Deviancy Up," *New Republic*, November 22, 1993, 20–25; Ellen Bass and Laura Davis, *The Courage to Heal: A Guide for Women*

Survivors of Child Sexual Abuse (New York: Harper & Row, 1988), 21. See also Richard J. McNally, *Remembering Trauma* (Cambridge: Belknap Press of Harvard University Press, 2003) and Dorothy Rabinowitz, *No Crueler Tyrannies: Accusation, False Witness, and Other Terrors of Our Times* (New York: Wall Street Journal Books, 2003).

26. Naomi Wolf, *The Beauty Myth: How Images of Female Beauty Are Used Against Women* (New York: HarperCollins, 1991), 167.

27. Roger Kimball, *Tenured Radicals: How Politics Has Corrupted Our Higher Education*, rev. ed. (Chicago: Ivan R. Dee, 1998), xix; Gilder quoted in David Brooks, *Bobos in Paradise: The New Upper Class and How They Got There* (New York: Simon and Schuster, 2000), 196; Robert H. Bork, *Slouching Towards Gomorrah: Modern Liberalism and American Decline* (New York: Regan Books, 1996), 2; and William J. Bennett, *De-Valuing of America: The Fight for Our Culture and Our Children* (New York: Simon and Schuster, 1992), 258.

28. On the reality of the culture war, see Alan Abramowitz and Kyle Saunders, "Why Can't We All Just Get Along? The Reality of a Polarized America" and John H. Evans and Lisa M. Nunn, "The Deeper 'Culture Wars' Questions," both in the electronic journal *The Forum*, vol. 3: issue 2 (2005). For the contrary argument that there never was a culture war in any meaningful sense of that term, see Morris P. Fiorina, with Samuel J. Abrams and Jeremy C. Pope, *Culture War? The Myth of a Polarized America* (New York: Pearson Longman, 2005).

29. Alan Wolfe, *One Nation After All: What Middle-Class Americans Really Think About: God, Country, Family, Racism, Welfare, Immigration, Homosexuality, Work, the Right, the Left, and Each Other* (New York: Penguin, 1998), 279; and Brooks, *Bobos in Paradise*, 198, 200.

30. Gertrude Himmelfarb, *One Nation, Two Cultures* (New York: Vintage Books, 2001).

31. Paul Weyrich, "The Moral Minority," *Christianity Today*, September 6, 1999, 44; Cal Thomas and Ed Dobson, *Blinded by Might: Can the Religious Right Save America?* (Grand Rapids, Mich.: Zondervan Publishing House, 1999); Irving Kristol, "Faith a la Carte," *Times Literary Supplement*, May 26, 2000, 14.

32. Quoted in Ralph Z. Hallow, "Buchanan Sees 'War' Within Conservatism," *Washington Times*, May 17, 2005.

33. Stephen A. Borrelli, "Finding the Third Way: Bill Clinton, the DLC, and the Democratic Party Platform of 1992," *Journal of Policy History* 13, no. 4 (2001): 429–62.

34. Kenneth S. Baer, *Reinventing Democrats*, 2.

35. Ibid., 82.

36. Quoted in Skowronek, *Politics Presidents Make*, 531, n. 2.

37. Michael Kelly and Maureen Dowd, "The Company He Keeps," *New York Times*, January 17, 1993.

38. James Adams, "I've Lost that Leader Feeling," *Sunday Times* (London), January 8, 1995.

39. Ibid.; "Let a Thousand Gurus Bloom," *Washington Post Magazine*, February 12, 1995; and Philip Gailey, "Bill Clinton's Hapless Days," *St. Petersburg Times*, January 29, 1995.

40. Ad for the Conservative Book Club, *Weekly Standard*, December 29, 2003–January 5, 2004, 40.

41. Quoted in James L. Nolan, Jr., "Contrasting Styles of Political Discourse in America's Past and Present Culture Wars," in *The American Culture Wars: Current Contests and Future Prospects*, ed. Nolan (Charlottesville, Va.: University Press of Virginia, 1996), 165.

42. "Sob Sisters and Firewalkers," *San Francisco Chronicle*, January 12, 1995; Adams, "I've Lost that Leader Feeling"; "Let a Thousand Gurus Bloom."

43. Geoffrey Layman, *The Great Divide: Religious and Cultural Conflict in American Party Politics* (New York: Columbia University Press, 2001), 333–34.

INDEX

Tennessee Valley Authority (TVA), 37
Terry, Randall A., 190–92
text, postmodernist view of, 148–49
textbooks, 177
Thatcher, Margaret, 200, 207, 217, 225, 226
Therapeutic Abortion Act of 1967, 41
therapeutic culture, 5, 151–57; celebration of
    liberated self, 152–53; Clinton and, 252–54;
    pathologization of human behavior, 155–
    57; professional specialists, 155; repressed
    memories issue, 247; self-esteem, 154;
    self-help groups, 156–57; Tony Robbins,
    168–69; victimhood, 156–57, 183–84
think tanks, 47
Third World, Cold War and, 196, 209–11
Thomas, Cal, 249
Thomas, Clarence, 241
Thomas Road Baptist Church, 175
Thompson, Robert, 167
thrift industry. *See* savings and loan associa-
    tions (S&Ls)
Thriller (Jackson), 166
Time, 17, 124; machine of the year award,
    106–7, 109; Reagan interview (1966), 44
Tocqueville, Alexis de, 131, 152, 157–58
Topping, Norman, 42
Total Quality Management (TQM), 114
Toward a State of Esteem (California Task
    Force), 154
Tower, John, 228
trade, globalization and, 102
transportation sector, 75, 101
Tribe, Laurence, 190
Trident missile submarines, 197
Triumph of the Therapeutic, The (Rieff), 152
Trollope, Frances, 158
*Truly Disadvantaged, The: The Inner City, the
    Underclass, and Public Policy* (Wilson),
    126–28
Truman, Harry S., 37, 131
Tsongas, Paul, 243
Tunney, Gene, 71
Turner, Ted, 164
Tuttle, Holmes, 38–39
Tyson's Corner Center, 159

Uhler, Lewis, 42, 43
underclass, 124–30; absolute numbers of poor
    people, 129; cultural dimension of, 127–29;
    culture of poverty model of explanation,

126–27, 128; joblessness as cause of, 128,
    129; racism model of explanation, 127; turn-
    around in 2000, 129; welfare dependency
    model of explanation, 125, 127; white, 130
unemployment rate, 8
unions: air traffic controllers, 72; United Auto
    Workers, 114. *See also* Screen Actors Guild
UNITA, 217
United Auto Workers (UAW), 114
United States, centralizing tendencies, 14–17
United States Information Agency, 205
universities: culture war and, 179–86;
    multiculturalism and, 181–86; political
    correctness, 184–85; scholarship, declinist,
    238; speech codes, 184; women's studies
    programs, 16
University of Connecticut, 184
University of Pennsylvania, 184–85
Unlimited Power (Robbins), 168
Unruh, Jesse "Big Daddy," 40, 41
Urban Institute, 124, 129
U.S. Steel (firm), 9
USA Cable Network, 167

Van Halen, Eddie, 166
Vatican, 209
Veblen, Thorstein, 161–62
Venturi, Robert, 150
VH-1 (television channel), 164–65
victimhood, 156–57, 183–84
"Video Killed the Radio Star" (the Buggles),
    164
Vietnam, withdrawal from, 11–13
Vietnam War, Reagan on, 48
Vietor, Richard H. K., 82
Village People, 134
violence, escalation of, 246
Viscott, David, 155
Vishny, Robert W., 112
VisiCalc (computer program), 105
Vogel, Ezra, 9
Voice of America, 205
Volcker, Paul, 63, 72
Von Damm, Helene, 52
voodoo economics, 68
Voting Rights Act of 1965, 240

wage inequality, 131
Waldman, Steven, 151
Walesa, Lech, 209